The
Oxford Book of
Ballads

Impression of 1932
First edition, 1910

Printed in Great Britain

The Oxford Book of Ballads

Chosen & Edited by

Arthur Quiller-Couch

Oxford

At the Clarendon Press

TO

THE ONE SURVIVOR

OF THREE MEN

TO WHOM ALL LOVERS OF THE BALLAD

OWE MOST IN THESE TIMES

FRANCIS JAMES CHILD

FREDERICK JAMES FURNIVALL

AND

JOHN WESLEY HALES

PREFACE

AS in *The Oxford Book of English Verse* I tried to range over the whole field of the English Lyric, and to choose the best, so in this volume I have sought to bring together the best Ballads out of the whole of our national stock. But the method, order, balance of the two books are different perforce, as the fates of the Lyric and the Ballad have been diverse. While the Lyric in general, still making for variety, is to-day more prolific than ever and (all cant apart) promises fruit to equal the best, that particular offshoot which we call the Ballad has been dead, or as good as dead, for two hundred years. It would seem to have discovered, almost at the start, a very precise Platonic pattern of what its best should be; and having exhausted itself in reproducing that, it declined (through a crab-apple stage of Broadsides) into sterility. Therefore this anthology cannot be brought down to the present day, and therefore the first half of it contains far finer poetry than the second.

But it may be objected that among Ballads no such thing as chronological order is possible; and that, if it were, I have not attempted it. 'Why then did I not boldly mix up all my flowers in a heap and afterwards sit down to re-arrange them, disregarding history, studious only that one flower should set off another and the whole wreath be a well-balanced circle ? ' I will try to answer this, premising only that tact is nine-tenths of the anthologist's business. It is very true that the Ballads have no chronology : that no one can say when *Hynd Horn* was composed, or assert with proof that *Clerk Saunders* is younger than *Childe Maurice* or *Tam Lin* older than *Sir Patrick Spens*, though that all five are older than *The Children in the Wood* no one with an ounce of literary sense would deny. Even of our few certainties we have to remember that, where almost everything depends on oral tradition, it may easily happen—in fact happens not seldom—that a really old ballad ' of the best period ' has reached us late and in a corrupted form, its original gold overlaid with silver and bronze. It is true, moreover, that these pages, declining an impossible order, decline also the pretence to it. I have arranged the ballads in seven books : of which the first deals with Magic, the ' Seely Court ', and the supernatural ; the second (and on the whole the most beautiful) with stories of absolute romance such as *Childe Waters, Lord Ingram, Young Andrew* ; the third with romance shading off into real history, as in *Sir Patrick Spens, Hugh of Lincoln, The Queen's Marie* ; the fourth with Early Carols and ballads of Holy Writ. This closes Part I. The fifth book is all of the Greenwood and Robin Hood ; the sixth follows history down from Chevy Chase and the Homeric deeds of Douglas and Percy to less renowned if not less spirited Border feuds ; while the seventh and last book presents the Ballad in various aspects of false beginning and decline—*The Old Cloak*, which deserved a long line of children but in fact has had few ; *Barbara Allen*, late but exquisite ; *Lord Lovel*, which is silly sooth ; and *The Suffolk Tragedy*, wherein a magnificent ballad-theme is ambled to market like so much butter. My hope is that this arrangement, while it avoids mixing up things that differ and keeps consorted those (the Robin Hood Ballads for example) which naturally go together, does 'in round numbers' give a view of the Ballad in its perfection and decline, and that so my book may be useful to the student as well as to the disinterested lover of poetry for whom it is chiefly intended.

This brings me to the matter of text. To make a 'scientific' anthology of the Ballads was out of the question. In so far as scientific treatment could be brought to them the work had been done, for many generations to come, if not finally, by the late Professor Child [1] in his monumental edition, to which at every turn I have been indebted for guidance back to the originals. Child's method was to get hold of every ballad in every extant version, good, bad, or indifferent, and to print these versions side by side, with a foreword on the ballad's history, packed with every illustration that could be contributed out of his immense knowledge of the folk-poetry of every race and country. His work, as I say, left no room for follower or imitator ; but

---

[1] A smaller edition of 'Child', excellently planned, by Helen Child Sargent and George Lyman Kittredge, is published in England by Mr. Nutt.

fortunately it lies almost as wide of my purpose as of my learning. My reader did not require *Sir Patrick Spens* or *May Colvin* in a dozen or twenty versions : he wanted one ballad, one *Sir Patrick Spens*, one *May Colvin*, and that the best. How could I give him the best in my power?

There is only one way. It was Scott's way, and the way of William Allingham, who has been at pains to define it in the preface to his *Ballad Book* (Macmillan) :—

> The various oral versions of a popular ballad obtainable throughout England, Scotland, and Ireland, are perhaps, even at this late day,[1] practically innumerable— one as 'authentic' as another. What then to do? . . . The right course has appeared to be this, to make oneself acquainted with all attainable versions of a ballad. Then (granting a 'turn' for such things, to begin; without which all were labour in vain) the editor may be supposed to get as much insight as may be into the origin and character of the ballad in question; he sees or surmises more or less as to the earliest version or versions, as to blunders, corruptions, alterations of every sort (national, local, personal) on the part of the reciters ; he then comes to investigate the doings of former editors, adopting thankfully what he finds good, correcting at points whereupon he has attained better information, rejecting (when for the worse) acknowledged or obvious interpolations or changes. He has to give it in *one* form —the best according to his judgement and feeling—in firm black and white, for critics, and for readers cultivated and simple.

This fairly describes Scott's method as well as Allingham's own. But while I must claim along with

[1] 1864.

them 'a " turn" for such things' (the claim is implicit in
my attempt), these two men were poets, and could dare
more boldly than I to rewrite a faulty stanza or to supply
a missing one. Of this ticklish license I have been
extremely chary, and have used it with the double precaution
(1) of employing, so far as might be, words and phrases
found elsewhere in the text of the ballad, and (2) of printing
these experiments in square brackets,[1] that the reader may
not be misled. Maybe I should have resisted the
temptation altogether but for the necessity—in a work
intended for all sorts of readers, young and old—of
removing or reducing here and there in these eight hundred
and sixty-five pages a coarse or a brutal phrase. To those
who deny the necessity I will only answer that while no
literature in the world exercises a stronger or on the whole
a saner fascination upon imaginative youth than do these
ballads, it seems to me wiser to omit a stanza from
Glasgerion, for example, or to modify a line in *Young
Hunting*, than to withhold these beautiful things altogether
from boy or maid.

Before leaving this subject of texts and their handling,
I must express my thanks for the permission given me to
make free use of the text of the Percy Folio MS., edited
by Professors Hales and Furnivall some forty years ago.
This was of course indispensable. In the history of our

---

[1] This does not hold of small transpositions, elisions of
superfluous words, or corrections of spelling. In these matters
I have allowed myself a free hand.

ballad-literature the *Reliques* themselves are, if something more of a landmark, much less of a trophy than the three famous volumes so romantically achieved by Professor Child and their two editors, whose labour has been scarcely more honourable than their liberality which has ever laid its results open to men's benefit. Mr. Child died in 1896; Mr. Furnivall a few months ago. To Mr. Hales, survivor of the famous three, I owe the permission given with a courtesy which set a fresh value on what was already beyond value. I must also thank the Rev. Sabine Baring-Gould for leave to include *The Brown Girl* and other ballads from his *Songs of the West* and *A Garland of Country Song* (Methuen). It were idle to quote all the scholars—Ritson, Herd, Scott, Jamieson and the rest— to whose labours every ballad-editor must be indebted: but among younger men I wish to thank Mr. F. Sidgwick, whose method in his two volumes of Ballads (Bullen) I can admire the more unreservedly because it differs from mine.

I hope, at any rate, that in presenting each ballad as *one*, and reconstructing it sometimes from many versions, I have kept pretty constantly to the idea, of which Professor Ker[1] says—'The truth is that the Ballad is an Idea, a Poetical Form, which can take up any matter, and does not leave that matter as it was before.' If the reader interrogate me concerning this Idea of the Ballad, as

[1] *On the History of the Ballads, 1100–1500*, by W. P. Ker, Proceedings of the British Academy, vol. iv.

PREFACE

Mr. Pecksniff demanded of Mrs. Todgers her Notion of a Wooden Leg, Professor Ker has my answer prepared :—

> In spite of Socrates and his logic we may venture to say, in answer to the question ' What is a ballad ? '— ' A Ballad is *The Milldams of Binnorie* and *Sir Patrick Spens* and *The Douglas Tragedy* and *Lord Randal* and *Childe Maurice*, and things of that sort.'

There the reader has it, without need of the definition or of the historical account which this Preface must not attempt. Its author, no doubt, is destined to consign, some day, and ' come to dust ' with more learned editors : but meanwhile, if one ask ' What is a Ballad ? '—I answer, It is these things ; and it is

> About the dead hour o' the night
> She heard the bridles ring. *(Tam Lin)*

and

> But this ladye is gone to her chamber,
> Her maydens following bright. *(Sir Cawline)*

It is

> ' O we were sisters, sisters seven ;
> We were the fairest under heaven.' *(Cospatrick)*

and

> ' I see no harm by you, Margaret,
> Nor you see none by me.'
> *(Fair Margaret and Sweet William)*

and

> In somer, when the shawes be sheyne,
> And leves be large and long.
> *(Robin Hood and the Monk)*

and

> O there was horsing, horsing in haste,
>   And cracking of whips out owre the lee.
>
> *(Archie of Cawfield)*

It is even

> And there did he see brave Captain Ogilvie
>   A-training of his men on the green.
>
> *(The Duke of Gordon's Daughter)*

Like the Clown in *Twelfth Night*, it can sing both high and low: but the note is unmistakable whether it sing high:

> O cocks are crowing on merry middle-earth;
>   I wot the wild fowls are boding day.
>
> *(Clerk Saunders)*

> Half-owre, half-owre to Aberdour,
>   'Tis fifty fathoms deep;
> And there lies gude Sir Patrick Spens,
>   Wi' the Scots lords at his feet!
>
> *(Sir Patrick Spens)*

> 'O Earl Bran', I see your heart's bloud!'—
>   *Ay lally, o lilly lally*
> 'It's na but the glent o' my scarlet hood'
>   *All i' the night sae early.*   *(Earl Brand)*

or low

> Then up bespake the bride's mother—
>   She never was heard to speak so free:
> 'Ye'll not forsake my only daughter,
>   Though Susie Pye has cross'd the sea.'
>
> *(Young Beichan)*

> 'An' thu sall marry a proud gunner,
>   An' a proud gunner I'm sure he'll be.'
>
> *(The Great Silkie of Sule Skerrie)*

PREFACE

> Rise up, rise up, brother Dives,
>   And go with us to see
> A dismal place, prepared in hell,
>   To sit on a serpent's knee.   (*Dives and Lazarus*)

or, merely flat and pedestrian:

> There was slayne upon the English part
>   For sooth as I you say,
> Of ninè thousand English men
>   Five hundred came away.   (*Otterburn*)

But it is always unmistakable and like no other thing in poetry; in proof of which let me offer one simple, practical test. If any man ever steeped himself in balladry, that man was Scott, and once or twice, as in *Proud Maisie* and *Brignall Banks*, he came near to distil the essence. If any man, taking the Ballad for his model, has ever sublimated its feeling and language in a poem

> seraphically free
> From taint of personality,

that man was Coleridge and that poem his *Ancient Mariner*. If any poet now alive can be called a ballad-writer of genius, it is the author of *Danny Deever* and *East and West*. But let the reader suppose a fascicule of such poems bound up with the present collection, and he will perceive that I could have gone no straighter way to destroy the singularity of the book.

In claiming this singularity for the Ballad I do not seek to exalt it above any other lyrical form. Rather I am ready to admit, out of some experience in anthologizing,

xv

that when a ballad is set in a collection alongside the best of Herrick, Gray, Landor, Browning—to name four poets opposite as the poles and to say nothing of such master-work as Spenser's *Epithalamion* or Milton's *Lycidas*—it is the ballad that not only suffers by the apposition but suffers to a surprising degree; so that I have sometimes been forced to reconsider my affection, and ask 'Are these ballads really beautiful as they have always appeared to me?' In truth (as I take it) the contrast is unfair to them, much as any contrast between children and grown folk would be unfair. They appealed to something young in the national mind, and the young still ramp through Percy's *Reliques*— as I hope they will through this book—'trailing clouds of glory,' following the note in Elmond's wood—

> May Margaret sits in her bower door
>   Sewing her silken seam ;
> She heard a note in Elmond's wood,
>   And wish'd she there had been.
>
> She loot the seam fa' frae her side,
>   The needle to her tae,
> And she is on to Elmond's wood
>   As fast as she could gae.

A. Q. C.

CONTENTS

PART I

BOOK I

xvii

CONTENTS

BOOK II

CONTENTS

BOOK III

xix

CONTENTS

BOOK IV

CONTENTS

PART II

BOOK V

BOOK VI

CONTENTS

CONTENTS

Certainly, I must confesse my own barbarousnes, I neuer heard the olde song of Percy *and* Duglas *that I found not my heart mooued more then with a* Trumpet.

SIR PHILIP SIDNEY.

BOOK I

1. ## *Thomas the Rhymer*

I

TRUE Thomas lay on Huntlie bank;
  A ferlie he spied wi' his e'e;
And there he saw a ladye bright
  Come riding down by the Eildon Tree.

II

Her skirt was o' the grass-green silk,
  Her mantle o' the velvet fyne;
At ilka tett o' her horse's mane
  Hung fifty siller bells and nine.

III

True Thomas he pu'd aff his cap,
  And louted low down on his knee:
'Hail to thee, Mary, Queen of Heaven!
  For thy peer on earth could never be.'

IV

'O no, O no, Thomas,' she said,
  'That name does not belang to me;
I'm but the Queen o' fair Elfland,
  That am hither come to visit thee.

V

'Harp and carp, Thomas,' she said;
  'Harp and carp along wi' me;
And if ye dare to kiss my lips,
  Sure of your bodie I will be.'

ferlie] marvel.   tett] tuft.   harp and carp] play
and recite (as a minstrel).

1225   B   1

VI

'Betide me weal, betide me woe,
   That weird shall never daunten me.'
Syne he has kiss'd her rosy lips,
   All underneath the Eildon Tree.

VII

'Now ye maun go wi' me,' she said,
   'True Thomas, ye maun go wi' me ;
And ye maun serve me seven years,
   Thro' weal or woe as may chance to be.'

VIII

She's mounted on her milk-white steed,
   She's ta'en true Thomas up behind ;
And aye, whene'er her bridle rang,
   The steed gaed swifter than the wind.

IX

O they rade on, and farther on,
   The steed gaed swifter than the wind ;
Until they reach'd a desert wide,
   And living land was left behind.

X

'Light down, light down now, true Thomas,
   And lean your head upon my knee ;
Abide ye there a little space,
   And I will show you ferlies three.

XI

'O see ye not yon narrow road,
   So thick beset wi' thorns and briers ?
That is the Path of Righteousness,
   Though after it but few inquires.

weird] doom.

THOMAS THE RHYMER

XII

'And see ye not yon braid, braid road,
  That lies across the lily leven?
That is the Path of Wickedness,
  Though some call it the Road to Heaven.

XIII

'And see ye not yon bonny road
  That winds about the fernie brae?
That is the Road to fair Elfland,
  Where thou and I this night maun gae.

XIV

'But, Thomas, ye sall haud your tongue,
  Whatever ye may hear or see;
For speak ye word in Elflyn-land,
  Ye'll ne'er win back to your ain countrie.'

XV

O they rade on, and farther on,
  And they waded rivers abune the knee;
And they saw neither sun nor moon,
  But they heard the roaring of the sea.

XVI

It was mirk, mirk night, there was nae starlight,
  They waded thro' red blude to the knee;
For a' the blude that 's shed on the earth
  Rins through the springs o' that countrie.

XVII

Syne they came to a garden green,
  And she pu'd an apple frae a tree:
'Take this for thy wages, true Thomas;
  It will give thee the tongue that can never lee.'

leven]? lawn.

3

XVIII

'My tongue is my ain,' true Thomas he said;
  'A gudely gift ye wad gie to me!
I neither dought to buy or sell
  At fair or tryst where I might be.

XIX

'I dought neither speak to prince or peer,
  Nor ask of grace from fair ladye!'—
'Now haud thy peace, Thomas,' she said,
  'For as I say, so must it be.'

XX

He has gotten a coat of the even cloth,
  And a pair o' shoon of the velvet green;
And till seven years were gane and past,
  True Thomas on earth was never seen.

2. *Tam Lin*

I

'O I forbid you, maidens a',
  That wear gowd on your hair,
To come or gae by Carterhaugh,
  For young Tam Lin is there.

II

'For even about that knight's middle
  O' siller bells are nine;
And nae maid comes to Carterhaugh
  And a maid returns again.'
  dought] could.   even cloth] smooth cloth.

4

TAM LIN

III

Fair Janet sat in her bonny bower,
  Sewing her silken seam,
And wish'd to be in Carterhaugh
  Amang the leaves sae green.

IV

She's lat her seam fa' to her feet,
  The needle to her tae,
And she's awa' to Carterhaugh
  As fast as she could gae.

V

And she has kilted her green kirtle
  A little abune her knee;
And she has braided her yellow hair
  A little abune her bree;
And she has gaen for Carterhaugh
  As fast as she can hie.

VI

She hadna pu'd a rose, a rose,
  A rose but barely ane,
When up and started young Tam Lin;
  Says, 'Ladye, let alane.

VII

'What gars ye pu' the rose, Janet?
  What gars ye break the tree?
What gars ye come to Carterhaugh
  Without the leave o' me?'

tae] toe.   bree] eye-brow.

5

TAM LIN

VIII

'Weel may I pu' the rose,' she says,
    'And ask no leave at thee;
For Carterhaugh it is my ain,
    My daddy gave it me.'

IX

He's ta'en her by the milk-white hand,
    And by the grass-green sleeve,
He's led her to the fairy ground
    At her he ask'd nae leave.

X

Janet has kilted her green kirtle
    A little abune her knee,
And she has snooded her yellow hair
    A little abune her bree,
And she is to her father's ha'
    As fast as she can hie.

XI

But when she came to her father's ha',
    She look'd sae wan and pale,
They thought the lady had gotten a fright,
    Or with sickness she did ail.

XII

Four and twenty ladies fair
    Were playing at the ba',
And out then came fair Janet
    Ance the flower amang them a'.

XIII

Four and twenty ladies fair
    Were playing at the chess,
And out then came fair Janet
    As green as onie glass.

6

XIV

Out then spak' an auld grey knight
  'Lay owre the Castle wa',
And says, 'Alas, fair Janet !
  For thee we'll be blamèd a'.'

XV

'Hauld your tongue, ye auld-faced knight,
  Some ill death may ye die !
Father my bairn on whom I will,
  I'll father nane on thee.

XVI

'O if my love were an earthly knight,
  As he is an elfin gay,
I wadna gie my ain true-love
  For nae laird that ye hae.

XVII

'The steed that my true-love rides on
  Is fleeter nor the wind ;
Wi' siller he is shod before,
  Wi' burning gold behind.'

XVIII

Out then spak' her brither dear—
  He meant to do her harm :
'There grows an herb in Carterhaugh
  Will twine you an' the bairn.'

XIX

Janet has kilted her green kirtle
  A little abune her knee,
And she has snooded her yellow hair
  A little abune her bree,
And she's awa' to Carterhaugh
  As fast as she can hie.

  twine] part, sunder.

XX

She hadna pu'd a leaf, a leaf,
    A leaf but only twae,
When up and started young Tam Lin,
    Says, ' Ladye, thou 's pu' nae mae.

XXI

' How dar' ye pu' a leaf ? ' he says,
    ' How dar' ye break the tree ?
How dar' ye scathe my babe,' he says,
    ' That 's between you and me ? '

XXII

' O tell me, tell me, Tam,' she says,
    ' For His sake that died on tree,
If ye were ever in holy chapel
    Or sain'd in Christentie ? '

XXIII

' The truth I'll tell to thee, Janet,
    Ae word I winna lee ;
A knight me got, and a lady me bore,
    As well as they did thee.

XXIV

' Roxburgh he was my grandfather,
    Took me with him to bide ;
And ance it fell upon a day,
    As hunting I did ride,

XXV

' There came a wind out o' the north,
    A sharp wind an' a snell,
A dead sleep it came over me
    And frae my horse I fell ;
And the Queen o' Fairies she took me
    In yon green hill to dwell.

scathe] harm.   sain'd] blessed, baptised.   snell] keen, cold.

TAM LIN

XXVI

' And pleasant is the fairy land
    For those that in it dwell,
But ay at end of seven years
    They pay a teind to hell;
I am sae fair and fu' o' flesh
    I'm fear'd 'twill be mysell.

XXVII

' But the night is Hallowe'en, Janet,
    The morn is Hallowday;
Then win me, win me, an ye will,
    For weel I wat ye may.

XXVIII

' The night it is gude Hallowe'en,
    The fairy folk do ride,
And they that wad their true-love win,
    At Miles Cross they maun bide.'—

XXIX

' But how should I you ken, Tam Lin,
    How should I borrow you,
Amang a pack of uncouth knights
    The like I never saw?'—

XXX

' You'll do you down to Miles Cross
    Between twel' hours and ane,
And fill your hands o' the holy water
    And cast your compass roun'.

teind] tithe.   borrow] ransom.   uncouth] unknown.

XXXI

'The first company that passes by,
  Say na, and let them gae;
The neist company that passes by,
  Say na, and do right sae;
The third company that passes by,
  Then I'll be ane o' thae.

XXXII

'O first let pass the black, ladye,
  And syne let pass the brown;
But quickly run to the milk-white steed,
  Pu' ye his rider down.

XXXIII

'For some ride on the black, ladye,
  And some ride on the brown;
But I ride on a milk-white steed,
  A gowd star on my crown:
Because I was an earthly knight
  They gie me that renown.

XXXIV

'My right hand will be gloved, ladye,
  My left hand will be bare,
And thae's the tokens I gie thee:
  Nae doubt I will be there.

XXXV

'Ye'll tak' my horse then by the head
  And let the bridle fa';
The Queen o' Elfin she'll cry out
  "True Tam Lin he's awa'!"

TAM LIN

XXXVI

'They'll turn me in your arms, ladye,
  An aske but and a snake;
But hauld me fast, let me na gae,
  To be your warldis make.

XXXVII

'They'll turn me in your arms, ladye,
  But and a deer so wild;
But hauld me fast, let me na gae,
  The father o' your child.

XXXVIII

'They'll shape me in your arms, ladye,
  A hot iron at the fire;
But hauld me fast, let me na go,
  To be your heart's desire.

XXXIX

'They'll shape me last in your arms, Janet,
  A mother-naked man;
Cast your green mantle over me,
  And sae will I be won.'

XL

Janet has kilted her green kirtle
  A little abune the knee;
And she has snooded her yellow hair
  A little abune her bree,
And she is on to Miles Cross
  As fast as she can hie.

XLI

About the dead hour o' the night
  She heard the bridles ring;
And Janet was as glad at that
  As any earthly thing.

aske] newt, lizard.   make] mate, husband.

TAM LIN

And first gaed by the black, black steed,
　　And syne gaed by the brown;
But fast she gript the milk-white steed
　　And pu'd the rider down.

XLIII

She's pu'd him frae the milk-white steed,
　　An' loot the bridle fa',
And up there rase an eldritch cry,
　　'True Tam Lin he's awa'!'

XLIV

They shaped him in her arms twa
　　An aske but and a snake;
But aye she grips and hau'ds him fast
　　To be her warldis make.

XLV

They shaped him in her arms twa
　　But and a deer sae wild;
But aye she grips and hau'ds him fast,
　　The father o' her child.

XLVI

They shaped him in her arms twa
　　A hot iron at the fire;
But aye she grips and hau'ds him fast
　　To be her heart's desire.

XLVII

They shaped him in her arms at last
　　A mother-naked man;
She cast her mantle over him,
　　And sae her love she wan.

loot] let.　　eldritch] unearthly.

12

TAM LIN

Up then spak' the Queen o' Fairies,
  Out o' a bush o' broom,
' She that has borrow'd young Tam Lin
  Has gotten a stately groom.'

XLIX

Out then spak' the Queen o' Fairies,
  And an angry woman was she,
' She 's ta'en awa' the bonniest knight
  In a' my companie !

L

' But what I ken this night, Tam Lin,
  Gin I had kent yestreen,
I wad ta'en out thy heart o' flesh,
  And put in a heart o' stane.

LI

' And adieu, Tam Lin ! But gin I had kent
  A ladye wad borrow'd thee,
I wad ta'en out thy twa grey e'en
  Put in twa e'en o' tree.

LII

' And had I the wit yestreen, yestreen,
  That I have coft this day,
I'd paid my teind seven times to hell
  Ere you had been won away ! '

tree] wood.   coft] bought.

13

Sir Cawline

3.

I

JESUS, Lord mickle of might,
   That dyed for us on roode,
So maintaine us in all our right
   That loves true English blood!

II

Sir Cawline [was an English knight]
   Curteous and full hardye;
[And our King has lent him] forth to fight,
   Into Ireland over the sea.

III

And in that land there dwells a King,
   Over all the bell does beare;
And he hath a ladye to his daughter,
   Of fashion she hath no peere;
Knights and lordes they woo'd her both,
   Trusted to have been her feere.

IV

Sir Cawline loves her best of onie,
   But nothing durst he say
To discreeve his councell to no man,
   But dearlye loved this may.

V

Till it befell upon a day,
   Great dill to him was dight;
The mayden's love removed his mind,
   To care-bed went the knight.

fashion] form, beauty.   feere] mate, consort.   discreeve]
discover.   may] maid.   dill] dole, grief.   dight] ordained.
care-bed] sick-bed.

14

SIR CAWLINE

VI

One while he spread his armes him fro,
  And cryed so pittyouslye :
' For the mayden's love that I have most minde
  This day shall comfort mee,
Or else ere noone I shall be dead ! '
  Thus can Sir Cawline say.

VII

When the parish mass that itt was done,
  And the King was bowne to dine,
Says, 'Where is Sir Cawline, that was wont
  To serve me with ale and wine ?'

VIII

But then answer'd a curteous knight
  Fast his hands wringinge :
' Sir Cawline 's sicke and like to be dead
  Without and a good leechinge.'

IX

' Feitch ye downe my daughter deere,
  She is a leeche full fine ;
Ay, and take you doe and the baken bread,
  And [drinke he of] the wine soe red,
And looke no daynty's for him too deare,
  For full loth I wo'ld him tine.'

X

This ladye is gone to his chamber,
  Her maydens following nye ;
' O well,' she saith, ' how doth my lord ?'
  ' O sicke ! ' againe saith hee.

bowne] made ready, gone.
have a good leech, or physician.

without and, &c.] unless he
tine] lose.

15

XI

‘ But rise up wightlye, man, for shame !
  Ne’er lie here soe cowardlye !
Itt is told in my father’s hall
  For my love you will dye.’—

XII

‘ Itt is for your love, fayre ladye,
  That all this dill I drie ;
For if you wo’ld comfort me with a kisse,
Then were I brought from bale to bliss,
  No longer here wo’ld I lye.’—

XIII

‘ Alas ! soe well you know, Sir Knight,
  I cannot be your feere.’—
‘ Yet some deeds of armes fain wo’ld I doe
  To be your bacheleere.’—

XIV

‘ On Eldritch Hill there grows a thorn,
  Upon the mores brodinge ;
And wo’ld you, Sir Knight, wake there all night
  To day of the other morninge ?

XV

‘ For the Eldritch King, that is mickle of might,
  Will examine you beforne :
There was never a man bare his life away
  Since the day that I was born.’—

XVI

‘ But I will for your sake, ladye,
  Walk on the bents soe browne,
And I’ll either bring you a readye token,
  Or I’ll ne’er come to you again.’

wightlye] briskly, stoutly.   mores] moors.   brodinge]
growing, sprouting.   examine] put to the test.   beforne]
before (morning).   bents] rough grasses.

16

SIR CAWLINE

XVII

But this ladye is gone to her chamber,
    Her maydens following bright;
And Sir Cawline's gone to the mores soe broad,
    For to wake there all night.

XVIII

Unto midnight that the moone did rise
    He walkèd up and downe,
And a lightsome bugle then heard he blow
    Over the bents so browne;
Sayes he, ' And if cryance come to my heart,
    I am farr from any good towne.'

XIX

And he spyèd, e'en a little him by,
    A furyous king and a fell,
And a ladye bright his brydle led
    [More] seemlye [than onie can tell].

XX

Soe fast he call'd on Sir Cawline,
    ' O man, I rede thee flye !
For if cryance come untill thy heart
    I'm afeard lest thou maun dye !'—

XXI

He sayes, ' No cryance comes to my heart,
    Nor i'faith I fear not thee;
For because thou ming'd not Christ before,
    The lesse me dreadeth thee.'

cryance] yielding, cowardice.   ming'd] mentioned, spoke the name of.

17

SIR CAWLINE

XXII

But Sir Cawline then he shooke a speare ;
    The King was bold, and abode :
And the timber those two children bare
    Soe soon in sunder slode :
Forth they tooke and two good swords,
    And they layden on good loade.

XXIII

The Eldritch King was mickle of might,
    And stiffly to the ground did stand ;
But Sir Cawline with an aukeward stroke
    He brought from him his hand—
Ay, and flying over his head so hye
    It fell down of that lay land.

XXIV

His ladye stood a little thereby,
    Fast her hands wringinge :
' For the mayden's love that you have most minde,
    Smyte you noe more [this King].

XXV

' And he's never come upon Eldritch Hill
    Him to sport, gammon or play,
And to meet no man of middle-earth
    That lives on Christ his lay.'

XXVI

But he then up, that Eldritch King,
    Set him in his sadle againe,
And that Eldritch King and his ladye
    To their castle are they gone.

slode] split.   good loade] heavily   aukeward] back-handed.   lay land] lea, land not under cultivation ; here =ground.   he's never] he will never.   middle-earth] this earth, as midway between heaven and hell.   lay] law, faith.

SIR CAWLINE

XXVII

Sir Cawline took up that eldritch sword
  As hard as any flynt,
Soe did he [the hand with] ringès five
  Harder than fyer, and brent.

XXVIII

The watchmen cryed upon the walls
  And sayd, ' Sir Cawline's slaine !'
Then the King's daughter she fell downe,
  ' For peerlesse is my payne !'—

XXIX

' O peace, my ladye !' sayes Sir Cawline,
  ' I have bought thy love full deare ;
O peace, my ladye !' sayes Sir Cawline,
  ' Peace, ladye, for I am heere !'

XXX

He 's presented to the King's daughter
  The hand, and then the sword
[And he has claimed the King's daughter
  According to her word].

XXXI

And the King has betaken him his broad lands
  And all his venison ;
[Sayes] ' Thou shalt have my daughter deare,
  [And be my onelye son '].

brent] smooth.   betaken] given, made over.   venison]
i. e. deer-forests.

19

Sir Aldingar

I

OUR King he kept a false steward,
  Men call'd him Sir Aldingar;
[He would have woo'd our comely Queene
  To be his paramour].

II

He would have woo'd our comely Queene,
  Her deere worship to betray:
Our Queene she was a good woman
  And evermore said him nay.

III

Sir Aldingar was offended in 's mind,
  With her he was ne'er content,
But he sought what meanès he could find
  In a fyer to have her brent.

IV

There came a lame lazar to the King's gate,
  A lazar 'was blind and lame;
He took the lazar upon his backe,
  Upon the Queene's bed did him lay.

V

Said, 'Lye still, lazar, whereas thou lyest,
  Looke thou goe not away;
I'le make thee a whole man and a sound
  In two howres of a day.'

VI

And then went forth Sir Aldingar
  Our Queene for to betray,
And then he met with our comely King;
  Says, 'God you save and see!

brent] burnt.

SIR ALDINGAR

VII

' If I had space, as I have grace,
  A message I'd say to thee.'—
' Say on, say on, Sir Aldingar,
  Say thou on and unto me.'

VIII

' I can shew you one of the grievous't sights
  Ever Christian King did see ;
Our Queene hath chosen a new, new love,
  She will have none of thee.

IX

' If she had chosen a right good knight,
  The lesse had beene her shame ;
But she hath chosen a lazar man
  Which is both blind and lame.'--

X

' If this be true, Sir Aldingar,
  That thou dost tell to me,
Then will I make thee a rich knight
  Both of gold and fee.

XI

' But if it be false, Sir Aldingar,
  That thou dost tell to me,
Then looke thou for no other death
  But to be hang'd on tree.'

XII

When the King came into the Queene's chamber,
  Standing her bed before,
' There 's a lodly lome,' says Harry the King
  For our dame Queene Elinor !

lodly] loathly.   lome] thing.

21

XIII

' If thou were a man, as thou art none,
    It is here thou shouldest dye ;
But a paire of new gallowes shall be built,
    Thou'st hang on them soe hye.

XIV

' And a fayre fyer there shall be bett,
    And brent our Queene shall been.'
Forth then walk'd our comely King,
    And met with our comely Queene.

XV

Saies, ' God you save our Queene, Madam,
    And Christ you save and see !
Here you have chosen a new, new love,
    And you will have none of mee.

XVI

' If you had chosen a right good knight,
    The lesse had beene your shame ;
But you have chosen a lazar man
    That is both blind and lame.'

XVII

' Ever alacke ! ' said our comely Queene,
    ' Sir Aldingar he is false ;
But ever alacke !' said our comely Queene,
    ' And woe is me, and alas !

XVIII

' I had thought swevens had never been true
    I have proved them true [today]:
I dream'd in my swevens on Thursday at even
    In my bed wheras I lay,

bett] kindled.   swevens] dreams.

22

SIR ALDINGAR

XIX

'I dreamèd a grype and a grimlie beast
  Had carried my crowne away,
My gorget and my kirtle of golde,
  And all my heade-geare [gay].

XX

'He wo'ld have worryed me with his tush,
  And borne me into his nest,
Saving there came a little hawke
  Flying out of the east.

XXI

'—Saving there came a little hawke
  Which men call a merlion;
He stroke him downe untill the ground,
  That deade he did fall downe.

XXII

'Gif I were a man, as I am none,
  A battell I wo'ld prove;
I wo'ld fight with that false traitor;
  At him I cast my glove!

XXIII

'Seeing I am able noe battell to make,
  You must grant me, my liege, a knight,
To fight with that traitor, Sir Aldingar,
  To maintaine me in my right.'

XXIV

'I'le give thee forty dayes,' said our King,
  'To seeke thee a man therein;
If thou find not a man in forty dayes,
  In a hott fyer thou shalt brenn.'

grype] gryphon.　　tush] tusk, beak.　　merlion] merlin,
a small falcon.

SIR ALDINGAR

XXV

Our Queene sent forth a messenger ;
    He rode fast into the south ;
He rode the countryes through and through
    Soe far unto Portsmouth.

XXVI

[But for all his riding ne'er sped he
    To fetch help to our Queene ;]
He co'ld find noe man in the south country
    'Wo'ld fight with the knight soe keene.

XXVII

The second messenger shee sent forth,
    Rode far into the east ;
But—blessèd be God 'made sunn and moone ! —
    He sped then all of the best.

XXVIII

As he rode then by one river side,
    There he mett with a little Child ;
He seemèd noe more in a man's likenesse
    Than a child of four yeeres old.

XXIX

He ask'd the messenger how far he rode ;
    Loth he was him to tell ;
The little one was offended att him,
    Bade him adieu, farewell.

XXX

Said, ' Turne thou againe, thou messenger,
    Greete our Queen well from me ;
When bale is at hyest, boote is at nyest—
    Helpe enough there may bee.

bale] evil, trouble.   boote] help, remedy.

24

XXXI

' Bid our Queene remember what she did dreame
    In her bedd wheras shee lay ;
She dreamèd the grype and the grimlie beast
    Had carryed her crowne away ;

XXXII

' Her gorgett and her kirtle of gold,
    Her head-geare [all soe drest]
He wo'ld have worryed her with his tush,
    And borne her into his nest.

XXXIII

' Saving there came a little hawke,
    Men call him a merlion ;
'Did strike him downe untill the ground
    That dead he did fall downe.

XXXIV

' Bidd the Queene be merry att her heart,
    Evermore light and glad ;
When bale is at hyest, boote is at nyest,
    Helpe enough [shall be had '].

XXXV

Then the Queen's messenger rode backe,
    A gladded man then was hee ;
When that he came before our Queene,
    A gladd woman then was shee.

XXXVI

She gave the messenger twenty pound,
    O Lord, in gold and fee ;
Saies, 'Spend, nor spare while this doth last,
    Then fetch thou more of me.'

XXXVII

Our Queene was put in a tunne to burn;
　　She thought noe thing but death :
When they were ware of the Little One
　　'Came ryding forth of the east.

XXXVIII

With a mu[le and a bridle all of bells]
　　A lovelye child was hee ;
When that he came to that fyér
　　He lighted the Queene full nigh.

XXXIX

Sayd, 'Draw away these brands of fyer
　　'Lie burning before our Queene,
And fetch me hither Sir Aldingar
　　That is a knight soe keene.'

XL

When Aldingar saw that Little One,
　　Full little of him hee thought ;
If there had been halfe a hundred such
　　Of them he would not have wrought.

XLI

He sayd, 'Come hither, Sir Aldingar,
　　Thou seemest as big as a fooder ;
I trust God ere I have done with thee
　　God will send us an auger.'

XLII

Sayes, 'The first stroke that's given, Sir Aldingar,
　　I will give unto thee ;
And if the second give thou may,
　　Looke then thou spare not mee.'

tunne] barrel.　　　wrought] recked.　　　fooder] tun.

26

SIR ALDINGAR

XLIII

This Little One pull'd forth a well good sword,
    I wis it well all of gilte.
It cast a light there over that field,
    It shone soe all of gilte.

XLIV

He stroke the first stroke at Aldingar;
    [Noe second needed hee;
At the first stroke] he stroke away
    His leggs [all] by the knee.

XLV

Sayes, ' Stand up, stand up, thou false traitor,
    And fight upon thy feete;
For, an thou thrive as thou begins,
    Of a height we shall be meete.'

XLVI

' A priest, a priest,' sayes Aldingar,
    ' Me for to housel and shrive !
A priest, a priest,' sayes Aldingar,
    ' While I am a man living alive !

XLVII

' I would have courted our comely Queene ;
    To it shee wo'ld never consent ;
I thought to betray her to our King
    In a fyer to have her brent.

XLVIII

' There came a lame lazar to the King's gate,
    A lazar both blind and lame ;
I took the lazar upon my back,
    Upon the Queene's bedd had him layn.

meete] matched, equal.

27

XLIX

'I bade him, *Lye still, lazar,* where he lay,
  Looke he went not away ;
I wo'ld make him a whole man and a sound
  In two houres of a day.

L

' A priest, a priest,' sayes Aldingar,
  ' To shrive me cleane of hell !
Ever alacke !' sayes Sir Aldingar,
  ' Falsing never doth well.

LI

' Forgive, forgive me, Queene, Madam !
  For Christ's love forgive me !'—
' God forgave his death, Aldingar,
  And freely I forgive thee.'—

LII

' Now take thy wife, thou King Harry,
  And love her as thou sho'ld ;
Thy wife shee is as true to thee
  As stone lies in castle wall.'

LIII

The lazar under the gallow tree
  [Grew] a pretty man and small :
The lazar under the gallow tree
  Was made steward in King Harry's hall.

5

Cospatrick

I

COSPATRICK has sent o'er the faem :
Cospatrick brought his ladye hame.

II

Full seven score ships have come her wi',
The ladye by the grene-wood tree.

III

There was twal' and twal' wi' baken bread,
And twal' and twal' wi' the goud sae red :

IV

And twal' and twal' wi' beer and wine,
And twal' and twal' wi' muskadine :

V

And twal' and twal' wi' bouted flour,
And twal' and twal' wi' paramour.

VI

Sweet Willy was a Widow's son,
And at her stirrup he did run.

VII

And she was clad in the finest pall,
But aye she let the tears down fall.

VIII

'O lady, sits your saddle awry ?
Or is your steed for you owre high ?

IX

'Or are you mourning in your tide
That you suld be Cospatrick's bride ?'

X

'I am not mourning at this tide
That I suld be Cospatrick's bride :

bouted] bolted, sifted.   paramour] *meaning here uncertain.*
pall] fine cloth.

29

COSPATRICK

XI

' But I a.n mourning in my mood
That ever I left my mother good.

XII

' But, bonny boy, come tell to me
What is the custom o' your countrie ?'

XIII

' The custom thereof, my dame,' he says,
' Will ill a gentle ladye please.

XIV

' Seven King's daughters has our lord wedded,
And seven King's daughters has our lord bedded:

XV

' But he 's cutted their breasts frae their breast-bane,
And sent them mourning hame again.

XVI

' But when you come to the palace yett,
His mother a gowden chair will set:

XVII

' And be you maid or be you nane,
O sit you there till the day be dane.

XVIII

' And gin you're sure that you're a maid,
Ye may gae safely him to wed:

XIX

' But gif o' that ye be na sure,
Then hire some damsel o' your bour.'—

XX

O when she came to the palace yett,
His mother a gowden chair did set:

yett] gate.

30

XXI

The bonnie may was tired wi' ridin',
Gae'd sit her down ere she was bidden.

XXII

And was she maid or was she nane,
She sat in it till the day was dune.

XXIII

And she's call'd on her bour-woman,
That waiting was into her train :

XXIV

' Five thousand marks I'll gie to thee,
To sleep this night with my lord for me.'—

XXV

[' But will it for my ladye plead,
I'se be the bride in my ladye's stead.']—

XXVI

When bells were rung and mass was sayne,
And a' men unto bed were gane,

XXVII

Cospatrick and the bonny maid
Into ae chamber they were laid.

XXVIII

' Now speak to me, blankets, and speak to me, bed,
And speak, thou sheet, inchanted web,

XXIX

' And speak, my brown sword, that winna lee,
Is this a leal maiden that lies by me ? '

XXX

' It is not a maid that you hae wedded,
But it is a maid that you hae bedded :

into] in.   lee] lie.

31

COSPATRICK

XXXI
'It is a leal maiden that lies by thee,
But not the maiden that it should be.'

XXXII
Then out he sprang o' his bridal bed,
And wrathfully his claiths on did:

XXXIII
And he has ta'en him through the ha',
And on his mother he did ca'.

XXXIV
'I am the most unhappy man
That ever was in Christen land:

XXXV
'I courted a maiden meik and mild,
And I've gat but a woman great wi' child.'—

XXXVI
'O stay, my son, into this ha',
And sport ye wi' your merry men a'.

XXXVII
'And I'll gang to your painted bour,
To see how it fares wi' your paramour.'

XXXVIII
The carline queen was stark and strang
She gar'd the door flee aff the ban.

XXXIX
'O is your bairn to laird or loun,
Or is it to your father's groom?'—

XL
'O hear me, mother, on my knee,
Till my sad story I tell to thee.

carline] old woman.   ban] band, hinge.   laird or loun]
squire or common fellow.

32

COSPATRICK

'O we were sisters, sisters seven;
We were the fairest under heaven.

' We had nae mair for our seven years' wark
But to shape and sew the King's son a sark.

' It fell on a summer's afternoon,
When a' our langsome task was done,

' We cast the kevils us amang
To see which suld to the grene-wood gang.

' Ohone, alas ! for I was the youngest,
And aye my weird it was the hardest.

' The kevil it did on me fa',
Which was the cause of a' my wae.

' For to the grene-wood I must gae,
To pu' the red rose and the slae ;

' To pu' the red rose and the thyme
To deck my mother's bour and mine.

' I hadna pu'd a flower but ane,
When by there came a gallant hende,

' Wi' high-coll'd hose and laigh-coll'd shoon,
And he seem'd to be some Kingis son.

kevils] lots.   hende] courteous youth.   high-coll'd,
laigh-coll'd] high-cut, low-cut.

LI

'And be I a maid, or be I nae,
He kept me there till the close o' day:

LII

'And be I a maid or be I nane,
He kept me there till the day was done.

LIII

'He gae me a lock o' his yellow hair,
And bade me keep it for ever mair:

LIV

'He gae me a carknet o' bonny beads,
And bade me keep it against my needs.

LV

'He gae to me a gay gold ring,
And bade me keep it abune a' thing.

LVI

'He gae to me a little pen-knife,
And bade me keep it as my life.'—

LVII

'What did you wi' the tokens rare
That ye got frae that gallant there?'—

LVIII

'O bring that coffer here to me,
And a' the tokens ye sall see.'

LIX

And aye she sought, and aye she flang
Until these four things cam' to her hand.

LX

'Now stay here, daughter, your bour within,
Till I gae parley with my son.'

carknet] necklace.   flang] flung about, rummaged violently.

COSPATRICK

LXI

O she has ta'en her thro' the ha',
And on her son began to ca'.

LXII

' What did you wi' that gay gold ring
I bade you keep abune a' thing?

LXIII

' What did you wi' that little pen-knife
I bade you keep while you had life?

LXIV

' What did you wi' the bonny beads
I bade you keep against your needs?'—

LXV

'I gae them to a ladye gay
I met i' the grene-wood on a day.

LXVI

' But I wad gie a' my ha's and tours,
I had that bright burd in my bours:

LXVII

' But I wad gie my very life
I had that ladye to my wife!'

LXVIII

'Now keep, my son, your ha's and tours;
Ye have that bright burd in your bours.

LXIX

' And keep, my son, your very life,
Ye have that ladye to your wife.'

LXX

Now, or a month was come and gane,
The ladye bore him a bonny son.

LXXI

And it was well written on his breast-bane,
' Cospatrick is my father's name.'

LXXII

O rowe my ladye in satin and silk,
And wash my son in the morning milk !

6.   *Willy's Lady*

I

SWEET Willy's ta'en him o'er the faem,
He's woo'd a wife and brought her hame.

II

He's woo'd her for her yellow hair,
But his mither wrought her mickle care;

III

And mickle dolour gar'd her drie,
For lighter she can never be.

IV

But in her bower she sits wi' pain,
And Willy mourns o'er her in vain.

V

And to his mither he has gane;
That vile rank witch of vilest kind.

VI

He says: ' My ladie has a cup
Wi' gowd and silver set about.

VII

' This goodlie gift shall be your ain,
And let her be lighter o' her young bairn.'—

rowe] roll, wrap.   gar'd her drie] caused her to suffer.
lighter] i.e. delivered of her child.

36

WILLY'S LADY

VIII

'Of her young bairn she'll ne'er be lighter,
Nor in her bower to shine the brighter:

IX

'But she shall die and turn to clay,
And you shall wed another may.'—

X

'Another may I'll marry nane,
Another may I'll ne'er bring hame.'

XI

But sighing says his bonnie wife,
'I wish this was an end o' my life!

XII

'Yet gae ye unto your mither again,
That vile rank witch of vilest kind.

XIII

'And say: **My** ladie has a steed,
The like o' him 's no in the lands of Leed.

XIV

'For at ilka tett o' that horse's mane
There's a golden chess and a bell ringíng.

XV

'This goodlie gift shall be your ain,
And let her be lighter o' her young bairn.'—

XVI

'O' her young bairn she'll ne'er be lighter,
Nor in her bower to shine the brighter;

XVII

'But she shall die and turn to clay,
And ye shall wed another may.'—

tett] tuft.   chess] ? jess, strap.

37

XVIII

'Another may I'll marry nane,
Another may I'll ne'er bring hame.'

XIX

But sighing says his bonnie wife,
'I wish this was an end o' my life!

XX

'Yet gae ye unto your mither again,
That vile rank witch of vilest kind:

XXI

'And say: My ladie has a girdle,
It's a' red gowd unto the middle.

XXII

'And ay at every silver hem
Hangs fifty silver bells and ten.

XXIII

'That goodlie gift shall be your ain,
But let her be lighter o' her young bairn.'—

XXIV

'O' her young bairn she's ne'er be lighter,
Nor in her bower to shine the brighter:

XXV

'But she shall die and turn to clay,
And you shall wed another may.'—

XXVI

'Another may I'll never wed nane,
Another may I'll never bring hame.'

XXVII

But sighing says his bonnie wife,
'I wish this was an end o' my life!'

XXVIII

Then out and spake the Billy Blind—
He spake aye in a good time;

Billy Blind] a Brownie, or friendly House-spirit.

XXIX

'Ye doe ye to the market-place,
And there buy ye a loaf o' wax;

XXX

'Ye shape it bairn and bairnly like,
And in twa glasses e'en ye'll pit.

XXXI

'And do ye to your mither then,
And bid her come to your boy's christ'nen,

XXXII

'For dear's the boy he's been to you:
Then notice weel what she shall do:

XXXIII

'And do you stand a little away,
And listen weel what she shall say.'

XXXIV

He did him to the market-place,
And there he bought a loaf o' wax.

XXXV

He shaped it bairn and bairnly-like,
And in 't twa glasses e'en he pat.

XXXVI

He did him till his mither then,
And bade her to his boy's christ'nen.

XXXVII

And he did stand a little forbye,
And noticed well what she did say.

XXXVIII

'O wha has loosed the nine witch-knots
That was among that ladie's locks?

pit] put.   pat] did put.   forbye] aside.

WILLY'S LADY

XXXIX

' And wha has ta'en out the kaims o' care
That hangs among that ladie's hair?

XL

' And wha's ta'en down the bush o' woodbine
That hangs atween her bower and mine?

XLI

' And wha has kill'd the master kid
That ran aneath that ladie's bed?

XLII

' And wha has loosed her left-foot shee
And letten that ladie lighter be?'

XLIII

Syne Willy has loosed the nine witch-knots
That was among his ladie's locks:

XLIV

And Willy's ta'en out the kaims o' care
That hang among his ladie's hair:

XLV

And Willy's ta'en down the bush o' woodbine
That hang atween her bower and thine:

XLVI

And Willy has kill'd the master kid
That ran aneath his ladie's bed:

XLVII

And Willy has loosed her left-foot shee,
And letten his ladie lighter be.

XLVIII

And now he's gotten a bonny young son,
And mickle grace be him upon!

kaims] combs.   shee] shoe.

7. *The Queen of Elfland's Nourice*

I

'*I* HEARD *a cow low, a bonnie cow low,*
  And a cow low down in yon glen :
Lang, lang will my young son greet
  Or his mither bid him come ben !

II

'*I heard a cow low, a bonnie cow low,*
  And a cow low down in yon fauld :
Lang, lang will my young son greet
  Or his mither take him frae cauld !'

III

[The Queen of Elfan's nourice
  She sits and sings her lane]
'Waken, Queen of Elfan
  And hear your nourice moan.'—

IV

'O moan ye for your meat,
  Or moan ye for your fee,
Or moan ye for the ither bounties
  That ladies are wont to gie ? '—

V

'I moan na for my meat,
  Nor moan I for my fee,
Nor moan I for the ither bounties
  That ladies are wont to gie.

VI

['But I heard a bonnie cow
  Low down in yonder fauld]
And I moan for my young son
  I left in four nights auld.

greet] cry.   *ben*] to the inner room.   nourice] nurse.

VII

'I moan na for my meat,
  Nor yet for my fee;
But I moan for Christen land;
  It's there I fain would be.'

VIII

'O nurse my bairn, nourice,
  Till he stan' at your knee,
An ye's win hame to Christen land
  Whar fain it's ye wad be.

IX

'O keep my bairn, nourice,
  Till he gang by the hauld,
An ye's win hame to your young son
  Ye left in four nights auld.

X

'O nourice lay your head
  [Here] upo' my knee:
See ye not that narrow road
  Up by yonder tree?

XI

['See ye not the narrow road
  By yon lillie leven?]
That's the road the righteous goes
  And that's the road to heaven.

XII

'An' see na ye that braid road
  Down by yon sunny fell?
Yon's the road the wicked gae,
  An' that's the road to hell.

gang by the hauld] walk by holding on to the hand.

42

XIII

[An' see na ye that bonny road
About the fernie brae ?
That wins back frae Elfland
Where you must wait to gae.]

8. *Lady Isabel and the Elf-Knight*

I

*M*Y *plaid awa', my plaid awa',*
And o'er the hill and far awa';
And far awa' to Norrowa',
My plaid shall not be blown awa'!

II

Lady Isabel sits in her bower sewing,
Aye as the gowans grow gay—
She heard an elf-knight his horn blawing,
The first morning in May.

III

The elfin-knight sits on yon hill,
He blaws his horn baith loud and shrill.

IV

He blaws it east, he blaws it west,
He blaws it where he lyketh best.

V

' I wish that horn were in my kist,
Yea, and the knight in my arms niest.'

VI

She had no sooner these words said,
When that knight came to her bed.

gowans] daisies.   kist] chest.   niest] next.

43

VII

'Thou art owre young a maid,' quoth he,
'Married with me thou ill wouldst be.'—

VIII

'I have a sister younger than I,
And she was married yesterday.'—

IX

'Married with me if thou wouldst be,
A courtesie thou must do to me.

X

'For thou must shape a sark to me
Without any cut or hem,' quoth he ·

XI

'It's ye maun shape it knife-and-shurlesse,
And also sew it needle-threedlesse.

XII

'And ye maun wash it in yonder well,
Where the dew never wat nor the rain never fell.

XIII

'And ye maun dry it upon a thorn
That never budded sin Adam was born.'—

XIV

'Now sin ye have asked some things o' me,
It's right I ask as mony o' thee.

XV

'My father he ask'd me an acre o' land
Between the saut sea and the strand.

XVI

'And ye maun are it wi' your blawin' horn,
And ye maun sow it wi' pepper corn.

sark] shirt.　　　wat] wetted.　　　are] plough.

LADY ISABEL AND THE ELF-KNIGHT

XVII

' And ye maun harrow it with ae tyne,
And ye maun shear it with ae horse bane.

XVIII

' And ye maun stack it in yon mouse-hole,
And ye maun thresh it in yon shoe-sole.

XIX

' And ye maun winnow it in your loof,
And ye maun sack it in your glove.

XX

' And ye maun bring it owre the sea,
Fair and clean and dry to me.

XXI

' And when ye've done an' finish'd your wark,
Come to me, love, an' get your sark.'

XXII

' It 's I'll not quit my plaid for my life ;
It haps my seven bairns and my wife.'
   The wind sall not blaw my plaid awa':
' And it 's I will keep me a maiden still,
Let the elfin knight do what he will'—
   The wind has not blawn my plaid awa'!

ae tyne] one harrow-point.   loof] palm.

The Riddling Knight

I

THERE were three sisters fair and bright,
    Jennifer, Gentle and Rosemary,
And they three loved one valiant knight—
    As the dow flies over the mulberry-tree.

II

The eldest sister let him in,
And barr'd the door with a silver pin.

III

The second sister made his bed,
And placed soft pillows under his head.

IV

The youngest sister that same night
Was resolved for to wed wi' this valiant knight.

V

'And if you can answer questions three,
O then, fair maid, I'll marry wi' thee.

VI

'O what is louder nor a horn,
Or what is sharper nor a thorn?

VII

'Or what is heavier nor the lead,
Or what is better nor the bread?

VIII

'Or what is longer nor the way,
Or what is deeper nor the sea?'—

IX

'O shame is louder nor a horn,
And hunger is sharper nor a thorn.

dow] dove.

X

'O sin is heavier nor the lead,
The blessing 's better nor the bread.

XI

'O the wind is longer nor the way
And love is deeper nor the sea.'

XII

['You have answer'd aright my questions three,]
Jennifer, Gentle and Rosemary;
And now, fair maid, I'll marry wi' thee,
  As the dow flies over the mulberry-tree.

10. ## *May Colvin*

I

FALSE Sir John a-wooing came
  To a maid of beauty fair;
May Colvin was this lady's name,
  Her father's only heir.

II

He woo'd her but, he woo'd her ben,
  He woo'd her in the ha';
Until he got the lady's consent
  To mount and ride awa'.

III

'Go fetch me some of your father's gold,
  And some of your mother's fee,
And I'll carry you into the north land,
  And there I'll marry thee.'

but, ben] both in the outer and inner rooms.

IV

She's gane to her father's coffers
　　Where all his money lay,
And she's taken the red, and she's left the white,
　　And so lightly she's tripp'd away.

V

She's gane to her father's stable
　　Where all the steeds did stand,
And she's taken the best, and she's left the warst
　　That was in her father's land.

VI

She's mounted on a milk-white steed,
　　And he on a dapple-grey,
And on they rade to a lonesome part,
　　A rock beside the sea.

VII

'Loup off the steed,' says false Sir John,
　　'Your bridal bed you see;
Seven ladies I have drownèd here,
　　And the eight' one you shall be.

VIII

'Cast off, cast off your silks so fine
　　And lay them on a stone,
For they are too fine and costly
　　To rot in the salt sea foam.

IX

'Cast off, cast off your silken stays,
　　For and your broider'd shoon,
For they are too fine and costly
　　To rot in the salt sea foam.

loup] leap.

MAY COLVIN

X

'Cast off, cast off your Holland smock
  That's border'd with the lawn,
For it is too fine and costly
  To rot in the salt sea foam.'—

XI

'O turn about, thou false Sir John,
  And look to the leaf o' the tree;
For it never became a gentleman
  A naked woman to see.'

XII

He turn'd himself straight round about
  To look to the leaf o' the tree;
She's twined her arms about his waist
  And thrown him into the sea.

XIII

'O hold a grip o' me, May Colvín,
  For fear that I should drown;
I'll take you home to your father's bower
  And safe I'll set you down.'

XIV

'No help, no help, thou false Sir John,
  No help, no pity thee!
For you lie not in a caulder bed
  Than you thought to lay me.'

XV

She mounted on her milk-white steed,
  And led the dapple-grey,
And she rode till she reach'd her father's gate,
  At the breakin' o' the day.

XVI

Up then spake the pretty parrot,
   'May Colvin, where have you been?
What has become o' false Sir John
   That went with you yestreen?'—

XVII

'O hold your tongue, my pretty parrot!
   Nor tell no tales o' me;
Your cage shall be made o' the beaten gold
   And the spokes o' ivorie.'

XVIII

Up then spake her father dear,
   In the bed-chamber where he lay:
'What ails the pretty parrot,
   That prattles so long ere day?'—

XIX

'There came a cat to my cage, master,
   I thought 't would have worried me,
And I was calling to May Coivín
   To take the cat from me.'

The Wee Wee Man

I

AS I was walking mine alane
 Atween a water and a wa',
There I spied a wee wee man,
 And he was the least that ere I saw.

II

His legs were scant a shathmont's length,
 And thick and thimber was his thie;
Atween his brows there was a span,
 And atween his shoulders there was three.

III

He 's ta'en and flung a meikle stane,
 And he flang 't as far as I could see;
Though I had been a Wallace wight
 I couldna liften 't to my knee.

IV

'O wee wee man, but ye be strang !
 O tell me where your dwelling be ? '
'My dwelling 's down by yon bonny bower;
 Fair lady, come wi' me and see.'

V

On we lap, and awa' we rade,
 Till we came to yon bonny green;
We lighted down to bait our steed,
 And out there came a lady sheen;

VI

Wi' four and twenty at her back
 A' comely clad in glisterin' green;
Tho' the King of Scotland had been there,
 The warst o' them might ha' been his queen.

shathmont] measure from the point of the extended thumb to
the extremity of the palm, six inches.   thimber] stout.   thie]
thigh.   lap] leapt.   sheen] shining, beautiful.

VII

On we lap, and awa' we rade,
  Till we came to a bonny ha';
The roof was o' the beaten gowd,
  And the floor was o' the cristal a'.

VIII

When we came to the stair-foot,
  Ladies were dancing jimp and sma',
But in the twinkling of an eie
  My wee wee man was clean awa'.

IX

Out gat the lights, on came the mist,
  Ladies nor mannie mair cou'd I see :
I turn'd about, and gae a look
  Just at the foot o' Benachie.

12.   *Alison Gross*

I

O ALISON GROSS, that lives in yon tow'r,
  The ugliest witch i' the north countrie,
Has trysted me ae day up till her bow'r
  And mony fair speeches she made to me.

II

She straik'd my head an' she kaim'd my hair,
  An' she set me down saftly on her knee ;
Says, 'Gin ye will be my lemman sae true,
  Sae mony braw things as I would you gie !'

    jimp] slim, slender.   trysted] invited.
  52

ALISON GROSS

She show'd me a mantle o' red scarlét,
  Wi' gouden flowers an' fringes fine ;
Says, ' Gin ye will be my lemman sae true,
  This gudely gift it sall be thine.'—

IV

' Awa', awa', ye ugly witch,
  Haud far awa', an' lat me be !
I never will be your lemman sae true,
  An' I wish I were out o' your company.'

V

She neist brought a sark o' the saftest silk,
  Well wrought wi' pearls about the band ;
Says, ' Gin ye will be my lemman sae true,
  This gudely gift ye sall command.'

VI

She show'd me a cup o' the good red gowd,
  Well set wi' jewels sae fair to see ;
Says, ' Gin ye will be my lemman sae true,
  This gudely gift I will you gie.'—

VII

' Awa', awa', ye ugly witch,
  Haud far awa', an' lat me be !
For I wouldna once kiss your ugly mouth
  For a' the gifts that ye could gie.'

VIII

She 's turn'd her right an' roun' about,
  An' thrice she blaw on a grass-green horn ;
An' she sware by the moon an' the stars abune
  That she'd gar me rue the day I was born.

lemman] sweetheart.   haud] hold, keep.

ALISON GROSS

IX

Then out has she ta'en a silver wand,
    An' she's turn'd her three times roun' and roun';
She mutter'd sic words till my strength it fail'd,
    An' I fell down senseless upon the groun'.

X

She's turn'd me into an ugly worm,
    And gar'd me toddle about the tree;
An' ay, on ilka Saturday's night,
    My sister Maisry came to me,

XI

Wi' silver bason an' silver kaim
    To kaim my headie upon her knee;
But or I had kiss'd [wi' Alison Gross]
    I'd sooner ha' toddled about the tree.

XII

But as it fell out, on last Hallowe'en,
    When the Seely Court was ridin' by,
The Queen lighted down on a gowany bank
    Nae far frae the tree where I wont to lye.

XIII

She took me up in her milk-white han',
    An' she's straik'd me three times o'er her knee;
She changed me again to my ain proper shape,
    An' nae mair I toddle about the tree.

Seely Court] the Happy Court (of the Fairies).   gowany]
daisied.

Kemp Owyne

I

HER mother died when she was young,
  Which gave her cause to make great moan;
Her father married the warst woman
  That ever lived in Christendom.

II

She servèd her wi' foot and hand
  In everything that she could dee,
Till once, in an unlucky time
  She threw her owre a craig o' the sea.

III

Says, ' Lie you there, dove Isabel,
  And all my sorrows lie wi' thee !
Till Kemp Owyne come to the craig,
  And borrow you wi' kisses three.'

IV

Her breath grew strang, her hair grew lang
  And twisted thrice about the tree,
And all the people, far and near,
  Thought that a savage beast was she.

V

And aye she cried for Kemp Owyne
  Gin that he would but com' to her hand:—
Now word has gane to Kemp Owyne
  That siccan a beast was in his land.

VI

' Now by my sooth,' says Kemp Owyne,
  ' This fiery beast I'll gang to see ';
' And by my sooth,' says Segramour,
  ' My ae brother, I'll gang you wi'.'

dee] do.   craig] rock.   Kemp] champion, knight.
borrow] ransom.   siccan] such.

KEMP OWYNE

VII

O they have biggit a bonny boat,
　And they have set her to the sea;
But a mile before they reach'd the shore
　I wot she gar'd the red fire flee.

VIII

' O brother, keep my boat afloat,
　An' lat her na the land so near!
For the wicked beast she'll sure go mad,
　An' set fire to the land an' mair.'

IX

Syne he has bent an arblast bow
　And aim'd an arrow at her head,
And swore, if she didna quit the land,
　Wi' that same shaft to shoot her dead.

X

' O out o' my stythe I winna rise—
　And it is na for the fear o' thee—
Till Kemp Owyne, the kingis son,
　Come to the craig an' thrice kiss me.'

XI

Her breath was strang, her hair was lang
　And twisted thrice about the tree,
And with a swing she came about:
　' Come to the craig, an' kiss with me!

XII

' Here is a royal belt,' she cried,
　' That I have found in the green sea;
And while your body it is on,
　Drawn shall your blood never be;
But if you touch me, tail or fin,
　I swear my belt your death shall be.'

biggit] built.　　gar'd] made.　　stythe] place, station.
56

XIII

He 's louted him o'er the Eastmuir craig,
    As out she swang and about the tree ;
He steppèd in, gave her a kiss,
    The royal belt he brought him wi'.

XIV

Her breath was strang, her hair was lang
    And twisted twice about the tree,
As awa' she gid, and again she swang—
    ' Come to the craig, an' kiss with me !

XV

' Here is a royal ring,' she said,
    ' That I have found in the green sea ;
And while your finger it is on,
    Drawn shall your blood never be ;
But if you touch me, tail or fin,
    I swear my ring your death shall be.'

XVI

He 's louted him o'er the Eastmuir craig,
    As out she swang and about the tree ;
He stepped in, gave her a kiss,
    The royal ring he brought him wi'.

XVII

Her breath was strang, her hair was lang
    And twisted ance about the tree,
As awa' she gid and again she swang—
    'Come to the craig, an' kiss with me !

louted] bowed.   gid] went.

KEMP OWYNE

XVIII

'Here is a royal brand,' she said,
  'That I have found in the green sea;
And while your body it is on,
  Drawn shall your blood never be;
But if you touch me, tail or fin,
  I swear my brand your death shall be.'

XIX

He's louted him o'er the Eastmuir craig,
  As out she swang and about the tree;
He steppèd in, gave her a kiss
  That royal brand he brought him wi'.

XX

Her breath was sweet, her hair grew short,
  And twisted nane about the tree,
As awa' she gid and again she came
  The fairest lady that ever could be.

XXI

'O was it a wer-wolf into the wood,
  Or was it a mermaid into the sea,
Or was it a man or a vile woman,
  My true love, that mis-shapit thee?'—

XXII

'It was na wer-wolf into the wood,
  Nor was it mermaid into the sea,
But and it was my vile stepmother,
  And wae and weary mote she be!

XXIII

'O a heavier weird shall light her on,
  Her hair sall grow rough an' her teeth grow lang,
And [aye] on her four feet sall she gang,
  And aye in Wormeswood sall she won!'

            into] in.   won] dwell.
58

The Laily Worm
and the Machrel of the Sea

I

' I WAS but seven year auld
   When my mither she did dee;
My father married the ae warst woman
   The warld did ever see.

II

' For she has made me the laily worm,
   That lies at the fit o' the tree,
An' my sister Masery she 's made
   The machrel of the sea.

III

' An' every Saturday at noon
   The machrel comes to me,
An' she takes my laily head
   An' lays it on her knee,
She kaims it wi' a siller kaim,
   An' washes 't in the sea.

IV

' Seven knights hae I slain,
   Sin I lay at the fit of the tree,
An' ye war na my ain father,
   The eighth ane ye should be.'—

V

' Sing on your song, ye laily worm,
   That ye did sing to me.'—
' I never sung tnat song but what
   I would sing it to thee.

laily] loathly.

59

THE LAILY WORM

'I was but seven year auld,
  When my mither she did dee ;
My father married the ae warst woman
  The warld did ever see.

VII

'For she changed me to the laily worm,
  That lies at the fit o' the tree,
And my sister Masery
  To the machrel of the sea.

VIII

'And every Saturday at noon
  The machrel comes to me,
An' she takes my laily head
  An' lays it on her knee,
An' kames it wi' a siller kame,
  An' washes it i' the sea.

IX

'Seven knights hae I slain
  Sin I lay at the fit o' the tree ;
An' ye war na my ain father,
  The eighth ane ye should be.'

X

He sent for his lady,
  As fast as send could he :
'Whar is my son that ye sent frae me,
  And my daughter, Lady Masery ?'—

XI

'Your son is at our king's court,
  Serving for meat an' fee,
An' your daughter's at our queen's court,
  The queen's maiden to be.'—

THE LAILY WORM

'Ye lee, ye lee, ye ill woman,
    Sae loud as I hear ye lee ;
My son 's the laily worm,
    That lies at the fit o' the tree,
And my daughter, Lady Masery,
    Is the machrel of the sea !'

XIII

She has tane a siller wan',
    An' gi'en him strokès three,
And he 's started up the bravest knight
    That ever your eyes did see.

XIV

She has ta'en a small horn,
    An' loud an' shrill blew she,
An' a' the fish came her untill
    But the machrel of the sea :
' Ye shapeit me ance an unseemly shape,
    An' ye 's never mare shape me.'

XV

He has sent to the wood
    For whins and for hawthorn,
An' he has ta'en that gay lady,
    An' there he did her burn.

King Orfeo

A Shetland Ballad.

I

DER lived a king inta da aste,
    Scowan ürla grün
Der lived a lady in da wast.
    Whar giorten han grün oarlac.

II

Dis king he has a huntin gaen,
He's left his Lady Isabel alane.

III

'Oh I wis ye'd never gaen away,
For at your hame is döl an wae.

IV

'For da king o Ferrie we his daert,
Has pierced your lady to da hert.'

   .   .   .   .

V

And aifter dem da king has gaen,
But when he cam it was a grey stane.

VI

Dan ne took oot his pipes ta play,
Bit sair his hert wi döl an wae.

VII

And first he played da notes o noy,
An dan he played da notes o jov.

VIII

An dan he played da göd gabber reel,
Dat meicht ha made a sick hert hale.

   .   .   .   .

aste] east.   *Scowan* &c.] Early green's the wood.   *Whar giorten* &c.] Where the hart goes yearly.   noy] grief.   da göd gabber reel] the rollicking dance-tune.

KING ORFEO

IX

'Noo come ye in inta wir ha',
An come ye in among wis a'.'

X

Now he's gaen in inta der ha',
An he's gaen in among dem a'.

XI

Dan he took out his pipes to play,
Bit sair his hert wi döl an wae.

XII

An first he played da notes o noy,
An dan he played da notes o joy.

XIII

An dan he played da göd gabber reel,
Dat meicht ha made a sick hert hale.

XIV

'Noo tell to us what ye will hae:
What sall we gie you for your play?'—

XV

'What I will hae I will you tell,
An dat's me Lady Isabel.'—

XVI

'Yees tak your lady, an yees gaeng hame,
An yees be king ower a' your ain.'

XVII

He's taen his lady, an he's gaen hame,
An noo he's king ower a' his ain.

wir] our.   wis] us.

63

I

LET never a man a wooing wend
  That lacketh thingis three;
A routh o' gold, an open heart
  And fu' o' courtesye.

II

As this I speak of King Henry,
  For he lay burd-alone;
An' he's doen him to a jelly hunt's ha'
  Was seven mile frae a town.

III

He's chased the deer down him before,
  An' the roe down by the den,
Till the fattest buck in a' the flock
  King Henry he has slain.

IV

O he has doen him to his ha'
  To make him bierly cheer;
An' in it came a griesly ghost
  Steed stappin' i' the fleer.

V

Her head hat the roof-tree o' the house,
  Her middle ye weel mot span;
He's thrown to her his gay mantle,
  Says, 'Lady, hap your lingcan.'

routh] plenty.   burd-alone] lone as a maid.   jelly] jolly, jovial.   bierly] stout, handsome.   fleer] floor.   hat] hit.   mot] might.   hap] cover.   lingcan *for* lycam] body.

VI

Her teeth were a' like teather stakes,
    Her nose like club or mell;
An' I ken naething she 'pear'd to be
    But the fiend that wons in hell.

VII

'Some meat, some meat, ye King Henry,
    Some meat ye gie to me!'—
'An' what meat's in this house, ladye,
    That ye're not welcome tae?'—
'O ye'se gae kill your berry-brown steed,
    And serve him up to me.'

VIII

O whan he slew his berry-brown steed,
    Wow but his heart was sair!
She ate him a' up, skin an' bane,
    Left naething but hide an' hair.

IX

'Mair meat, mair meat, ye King Henry,
    Mair meat ye gie to me!'—
'An' what meat's in this house, ladye,
    That ye're not welcome tae?'—
'O do ye slay your good grey-hounds
    An' bring them a' to me.'

X

O whan he slew his good grey-hounds,
    Wow but his heart was sair!
She ate them a' up, skin an' bane,
    Left naething but hide an' hair.

teather stakes] tether pegs.   mell] mallet.   wons] dwells.
ye'se gae] you shall go.

XI

'Mair meat, mair meat, ye King Henry,
    Mair meat ye gie to me ! '—
'An' what meat's in this house, ladye,
    That ye're not welcome tae ? '—
'O do ye kill your gay goss-hawks
    An' bring them a' to me.'

XII

O whan he fell'd his gay goss-hawks,
    Wow but his heart was sair !
She's ate them a' up, skin an' bane,
    Left naethin' but feathers bare.

XIII

'Some drink, some drink, now, King Henry,
    Some drink ye bring to me ! '—
'O what drink's in this house, ladye,
    That ye're not welcome tae ? '—
'O ye sew up your horse's hide,
    An' bring in drink to me.'

XIV

O he's sew'd up the bluidy hide,
    A puncheon o' wine put in ;
She's drunk it a' up at a waught,
    Left na ae drap ahin'.

XV

'A bed, a bed, now King Henry,
    A bed ye'se mak' to me ! '—
'An' what's the bed in this house, ladye,
    That ye're not welcome tae ? '—

      waught] draught.   ahin'] behind.

'O ye maun pu' the heather green,
    An' mak' a bed to me.'

XVI

Syne pu'd he has the heather green,
    An' made to her a bed,
An' up has he ta'en his gay mantle,
    An' o'er it he has spread.

XVII

'Tak' off your claiths now, King Henry,
    An' lie down by my side!'—
'O God forbid,' says King Henry,
    'That ever the like betide;
That ever a fiend that wons in hell
    Shou'd streak down by my side!'

XVIII

But whan day was come, and night was gane,
    An' the sun shone thro' the ha',
The fairest ladye that ever was seen
    [Cam' to his armès twa].

XIX

'O weel is me!' says King Henry,
    'How lang 'll this last wi' me?'
Then out an' spake that fair ladye,
    'Even till the day you dee.

XX

'For I've met wi' many a gentle knight
    That's gien me sic a fill;
But never before wi' a courteous knight
    That ga'e me a' my will.'

streak] stretch.

The Boy and the Mantle

A Ballad of King Arthur's Court.

I

IN the third day of May
To Carleile did come
A kind curteous child
  That co'ld much of wisdome.

II

A kirtle and a mantle
This child had uppon,
With brauches and ringes
  Full richelye bedone.

III

He had a sute of silke
  About his middle drawne ;
Without he co'ld of curtesye
  He thought it much shame.

IV

' God speed thee, King Arthur,
  Sitting at thy meate ;
And the goodly Queene Guenever !
  I cannot her forget.

V

' I tell you, lords in this hall,
  I hett you all heed,
Except you be the more surer
  Is for you to dread.'

co'ld] could, knew.   bedone] adorned.   hett] bid.

VI

He pluck'd out of his potener,
    And longer wo'ld not dwell,
He pull'd forth a pretty mantle
    Betweene two nut-shells.

VII

' Have thou here, King Arthur,
    Have thou here of mee :
Give itt to thy comely queene
    Shapen as itt is alreadye.

VIII

' Itt shall never become that wiffe
    That hath once done amisse.'
Then every knight in the king's court
    Began to care for his.

IX

Forth came dame Guenever,
    To the mantle she her bed ;
The ladye shee was new fangle
    But yett she was affrayd.

X

When shee had taken the mantle,
    She stoode as shee had beene madd ;
It was from the top to the toe
    As sheeres had it shread.

XI

One while was it gaule,
    Another while was itt greene,
Another while was it wadded ;
    Ill itt did her beseeme.

potener] pouch, purse. care] bethink him. bed] bid, offered.
new fangle] capricious.   gaule] gules, red.   wadded] of
woad colour, blue.

XII

Another while it was blacke,
　　And bore the worst hue :
' By my troth,' quoth King Arthur,
　　' I thinke thou be not true.'

XIII

Shee threw downe the mantle,
　　That bright was of blee ;
Fast with a rudd red
　　To her chamber can she flee.

XIV

She cursed the weaver and the walker
　　That cloth that had wrought,
And bade a vengeance on his crowne
　　That hither hath itt brought.

XV

' I had rather be in a wood,
　　Under a greenè tree,
Than in King Arthur's court
　　Shamèd for to bee.'

XVI

Kay call'd forth his ladye
　　And bade her come neere ;
Saies, ' Madam, and thou be guiltye
　　I pray thee hold thee here.'

XVII

Forth came his ladye
　　Shortlye and anon ;
Boldlye to the mantle
　　Then is she gone.

blee] hue.　　　can] did.　　　walker] fuller.

XVIII

When she had tane the mantle,
  And her about it cast
Then was she bare
  All unto the waist.

XIX

Then every knight
  That was in the King's court
Talk'd, laugh'd and showted
  Full oft att that sport.

XX

She threw down the mantle
  That bright was of blee,
Fast with a red rudd
  To her chamber can she flee.

XXI

Forth came an old Knight
  Pattering ore a creede,
And he proferr'd to this little Boy
  Twenty markes to his meede;

XXII

And all the time of Christmasse
  Willingly to ffeede;
For why this mantle might
  Doe his wiffe some need.

XXIII

When shee had tane the mantle
  Of cloth that was made,
Shee had no more left on her
  But a tassell and a threed:
That every knight in the King's court
  Bade evill might shee speed.

rudd] complexion.   For why] because.

XXIV

She threw downe the mantle,
   That bright was of blee,
Fast with a red rudd
   To her chamber can she flee.

XXV

Craddocke call'd forth his ladye
   And bade her come in ;
Saith, ' Winne this mantle, ladye,
   With a little dinne.

XXVI

' Winne this mantle, ladye,
   And it shal be thine
If thou never did amisse
   Since thou wast mine.

XXVII

Forth came Craddocke's ladye
   Shortlye and anon,
But boldlye to the mantle
   Then is shee gone.

XXVIII

When she had tane the mantle
   And cast it her about,
Up at her great toe
   It began to crinkle and crowt :
Shee said, ' Bowe downe, mantle,
   And shame me not for nought.

XXIX

' Once I did amisse,
   I tell you certainlye,
When Craddocke's mouth I kist
   Under a greenè tree ;

dinne] noise, i. e. ado.   crowt] pucker.

When I kist Craddocke's mouth
Before he marryed mee.'

XXX

When shee had her shreeven
And her sinnes shee had tolde,
The mantle stood about her
Right as she wo'ld ;

XXXI

Seemelye of coulour,
Glittering like gold
Then every knight in Arthur's court
Did her behold.

    .   .   .   .

XXXII

The little Boy stoode
Looking over a dore ;
[There as he look'd
He was ware of a wyld bore.]

XXXIII

He was ware of a wyld bore
Wo'ld have werryed a man :
He pull'd forth a wood-kniffe
Fast thither that he ran :
He brought in the bore's head
And quitted him like a man.

XXXIV

He brought in the bore's head,
And was wonderous bold ;
He said there was never a cuckold's kniffe
Carve itt that co'ld.

shreeven] shriven, confessed.   werryed] worried

XXXV

Some rubb'd their knives
  Uppon a whetstone ;
Some threw them under the table,
  And said they had none.

XXXVI

King Arthur and the child
  Stood looking them upon ;
All their knives' edges
  Turnèd backe againe.

XXXVII

Craddocke had a litle kniffe
  Of iron and of steele ;
He birtled the bore's head
  Wonderous weale,
That every knight in the King's court
  Had a morssell.

XXXVIII

The litle Boy had a horne,
  Of red gold that ronge ;
He said, ' There was noe cuckolde
  Shall drinke of my horne,
But he sho'ld itt sheede
  Either behind or beforne.'

XXXIX

Some shedd it on their shoulder
  And some on their knee ;
He that co'ld not hitt his mouth
  Put it in his e'e ;
And he that was a cuckold
  Every man might him see.

birtled] brittled, cut up.　　ronge] rung, resounded.　　sheede]
shed, spill.

74

XL

Craddocke wan the horne
And the bore's head;
His ladye wan the mantle
Unto her meede;
Everye such a lovely ladye
God send her well to speede!

18. *King Arthur and King Cornwall*
A Fragment

King Arthur of Little Britain unwisely boasts the beauty of
his famous Round Table.

I

SAIES, 'Come here, cuzen Gawaine so gay,
My sisters sonne be yee;
Ffor you shall see one of the fairest round tables
That ever you see with your eye.'

II

Then bespake Lady Queen Guenever,
And these were the words said shee:
'I know where a round table is, thou noble king,
Is worth thy round table and other such three.

III

'The trestle that stands under this round table,' she said,
'Lowe downe to the mould,
It is worth thy round table, thou worthy king,
Thy halls, and all thy gold.

IV

'The place where this round table stands in,
[Is fencèd round amaine]
It is worth thy castle, thy gold, thy fee,
And all good Litle Britaine.'

V

'Where may that table be, lady?' quoth hee,
  'Or where may all that goodly building be?'
'You shall it seeke,' shee says, 'till you it find;
  You shall never gett more of me.'

VI

Then bespake him noble King Arthur
  These were the words said hee:
'I'le make mine avow to God,
  And alsoe to the Trinity,

VII

'I'le never sleepe one night there as I doe another
  'Till that round table I see:
Sir Marramiles and Sir Tristeram,
  Fellowes that ye shall bee.

VIII

['Sir Gawaine and Sir Bredbettle
  Be fellowes eke with me,]
Weele be clad in palmers' weede,
  Five palmers we will bee;

IX

'There is noe outlandish man will us abide,
  Nor will us come nye.'
Then they rived east and they rived west,
  In many a strange country.

X

Then they tranckled a litle further,
  They saw a battle new sett:
'Now, by my faith,' saies noble King Arthur,
  [These armies be well met.']

rived] arrived, travelled.   tranckled] travelled.

KING ARTHUR AND KING CORNWALL

After travelling in many strange lands they arrive at the
castle of King Cornwall, not a great way from home.

XI

But when he cam to this [Cornwall castle]
    And to the palace gate,
Soe ready was ther a proud portèr,
    And met him soone therat.

XII

Shooes of gold the porter had on,
    And all his other rayment was unto the same:
'Now, by my faith,' saies noble King Arthur,
    'Yonder is a minion swaine.'

XIII

Then bespake noble King Arthur,
    These were the words says hee:
'Come thou hither, thou proud portèr,
    I pray thee come hither to me.

XIV

'I have two poore rings, of my finger,
    The better of them I'le give to thee;
Tell who may be lord of this castle,
    Or who is lord in this cuntry?'

XV

'Cornewall King,' the porter sayes,
    'There is none soe rich as hee;
Neither in christendome, nor yet in heathendom,
    None hath soe much gold as he.'

XVI

And then bespake him noble King Arthur,
    These were the words sayes hee:
'I have two poore rings of my finger,
    The better of them I'le give thee,

If thou wilt greete him well, Cornewall King,
    And greete him well from me.

XVII

' Pray him for one night's lodging and two meales' meate,
    For his love that dyed uppon a tree ;
Of one ghesting and two meales' meate,
    For his love that dyed uppon tree.

XVIII

' Of one ghesting, of two meales' meate,
    For his love that was of virgin borne,
And in the morning that we may scape away,
    Either without scath or scorne.'

XIX

Then forth is gone this proud portèr,
    As fast as he co'ld hye,
And when he came befor Cornewall King,
    He kneelèd downe on his knee.

XX

Sayes, ' I have beene porter-man at thy gate
    This thirty winter and three,
[But there is ffive knights before itt now,
    The like I never did see.']

King Cornwall questioning the strangers, they happen to speak
of a certain shrine of Our Lady, from which he gathers that they
have been in Little Britain. This leads him to question them
concerning King Arthur.

XXI

.   .   .   .

Our Lady was borne ; then thought Cornewall King
    ' These palmers had beene in Brittaine.'

            ghesting] guesting, lodging.

XXII

Then bespake him Cornewall King,
  These were the words he said there:
'Did you ever know a comely king,
  His name was King Arthùr?'

XXIII

And then bespake him noble King Arthùr,
  These were the words said hee:
'I doe not know that comly king,
  But once my selfe I did him see.'
Then bespake Cornewall King againe,
  These were the words said he:

XXIV

Sayes, 'Seven yeere I was clad and fed,
  In Litle Brittaine, in a bower;
I had a daughter by King Arthur's wife,
  That now is called my flower;
For King Arthur, that kindly cockward,
  Hath none such in his bower.

XXV

'For I durst sweare, and save my othe,
  That same lady soe bright,
That a man that were laid on his death bed
  Wo'ld open his eyes on her to have sight.'—
'Now, by my faith,' sayes noble King Arthur,
  'And that's a full faire wight!'

XXVI

And then bespake Cornewall [King] againe,
  And these were the words he said:
'Come hither, five or three of my knights,
  And feitch me downe my steed;
King Arthur, that foule cockeward,
  Hath none such, if he had need.

XXVII

' For I can ryde him as far on a day
    As King Arthur can any of his on three ;
And is it not a pleasure for a king
    When he shall ryde forth on his journèy ?

XXVIII

' For the eyes that beene in his head,
    They glister as doth the gleed.'
' Now, by my faith,' says noble King Arthur,
    ' That is a well faire steed.'

After showing them other of his possessions, King Cornwall has the strangers conducted to bed ; but first takes the precaution to conceal the Burlow Beanie, or Billy Blind—friendly household spirit — in a rubbish-barrel by the bedside, to listen and overhear their conversation.

XXX

Then King Arthur to his bed was brought,
    A greivèd man was hee ;
And soe were all his fellowes with him,
    From him they thought never to flee.

XXXI

Then take they did that lodly groome,
    And under the rub-chadler closed was hee,
And he was set by King Arthur's bed-side,
    To heere theire talke and theire comunye ;

XXXII

That he might come forth, and make proclamation,
    Long before it was day ;
It was more for King Cornewall's pleasure,
    Then it was for King Arthur's pay.

gleed] live coal.   lodly] loathly.   rub-chadler] rubbish-tub.   pay] satisfaction.

XXXIII

And when King Arthur in his bed was laid,
    These were the words said hee:
' I'le make mine avow to God,
    And alsoe to the Trinity,
That I'le be the bane of Cornewall Kinge
    Litle Brittaine or ever I see!'

XXXIV

' It is an unadvised vow,' saies Gawaine the gay,
    ' As ever king hard make I;
But wee that beene five christian men,
    Of the christen faith are wee,
And we shall fight against anoynted king
    And all his armorie.'

XXXV

And then bespake him noble Arthur,
    And these were the words said he:
' Why, if thou be afraid, Sir Gawaine the gay,
    Goe home, and drinke wine in thine owne country.'

XXXVI

And then bespake Sir Gawaine the gay,
    And these were the words said hee:
' Nay, seeing you have made such a hearty vow,
    Heere another vow make will I.

XXXVII

' I'le make mine avow to God,
    And alsoe to the Trinity,
That I will have yonder faire lady
    To Litle Brittaine with mee.

While they lie talking, an unguarded movement of the sprite in the barrel leads to his discovery. Then follows a great combat.

XXXIX

[O then bespake Sir Tristram,]
    These were the words sayd hee :
' Befor I wold wrestle with yonder feend,
    It is better to be drown'd in the sea.'

XL

And then bespake Sir Bredbeddle,
    And these were the words said he :
' Why, I will wrestle with yon lodly feend,
    God, my governor thou wilt bee ! '

XLI

Then bespake him noble Arthur,
    And these were the words said he :
' What weapons wilt thou have, thou gentle knight ?
    I pray thee tell to me.'

XLII

He sayes, ' Collen brand I'le have in my hand,
    And a Millaine knife fast by my knee,
And a Danish axe fast in my hands,
    That a sure weapon I thinke will be.'

XLIII

Then with his Collen brand that he had in his hand,
    The bunge of that rub-chandler he burst in three ;
With that start out a lodly feend,
    With seven heads, and one body.

XLIV

The fyer towards the element flew,
    Out of his mouth, where was great plentie ;
The knight stoode in the middle and fought,
    That it was great joy to see.

Collen brand] sword of Cologne steel.   Millaine] Milanese
element] sky.

XLV

Till his Collaine brand brake in his hand,
    And his Millaine knife burst on his knee,
And then the Danish axe burst in his hand first,
    That a sure weapon he thought sho'ld be.

XLVI

But now is the knight left without any weapons,
    And alacke! it was the more pittye;
But a surer weapon then he had one,
    Had neuer lord in Christentye;
And all was but one litle booke,
    He found it by the side of the sea.

XLVII

He found it at the sea-side,
    Wruckèd upp in a floode;
Our Lord had written it with his hands,
    And sealed it with his bloode.

With this book of Evangiles Sir Bredbittle, otherwise the
Green Knight, overcomes the sprite, and having conjured him into
a wall of stone, returns with report to King Arthur.

XLVIII

[Saies] 'That thou doe not [stir a foot]
    But ly still in that wall of stone,
Till I have beene with noble King Arthur,
    And told him what I have done.'

XLIX

And when he came to the king's chamber,
    He co'ld of his curtesie:
Says, 'Sleepe you, wake you, noble King Arthur?
    And ever Jesus waken yee!'

L

'Nay, I am not sleeping, I am waking,'
 These were the words said hee;
'Ffor thee I have car'd; how hast thou fared?
 O gentle knight, let me see.'

LI

The knight wrought the king his booke,
 Bad him behold, reede and see;
And ever he found it on the back of the leafe
 As noble Arthur wo'ld wish it to be.

LII

And then bespake him King Arthur,
 'Alas! thow gentle knight, how may this be,
That I might see him in the same licknesse
 That he stood unto thee?'

LIII

And then bespake him the Greene Knight,
 These were the words said hee:
'If you'le stand stifly in the battell stronge,
 For I have won all the victory.'

LIV

Then bespake him the king againe,
 And these were the words said hee:
'If wee stand not stifly in this battell strong,
 Wee are worthy to be hang'd on a tree.'

LV

Then bespake him the Greene Knight,
 These were the words said he:
Saies, 'I doe conjure thee, thou fowle feend,
 In the same licknesse thou stood unto me.'

84

LVI

With that start out a lodly feend,
  With seven heads, and one bodỳ;
The fier towards the element flew
  Out of his mouth, where was great plentie.

But now with the aid of the book Sir Bredbittle has the fiend
wholly at command.   He is sent first to fetch the steed.

LIX

And then bespake him the Greene Knight,
  And these were the words said he:
Saith, 'I conjure thee, thou fowle feend,
  That thou feitch downe the steed, that we see.'

LX

And then forth is gone Burlow-beanie,
  As fast as he co'ld hie,
And feitch he did that fairè steed,
  And came againe by and by.

LXI

Then bespake him Sir Marramiles,
  And these were the words said hee:
'Ryding of this steed, brother Bredbeddle,
  The mastery belongs to me.'

LXII

Marramiles tooke the steed to his hand,
  To ryd him he was full bold;
He co'ld noe more make him goe
  Then a child of three yeere old.

LXIII

He laid uppon him with heele and hand,
  With yard that was soe fell;
'Helpe! brother Bredbeddle,' says Marramile,
  'For I thinke he be the devill of hell.

LXIV

'Helpe! brother Bredbeddle,' says Marramile,
　'Helpe! for Christ's pittye;
Ffor without thy help, brother Bredbeddle,
　He will never be rydden for me.'

LXV

Then bespake him Sir Bredbeddle,
　These were the words said he:
'I conjure thee tell, thou Burlow-beanie,
　How this steed was riddin in his country.'

LXVI

'In Cornewall's window is a gold wand;
　Let him strike three strokes on that steed,
And then he will spring forth of his hand
　As sparke doth out of gleede.'

Then Sir Tristram requires a horn. At Sir Bredbittle's command
the sprite fetches it; but the horn will not sound until anointed
with a certain powder. This also the sprite is sent to fetch.

LXX

And then bespake Sir Bredebeddle,
　To the ffeend these words said hee:
Says, 'I conjure thee, thou Burlow-beanie,
　The powder-box thou feitch me.'

LXXI

Then forth is gone Burlow-beanie,
　As fast as he co'ld hie,
And feich he did the powder-box,
　And came againe by and by.

gleede] live coal.

86

LXXII

Then Sir Tristeram tooke powder forth of that box,
　　And blent it with warme sweet milke,
And there put it unto that horne,
　　And swill'd it about in that ilke.

LXXIII

Then he tooke the horne into his hand,
　　And a lowd blast he blew;
He rent the horne up to the midst,
　　All his ffellowes this they knew.

LXXIV

Then bespake him the Greene Knight,
　　These were the words said he:
Saies, 'I conjure thee, thou Burlow-beanie,
　　That thou feitch me the sword, that I see.'

LXXV

Then forth is gone Burlow-beanie,
　　As fast as he co'ld hie,
And feitch he did that fairè sword,
　　And came againe by and by.

LXXVI

Then bespake him Sir Bredbeddle,
　　To the king these words said he:
'Take this sword in thy hand, thou noble King Arthur,
　　For thy vowes sake I'le give it thee,
And goe strike off King Cornewall's head,
　　In bed where he doth lye.'

LXXVII

Then forth is gone noble King Arthur,
As fast as he co'ld hye,
And strucken he hath off King Cornewall's head,
And came againe by and by.

So King Arthur fulfils his vow; and, if the rest of the Ballad had been preserved, no doubt it would have told us how his companions fulfilled theirs.

19.   *The Marriage of Sir Gawain*

[*A Fragment*]

I

KINGE Arthur lives in merry Carleile,
And seemely is to see,
And there he hath with him Queene Genever,
That bride soe bright of blee.

II

And there he hath with him Queene Genever,
That bride soe bright in bower,
And all his barons about him stoode,
That were both stiffe and stowre.

III

The king kept a royall Christmasse,
Of mirth and great honor.

blee] hue, complexion.   stowre] strong: or perhaps we should read 'stiff in stowre' = sturdy in fight.

THE MARRIAGE OF SIR GAWAIN

Soon after Christmas the King chanced to ride by Tarn Wadling, in the forest of Inglewood, when he was met by a fierce baron armed with a club, who offered him choice between fighting and ransom. For ransom, the King must return on New Year's Day—

IV

'And bring me word what thing it is
    That a woman will most desire;
This shalbe thy ransome, Arthur,' he sayes,
    'For I'le have noe other hier.'

V

King Arthur then held up his hand,
    According thene as was the law;
He tooke his leave of the baron there,
    And homward can he draw.

VI

And when he came to merry Carleile,
    To his chamber he is gone,
And ther came to him his cozen Sir Gawaine,
    As he did make his mone.

VII

And there came to him his cozen Sir Gawaine,
    That was a curteous knight;
'Why sigh you soe sore, unckle Arthur,' he said,
    'Or who hath done thee unright?'—

VIII

'O peace, O peace, thou gentle Gawaine,
    That faire may thee beffall!
For if thou knew my sighing soe deepe,
    Thou wo'ld not mervaile att all.

Tarn Wadling] The place—near Hesketh in Cumberland, on the road from Carlisle to Penrith—keeps its name to this day. But the tarn has been drained and its site is now a pasture for sheep.

IX

' Ffor when I came to Tearne Wadling,
    A bold barron there I fand,
With a great club upon his backe,
    Standing stiffe and strong.

X

' And he asked me wether I wo'ld fight
    Or from him I shold begone,
Or else I must him a ransome pay,
    And soe depart him from.

XI

' To fight with him I saw noe cause ;
    Methought it was not meet ;
For he was stiffe and strong with-all,
    His strokes were nothing sweete.

XII

' Therefor this is my ransome, Gawaine,
    I ought to him to pay ;
I must come againe, as I am sworne,
    Upon the New Yeer's day ;

XIII

' And I must bring him word what thing it is
    [That a woman will most desire].

Arthur, having collected and written down many answers to
the baron's riddle, was true to his promise, thus—

XIV

Then king Arthur drest him for to ryde,
    In one soe rich array,
Toward the fore-said Tearne Wadling,
    That he might keepe his day.

XV

And as he rode over a more,
    Hee see a lady where shee sate
Betwixt an oke and a greene hollen;
    She was cladd in red scarlett.

XVI

Then thereas shold have stood her mouth,
    Then there was sett her eye;
The other was in her forhead fast,
    The way that she might see.

XVII

Her nose was crooked and turn'd outward,
    Her mouth stood foule a-wry;
A worse form'd lady than shee was,
    Never man saw with his eye.

XVIII

To halch upon him, King Arthur,
    This lady was full faine,
But King Arthur had forgott his lesson,
    What he sho'ld say againe.

XIX

'What knight art thou,' the lady sayd,
    'That will not speak to me?
Of me be thou nothing dismay'd,
    Tho I be ugly to see.

XX

' For I have halched you curteouslye,
    And you will not me againe;
Yett I may happen Sir Knight,' shee said,
    'To ease thee of thy paine.'

hollen] holly-tree.   halch upon] salute.

XXI

'Give thou ease me, lady,' he said,
  'Or helpe me any thing,
Thou shalt have gentle Gawaine, my cozen,
  And marry him with a ring.'

The hag thereupon gave him the right answer and he rode forward.

XXIII

And when he came to the Tearne Wadling,
  The baron there co'ld he finde,
With a great weapon on his backe,
  Standing stiffe and stronge.

XXIV

And then he tooke King Arthur's letters in his hands,
  And away he co'ld them fling,
And then he puld out a good browne sword,
  And cryd himselfe a king.

XXV

And he sayd, 'I have thee and thy land, Arthur,
  To doe as it pleaseth me,
For this is not thy ransome sure,
  Therfore yeeld thee to me.'

XXVI

And then bespoke him noble Arthur,
  And bad him hold his hand :
'And give me leave to speake my mind
  In defence of all my land.'

XXVII

He said, 'As I came over a more,
  I see a lady where shee sate
Betweene an oke and a green hollen ;
  Shee was clad in red scarlett.

XXVIII

'And she says a woman will have her will,
  And this is all her cheef desire:
Doe me right, as thou art a baron of sckill,
  This is thy ransome and all thy hyer.'

XXIX

He sayes, 'An early vengeance light on her!
  She walkes on yonder more;
It was my sister that told thee this,
  [As shee heard it of me before.]

XXX

'But heer I'le make mine avow to God
  To doe her an evill turne;
For an' ever I may thate fowle theefe get,
  In a fyer I will her burne.'

The King, having returned home, told his knights that he
had in the forest a bride for one of them, and a number rode out
in his company to find her.

XXXI

Sir Lancelott and Sir Steven bold,
  They rode with them that day,
And the formost of the company
  There rode the steward Kay.

XXXII

Soe did Sir Banier and Sir Bore,
  Sir Garrett with them soe gay,
Soe did Sir Tristeram that gentle knight,
  To the forrest fresh and gay.

sckill] wit, judgement.

XXXIII

And when he came to the greene forrest,
  Underneath a greene holly tree,
Their sate that lady in red scarlet
  That unseemly was to see.

XXXIV

Sir Kay beheld this lady's face,
  And looked uppon her swire;
'Whosoever kisses this lady,' he sayes,
  'Of his kisse he stands in feare.'

XXXV

Sir Kay beheld the lady againe,
  And looked upon her snout;
'Whosoever kisses this lady,' he saies,
  'Of his kisse he stands in doubt.'

XXXVI

'Peace, cozen Kay,' then said Sir Gawaine,
  'Amend thee of thy life;
For there is a knight amongst us all
  That must marry her to his wife.'

XXXVII

'What! wedd her to wiffe!' then said Sir Kay,
  'In the divell's name anon!
Gett me a wiffe where-ere I may,
  For I had rather be slaine!'

XXXVIII

Then some tooke up their hawkes in hast.
  And some tooke up their hounds,
And some sware they wo'ld not marry her
  For citty nor for towne.

swire] neck.

THE MARRIAGE OF SIR GAWAIN

XXXIX

And then be-spake him noble King Arthur,
   And sware there by this day,
For a litle foule sight and misliking
   [They should not say her Nay].

At length Sir Gawain, for Arthur's sake, consented. The
ugly bride was taken home and bedded, when to Gawain's
delight in his arms she turned to a beautiful woman. She then
offered him a choice.—

XL

Then shee said, 'Choose thee, gentle Gawaine,
   Truth as I doe say,
Wether thou wilt have me in this liknesse
   In the night or else in the day.'

XLI

And then bespake him gentle Gawaine,
   Was one soe mild of moode,
Sayes, 'Well I know what I wo'ld say,
   God grant it may be good!

XLII

'To have thee fowle in the night
   When I with thee sho'ld play —
Yet I had rather, if I might,
   Have thee fowle in the day.'

XLIII

'What! when lords goe with ther feires,' shee said,
   'Both to the ale and wine,
Alas! then I must hyde my selfe,
   I must not goe withinne.'

feires] mates.

XLIV

And then bespake him gentle Gawaine,
  Said, 'Lady, that's but skill;
And because thou art my owne lady,
  Thou shalt have all thy will.'

XLV

Then she said, 'Blesed be thou, gentle Gawain,
  This day that I thee see!
For as thou seest me att this time,
  From hencforth I wilbe.

XLVI

'My father was an old knight,
  And yett it chancèd soe
That he marryed a younge lady
  That brought me to this woe.

XLVII

'Shee witched me, being a faire young lady,
  To the greene forrest to dwell,
And there I must walke in woman's liknesse,
  Most like a feend of hell.

XLVIII

'She witched my brother to a carlish [boore]

Being thus given what a woman most desires (that is, her will) she
is released from the spell and becomes beautiful at all times:
and Sir Gawain leads his lady in triumph among the knights, to
present her to the King and Queen.

L

'Come kisse her, brother Kay,' then said Sir Gawaine,
  'And amend thé of thy liffe;
I sweare this is the same lady
  That I marryed to my wiffe.'
    96

LI

Sir Kay kissed that lady bright,
    Standing upon his ffeete ;
He swore, as he was trew knight,
    The spice was never soe sweete.

LII

'Well, cozen Gawaine,' sayes Sir Kay,
    'Thy chance is fallen arright,
For thou hast gotten one of the fairest maids
    I ever saw with my sight.'—

LIII

'It is my fortune,' said Sir Gawaine ;
    'For my unckle Arthurs sake
I am glad as grasse wold be of raine,
    Great joy that I may take.'

LIV

Sir Gawaine tooke the lady by the one arme,
    Sir Kay tooke her by the tother,
They led her straight to King Arthur,
    As they were brother and brother.

LV

King Arthur welcomed them there all,
    And soe did Lady Genever his queene,
With all the knights of the Round Table,
    Most seemly to be seene.

LVI

King Arthur beheld that lady faire
    That was soe faire and bright,
He thanked Christ in Trinity
    For Sir Gawaine that gentle knight.

LVII

Soe did the knights, both more and lesse,
   Rejoyced all that day
For the good chance that hapened was
   To Sir Gawaine and his lady gay.

20.   *Bonnie Annie*

I

THERE was a rich lord, and he lived in Forfar,
  He had a fair lady and one only dochter.

II

O she was fair!   O dear, she was bonnie!
A ship's captain courted her to be his honey.

III

'Ye'll steal your father's gowd, and your mother's money,
And I'll make ye a lady in Ireland bonnie.'

IV

She's stown her father's gowd, and her mother's money,
But she was never a lady in Ireland bonnie.

V

They hadna sail'd far till the young thing cried ' Woman!'
' What can a woman do, love, I will do for ye.

VI

' Lay about, steer about, lay our ship cannie,
Do all ye can to save my dear Annie.'

VII

'There's fey folk in our ship, she winna sail for me,
There's fey folk in our ship, she winna sail [ony].'

        cannie] gently.   fey] destined to die.

BONNIE ANNIE

They've castin' black bullets twice six and forty,
And ae the black bullet fell on bonnie Annie.

IX

' Ye'll tak me in your arms twa, lo, lift me cannie,
Throw me out owre-board, your ain dear Annie.'

X

He has ta'en her in his arms twa, lo, lifted her cannie,
He has laid her on a bed of down, his ain dear Annie.

XI

' What can a woman do, love, I'll do for ye : '
' Muckle can a woman do, ye canna do for me.'

XII

' Lay about, steer about, lay our ship cannie,
Do all ye can to save my dear Annie.'

XIII

' I've laid about, steer'd about, laid about cannie,
Our ship's on a sand-bank, she winna sail [ony]—

XIV

' Ye'll take her in your arms twa, lo, lift her cannie,
And throw her out owre-board, your ain dear Annie.'

XV

He has ta'en her in his arms twa, lo, lifted her cannie,
He has thrown her out owre-board, his ain dear Annie.

XVI

[The corse it did float, the ship it did follow]
Until that they came to the high banks o' Yarrow.

Yarrow] ? Jarrow.

99

XVII

' O I'd bury my love on the high banks o' Yarrow,
But the wood it is dear, and the planks they are narrow.'

XVIII

He made his love a coffin o' the gowd sae yellow,
And buried his bonnie love doun in a sea valley.

21. *Brown Robyn's Confession*

I

IT fell upon a Wadensday
Brown Robyn's men went to sea ;
But they saw neither moon nor sun
    Nor starlight wi' their e'e.

II

' We'll cast kevels us amang ;
    See wha the man may be.'—
The kevel fell on Brown Robyn,
    The master-man was he.

III

' It is nae wonder,' said Brown Robyn,
    ' Altho' I dinna thrive ;
[For at hame I murder'd my ain father-—
    I would he were on live.]

IV

' But tie me to a plank o' wude,
    And throw me in the sea ;
And if I sink, ye may bid me sink,
    But if I swim, let be.'

        kevels] lots.

V

They've tied him to a plank o' wude
    And thrown him in the sea;
He didna sink, tho' they bade him sink,
    He swim'd, and they bade let be.

VI

He hadna been into the sea
    An hour but barely three,
Till by it came Our Blessed Ladie
    Her dear young son her wi'.

VII

' Will ye gang to your men again,
    Or will ye gang wi' me ?
Will ye gang to the high heavens
    Wi' my dear son and me ? '—

VIII

' I winna gang to my men again,
    For they would be fear'd at me ;
But I would gang to the high heavens,
    Wi' thy dear son and thee.'

IX

' It 's for nae honour ye did, Brown Robyn,
    It 's for nae gude ye did to me ;
But a' is for your fair confession
    You've made upon the sea.'

The Cruel Mother

I

SHE lean'd her back unto a thorn ;
Fine flowers in the valley
And there she has her two babes born,
And the green leaves they grow rarely.

II

She's ta'en the ribbon frae her hair,
And bound their bodies fast and sair.

III

' Smile na sae sweet, my bonny babes,
An' ye smile sae sweet, ye'll smile me dead.

IV

' And, O bonny babes, if ye suck sair,
Ye'll never suck by my side mair.'

V

She 's ta'en out her little penknife
And twinn'd the sweet babes o' their life.

VI

She 's howket a grave baith deep and wide,
And there she 's buried them side by side.

VII

She 's buried them baith beneath the brier,
And washed her hands wi' mony a tear.

VIII

' O ay, my God, as I look to thee,
My babes be atween my God and me !

IX

' And ay their smiles wad win me in,
But I am borne down by deadly sin.'

twinn'd] robbed, deprived.

THE CRUEL MOTHER

X

She 's cover'd them o'er wi' a marble stane,
Thinking she wad gang maiden hame.

XI

She lookit out owre her castle wa'
And saw twa naked boys play at the ba.'

XII

' O bonny boys, gin ye were mine
I wad cleed you in silk and sabelline.

XIII

' O I would dress you in the silk,
And wash you ay in morning milk.'—

XIV

' O mother dear, when we were thine,
You didna prove to us sae kind.

XV

' O cruel mother, we were thine
And thou made us to wear the twine.

XVI

' But now we're in the heavens hie,
    Fine flowers in the valley
And ye have the pains o' hell to drie '—
    And the green leaves they grow rarely ;
Ten thousand times good night and be wi' thee !

cleed] clothe.   sabelline] sable.   twine] twine-cloth,
shroud.

Binnorie

I

THERE were twa sisters sat in a bour ;
 Binnorie, O Binnorie !
There cam a knight to be their wooer,
 By the bonnie milldams o' Binnorie.

II

He courted the eldest with glove and ring,
But he lo'ed the youngest abune a' thing.

III

The eldest she was vexèd sair,
And sair envìed her sister fair.

IV

Upon a morning fair and clear,
She cried upon her sister dear :

V

' O sister, sister, tak my hand,
And we'll see our father's ships to land.'

VI

She 's ta'en her by the lily hand,
And led her down to the river-strand.

VII

The youngest stood upon a stane,
The eldest cam and push'd her in.

VIII

' O sister, sister, reach your hand !
And ye sall be heir o' half my land :

IX

' O sister, reach me but your glove !
And sweet William sall be your love.'—

BINNORIE

X

'Foul fa' the hand that I should take;
It twin'd me o' my warldis make.

XI

'Your cherry cheeks and your yellow hair
Gar'd me gang maiden evermair.'

XII

Sometimes she sank, sometimes she swam,
Until she cam to the miller's dam.

XIII

Out then cam the miller's son,
And saw the fair maid soummin' in.

XIV

'O father, father, draw your dam!
There's either a mermaid or a milk-white swan.'

XV

The miller hasted and drew his dam,
And there he found a drown'd woman.

XVI

You couldna see her middle sma',
Her gowden girdle was sae braw.

XVII

You couldna see her lily feet,
Her gowden fringes were sae deep.

XVIII

You couldna see her yellow hair
For the strings o' pearls was twisted there.

XIX

You couldna see her fingers sma',
Wi' diamond rings they were cover'd a'.

---

twin'd] robbed, deprived.   my warldis make] my one mate
in the world.   soummin'] swimming.

XX

And by there cam a harper fine,
That harpit to the king at dine.

XXI

And when he look'd that lady on,
He sigh'd and made a heavy moan.

XXII

He 's made a harp of her breast-bane,
Whose sound wad melt a heart of stane.

XXIII

He 's ta'en three locks o' her yellow hair,
And wi' them strung his harp sae rare.

XXIV

He went into her father's hall,
And there was the court assembled all.

XXV

He laid his harp upon a stane,
And straight it began to play by lane.

XXVI

' O yonder sits my father, the King,
And yonder sits my mother, the Queen ;

XXVII

' And yonder stands my brother Hugh,
And by him my William, sweet and true.'

XXVIII

But the last tune that the harp play'd then—
Binnorie, O Binnorie !
Was, ' Woe to my sister, false Helèn ! '
By the bonnie milldams o' Binnorie.

by lane] alone, of itself.

I

THERE was a knight and a lady bright
    Set trysts amang the broom,
The ane to come at morning ear,
    The other at afternoon.

II

' I'll wager, I'll wager, I'll wager wi' you
    Five hundred merks and ten
That a maid shanna gae to the bonny broom
    And a maiden return again.'—

III

' I'll wager, I'll wager, I'll wager wi' you
    Five hundred merks and ten
That a maid shall gae to the bonny green broom
    And a maiden return again.'

IV

The may she sat at her mother's bower door
    And aye she made her mane :
' O whether shou'd I gang to the Broomfield Hill,
    Or should I stay at hame ?

V

' For if I do gang to the Broomfield Hill,
    A maid I'll not return ;
But if I stay frae the Broomfield Hill,
    My love will ca' me man-sworn.'

VI

Up then spake an auld witch-wife,
    Sat in the bower abune :
' O ye may gang to the Broomfield Hill,
    And yet come maiden hame,

trysts] assignations.   ear] early.

THE BROOMFIELD HILL

VII

'For when ye gang to the Broomfield Hill,
  Ye'll find your love asleep,
Wi' a silver belt above his head,
  And a broom-cow at his feet.

VIII

'Tak' ye the bloom frae aff the broom,
  Strew't at his head an' feet,
And aye the thicker that ye do strew,
  The sounder he will sleep.

IX

'Tak' ye the rings aff your fingers,
  Put them in his right hand,
To let him know when he does wake,
  His love was at his command.'

X

Lord John has ta'en his milk-white steed
  And his hawk wi' his bells sae bright,
And he's ridden swift to the Broomfield Hill,
  [Was never a baulder] knight.

XI

'Now rest, now rest, my milk-white steed,
  My lady will soon be here,
And I'll lay my head by this rose sae red,
  And the bonny burn sae near.'

XII

She's pu'd the broom-flower on Hive Hill,
  And strew'd on 's white breast-bane,
And that was to be wittering true
  That maiden she had gane.

broom-cow] branch of broom.   wittering] information,
token.

108

THE BROOMFIELD HILL

XIII

'O where were ye, my milk-white steed,
   That I hae coft sae dear,
That wadna watch and waken me
   When there was maiden here?'—

XIV

'I stampèd wi' my foot, master,
   And gar'd my bridle ring,
But no kin' thing wald waken ye
   Till she was past and gane.'—

XV

'And wae betide ye, my gay goss-hawk,
   That I hae coft sae dear,
That wadna watch an' waken me
   When my true-love was here.'—

XVI

'I clappèd wi' my wings, master,
   And aye my bells I rang,
And aye cried, *Waken, waken, master,*
   Before the ladye gang!'—

XVII

'But haste, but haste, my gude white steed,
   To come the maiden till,
Or a' the birds of the gude greenwood
   O' your flesh shall have their fill!'—

XVIII

'Ye needna burst your gude white steed
   Wi' racing o'er the howm;
Nae bird flies faster thro' the wood
   Than she fled thro' the broom.'

coft] bought.   howm] holm, river-mead.

I

IT was intill a pleasant time,
  Upon a simmer's day,
The noble Earl Mar's daughter
  Went forth to sport and play.

II

And while she play'd and sported
  Below a green aik tree,
There she saw a sprightly doo
  Set on a tower sae hie.

III

' O Coo-me-doo, my love sae true,
  If ye'll come doun to me,
Ye'se hae a cage o' gude red gowd
  Instead o' simple tree.

IV

' I'll put gowd hingers roun' your cage,
  And siller roun' your wa';
I'll gar ye shine as fair a bird
  As ony o' them a'.'

V

But she had nae these words well spoke,
  Nor yet these words well said,
Till Coo-me-doo flew frae the tower
  And lichted on her head.

VI

Then she has brought this pretty bird
  Hame to her bowers and ha',
And made him shine as fair a bird
  As ony o' them a'.

doo] dove.   hingers] hangings, curtains.

VII

When day was gone, and night was come,
  About the evening-tide,
This lady spied a gallant youth
  Stand straight up by her side.

VIII

'From whence cam' ye, young man?' she said;
  'That does surprise me sair;
My door was bolted right secure,
  What way hae ye come here?'—

IX

'O haud your tongue, ye lady fair,
  Lat a' your folly be;
Mind ye not o' your turtle-doo
  Ye wiled from aff the tree?'—

X

'What country come ye frae?' she said,
  'An' what's your pedigree?'—
'O it was but this verra day
  That I cam' ower the sea.

XI

'My mither lives on foreign isles,
  A queen o' high degree;
And by her spells I am a doo
  With you to live an' dee.'—

XII

'O Coo-me-doo, my love sae true,
  Nae mair frae me ye'se gae.'—
'That's never my intent, my love;
  As ye said, it shall be sae.'

EARL MAR'S DAUGHTER

XIII

Then he has stay'd in bower wi' her
  For six lang years and ane,
Till six young sons to him she bare,
  And the seventh she 's brought hame.

XIV

But aye, as ever a child was born,
  He carried them away,
And brought them to his mither's care
  As fast as he could fly.

XV

When he had stay'd in bower wi' her
  For seven lang years an' mair
There cam' a lord o' high renown
  To court this lady fair.

XVI

But still his proffer she refused
  And a' his presents too ;
Says, ' I'm content to live alane
  Wi' my bird Coo-me-doo.'

XVII

Her father swore a michty oath
  Amang the nobles all,
' The morn, or ere I eat or drink,
  This bird I will gar kill.'

XVIII

The bird was sitting in his cage
  And heard what they did say ;
Says, ' Wae is me, and you forlorn,
  If I do langer stay ! '

EARL MAR'S DAUGHTER

XIX

Then Coo-me-doo took flight and flew
    And afar beyond the sea,
And lichted near his mither's castle
    On a tower o' gowd sae hie.

XX

His mither she was walking out
    To see what she could see,
And there she saw her one young son
    Set on the tower sae hie.

XXI

' Get dancers here to dance,' she said,
    ' And minstrels for to play ;
For here's my young son Florentine
    Come hame wi' me to stay.'—

XXII

' Get nae dancers to dance, mither,
    Nor minstrels for to play ;
For the mither o' my seven sons,
    The morn's her wedding-day.'—

XXIII

' O tell me, tell me, Florentine,
    Tell me, an tell me true ;
Tell me this day without a flaw
    What I will do for you ?'—

XXIV

' Instead of dancers to dance, mither,
    Or minstrels for to play,
Turn four-and-twenty well-wight men
    Like storks in feathers gray :

      well-wight] strong, lusty.

113

XXV

'My seven sons in seven swans
  Aboon their heads to flee;
And I mysell a gay goshawk,
  A bird o' high degree.'

XXVI

Then siching said the Queen hersel',
  'That thing 's too high for me!'
But she applied to an auld woman
  Wha had mair skill than she.

XXVII

Instead o' dancers to dance a dance,
  Or minstrels for to play,
Four-and-twenty well-wight men
  Turn'd birds o' feathers gray.

XXVIII

Her seven sons in seven swans,
  Aboon their heads to flee;
And he himsel' a gay goshawk,
  A bird o' high degree.

XXIX

This flock o' birds took flight and flew
  Beyond the raging sea,
And landed near the Earl Mar's castle,
  Took shelter in every tree.

XXX

They were a flock o' pretty birds
  Right comely to be seen;
The people view'd them wi' surprise
  As they dancèd on the green.

XXXI

These birds flew out frae every tree
  And lichted on the ha',
And [frae the roof] with force did flee
  Amang the nobles a'.

XXXII

The storks there seized [ilk wedding-guest]
  —They could not fight nor flee ;
The swans they bound the [bridegroom fast]
  Below a green aik tree.

XXXIII

They lichted next on the [bride-] maidens,
  Then on the bride's own head ;
And wi' the twinkling o' an e'e
  The bride an' them were fled.

XXXIV

There 's ancient men at weddings been
  For sixty years or more,
But siccan a curious wedding-day
  They never saw before.

XXXV

For naething could the companie do,
  Nor naething could they say ;
But they saw a flock o' pretty birds
  That took their bride away.

Proud Lady Margaret

I

FAIR Margret was a proud ladye,
    The King's cousin was she ;
Fair Margret was a rich ladye,
    An' vain as vain cou'd be.

II

Ae night she sat in her stately ha'
    Kaimin' her yellow hair,
When in there cam' a gentle Knight,
    An' a white scarf he did wear.

III

'O what 's your will wi' me, Sir Knight ?
    O what 's your will wi' me ?
You're the likest to my ae brither
    That ever I did see.

IV

' You're the likest to my ae brither
    That ever I hae seen ;
But he 's buried in Dunfermline kirk
    A month an' mair bygane.'—

V

' I'm the likest to your ae brither
    That ever ye did see ;
But I canna get rest in my grave,
    A' for the pride o' thee.

VI

'Leave pride, Margret, leave pride, Margret,
  Leave pride an' vanity;
Cou'd ye see the sights that I hae seen
  Sair warnèd ye wou'd be.

VII

'For the wee worms are my bedfellows,
  An' cauld clay is my sheets,
An' when the stormy winds do blow
  My body lies and sleeps.

VIII

'O ye come in at the kirk-door
  Wi' the red gowd on your crown;
But when you come where I have been,
  You'll wear it laigher down.

IX

'O ye come in at the kirk-door
  Wi' the gowd prins i' your sleeve,
But when you come where I have been
  Ye maun gie them a' their leave.

X

'Leave pride, Margret, leave pride, Margret,
  Leave pride an' vanity;
Ere ye see the sights that I hae seen,
  Sair alter'd ye maun be.'

XI

He got her in her stately ha',
  Kaimin' her yellow hair;
He left her on her sick, sick bed
  Mournin' her sins sae sair.

laigher] lower.   prins] pins.

PART I

I

CLERK SAUNDERS and may Margaret
  Walk'd owre yon garden green;
And deep and heavy was the love
    That fell thir twa between.

II

'A bed, a bed,' Clerk Saunders said,
  ' A bed for you and me! '
' Fye na, fye na,' said may Margaret,
  'Till anes we married be! '—

III

'Then I'll take the sword frae my scabbard
  And slowly lift the pin;
And you may swear, and save your aith,
  Ye ne'er let Clerk Saunders in.

IV

'Take you a napkin in your hand,
  And tie up baith your bonnie e'en,
And you may swear, and save your aith,
  Ye saw me na since late yestreen.'

V

It was about the midnight hour,
  When they asleep were laid,
When in and came her seven brothers,
  Wi' torches burning red:

VI

When in and came her seven brothers,
  Wi' torches burning bright:
They said, 'We hae but one sister,
  And behold her lying with a knight! '

CLERK SAUNDERS

VII

Then out and spake the first o' them,
  ' I bear the sword shall gar him die.'
And out and spake the second o' them,
  ' His father has nae mair but he.'

VIII

And out and spake the third o' them,
  ' I wot that they are lovers dear.'
And out and spake the fourth o' them,
  ' They hae been in love this mony a year.'

IX

Then out and spake the fifth o' them,
  ' It were great sin true love to twain.'
And out and spake the sixth o' them,
  ' It were shame to slay a sleeping man.'

X

Then up and gat the seventh o' them,
  And never a word spake he ;
But he has striped his bright brown brand
  Out through Clerk Saunders' fair bodye.

XI

Clerk Saunders he started, and Margaret she turn'd
  Into his arms as asleep she lay ;
And sad and silent was the night
  That was atween thir twae.

XII

And they lay still and sleepit sound
  Until the day began to daw' ;
And kindly she to him did say,
  ' It is time, true love, you were awa'.'

striped] thrust.

XIII

But he lay still, and sleepit sound,
    Albeit the sun began to sheen ;
She look'd atween her and the wa',
    And dull and drowsie were his e'en.

XIV

Then in and came her father dear ;
    Said, 'Let a' your mourning be ;
I'll carry the dead corse to the clay,
    And I'll come back and comfort thee.'

XV

'Comfort weel your seven sons,
    For comforted I will never be :
I ween 'twas neither knave nor loon
    Was in the bower last night wi' me.'

PART II

I

The clinking bell gaed through the town,
    To carry the dead corse to the clay ;
And Clerk Saunders stood at may Margaret's window,
    I wot, an hour before the day.

II

'Are ye sleeping, Marg'ret ? ' he says,
    ' Or are ye waking presentlie ?
Give me my faith and troth again,
    I wot, true love, I gied to thee.'

III

' Your faith and troth ye sall never get,
    Nor our true love sall never twin,
Until ye come within my bower,
    And kiss me cheik and chin.'

twin] break in two.

CLERK SAUNDERS

IV

'My mouth it is full cold, Marg'ret;
  It has the smell, now, of the ground;
And if I kiss thy comely mouth,
  Thy days of life will not be lang.

V

'O cocks are crowing on merry middle-earth,
  I wot the wild fowls are boding day;
Give me my faith and troth again,
  And let me fare me on my way.'

VI

'Thy faith and troth thou sallna get,
  And our true love sall never twin,
Until ye tell what comes o' women,
  I wot, who die in strong traivelling?'

VII

'Their beds are made in the heavens high,
  Down at the foot of our good Lord's knee,
Weel set about wi' gillyflowers;
  I wot, sweet company for to see.

VIII

'O cocks are crowing on merry middle-earth,
  I wot the wild fowls are boding day;
The psalms of heaven will soon be sung,
  And I, ere now, will be miss'd away.'

IX

Then she has taken a crystal wand,
  And she has stroken her troth thereon;
She has given it him out at the shot-window,
  Wi' mony a sad sigh and heavy groan.

X

'I thank ye, Marg'ret; I thank ye, Marg'ret;
  And ay I thank ye heartilie;
Gin ever the dead come for the quick,
  Be sure, Marg'ret, I'll come for thee.'

XI

It's hosen and shoon, and gown alone,
  She climb'd the wall, and follow'd him,
Until she came to the green forèst,
  And there she lost the sight o' him.

XII

'Is there ony room at your head, Saunders?
  Is there ony room at your feet?
Or ony room at your side, Saunders,
  Where fain, fain, I wad sleep?'

XIII

'There's nae room at my head, Marg'ret,
  There's nae room at my feet;
My bed it is fu' lowly now,
  Amang the hungry worms I sleep.

XIV

'Cauld mould is my covering now,
  But and my winding-sheet;
The dew it falls nae sooner down
  Than my resting-place is weet.

XV

'But plait a wand o' bonny birk,
  And lay it on my breast;
And shed a tear upon my grave,
  And wish my saul gude rest.'

CLERK SAUNDERS

XVI

Then up and crew the red, red cock,
　And up and crew the gray:
' 'Tis time, 'tis time, my dear Marg'ret,
　That you were going away.

XVII

' And fair Marg'ret, and rare Marg'ret,
　And Marg'ret o' veritie,
Gin e'er ye love another man,
　Ne'er love him as ye did me.'

28.　　*The Daemon Lover*

I

' O WHERE hae ye been, my long, long love,
　These seven long years and more?'—
' O I'm come to seek my former vows,
　That ye promised me before.'—

II

' Awa' wi' your former vows,' she says,
　' For they will breed but strife;
Awa' wi' your former vows,' she says,
　' For I am become a wife.

III

' I am married to a ship-carpenter,
　A ship-carpenter he's bound;
I wadna he kenn'd my mind this nicht
　For twice five hundred pound.'

IV

He turn'd him round and round about,
　And the tear blinded his e'e:
' I wad never hae trodden on Irish ground
　If it hadna been for thee.

123

V

' I might hae had a noble lady,
  Far, far beyond the sea ;
I might hae had a noble lady,
  Were it no for the love o' thee.'—

VI

' If ye might hae had a noble lady,
  Yoursel' ye had to blame ;
Ye might hae taken the noble lady,
  For ye kenn'd that I was nane.'—

VII

' O fause are the vows o' womankind,
  But fair is their fause bodie :
I wad never hae trodden on Irish ground,
  Were it no for the love o' thee.'—

VIII

' If I was to leave my husband dear,
  And my wee young son alsua,
O what hae ye to tak' me to,
  If with you I should gae ?'—

IX

' I hae seven ships upon the sea,
  The eighth brought me to land ;
With mariners and merchandise,
  And music on every hand.

X

' The ship wherein my love sall sail
  Is glorious to behowd ;
The sails sall be o' the finest silk,
  And the mast o' beaten gowd.'

THE DAEMON LOVER

XI

She has taken up her wee young son,
    Kiss'd him baith cheek and chin ;
'O fare ye weel, my wee young son,
    For I'll never see you again ! '

XII

She has put her foot on gude ship-board,
    And on ship-board she has gane,
And the veil that hangit ower her face
    Was a' wi' gowd begane.

XIII

She hadna sail'd a league, a league,
    A league but barely twa,
Till she minded on her husband she left
    And her wee young son alsua.

XIV

'O haud your tongue o' weeping,' he says,
    'Let a' your follies a-bee ;
I'll show where the white lilies grow
    On the banks o' Italie.'

XV

She hadna sail'd a league, a league,
    A league but barely three,
Till grim, grim grew his countenance
    And gurly grew the sea.

XVI

'What hills are yon, yon pleasant hills,
    The sun shines sweetly on ? '—
'O yon are the hills o' Heaven,' he said,
    'Where you will never won.'—

begane] overlaid.   gurly] rough, surly.

125

XVII

' O whaten-a mountain is yon,' she said,
    Sae dreary wi' frost and snae ?'—
' O yon is the mountain o' Hell,' he said,
    Where you and I will gae.

XVIII

' But haud your tongue, my dearest dear,
    Let a' your follies a-bee,
I'll show where the white lilies grow,
    In the bottom o' the sea.'

XIX

And aye as she turn'd her round about,
    Aye taller he seem'd to be ;
Until that the tops o' that gallant ship
    Nae taller were than he.

XX

He strack the top-mast wi' his hand,
    The fore-mast wi' his knee ;
And he brake that gallant ship in twain,
    And sank her in the sea.

29.   *Clerk Colven*

I

CLERK COLVEN, and his gay ladie,
    As they walk'd in yon garden green,
The belt about her middle jimp
    It cost Clerk Colven crowns fifteen.

snae] snow.   jimp] slim, slender.

126

CLERK COLVEN

II

'O hearken weel now, my good lord,
  O hearken weel to what I say;
When ye gang to the wall o' Stream
  O gang nae near the weel-faur'd may.'

III

'O haud your tongue, my gay ladie,
  Now speak nae mair of that to me;
For I nae saw a fair woman
  [That I cou'd] like so well as thee.'

IV

He's mounted on his berry-brown steed,
  And merry, merry rade he on,
Till that he came to the wall o' Stream,
  And there he saw the mermaiden.

V

'Ye wash, ye wash, ye bonny may,
  And ay's ye wash your sark o' silk.'—
'It's a' for ye, you gentle knight,
  My skin is whiter than the milk.'

VI

He's ta'en her by the milk-white hand,
  He's ta'en her by the sleeve sae green,
And he's forgotten his gay ladie,
  And he's awa' wi' the mermaiden.

VII

—'Ohone, alas!' says Clerk Colven,
  'And aye so sair as akes my head!'
And merrily leugh the mermaiden,
  'O 'twill win on till you be dead.

wall] well.   weel-faur'd may] well-favoured maiden.
leugh] laughed.   win on] continue.

VIII

'But out ye tak' your little pen-knife,
　　And frae my sark ye shear a gare ;
Row that about your lovely head,
　　And the pain ye'll never feel nae mair.'

IX

Out he has ta'en his little pen-knife,
　　And frae her sark he's shorn a gare ;
She's ty'd it round his whey-white face,
　　But and ay his head it akèd mair.

X

'Ohone, alas !　says Clerk Colven,
　　O sairer, sairer akes my head ! '—
'And sairer, sairer ever will,
　　And aye be war' till ye be dead.'

XI

Then out he drew his shining blade
　　And thought wi' it to be her deid,
But she's become a fish again,
　　And merrily sprang into the fleed.

XII

He's mounted on his berry-brown steed,
　　And dowie, dowie rade he hame,
And heavily, heavily lighted down
　　When to his ladie's bower he came.

XIII

'O mither, mither, mak' my bed,
　　And, gentle ladie, lay me down ;
O brither, brither, unbend my bow,
　　'Twill never be bent by me again ! '

gare] gore, strip.　　row] roll, wrap.　　war'] worse.　　deid]
death.　　fleed] flood.　　dowie] dolefully.

XIV

His mither she has made his bed,
  His gentle ladie laid him down,
His brither he has unbent his bow,
  —'Twas never bent by him again.

30.   *Young Hunting*

I

'O LADY, rock never your young son young
  One hour longer for me ;
For I have a sweetheart in Gareloch Wells
  I love thrice better than thee.

II

' The very sole o' that lady's foot,
  Than thy face is mair white.'—
' But nevertheless now, Young Hunting,
  Ye'll bide in my bower this night ? '

III

She has birl'd in him Young Hunting
  The good ale and the wine,
Till he was as fou drunken
  As any wild-wood swine.

IV

[She has kiss'd him by] the candle-light
  And the charcoal burning red,
And up she has ta'en Young Hunting,
  And she 's had him to her bed.

birl'd] poured.

YOUNG HUNTING

V

And she's minded her on a little pen-knife
    That hang'd below her gare,
And she has gi'en Young Hunting
    A deep wound and a sair.

VI

Then up and spake the popinjay
    That flew abune her head :
' Lady, keep well your green cleiding
    Frae good Young Hunting's bleid ! '—

VII

' O better I'll keep my green cleiding
    Frae good Young Hunting's bleid
Than thou canst keep thy clattering tongue
    That trattles in thy head.'

VIII

' O lang, lang is the winter's night,
    And slowly daws the day!
There lies a dead man in my bower,
    And I wish he were away.'

IX

She has call'd upon her bower-maidens,
    She has call'd them ane by ane :
' There lies a dead man in my bower,
    I wish that he were gane.'

X

They have booted and spurr'd Young Hunting
    As he was wont to ride—
A hunting-horn about his neck,
    And a sharp sword by his side ;
And they've had him to the wan water,
    Where a' men ca's it Clyde.

gare] gore, in the skirt.   cleiding] clothing.   daws]
dawns.

YOUNG HUNTING

XI

In the deepest pot of Clyde-water
    It 's there they flang him in,
And put a turf on his breast-bane
    To hold Young Hunting down.

XII

Then up and spake the popinjay
    That sat upon the tree ;
' Gae hame, gae hame, ye fause lady,
    And pay your maids their fee.'—

XIII

' Come down, come down, my pretty bird,
    That sits upon the tree ;
I have a cage o' beaten gold,
    I'll gie it unto thee.'—

XIV

' How shall I come down, how can I come down,
    How shall I come down to thee ?
The things ye said to Young Hunting,
    The same ye're saying to me.'

XV

She hadna cross'd a rigg o' land,
    A rigg but barely ane,
When she met wi' his auld father,
    Came riding all alane.

XVI

' Where has ye been, now, lady fair,
    Where has ye been sae late ?
We hae been seeking Young Hunting,
    But him we canna get.'—

rigg] ridge.

YOUNG HUNTING

XVII

'Young Hunting kens a' the fords o' Clyde,
    He'll ride them ane by ane;
And though the night was ne'er so mirk,
    Young Hunting will be hame.'

XVIII

O there came seeking Young Hunting
    Mony a lord and knight,
And there came seeking Young Hunting
    Mony a lady bright.

XIX

And it fell ance upon a day
    The King was bound to ride,
And he has miss'd Young Hunting,
    Should hae ridden on his right side.

XX

And they have to his true love gane;
    But she sware by the thorn,
'O I have not seen Young Hunting
    Since yesterday at morn.

XXI

'It fears me sair in Clyde Water
    That he is drown'd therein!'
O they have sent for the King's divers,
    To dive for Young Hunting.

XXII

'Gar dive, gar dive!' the King he cried,
    'Gar dive for gold and fee!
O wha will dive for Young Hunting's sake,
    Or wha will dive for me?'

YOUNG HUNTING

XXIII

They dived in at the tae water-bank,
    They dived in at the tither:
'We can dive no more for Young Hunting,
    Altho' he were our brither.'

XXIV

It fell that in that lady's castle
    The King was boun to bed,
And out it spake the popinjay
    That flew abune his head:

XXV

'Leave off, leave off, your day diving,
    And dive upon the night;
And where that sackless Knight lies slain
    The candles will burn bright.'

XXVI

They left their diving on the day,
    And dived upon the night;
And over the place Young Hunting lay
    The candles shone fu' bright.

XXVII

The deepest pot in Clyde Water
    They got Young Hunting in,
With a green turf tied across his breast
    To keep that good lord down.

XXVIII

Then up and spake the King himsel',
    When he saw the deadly wound:
'O wha has slain my right-hand man,
    That held my hawk and hound?'

sackless] innocent.

YOUNG HUNTING

XXIX

Then up and spake the popinjay,
  Says, 'What needs a' this din?
It was his light leman took his life,
  And hided him in the linn.'

XXX

She sware her by the grass sae green,
  So did she by the corn,
She hadna seen Young Hunting
  Since Monanday at morn.

XXXI

'Put not the wyte on me,' she says,
  'It was my May Catheren.'
Then they have cut baith thorn and fern,
  To burn that maiden in.

XXXII

When they had ta'en her May Catheren,
  In the bonfire set her in;
It wouldna take upon her cheeks,
  Nor yet upon her chin,
Nor yet upon her yellow hair,
  To heal the deadly sin.

XXXIII

Out they have ta'en her May Catheren,
  And put the lady in :
O it took upon her cheek, her cheek,
  Took fast upon her chin,
Took fast upon her fair body—
  She burnt like hollins green.

linn] stream, pool.   wyte] blame.   May] Maid.
hollins] holly.
  134

31. *The Great Silkie of Sule Skerrie*

I

AN earthly nourrice sits and sings,
  And aye she sings, ' Ba, lily wean !
Little ken I my bairn's father,
  Far less the land that he staps in.'

II

Then ane arose at her bed-fit,
  An' a grumly guest I'm sure was he :
' Here am I, thy bairn's father,
  Although that I be not comèlie.

III

I am a man, upo' the lan',
  An' I am a silkie in the sea ;
And when I'm far and far frae lan',
  My dwelling is in Sule Skerrie.'

IV

' It was na weel,' quo' the maiden fair,
  ' It was na weel, indeed,' quo' she,
' That the Great Silkie of Sule Skerrie
  Suld hae come and aught a bairn to me.'

V

Now he has ta'en a purse of goud,
  And he has pat it upo' her knee,
Sayin', ' Gie to me my little young son,
  An' tak thee up thy nourrice-fee.

VI

' An' it sall pass on a simmer's day,
  When the sin shines het on evera stane,
That I will tak my little young son,
  An' teach him for to swim his lane.

nourrice] nurse. silkie] seal. aught] own. his lane]
alone, without assistance.

135

VII

'An' thu sall marry a proud gunner,
　　An' a proud gunner I'm sure he'll be,
An' the very first schot that ere he schoots,
　　He'll schoot baith my young son and me.'

32. *The Wife of Usher's Well*

I

THERE lived a wife at Usher's well,
　　And a wealthy wife was she;
She had three stout and stalwart sons,
　　And sent them o'er the sea.

II

They hadna been a week from her,
　　A week but barely ane,
When word came to the carline wife
　　That her three sons were gane.

III

They hadna been a week from her,
　　A week but barely three,
When word came to the carline wife
　　That her sons she'd never see.

IV

' I wish the wind may never cease,
　　Nor fashes in the flood,
Till my three sons come hame to me
　　In earthly flesh and blood ! '

　　carline] old woman.　　　　fashes] troubles.
136

THE WIFE OF USHER'S WELL

V

It fell about the Martinmas,
　When nights are lang and mirk,
The carline wife's three sons came hame,
　And their hats were o' the birk.

VI

It neither grew in syke nor ditch,
　Nor yet in ony sheugh;
But at the gates o' Paradise
　That birk grew fair eneugh.

VII

'Blow up the fire, my maidens!
　Bring water from the well!
For a' my house shall feast this night,
　Since my three sons are well.'

VIII

And she has made to them a bed,
　She's made it large and wide;
And she's ta'en her mantle her about,
　Sat down at the bedside.

IX

Up then crew the red, red cock,
　And up and crew the gray;
The eldest to the youngest said,
　''Tis time we were away.'

X

The cock he hadna craw'd but once,
　And clapp'd his wings at a',
When the youngest to the eldest said,
　'Brother, we must awa'.

　　　syke] marsh.　　　sheugh] trench.

F 3

XI

'The cock doth craw, the day doth daw,
  The channerin' worm doth chide;
Gin we be miss'd out o' our place,
  A sair pain we maun bide.'—

XII

'Lie still, lie still but a little wee while,
  Lie still but if we may;
Gin my mother should miss us when she wakes,
  She'll go mad ere it be day.'—

XIII

'Fare ye weel, my mother dear!
  Fareweel to barn and byre!
And fare ye weel, the bonny lass
  That kindles my mother's fire!'

33. *A Lyke-Wake Dirge*

I

THIS ae nighte, this ae nighte,
  —*Every nighte and alle,*
Fire and fleet and candle-lighte,
  And Christe receive thy saule.

II

When thou from hence away art past,
  —*Every nighte and alle,*
To Whinny-muir thou com'st at last:
  And Christe receive thy saule.

channerin'] fretting.   fleet] floor.   *Other readings are* 'sleet'
and 'salt'.
138

A LYKE-WAKE DIRGE

III

If ever thou gavest hosen and shoon,
  —*Every nighte and alle,*
Sit thee down and put them on :
  And Christe receive thy saule.

IV

If hosen and shoon thou ne'er gav'st nane
  —*Every nighte and alle,*
The whinnes sall prick thee to the bare bane ;
  And Christe receive thy saule.

V

From whinny-muir when thou may'st pass,
  —*Every nighte and alle,*
To Brig o' Dread thou com'st at last ;
  And Christe receive thy saule.

VI

From Brig o' Dread when thou may'st pass,
  —*Every nighte and alle,*
To Purgatory fire thou com'st at last ;
  And Christe receive thy saule.

VII

If ever thou gavest meat or drink,
  —*Every nighte and alle,*
The fire sall never make thee shrink ;
  And Christe receive thy saule.

VIII

If meat or drink thou ne'er gav'st nane,
  —*Every nighte and alle,*
The fire will burn thee to the bare bane ;
  And Christe receive thy saule.

IX

This ae nighte, this ae nighte,
  —*Every nighte and alle,*
Fire and fleet and candle-lighte,
  And Christe receive thy saule.

34. *The Unquiet Grave*

I

'THE wind doth blow to-day, my love,
  And a few small drops of rain;
I never had but one true-love;
  In cold grave she was lain.

II

' I'll do as much for my true-love
  As any young man may;
I'll sit and mourn all at her grave
  For a twelvemonth and a day.'

III

The twelvemonth and a day being up,
  The dead began to speak:
' Oh who sits weeping on my grave,
  And will not let me sleep?'—

IV

' 'Tis I, my love, sits on your grave,
  And will not let you sleep;
For I crave one kiss of your clay-cold lips,
  And that is all I seek.'—

140

THE UNQUIET GRAVE

V

'You crave one kiss of my clay-cold lips;
  But my breath smells earthy strong;
If you have one kiss of my clay-cold lips,
  Your time will not be long.

VI

''Tis down in yonder garden green,
  Love, where we used to walk,
The finest flower that ere was seen
  Is wither'd to a stalk.

VII

' The stalk is wither'd dry, my love,
  So will our hearts decay;
So make yourself content, my love,
  Till God calls you away.'

BOOK II

BOOK II

Hynd Horn

35.

I

HYND Horn's bound, love, and Hynd Horn's free,
With a hey lillelu and a how lo lan ;
Where was ye born, or in what countrie ?
And the birk and the broom blows bonnie.

II

'In good greenwood, there I was born,
And all my forbears me beforn.

III

'O seven long years I served the King,
And as for wages I never gat nane ;

IV

'But ae sight o' his ae daughter.
And that was thro' an auger-bore.'

V

Seven long years he served the King,
And it's a' for the sake of his daughter Jean.

VI

The King an angry man was he ;
He sent young Hynd Horn to the sea.

VII

He's gi'en his luve a silver wand
Wi' seven silver laverocks sittin' thereon.

VIII

She's gi'en to him a gay gold ring
Wi' seven bright diamonds set therein.

laverocks] larks.

HYND HORN.

IX

'As lang's these diamonds keep their hue,
Ye'll know I am a lover true:

X

'But when the ring turns pale and wan,
Ye may ken that I love anither man.'

XI

He hoist up sails and awa' sail'd he
Till that he came to a foreign countrie.

XII

One day as he look'd his ring upon,
He saw the diamonds pale and wan.

XIII

He's left the seas and he's come to the land,
And the first that he met was an auld beggar man.

XIV

'What news, what news? thou auld beggar man,
For it's seven years sin I've seen land.'

XV

'No news,' said the beggar, 'no news at a',
But there is a wedding in the King's ha'.

XVI

'But there is a wedding in the King's ha'
That has halden these forty days and twa.'

XVII

'Cast off, cast off thy auld beggar weed,
And I'll gi'e thee my gude grey steed:

XVIII

'And lend to me your wig o' hair
To cover mine, because it is fair.'—

weed] clothes.

143

XIX

'My begging weed is na for thee,
Your riding steed is na for me.'

XX

But part by right and part by wrang
Hynd Horn has changed wi' the beggar man.

XXI

The auld beggar man was bound for to ride,
But young Hynd Horn was bound for the bride.

XXII

When he came to the King's gate,
He sought a drink for Hynd Horn's sake.

XXIII

The bride came trippin' down the stair,
Wi' the scales o' red gowd in her hair;

XXIV

Wi' a cup o' the red wine in her hand,
And that she gae to the auld beggar man.

XXV

Out o' the cup he drank the wine,
And into the cup he dropt the ring.

XXVI

'O got ye this by sea or land?
Or got ye it of a dead man's hand?'——

XXVII

'I got it na by sea nor land,
But I got it, madam, of your own hand.

XXVIII

'O, I'll cast off my gowns o' brown,
And beg with you frae town to town.

XXIX

'O, I'll cast off my gowns o' red,
And I'll beg wi' you to win my bread.

XXX

' O I'll take the scales o' gowd frae my hair,
And I'll follow you for evermair.'

XXXI

She has cast awa' the brown and the red,
And she's follow'd him to beg her bread.

XXXII

She has ta'en the scales o' gowd frae her hair
And she's follow'd him for evermair.

XXXIII

But atween the kitchen and the ha'
He has let his cloutie cloak down fa'.

XXXIV

And the red gowd shinèd over him a',
With a hey lillelu, and a how lo lan;
And the bride frae the bridegroom was stown awa',
And the birk and the broom blows bonnie.

36.   *Hynd Etin*

I

MAY Margaret sits in her bower door
Sewing her silken seam;
She heard a note in Elmond's wood,
And wish'd she there had been.

II

She loot the seam fa' frae her side,
The needle to her tae,
And she is on to Elmond's wood
As fast as she could gae.

cloutie] full of clouts, patched.   stown] stolen.   loot] let.
tae] toe.

HYND ETIN

She hadna pu'd a nut, a nut,
  Nor broken a branch but ane,
Till by there came the Hynd Etin,
  Says, 'Lady, lat alane.

IV

'O why pu' ye the nut, the nut,
  Or why break ye the tree?
For I am forester o' this wood:
  Ye should spier leave at me.'—

V

I'll ask leave at nae living man,
  Nor yet will I at thee;
My father is king o'er a' this realm,
  This wood belongs to me.'

VI

The highest tree in Elmond's wood,
  He's pu'd it by the reet,
And he has built for her a bower
  Near by a hallow seat.

VII

He's kept her there in Elmond's wood
  For six lang years and ane,
Till six pretty sons to him she bare,
  And the seventh she's brought hame.

VIII

It fell out ance upon a day
  He's to the hunting gane,
And a' to carry his game for him
  He's tane his eldest son.

spier] ask.   reet] root.   hallow seat] holy man's or
hermit's cave.

IX

'A question I will ask, father,
  Gin ye wadna angry be.'—
'Say on, say on, my bonny boy,
  Ye'se nae be quarrell'd by me.'

X

'I see my mither's cheeks aye weet,
  I never can see them dry;
And I wonder what aileth my mither
  To mourn [sae constantly].'—

XI

'Your mither was a king's daughtèr,
  Sprung frae a high degree;
She might hae wed some worthy prince
  Had she na been stown by me.

XII

'Your mither was a king's daughtèr
  Of noble birth and fame,
But now she's wife o' Hynd Etin,
  Wha ne'er gat christendame.

XIII

'But we'll shoot the buntin' o' the bush,
  The linnet o' the tree,
And ye'se tak' them hame to your dear mither,
  See if she'll merrier be.'

XIV

It fell upon anither day,
  He's to the hunting gane
And left his seven [young] children
  To stay wi' their mither at hame.

stown] stolen.

HYND ETIN

XV

' O I will tell to you, mither,
Gin ye wadna angry be.'—
' Speak on, speak on, my little wee boy,
Ye'se nae be quarrell'd by me.'—

XVI

' As we came frae the hind-hunting,
We heard fine music ring.'—
'My blessings on you, my bonny boy,
I wish I'd been there my lane.'

XVII

They wistna weel where they were gaen,
Wi' the stratlins o' their feet;
They wistna weel where they were gaen,
Till at her father's yate.

XVIII

' I hae nae money in my pocket,
But royal rings hae three;
I'll gie them you, my little young son,
And ye'll walk there for me.

XIX

' Ye'll gi'e the first to the proud portèr
And he will let you in;
Ye'll gi'e the next to the butler-boy
And he will show you ben;

XX

' Ye'll gi'e the third to the minstrel
That plays before the King;
He'll play success to the bonny boy
Came thro' the wood him lane.'

stratlins] ? stragglings.   yate] gate.   ben] further in.

148

XXI

He ga'e the first to the proud portèr
    And he open'd and let him in;
He ga'e the next to the butler-boy,
    And he has shown him ben.

XXII

He ga'e the third to the minstrel
    That play'd before the King,
And he play'd success to the bonny boy
    Came thro' the wood him lane.

XXIII

Now when he came before the King,
    Fell low upon his knee;
The King he turn'd him round about,
    And the saut tear blint his e'e.

XXIV

'Win up, win up, my bonny boy,
    Gang frae my companie;
Ye look sae like my dear daughtèr,
    My heart will burst in three.'—

XXV

'If I look like your dear daughtèr,
    A wonder it is none;
If I look like your dear daughtèr,
    I am her eldest son.'—

XXVI

'Will ye tell me, ye little wee boy,
    Where may my Margaret be?'—
'She's just now standing at your yates,
    And my six brithers her wi'.'—

blint] blinded.

XXVII

'O where are a' my porter-boys
  That I pay meat and fee,
To open my yates baith wide and braid,
  Let her come in to me?'

XXVIII

When she cam' in before the King,
  Fell low down on her knee:
'Win up, win up, my daughter dear,
  This day ye'se dine wi' me.'—

XXIX

'Ae bit I canna eat, father,
  Nor ae drop can I drink,
Until I see my mither dear,
  For lang for her I think.'

XXX

When she cam' in before the queen,
  Fell low down on her knee;
'Win up, win up, my daughter dear,
  This day ye'se dine wi' me.'—

XXXI

'Ae bit I canna eat, mither,
  Nor ae drop can I drink,
Until I see my sister dear,
  For lang for her I think.'

XXXII

When that these twa sisters met,
  She hail'd her courteouslie;
'Come ben, come ben, my sister dear,
  This day ye'se dine wi' me.'—

HYND ETIN

XXXIII

'Ae bit I canna eat, sister,
    Nor ae drop can I drink,
Until I see my dear husband,
    So lang for him I think.'—

XXXIV

'O where are a' my rangers bold
    That I pay meat and fee,
To search the forest far an' wide,
    And bring Etin back to me?'

XXXV

Out it speaks the little wee boy:
    'Na, na, this mauna be;
Without ye grant a free pardon,
    I hope ye'll nae him see.'—

XXXVI

'O here I grant a free pardon,
    Well seal'd by my own han';
Ye may mak' search for Young Etin
    As soon as ever ye can.'

XXXVII

They search'd the country wide and braid,
    The forests far and near,
And they found him into Elmond's wood,
    Tearing his yellow hair.

XXXVIII

'Win up, win up now, Hynd Etin,
    Win up an' boun wi' me;
We're messengers come frae the court;
    The King wants you to see.'—

boun] go.

151

HYND ETIN

XXXIX

' O lat them tak' frae me my head,
  Or hang me on a tree ;
For since I've lost my dear lady,
  Life 's no pleasure to me.'—

XL

' Your head will na be touch'd, Etin,
  Nor you hang'd on a tree ;
Your lady 's in her father's court
  And a' he wants is thee.'

XLI

When he cam' in before the King,
  Fell low down on his knee ;
' Win up, win up now, Young Etin,
  This day ye'se dine wi' me.'

XLII

But as they were at dinner set
  The wee boy ask'd a boon :
' I wish we were in a good kirk
  For to get christendoun.

XLIII

' For we hae lived in gude green wood
  This seven years and ane ;
But a' this time since e'er I mind
  Was never a kirk within.'—

XLIV

' Your asking 's na sae great, my boy,
  But granted it sall be ;
This day to gude kirk ye sall gang
  And your mither sall gang you wi'. '

XLV

When unto the gude kirk she came,
  She at the door did stan';
She was sae sair sunk down wi' shame,
  She couldna come farther ben.

XLVI

Then out and spak' the parish priest,
  And a sweet smile ga'e he:
'Come ben, come ben, my lily-flower,
  Present your babes to me.'

XLVII

Charles, Vincent, Sam and Dick,
  And likewise John and James;
They call'd the eldest Young Etin,
  Which was his father's name.

37. *Erlinton*

I

ERLINTON had a fair daughter;
  I wat he wear'd her in a great sin;
For he has built a bigly bower,
  And a' to put that lady in.

II

An' he has warn'd her sisters six,
  An' sae has he her brethren se'en,
Outher to watch her a' the night,
  Or else to seek her morn an' e'en.

wear'd her in] led her into.

III

She hadna been i' that bigly bower,
  Na not a night but barely ane,
Till there was Willie, her ain true love,
  Chapp'd at the door, cryin' 'Peace within!'

IV

'O whae is this at my bower door,
  That chaps sae late, nor kens the gin?'—
'O it is Willie, your ain true love,
  I pray you rise an' let me in.'—

V

'For a' sae weel as I like ye, Willie,
  For a' sae weel as I ken the gin,
I wadna for ten thousand pounds, love,
  Na, no this night wad I let ye in.

VI

'But in the green-wood is a wake,
  And at the wake there is a wane,
An' there I'll come as sune the morn, love,
  Na no a mile but barely ane.

VII

'On-my right hand I'll have a glo', love,
  And on my left hand I'll have nane;
I'll have wi' me my sisters six, love,
  And we will wauk the wood our lane.'

VIII

Then she 's gane to her bed again,
  She has layen till the cock crew thrice,
An' then she said to her sisters a',
  'Maidens, 'tis time for us to rise.

chapp'd] knocked.   gin] trick, or sleight, of the door-latch.
wake (*obscure*).   wane] dwelling, arbor.   glo'] glove.   our
lane] we alone.

ERLINTON

IX

She pat on her back her silken gown,
  An' on her breast a siller pin,
An' she 's ta'en her sisters by the hand,
  An' to the green-wood she is gane.

X

They hadna wauk'd in the bonny green-wood,
  Na no an hour but barely ane,
Till up start Willie, her ain true love,
  Wha frae her sisters has her ta'en.

XI

An' he has kiss'd her sisters six,
  An' he has sent them hame again,
But he has keepit his ain true love,
  Sayin' ' We'll wauk the woods our lane.'

XII

They hadna wauk'd in the bonnie green-wood
  Na no an hour but barely ane,
Till up start fifteen o' the bravest outlaws
  That ever bare either blood or bane.

XIII

Then up bespake the foremost knight,—
  An' O but he spake angrilỳ :
Says, ' Yield to me thy ladye bright,
  This night shall wauk the woods wi' me.'—

XIV

' I like her weel, my ladye bright,
  And O my life but it lies me near !
But before I lose my ladye bright
  I'll rather lose my life sae dear.'

XV

But up an' spake the second knight—
  I wat he spake right boustruslie—
Says, 'Baith your life an' your ladye bright
  This night shall wauk the woods wi' me.'—

XVI

'My ladye is my warldis meed :
  My life I winna yield to nane ;
But if ye be men of your manheid,
  Ye'll only fight me ane by ane.—

XVII

'O sit ye down, my dearest dear,
  Sit down an' hold my milk-white steed,
An' see that ye dinna change your cheer
  Until ye see my body bleed.'

XVIII

He set his back unto an aik,
  He set his feet against a stane,
He 's feightin a' these fifteen outlaws,
  An' kill'd them a' but barely ane.

XIX

An' he has gane to his ladye dear,
  I wat he kiss'd her cheek an' chin—
'Thou art mine ain, I have bought thee dear,
  An' now we will wauk the woods our lane.

warldis meed] world's reward, most precious thing in the
world : *or perhaps corrupted from* warldis make, mate.   aik]
oak.

Earl Brand

ī

O DID ye ever hear o' brave Earl Brand?
    Ay lally, o lilly lally
He courted the King's daughter o' fair England
    All i' the night sae early.

II

She was scarcely fifteen years that tide
Till sae boldly she came to his bedside.

III

' O Earl Bran', fain wad I see
A pack of hounds let loose on the lea.'—

IV

' O lady, I have no steeds but one,
But thou shalt ride, and I will run.'—

V

' O Earl Bran', my father has two,
And thou shalt have the best of tho'.—

VI

They have ridden o'er moss and moor,
And they have met neither rich nor poor,

VII

Until they met with old Carl Hood :
—He's aye for ill and never for good.

VIII

' Earl Bran', if ye love me,
Seize this old carl, and gar him die.'—

IX

' O lady fair, it wad be sair
To slay an old man that has grey hair.

tide] time, season.

EARL BRAND

X

'O lady fair, I'll no do sae;
I'll gie him a pound and let him gae.'

XI

'O where hae ye ridden this lee-lang day?
Or where hae ye stolen this lady away?'—

XII

'I have not ridden this lee-lang day,
Nor yet have I stolen this lady away.

XIII

'She is my only, my sick sistèr,
Which I have brought from Winchester.'—

XIV

'If she be sick and like to dead,
Why wears she the ribbon sae red?

XV

'If she be sick and like to die,
Then why wears she the gold on high?'

XVI

When came the carl to this lady's yett,
Rudely, rudely he rapp'd thereat.

XVII

'O where's the lady o' this ha'?'—
'She's out with her maids to play at the ba'.'—

XVIII

'Ha, ha, ha! ye are a' mista'en;
Gae count your maidens o'er again.

XIX

'I met her far beyond the lea,
With the young Earl Brand, his leman to be.'

lee-lang] live-long.   yett] gate.

158

EARL BRAND

XX

Her father arm'd of his men fifteen,
And they're ridden after them all-by-dene.

XXI

O'er her left shoulder the lady look'd then :
' O Earl Bran', we both are ta'en ! '—

XXII

' If they come on me ane by ane,
Ye may stand by and see them slain.

XXIII

' But if they come on me ane and all,
Ye may stand by and see me fall.'

XXIV

They have come on him ane by ane,
And fourteen men he has them slain.

XXV

But the fifteenth man behind stole round,
And he 's gi'en him a deadly wound.

XXVI

But for a' sae wounded as Earl Brand was
He has set his lady on her horse.

XXVII

They rode till they came to the water o' Doune.
And there he lighted to wash his wound.

XXVIII

' O Earl Bran', I see your heart's bloud ! '—
' It 's na but the glent o' my scarlet hood.'

XXIX

They rode till they came to his mother's yett,
So faint and feebly he rapp'd thereat.

all-by-dene] all together.   glent] gleam.

XXX

'O my son 's slain, he 's falling to swoun,
And a' for the sake of an English loun ! '—

XXXI

' So say not sae, my dearest mother,
But marry her to my youngest brother.

XXXII

' This has not been the death o' ane,
But it 's been the death o' fair seventeen.'

39. *The Douglas Tragedy*

I

'RISE up, rise up, now Lord Douglas,' she says,
  ' And put on your armour so bright ;
Let it never be said that a daughter of thine
  Was married to a lord under night.

II

' Rise up, rise up, my seven bold sons,
  And put on your armour so bright,
And take better care of your youngest sister,
  For your eldest 's awa the last night.'

III

He 's mounted her on a milk-white steed,
  And himself on a dapple grey,
With a bugelet horn hung down his side ;
  And lightly they rode away.

IV

Lord William look'd o'er his left shoulder,
  To see what he could see,
And there he spy'd her seven brethren bold
  Come riding over the lea.

THE DOUGLAS TRAGEDY

V

'Light down, light down, Lady Margret,' he said,
  'And hold my steed in your hand,
Until that against your seven brethren bold,
  And your father, I mak' a stand.'

VI

O, there she stood, and bitter she stood,
  And never did shed one tear,
Until that she saw her seven brethren fa',
  And her father, who lov'd her so dear.

VII

'O hold your hand, Lord William!' she said,
  'For your strokes they are wondrous sair;
True lovers I can get many an ane,
  But a father I can never get mair.'

VIII

O she's ta'en out her handkerchief,
  It was o' the holland sae fine,
And aye she dighted her father's wounds,
  That were redder than the wine.

IX

'O chuse, O chuse, Lady Margret,' he said,
  'O whether will ye gang or bide?'
'I'll gang, I'll gang, Lord William,' she said,
  'For ye've left me no other guide.'

X

He's lifted her on a milk-white steed,
  And himself on a dapple grey,
With a bugelet horn hung down by his side;
  And slowly they baith rade away.

dighted] dressed.

THE DOUGLAS TRAGEDY

XI

O they rade on, and on they rade,
　And a' by the light of the moon,
Until they came to yon wan water,
　And there they lighted doun.

XII

They lighted doun to tak' a drink
　Of the spring that ran sae clear,
And doun the stream ran his gude heart's blood,
　And sair she gan to fear.

XIII

' Hold up, hold up, Lord William,' she says,
　' For I fear that you are slain.'—
' 'Tis naething but the shadow of my scarlet cloak,
　That shines in the water sae plain.'

XIV

O they rade on, and on they rade,
　And a' by the light of the moon,
Until they cam' to his mother's ha' door,
　And there they lighted doun.

XV

' Get up, get up, lady mother,' he says,
　' Get up, and let me in !
Get up, get up, lady mother,' he says,
　' For this night my fair lady I've win.

XVI

' O mak my bed, lady mother,' he says,
　' O mak it braid and deep,
And lay Lady Margret close at my back,
　And the sounder I will sleep.'

XVII

Lord William was dead lang ere midnight,
  Lady Margret lang ere day,
And all true lovers that go thegither,
  May they have mair luck than they!

XVIII

Lord William was buried in St. Mary's kirk,
  Lady Margret in Mary's quire;
Out o' the lady's grave grew a bonny red rose,
  And out o' the knight's a brier.

XIX

And they twa met, and they twa plat,
  And fain they wad be near;
And a' the warld might ken right weel
  They were twa lovers dear.

XX

But bye and rade the Black Douglas,
  And wow but he was rough!
For he pull'd up the bonny brier,
  And flang't in St. Mary's Lough.

40.   *Glasgerion*

I

GLASGERION was a King's own son,
  And a harper he was good;
He harpèd in the King's chamber
  Where cup and candle stood,
And so did he in the Queen's chamber,
  Till ladies waxèd wood.

plat] pleated.   wood] crazy, wild with delight.

GLASGERION

II

And then bespake the King's daughter
  And these words thus said she :
[' There's never a stroke comes over this harp,
  But it glads the heart of me. ']

III

Said, ' Strike on, strike on, Glasgerion,
  Of thy striking do not blin ;
There's never a stroke comes over thine harp
  But it glads my heart within.'

IV

' Fair might you fall, lady,' quoth he ;
  ' Who taught you now to speak ?
I have loved you, lady, seven year ;
  My heart I durst ne'er break.'—

V

' But come to my bower, my Glasgerion,
  When all men are at rest ;
As I am a lady true of my promise,
  Thou shalt be a welcome guest.'

VI

But home then came Glasgerion,
  A glad man, Lord, was he !
' And come thou hither, Jack, my boy,
  Come hither unto me.

VII

' For the King's daughter of Normandye
  Her love is granted me ;
And before the cock have crowen
  At her chamber must I be.'

blin] stint, cease.

VIII

'But come you hither, master,' quoth he,
    'Lay your head down on this stone;
For I will waken you, master dear,
    Afore it be time to gone.'

IX

But up then rose that lither lad,
    And did on hose and shoon;
A collar he cast upon his neck,
    He seemèd a gentleman.

X

And when he came to that lady's chamber
    He tirl'd upon a pin;
The lady was true of her promise,
    Rose up and let him in.

XI

He did not kiss that lady gay
    When he came nor when he yode;
And sore mistrusted that lady gay
    He was of some churle's blood.

XII

But home then came that lither lad,
    And did off his hose and shoon,
And cast that collar from 'bout his neck;
    He was but a churlè's son:
'Awaken,' quoth he, 'my master dear,
    I hold it time to be gone.

XIII

'For I have saddled your horse, master,
    Well bridled I have your steed;
Have not I served a good breakfast
    When time comes I have need?'

lither] rascally, vile.   tirl'd] rattled.   yode] went.

XIV

But up then rose good Glasgerion,
  And did on both hose and shoon,
And cast a collar about his neck ;
  He was a Kingé's son.

XV

And when he came to that lady's chamber,
  He tirl'd upon a pin ;
The lady was more than true of her promise,
  Rose up, and let him in.

XVI

Says, ' Whether have you left with me
  Your bracelet or your glove ?
Or are you back return'd again
  To know more of my love ? '

XVII

Glasgerion swore a full great oath
  By oak and ash and thorn,
' Lady, I was never in your chamber
  Sith the time that I was born.'—

XVIII

' O then it was your little foot-page
  Falsely hath beguiled me ' :
And then she pull'd forth a little pen-knife
  That hangèd by her knee,
Says, ' There shall never no churlè's blood
  Spring within my bodye.'

XIX

But home then went Glasgerion,
  A woe man, Lord, was he ;
Sayes, ' Come hither, thou Jack, my boy,
  Come thou hither to me.

XX

'For if I had kill'd a man to-night,
    Jack, I would tell it thee,
But if I have not kill'd a man to-night,
    Jack, thou hast killéd three!'

XXI

And he pull'd out his bright brown sword,
    And dried it on his sleeve,
And he smote off that lither lad's head
    And ask'd no man no leave.

XXII

He set the sword's point till his breast,
    The pommel till a stone;
Through the falseness of that lither lad
    These three lives wern all gone.

41.   *King Estmere*

I

HEARKEN to me, gentlemen,
    Come and you shall heare;
Ile tell you of two of the boldest brether
    That ever bornè were.

II

The tone of them was Adler Younge,
    The tother was Kyng Estmere;
They were as bolde men in their deeds
    As any were, farr and neare.

III

As they were drinking ale and wine
    Within his brother's hall,
'When will ye marry a wyfe, brother,
    A wyfe to glad us all?'

IV

Then bespake him Kyng Estmere,
    And answered him hartilye :
' I know not that ladye in any land,
    That's able to marrye with mee.'—

V

' Kyng Adland hath a daughter, brother,
    Men call her bright and sheene ;
If I were kyng here in your stead,
    That ladye shold be my queene.'—

VI

Saies, ' Reade me, reade me, deare brother,
    Throughout merry England,
Where we might find a messenger
    Betwixt us towe to sende.'—

VII

Saies, ' You shal ryde yourselfe, brother,
    Ile beare you companye ;
Many a man throughe fals messengers is deceived,
    And I feare lest soe shold wee.'

VIII

Thus they renisht them to ryde,
    Of twoe good renisht steeds,
And when they came to Kyng Adland's halle,
    Of redd gold shone their weeds.

renisht] *perhaps for* 'revisht', dressed, arrayed.   weeds]
garments.

KING ESTMERE

IX

And when they came to Kyng Adland's halle,
  Before the goodlye gate,
There they found good Kyng Adland
  Rearing himselfe theratt.

X

'Now Christ thee save, good Kyng Adland;
  Now Christ you save and see.'—
Sayd, 'You be welcome, Kyng Estmere,
  Right hartilye to mee.'

XI

'You have a daughter,' said Adler Younge,
  'Men call her bright and sheene;
My brother wold marrye her to his wiffe,
  Of Englande to be queene.'—

XII

'Yesterday was att my deere daughter
  Kyng Bremor his sonne of Spayn,
And then she nickèd him of naye,
  And I doubt sheele do you the same.'—

XIII

'The Kyng of Spayne is a foule paynim,
  And 'lieveth on Mahound,
And pitye it were that fayre ladye
  Shold marry a heathen hound.

XIV

'But grant to me,' sayes Kyng Estmere,
  'For my love I you praye,
That I may see your daughter deere
  Before I goe hence awaye.'—

rearing] leaning.   nicked] refused.

XV

' Although itt is seven yeers and more
   Since my daughter was in halle,
She shall come once downe for your sake,
   To glad my guestès alle.'

XVI

Downe then came that mayden fayre,
   With ladyes laced in pall,
And halfe a hundred of bold knightes,
   To bring her from bowre to hall,
And as many gentle squiers,
   To tend upon them all.

XVII

The talents of golde were on her head sette
   Hanged low downe to her knee,
And everye ring on her small finger
   Shone of the chrystall free.

XVIII

Saies, ' God you save, my deere madam,'
   Saies, ' God you save and see ! '—
Said, ' You be welcome, Kyng Estmere,
   Right welcome unto mee.

XIX

' And, if you love me, as you saye,
   Soe well and hartilee,
All that ever you are comen about
   Soone sped now itt shal bee.'

XX

Then bespake her father deare :
   ' My daughter, I saye naye ;
Remember well the Kyng of Spayne,
   What he sayd yesterdaye.

        pall] fine cloth.

XXI

'He wold pull downe my halles and castles,
  And reave me of my lyfe ;
I cannot blame him if he doe,
  If I reave him of his wyfe.'—

XXII

'Your castles and your towres, father,
  Are stronglye built aboute,
And therefore of the Kyng his sonne of Spaine
  Wee neede not stande in doubt.

XXIII

'Plight me your troth, nowe, Kyng Estmere,
  By heaven and your righte hand,
That you will marrye me to your wyfe,
  And make me queene of your land.'

XXIV

Then Kyng Estmere he plight his troth,
  By heaven and his righte hand,
That he wolde marrye her to his wyfe,
  And make her queene of his land.

XXV

And he tooke leave of that ladye fayre,
  To goe to his owne countree,
To fetche him dukes and lordes and knightes,
  That marryed they might bee.

XXVI

They had not ridden scant a myle,
  A myle forthe of the towne,
But in did come the Kyng of Spayne,
  With kempès many one.

kempès] fighting-men.

XXVII

But in did come the Kyng of Spayne,
    With manye a bold barone,
Tone day to marrye Kyng Adland's daughter,
    Tother daye to carrye her home.

XXVIII

Shee sent one after Kyng Estmere,
    In all the spede might bee,
That he must either turne againe and fighte,
    Or goe home and loose his ladye.

XXIX

One whyle then the page he went,
    Another while he ranne ;
Till he had oretaken Kyng Estmere,
    I-wis he never blanne.

XXX

' Tydings, tydings, Kyng Estmere ! '—
    ' What tydings nowe, my boye ? '—
' O tydinges I can tell to you,
    That will you sore annoye.

XXXI

' You had not ridden scant a mile,
    A mile out of the towne,
But in did come the Kyng of Spayne,
    With kempès many a one :

XXXII

' But in did come the Kyng of Spayne,
    With manye a bold barone,
Tone daye to marrye Kyng Adland's daughter,
    Tother daye to carry her home.

blanne] halted.

172

XXXIII

'My ladye fayre she greetes you well,
  And ever-more well by mee;
You must either turne againe and fighte,
  Or goe home and loose your ladye.'—

XXXIV

Saies, 'Reade me, reade me, deere brother,
  My reade shall ryse at thee;
Whether it is better to turne and fighte,
  Or goe home and loose my ladye.'

XXXV

'Now hearken to me,' sayes Adler Yonge,
  'And your reade must rise at me;
I quicklye will devise a waye
  To sette thy ladye free.

XXXVI

'My mother was a westerne woman,
  And learned in gramarye,
And when I learnèd at the schole,
  Something shee taught itt mee.

XXXVII

'There growes an hearbe within this field,
  And iff it were but knowne,
His color, which is whyte and redd,
  It will make blacke and browne.

XXXVIII

'His color, which is browne and blacke,
  Itt will make redd and whyte;
That sworde is not in all Englande
  Upon his coate will byte.

My reade shall ryse] my counsel shall arise, or spring, from thee.

KING ESTMERE

XXXIX

'And you shal be a harper, brother,
  Out of the north countrye,
And Ile be your boy, soe faine of fighte,
  And beare your harpe by your knee.

XL

'And you shal be the best harper
  That ever tooke harpe in hand,
And I wil be the best singer
  That ever sung in this lande.

XLI

'Itt shal be written in our forheads,
  All and in grammarye,
That we towe are the boldest men
  That are in all Christentye.'

XLII

And thus they renisht them to ryde,
  Of tow good renisht steedes,
And when they came to Kyng Adland's halle,
  Of redd gold shone their weedes.

XLIII

And whan they came to Kyng Adland's halle
  Untill the fayre hall yate,
There they found a proud portèr,
  Rearing himselfe thereatt.

XLIV

Sayes, 'Christ thee save, thou proud porter,'
  Sayes, 'Christ thee save and see!'—
'Nowe you be welcome,' sayd the porter,
  'Of what land soever ye bee.'

yate] gate.

174

KING ESTMERE

'Wee beenè harpers,' sayd Adler Younge,
   'Come out of the northe countrye ;
Wee beenè come hither untill this place
   This proud weddinge for to see.'—

XLVI

Sayd, 'And your color were white and redd,
   As it is blacke and browne,
I wold saye Kyng Estmere and his brother
   Were comen untill this towne.'

XLVII

Then they pulled out a ryng of gold,
   Layd itt on the porter's arme :
'And ever we will thee, proud portèr,
   Thow wilt saye us no harme.'

XLVIII

Sore he looked on Kyng Estmere,
   And sore he handled the ryng,
Then opened to them the fayre hall yates,
   He lett for no kind of thyng.

XLIX

Kyng Estmere he stabled his steede
   Soe fayre att the hall-bord ;
The froth that came from his brydle bitte
   Light in Kyng Bremor's beard.

L

Saies, 'Stable thy steed, thou proud harpèr,'
   Saies, 'Stable him in the stalle ;
It doth not beseeme a proud harpèr
   To stable his steed in a kyng's halle.'

LI

'My ladde he is so lither,' he said,
  'He will doe nought that's meete;
And is there any man in this hall
  Were able him to beate?'

LII

'Thou speakst proud words,'sayes the Kyng of Spaine,
  'Thou harper, here to mee;
There is a man within this halle
  Will beate thy ladd and thee.'—

LIII

'O let that man come downe,' he said,
  'A sight of him wold I see;
And when hee hath beaten well my ladd,
  Then he shall beate of mee.'

LIV

Downe then came the kemperye man,
  And lookèd him in the eare;
For all the gold that was under heaven,
  He durst not neigh him neare.

LV

'And how nowe, kempe,' said the Kyng of Spaine,
  'And how, what aileth thee?'—
He saies, 'It is writt in his forhead,
  All and in gramarye,
That for all the gold that is under heaven,
  I dare not neigh him nye.'

LVI

Then Kyng Estmere pull'd forth his harpe,
  And play'd a pretty thinge;
The ladye upstart from the borde,
  And wold have gone from the king.

lither] naughty.   neigh] come nigh, approach.
176

LVII

' Stay thy harpe, thou proud harpèr,
  For God's love I pray thee;
For and thou playes as thou beginns,
  Thou 'lt till my bryde from mee.'

LVIII

He stroake upon his harpe againe,
  And play'd a pretty thinge;
The ladye lough a loud laughter,
  As shee sate by the king.

LIX

Saies, ' Sell me thy harpe, thou proud harpèr,
  And thy stringës all;
For as many gold nobles thou shalt have,
  As heere bee ringes in the hall.'

LX

' What wold ye doe with my harpe,' he sayd,
  ' If I did sell itt yee?'—
' To playe my wiffe and me a fitt,
  When abed together wee bee.'

LXI

' Now sell me,' quoth hee, ' thy bryde soe gay,
  As shee sitts by thy knee;
And as many gold nobles I will give
  As leaves been on a tree.'

LXII

' And what wold ye doe with my bryde soe gay,
  Iff I did sell her thee?
More seemelye it is for her fayre bodye
  To lye by mee then thee.'

till] entice.   fitt] strain of music.

KING ESTMERE

LXIII

Hee played agayne both loud and shrille,
  And Adler he did syng,
' O ladye, this is thy owne true love,
  Noe harper, but a kyng.

LXIV

' O ladye, this is thy owne true love,
  As playnlye thou mayest see,
And Ile rid thee of that foule paynim
  Who partes thy love and thee.'

LXV

The ladye looked, the ladye blushte,
  And blushte and lookt agayne,
While Adler he hath drawne his brande,
  And hath the Sowdan slayne

LXVI

Up then rose the kemperye men,
  And loud they gan to crye :
' Ah ! traytors, yee have slayne our kyng,
  And therefore yee shall dye.'

LXVII

Kyng Estmere threwe the harpe asyde,
  And swith he drew his brand,
And Estmere he and Adler Yonge
  Right stiffe in stour can stand.

LXVIII

And aye their swordes soe sore can byte,
  Throughe help of gramarye,
That soone they have slayne the kempery men,
  Or forst them forth to flee.

swith] swiftly.   stour] press of fighting.

KING ESTMERE

LXIX

Kyng Estmere tooke that fayre ladye,
  And marryed her to his wiffe,
And brought her home to merry England,
  With her to lead his life.

42. *Fair Annie*

I

IT'S narrow, narrow, mak your bed,
  And learn to lie your lane;
For I'm gaun owre the sea, Fair Annie,
  A braw Bride to bring hame.
Wi' her I will get gowd and gear,
  Wi' you I ne'er gat nane.

II

' But wha will bake my bridal bread,
  Or brew my bridal ale?
And wha will become my bright Bride,
  That I bring owre the dale?'—

III

' It's I will bake your bridal bread,
  And brew your bridal ale;
And I will welcome your bright Bride,
  That you bring owre the dale.'—

IV

' But she that welcomes my bright Bride
  Maun gang like maiden fair;
She maun lace on her robe sae jimp,
  And comely braid her hair.

  jimp] slender, trim.

FAIR ANNIE

V

' Bind up, bind up your yellow hair,
  And tie it on your neck ;
And see you look as maiden-like
  As the day that first we met.'—

VI

' O how can I gang maiden-like,
  When maiden I am nane ?
Have I not borne six sons to thee,
  And am wi' child again ? '—

VII

' I'll put cooks into my kitchen,
  And stewards in my hall,
And I'll have bakers for my bread,
  And brewers for my ale ;
But you're to welcome my bright Bride,
  That I bring owre the dale.'

VIII

Three months and a day were gane and past,
  Fair Annie she gat word
That her love's ship was come at last,
  Wi' his bright young Bride aboard.

IX

She's ta'en her young son in her arms,
  Anither in her hand ;
And she's gane up to the highest tower,
  Looks over sea and land.

X

' Come doun, come doun, my mother dear,
  Come aff the castle wa' !
I fear if langer ye stand there,
  Ye'll let yoursell doun fa'.'

XI

She 's ta'en a cake o' the best bread,
    A stoup o' the best wine,
And a' the keys upon her arm,
    And to the yett is gane.

XII

'O ye're welcome hame, my ain gude lord,
    To your castles and your towers;
Ye're welcome hame, my ain gude lord,
    To your ha's, but and your bowers.
And welcome to your hame, fair lady!
    For a' that 's here is yours.'

XIII

'O whatna lady 's that, my lord,
    That welcomes you and me?
Gin I be lang about this place,
    Her friend I mean to be.'

XIV

Fair Annie served the lang tables
    Wi' the white bread and the wine;
But ay she drank the wan water
    To keep her colour fine.

XV

And aye sne served the lang tables
    Wi' the white bread and the brown,
And aye she turn'd her round about,
    Sae fast the tears fell doun.

XVI

She took a napkin lang and white,
    And hung it on a pin;
It was to wipe away the tears,
    As she gaed out and in.

        yett] gate.

FAIR ANNIE

XVII

When bells were rung and mass was sung,
  And a' men bound for bed,
The bridegroom and the bonny Bride
  In ae chamber were laid.

XVIII

Fair Annie's ta'en a harp in her hand,
  To harp thir twa asleep ;
But ay, as she harpit and she sang,
  Fu' sairly did she weep.

XIX

' O gin my sons were seven rats,
  Rinnin' on the castle wa',
And I mysell a great grey cat,
  I soon wad worry them a' !

XX

' O gin my sons were seven hares,
  Rinnin' owre yon lily lea,
And I mysell a good greyhound,
  Soon worried they a' should be ! '

XXI

Then out and spak the bonny young Bride,
  In bride-bed where she lay :
' That 's like my sister Annie,' she says ;
  ' Wha is it doth sing and play ?

XXII

' I'll put on my gown,' said the new-come Bride,
  ' And my shoes upon my feet ;
I will see wha doth sae sadly sing,
  And what is it gars her greet.

182

XXIII

'What ails you, what ails you, my housekeeper,
    That ye mak sic a mane?
Has ony wine-barrel cast its girds,
    Or is a' your white bread gane?'—

XXIV

'It isna because my wine is spilt,
    Or that my white bread's gane;
But because I've lost my true love's love,
    And he's wed to anither ane.'—

XXV

'Noo tell me wha was your father?' she says,
    'Noo tell me wha was your mither?
And had ye ony sister?' she says,
    'And had ye ever a brither?'—

XXVI

'The Earl of Wemyss was my father,
    The Countess of Wemyss my mither,
Young Elinor she was my sister dear,
    And Lord John he was my brither.'—

XXVII

'If the Earl of Wemyss was your father,
    I wot sae was he mine;
And it's O my sister Annie!
    Your love ye sallna tyne.

XXVIII

'Tak your husband, my sister dear;
    You ne'er were wrang'd for me,
Beyond a kiss o' his merry mouth
    As we cam owre the sea.

tyne] lose.

183

XXIX

'Seven ships, loaded weel,
　　Cam owre the sea wi' me;
Ane o' them will tak me hame,
　　And six I'll gie to thee.'

43.　　*The Lass of Lochroyan*

I

'O WHA will shoe my bonny foot?
　　And wha will glove my hand?
And wha will bind my middle jimp
　　Wi' a lang, lang linen band?

II

'O wha will kame my yellow hair,
　　With a haw bayberry kame?
And wha will be my babe's father
　　Till Gregory come hame?'—

III

'Thy father, he will shoe thy foot,
　　Thy brother will glove thy hand,
Thy mither will bind thy middle jimp
　　Wi' a lang, lang linen band.

IV

'Thy sister will kame thy yellow hair,
　　Wi' a haw bayberry kame;
The Almighty will be thy babe's father
　　Till Gregory come hame.'—

jimp] slim.　　kame] comb.　　haw bayberry] ? *a corruption for* 'braw ivory': *or* bayberry *may* = laurel-wood.

184

THE LASS OF LOCHROYAN

V

'And wha will build a bonny ship,
  And set it on the sea?
For I will go to seek my love,
  My ain love Gregory.'

VI

Up then spak her father dear,
  A wafu' man was he;
'And I will build a bonny ship,
  And set her on the sea.

VII

'And I will build a bonny ship,
  And set her on the sea,
And ye sal gae and seek your love,
  Your ain love Gregory.'

VIII

Then he's gart build a bonny ship,
  And set it on the sea,
Wi' four-and-twenty mariners,
  To bear her company.

IX

O he's gart build a bonny ship,
  To sail on the salt sea;
The mast was o' the beaten gold,
  The sails o' cramoisie.

X

The sides were o' the gude stout aik,
  The deck o' mountain pine,
The anchor o' the silver shene,
  The ropes o' silken twine.

  cramoisie] crimson.

XI

She hadna sail'd but twenty leagues,
 But twenty leagues and three,
When she met wi' a rank reiver,
 And a' his companie.

XII

'Now are ye Queen of Heaven hie,
 Come to pardon a' our sin?
Or are ye Mary Magdalane,
 Was born at Bethlehem?'—

XIII

'I'm no the Queen of Heaven hie,
 Come to pardon ye your sin,
Nor am I Mary Magdalane,
 Was born in Bethlehem.

XIV

'But I'm the lass of Lochroyan,
 That's sailing on the sea
To see if I can find my love,
 My ain love Gregory.'—

XV

'O see na ye yon bonny bower?
 It's a' covered owre wi' tin?
When thou hast sail'd it round about,
 Lord Gregory is within.'

XVI

And when she saw the stately tower,
 Shining both clear and bright,
Whilk stood aboon the jawing wave,
 Built on a rock of height,

reiver] robber.   jawing] surging.

XVII

Says, ' Row the boat, my mariners,
    And bring me to the land,
For yonder I see my love's castle,
    Close by the salt sea strand.'

XVIII

She sail'd it round, and sail'd it round,
    And loud and loud cried she.
' Now break, now break your fairy charms,
    And set my true-love free ! '

XIX

She 's ta'en her young son in her arms,
    And to the door she 's gane,
And long she knock'd, and sair she ca'd,
    But answer got she nane.

XX

' O open, open, Gregory !
    O open ! if ye be within ;
For here 's the lass of Lochroyan,
    Come far fra kith and kin.

XXI

' O open the door, Lord Gregory !
    O open and let me in !
The wind blows loud and cauld, Gregory,
    The rain drops fra my chin.

XXII

' The shoe is frozen to my foot,
    The glove unto my hand,
The wet drops fra my yellow hair,
    Na langer dow I stand.'

dow] can.

XXIII

O up then spak his ill mither,
   —An ill death may she die !
' Ye're no the lass of Lochroyan,
   She's far out-owre the sea.

XXIV

' Awa', awa', ye ill woman,
   Ye're no come here for gude ;
Ye're but some witch or wil' warlock,
   Or mermaid o' the flood.'—

XXV

' I am neither witch nor wil' warlock,
   Nor mermaid o' the sea,
But I am Annie of Lochroyan,
   O open the door to me ! '—

XXVI

' Gin ye be Annie of Lochroyan,
   As I trow thou binna she,
Now tell me of some love-tokens
   That pass'd 'tween thee and me.'

XXVII

' O dinna ye mind, love Gregory,
   As we sat at the wine,
We changed the rings frae our fingers ?
   And I can shew thee thine.

XXVIII

' O yours was gude, and gude enough,
   But ay the best was mine,
For yours was o' the gude red gowd,
   But mine o' the diamond fine.

THE LASS OF LOCHROYAN

XXIX

'Yours was o' the gude red gowd,
    Mine o' the diamond fine;
Mine was o' the purest troth,
    But thine was false within.'—

XXX

'If ye be the lass of Lochroyan,
    As I kenna thou be,
Tell me some mair o' the love-tokens
    Pass'd between thee and me.'—

XXXI

'And dinna ye mind, love Gregory!
    As we sat on the hill,
Thou twin'd me o' my maidenheid,
    Right sair against my will?

XXXII

'Now open the door, love Gregory!
    Open the door! I pray;
For thy young son is in my arms,
    And will be dead ere day.'—

XXXIII

'Ye lie, ye lie, ye ill woman,
    So loud I hear ye lie;
For Annie of the Lochroyan
    Is far out-owre the sea.'

XXXIV

Fair Annie turn'd her round about:
    'Weel, sine that it be sae,
May ne'er woman that has borne a son
    Hae a heart sae fu' o' wae!

XXXV

'Tak down, tak down that mast o' gowd,
    Set up a mast of tree ;
It disna become a forsaken lady
    To sail sae royallie.'

XXXVI

When the cock had crawn, and the day did dawn,
    And the sun began to peep,
Up then raise Lord Gregory,
    And sair, sair did he weep.

XXXVII

'O I hae dream'd a dream, mither,
    I wish it may bring good !
That the bonny lass of Lochroyan
    At my bower window stood.

XXXVIII

'O I hae dream'd a dream, mither,
    The thought o't gars me greet !
That fair Annie of Lochroyan
    Lay dead at my bed-feet.'——

XXXIX

'Gin it be for Annie of Lochroyan
    That ye mak a' this mane,
She stood last night at your bower-door,
    But I hae sent her hame.'——

XL

'O wae betide ye, ill woman,
    An ill death may ye die !
That wadna open the door yoursell
    Nor yet wad waken me.'

THE LASS OF LOCHROYAN

XLI

O he's gane down to yon shore-side,
  As fast as he could dree,
And there he saw fair Annie's bark
  A rowing owre the sea.

XLII

' O Annie, Annie,' loud he cried,
  ' O Annie, O Annie, bide ! '
But ay the mair he cried ' Annie,'
  The braider grew the tide.

XLIII

' O Annie, Annie, dear Annie,
  Dear Annie, speak to me ! '
But ay the louder he 'gan call,
  The louder roar'd the sea.

XLIV

The wind blew loud, the waves rose hie
  And dash'd the boat on shore ;
Fair Annie's corpse was in the faem,
  The babe rose never more.

XLV

Lord Gregory tore his gowden locks
  And made a wafu' moan ;
Fair Annie's corpse lay at his feet,
  His bonny son was gone.

XLVI

O cherry, cherry was her cheek,
  And gowden was her hair,
And coral, coral was her lips,
  Nane might with her compare !

THE LASS OF LOCHROYAN

XLVII

Then first he kiss'd her pale, pale cheek,
  And syne he kiss'd her chin,
And syne he kiss'd her wane, wane lips,
  There was na breath within.

XLVIII

'O wae betide my ill mither,
  An ill death may she die !
She turn'd my true-love frae my door,
  Who cam so far to me.

XLIX

'O wae betide my ill mither,
  An ill death may she die !
She has no been the deid o' ane,
  But she 's been the deid of three.'

L

Then he 's ta'en out a little dart,
  Hung low down by his gore,
He thrust it through and through his heart,
  And words spak never more.

deid] death.   gore] skirt, waist.

I

YOUNG BEKIE was as brave a knight
   As ever sail'd the sea;
And he's doen him to the court of France,
   To serve for meat and fee.

II

He had nae been i' the court of France
   A twelvemonth nor sae long,
Til he fell in love with the king's daughter,
   And was thrown in prison strong.

III

The king he had but ae daughter,
   Burd Isbel was her name;
And she has to the prison-house gane,
   To hear the prisoner's mane.

IV

'O gin a lady wou'd borrow me,
   At her stirrup-foot I wou'd rin;
Or gin a widow wou'd borrow me,
   I wou'd swear to be her son.

V

'Or gin a virgin wou'd borrow me,
   I wou'd wed her wi' a ring;
I'd gie her ha's, I'd gie her bowers,
   The bonny towrs o' Linne.'

VI

O barefoot, barefoot gaed she but,
   And barefoot came she ben;
It was no for want o' hose and shoone,
   Nor time to put them on;

borrow] ransom.   but] out.   ben] in.

YOUNG BEKIE

But a' for fear that her father dear
    Had heard her making din :
She 's stown the keys o' the prison-house door
    And latten the prisoner gang.

VIII

O whan she saw him, Young Bekie,
    Her heart was wondrous sair !
For the mice but and the bold rottons
    Had eaten his yallow hair.

IX

She 's gi'en him a shaver for his beard,
    A comber till his hair,
Five hunder pound in his pocket,
    To spen' and nae to spair.

X

She 's gi'en him a steed was good in need,
    An' a saddle o' royal bone,
A leash o' hounds o' ae litter,
    And Hector callèd one.

XI

Atween this twa a vow was made,
    'T was made full solemnly,
That or three years was come an' gane,
    Well married they should be.

XII

He had nae been in 's ain country
    A twelvemonth till an end,
Till he 's forc'd to marry a duke's daughter,
    Or than lose a' his land.

rottons] rats.   royal bone] ivory.   Or than] Or else.

YOUNG BEKIE

XIII

'Ohon, alas!' says Young Bekie,
   'I know not what to dee;
For I canno win to Burd Isbel,
   An' she kensnae to come to me.'

XIV

O it fell once upon a day
   Burd Isbel fell asleep,
And up it starts the Billy Blind,
   And stood at her bed-feet.

XV

'O waken, waken, Burd Isbel,
   How can you sleep so soun',
Whan this is Bekie's wedding day,
   An' the marriage gaïn on?

XVI

'Ye do ye to your mither's bowr,
   Think neither sin nor shame;
An' ye tak twa o' your mither's marys,
   To keep ye frae thinking lang.

XVII

'Ye dress yoursel' in the red scarlèt,
   An' your marys in dainty green,
An' ye pit girdles about your middles
   Wou'd buy an earldome.

XVIII

'O ye gang down by yon sea-side,
   An' down by yon sea-stran';
Sae bonny will the Hollan's boats
   Come rowin' till your han'.

Billy Blind] a friendly household fairy. See p. 80.   marys]
maids.

YOUNG BEKIE

XIX

'Ye set your milke-white foot abord,
   Cry, Hail ye, Domine!
An' I shal be the steerer o't,
   To row you o'er the sea.'

XX

She's tane her till her mither's bowr,
   Thought neither sin nor shame,
And she took twa o' her mither's marys,
   To keep her frae thinking lang.

XXI

She dress'd hersel' i' the red scarlèt,
   Her marys i' dainty green,
And they pat girdles about their middles
   Wou'd buy an earldome.

XXII

And they gid down by yon sea-side,
   And down by yon sea-stran';
Sae bonny did the Hollan's boats
   Come rowin' to their han'.

XXIII

She set her milke-white foot on board,
   Cried, Hail ye, Domine!
And the Billy Blind was the steerer o't,
   To row her o'er the sea.

XXIV

Whan she came to young Bekie's gate,
   She heard the music play;
Sae well she kent frae a' she heard,
   It was his wedding day.

196

YOUNG BEKIE

XXV

She's pitten her han' in her pocket,
　　Gi'en the porter guineas three;
'Hae, tak ye that, ye proud portèr,
　　Bid the bride-groom speake to me.'

XXVI

O whan that he cam up the stair,
　　He fell low down on his knee:
He hail'd the king, and he hail'd the queen,
　　And he hail'd him, Young Bekie.

XXVII

'O I've been porter at your gates
　　This thirty years an' three;
But there's three ladies at them now,
　　Their like I never did see.

XXVIII

'There's ane o' them dress'd in red scarlèt,
　　An' twa in dainty green,
An' they hae girdles about their middles
　　Wou'd buy an earldome.'

XXIX

Then out it spake the bierly bride,
　　Was a' goud to the chin;
'Gin she be braw without,' she says,
　　'We's be as braw within.'

XXX

Then up it starts him, Young Bekie,
　　And the tears was in his e'e:
'I'll lay my life it's Burd Isbel,
　　Come o'er the sea to me.'

bierly] stately.

YOUNG BEKIE

XXXI

O quickly ran he down the stair,
    And whan he saw 't was shee,
He kindly took her in his arms,
    And kiss'd her tenderly.

XXXII

'O hae ye forgotten, Young Bekie,
    The vow ye made to me,
Whan I took you out o' the prison strong,
    Whan ye was condemn'd to die?

XXXIII

'I gae you a steed was good in need,
    An' a saddle o' royal bone,
A leash o' hounds o' ae litter,
    An' Hector callèd one.'

XXXIV

It was well kent what the lady said,
    That it wasnae a lee,
For at ilka word the lady spake,
    The hound fell at her knee.

XXXV

'Tak hame, tak hame your daughter dear,
    A blessing gae her wi'!
For I maun marry my Burd Isbel,
    That's come o'er the sea to me.'

XXXVI

'Is this the custom o' your house,
    Or the fashion o' your lan',
To marry a maid in a May mornin',
    An' to send her back at even?'

Young Beichan

(Another version of the foregoing)

I

IN London was Young Beichan born,
  He long'd strange countries for to see ;
But he was ta'en by a savage Moor
  Who handled him right cruellie.

II

For he view'd the fashions of that land,
  Their way of worship viewèd he ;
But to Mahound or Termagant
  Would Beichan never bend a knee.

III

So thro' every shoulder they've bored a bore,
  And thro' every bore they've putten a tree,
And they have made him trail the wine
  And spices on his fair bodie.

IV

They've casten him in a dungeon deep,
  Where he could neither hear nor see ;
And fed him on nought but bread and water
  Till he for hunger 's like to die.

V

This Moor he had but ae daughter,
  Her name was callèd Susie Pye,
And every day as she took the air
  She heard Young Beichan sadly crie :

VI

' My hounds they all run masterless,
  My hawks they flie from tree to tree,
My youngest brother will heir my lands ;
  Fair England again I'll never see !

YOUNG BEICHAN

VII

' O were I free as I hae been,
    And my ship swimming once more on sea,
I'd turn my face to fair England
    And sail no more to a strange countrie ! '

VIII

Young Beichan's song for thinking on
    All night she never closed her e'e ;
She's stown the keys from her father's head
    Wi' mickle gold and white monie.

IX

And she has open'd the prison doors :
    I wot she open'd twa or three
Ere she could come Young Beichan at,
    He was lock'd up so curiouslie.

X

' O hae ye any lands or rents,
    Or cities in your own countrie,
Cou'd free you out of prison strong
    And cou'd maintain a lady free ? '—

XI

' O London city is my own,
    And other cities twa or three ;
I'll give them all to the lady fair
    That out of prison will set me free.'

XII

O she has bribed her father's men
    Wi' mickle gold and white monie,
She's gotten the keys of the prison strong,
    And she has set Young Beichan free.

stown] stolen.

XIII

She 's fed him upon the good spice-cake,
   The Spanish wine and the malvoisie ;
She 's broken a ring from off her finger
   And to Beichan half of it gave she.

XIV

' Go set your foot on good shipboard,
   And haste you back to your own countrie,
But before that seven years has an end,
   Come back again, love, and marry me.'

XV

It was long or seven years had an end
   She long'd full sore her love to see ;
So she 's set her foot on good ship-board
   And turn'd her back on her own countrie.

XVI

She 's sailèd east, she 's sailèd west,
   She 's sailèd all across the sea,
And when she came to fair England
   The bells were ringing merrilie.

XVII

' O whose are a' yon flock o' sheep ?
   And whose are a' yon flock o' kye ?
And whose are a' yon pretty castles,
   That I so often do pass by ?'

XVIII

' O they are a' Lord Beichan's sheep,
   And they are a' Lord Beichan's kye,
And they are a' Lord Beichan's castles
   That you so often do pass by.

kye] kine, cattle.

YOUNG BEICHAN

XIX

'O there's a wedding in yonder ha',
　　Has lasted thirty days and three;
Lord Beichan will not bed wi' his bride
　　For love of one that's 'yond the sea.'

XX

When she came to Young Beichan's gate
　　She tirlèd softly at the pin;
So ready was the proud portèr
　　To open and let this lady in.

XXI

'Is this Young Beichan's gates?' she says,
　　'Or is that noble lord within?'—
'He's up the stairs wi' his bonny bride,
　　For this is the day o' his weddin'.'—

XXII

'O has he taken a bonny bride,
　　And has he clean forgotten me?'
And sighing said that ladye gay,
　　'I wish I were in my own countrie!'

XXIII

She's putten her hand in her pockèt
　　And gi'en the porter guineas three;
Says, 'Take ye that, ye proud portèr,
　　And bid the bridegroom speak with me.'

XXIV

And she has ta'en her gay gold ring,
　　That with her love she brake so free;
Says, 'Gie him that, ye proud portèr,
　　And bid the bridegroom speak with me.'

tirlèd] rattled.

202

YOUNG BEICHAN

O when the porter came up the stair,
    He's kneelèd low upon his knee:
'Won up, won up, ye proud portèr,
    And what makes a' this courtesie?'—

XXVI

'O I've been porter at your gates
    I'm sure this thirty years and three,
But there is a lady stands thereat
    The fairest I did ever see.'

XXVII

It's out then spake the bride's mother,
    —Aye, and an angry woman was she—
'Ye might have excepted our bonny bride,
    And twa or three of our companie.'

XXVIII

'My dame, your daughter's fair enough,
    And aye the fairer mote she be!
But the fairest time that ever she was,
    She'll no compare wi' this ladye.

XXIX

'For on every finger she has a ring,
    And on the mid-finger she has three,
And as mickle gold she has on her brow
    'Would buy an earldome o' land to me.

XXX

'And this golden ring that's broken in twa,
    She sends the half o' this golden ring,
And bids you speak with a lady fair,
    That out o' prison did you bring.'

won] win, get.

XXXI

Then up and started Young Beichan
  And sware so loud by Our Ladye,
' It can be none but Susie Pye,
  That has come over the sea to me !

XXXII

O quickly ran he down the stair,
  Of fifteen steps he made but three ;
He 's ta'en his bonny love in his arms
  And kiss'd and kiss'd her tenderlie.

XXXIII

' O have ye ta'en another bride,
  And have ye quite forsaken me ?
And have ye clean forgotten her
  That gave you life and libertie ? '

XXXIV

She 's lookèd over her left shoulder
  To hide the tears stood in her e'e ;
' Now fare-thee-well, Young Beichan,' she says—
  ' I'll strive to think no more on thee.'

XXXV

' O never, never, Susie Pye,
  For surely this can never be,
That ever I shall wed but her
  That 's done and dreed so much for me ! '

XXXVI

Then up bespake the bride's mother—
  She never was heard to speak so free :
' Ye'll not forsake my only daughter,
  Though Susie Pye has cross'd the sea.'

dreed] suffered.

XXXVII

'Take home, take home your daughter, madam,
   She 's never a bit the worse for me ;
For saving a kiss of her bonny lips
   Of your daughter's body I am free.'

XXXVIII

He 's ta'en her by the milk-white hand
   And led her to yon fountain-stone ;
He 's changed her name from Susie Pye
   And call'd her his bonny love Lady Joan.

46. *Childe Waters*

I

CHILDE WATERS in his stable stood
   Stroking his milk-white steed :
To him came a fair young lady
   As ever wore woman's weed.

II

Says, 'Christ you save, Childe Waters ! '
   Says, 'Christ you save and see !
My girdle of gold, which was too long,
   Is now too short for me.

III

'And all is with one child of yours
   I feel stir at my side :
My gown of green, it is too strait ;
   Before it was too wide.'—

fountain-stone] font.

IV

'If the child be mine, Burd Ellen,' he said,
  'Be mine as you do swear,
Take you Cheshire and Lancashire both,
  And make that child your heir.'

V

She says, 'I would rather have one kiss,
  Childe Waters, of thy mouth
Than I would have Cheshire and Lancashire both,
  That lies by north and south.'—

VI

'To-morrow, Ellen, I must ride
  Far into the north countrye.'—
'Then I will run low by your side:
  Your foot-page let me be!'—

VII

'If you will be my foot-page, Ellen,
  As you do tell it me,
Then you must cut your gown of green
  An inch above your knee.'

VIII

Childe Waters leapt on his milk-white steed,
  And fast away did ride:
Burd Ellen has kilted her gay clothing,
  And ran low by his side.

IX

All this long day Childe Waters rode,
  She barefoot by his side;
Yet was he never so courteous a knight
  As to say, 'Burd Ellen, ride.'

CHILDE WATERS

X

He has ridden, and she has run,
  And barefoot through the broom;
Yet was he never so courteous a knight
  As to say, 'Put on your shoon.'

XI

'Ride softly,' she said, 'Childe Waters!
  O why do you ride so fast?
The child which is no man's but yours
  My body it will brast.'

XII

He has ridden on high horseback,
  And she's run low beside,
Until they came to a wan water—
  I think men call it Clyde.

XIII

Says, 'See'st yon water, Ellen,
  That flows from bank to brim?'—
'I trust to God, Childe Waters
  You will never see me swim.'

XIV

The firsten step Burd Ellen stept,
  The water came to her knee;
'Ochon, alas!' said Burd Ellen,
  'This water's o'er deep for me!'

XV

The neisten step Burd Ellen stept,
  The water came to her middle;
And sighing said Burd Ellen,
  'I've wetted my golden girdle!'

XVI

The thirden step Burd Ellen stept,
  The water came to her pap ;
And the bairn that was in her two sides
  For cold began to quake.

XVII

' Lie still, lie still, my own dear babe !
  Ye work your mother woe ;
Your father that rides on high horseback
  Cares little for us two.'

XVIII

About the midst of Clyde-water
  There was a yeard-fast stone :
He lightly turn'd his horse about
  And took Burd Ellen on.

XIX

When she over the water won,
  She then came to his knee :
Says, ' How far is it to your lodgin'
  Where we this night may be ? '—

XX

' Seest thou not yon castle, Ellen ?
  Of red gold shines the gate :
There is twenty-and-four fair ladies
  And one my worldly mate.

XXI

' Seest thou not yon castle, Ellen ?
  Of red gold shines the tower :
There is twenty-and-four fair ladies,
  And one my paramour.

yeard-fast] fast in earth.

CHILDE WATERS

XXII

'Seest thou not yon castle, Ellen,
  That shines so fair to see?
There's a lady in it, Ellen,
  Will sunder you and me.'—

XXIII

'I do see the castle, Childe Waters:
  Of red gold shines the gate.
God give you good then of yourself,
  And of your worldly mate!

XXIV

'I wish no ill to your lady;
  She ne'er wish'd none to me;
But I wish the maid most of your love
  Dries this and more for thee.

XXV

'I wish no ill to your lady;
  She ne'er comes in my thought;
But I wish the maid most of your love
  That dearest has you bought.'—

XXVI

'But my hounds shall eat of the bread of wheat,
  And you of the bread of bran;
And you shall curse the heavy hour
  That ever your love began.

XXVII

'But my horse shall drink of the good red wine,
  And you of the water wan;
And you will sigh and say "Alas,
  That ever I loved a man!"'—

Dries] endures.

XXVIII
'O, I will drink of the wan water,
  And eat of the bread of bran ;
And aye will I bless the happy hour
  That ever I loved a man.'

XXIX
O four-and-twenty gay ladies
  Were playing at the ball,
But Ellen, the fairest lady,
  Must bring his steed to stall.

XXX
And four-and-twenty gay ladies
  Were playing at the chess,
But Ellen, the fairest lady,
  Must bring his horse to grass.

XXXI
When bells were rung, and mass was sung,
  And a' men bound to meat,
Burd Ellen was at the bye-table
  Among the foot-men set.

XXXII
'O eat and drink, my bonny boy,
  The white bread and the beer.'—
'The never a bit can I eat or drink,
  My heart's so full of fear.'—

XXXIII
'O eat and drink, my bonny boy,
  The white bread and the wine.'—
'O I cannot eat nor drink, master,
  My heart's so full of pine.'

pine] pain.

XXXIV

But out and spake Childe Waters' mother,
  And a skilly dame was she :
' Where met ye with that little foot-page
  That looks so sad on thee ?

XXXV

' Sometimes his cheek is rosy red,
  And sometimes deadly wan ;
He 's liker a woman big with bairn
  Than a young lord's serving-man.'

XXXVI

And then bespake Childe Waters' sister,
  And these were the words said she :
' You have the prettiest foot-page, brother,
  Let him go into chamber with me.'—

XXXVII

' It is more meet for a little foot-page,
  That has run through moss and mire,
To take his supper upon his knee,
  And sit by the kitchen fire,
Than to go into chamber with any lady
  That wears so rich attire.

XXXVIII

' Rise up, rise up, my bonny boy ;
  Give my horse corn and hay.'—
' O that I will, my master dear,
  As quickly as I may.'

XXXIX

She 's ta'en the hay under her arm,
  The corn into her hand,
And she 's gone to the great stable
  As fast as e'er she can.

skilly] wise, knowledgeable.

XL

'O room ye round, my bonny brown steeds!
　　O room ye near the wall!
For this pain that strikes me through my sides
　　Full soon will gar me fall.'

XLI

She's lean'd her back against the wall,
　　Strong travail seized her on;
And even among the great horse' feet
　　Burd Ellen brought forth her son.

XLII

And that beheard Childe Waters' mother,
　　Sat in her bower alone.
'Rise up, rise up, Childe Waters,' she said,
　　'Seek neither hose nor shoon!'

XLIII

She said, 'Rise up, thou Childe Waters,
　　I think thou'rt a cursèd man;
For yonder's a ghost in thy stable
　　That grievously doth groan,
Or else some woman labours of child,
　　She is so woe-begone.'

XLIV

But up then rose Childe Waters,
　　Stay'd neither for hose nor shoon,
And he's doen him to the stable-door
　　Wi' the clear light of the moon.

XLV

And when he came to the stable-door,
　　Full still there he did stand,
That he might hear Burd Ellen,
　　How she made her monand.
　　　　　monand] moaning.

XLVI

She said, 'Lullabỳe, my own dear child!
  Lùllabye, dear child dear!
I would thy father were a king,
  Thy mother laid on a bier!'—

XLVII

'O open the door, Burd Ellen!
  O open and let me in!
I want to see if my steed be fed,
  Or my greyhounds fit to rin.'—

XLVIII

'How can I open, how shall I open,
  How can I open to thee,
When lying amang your great steeds' feet,
  Your young son on my knee?'

XLIX

He strack the door hard wi' his foot,
  And push'd it wi' his knee;
And iron locks and iron bars
  Into the floor flung he.
'Be not afraid, Burd Ellen,' he says,
  'There's none comes in but me.'

L

'An asking, an asking, Childe Waters,
  An asking I beg of thee:
May the meanest maid about your house
  Bring a glass o' water to me!'

LI

Up he has ta'en his bonny young son,
  Gar'd wash him wi' the milk;
And up he has taken his fair lady,
  Gar'd row her in the silk.

row] wrap.

LII

'Peace now,' he said, 'Burd Ellen,
And be of good cheer, I pray;
Your bridal and your churching both
Shall be upon one day.'

47. *Childe Maurice*

I

CHILDE MAURICE hunted the Silver Wood,
He whistled and he sang:
'I think I see the woman yonder
That I have lovèd lang.'

II

He callèd to his little man John,
'You don't see what I see;
For yonder I see the very first woman
That ever lovèd me.'

III

He says, 'Come hither, my little man John,
That I pay meat and fee,
For thou shalt go to John Steward's wife
And greet her well from me;

IV

'And as it falls as many times
As knots be knit in a kell,
Or merchantmen go to leeve Londòn
To buy ware or to sell;

kell] hair-net, i. e. give her as many greetings as there are
meshes in a net.   leeve] lovely.

CHILDE MAURICE

'And as it falls as many times
    As any heart can think,
Or school-masters are in any school
    Writing with pen and ink.

'Here is a glove, a glove,' he says,
    'Lined wi' the silver-gris;
Bid her to come to Silver Wood
    To speak with Childe Maurice.

'And here is a ring, a ring,' he says,
    'A ring of the precious stone:
He prays her come to Silver Wood
    And ask the leave of none.'—

'Well do I love your errand, master,
    But better I love my life.
Would ye have me go to John Steward's castle,
    To tryst away his wife?'—

'Do not I give you meat?' he says,
    'Do not I give you fee?
How daur you stop my errand
    When that I bid you flee?'

This little man John one while he yode,
    Another while he ran;
Until he came to John Steward's castle
    I wis he never blan.

silver-gris] a fur of silver-grey.   yode] walked.   blan]
stopped, stayed.

XI

He ask'd no porter's leave, but ran
    Up hall and bower free,
And when he came to John Steward's wife,
    Says, 'God you save and see!

XII

'I come, I am come from Childe Maurice—
    A message unto thee!
And Childe Maurice he greets you well,
    And ever so well from me,

XIII

'And as it falls as oftentimes
    As knots be knit in a kell,
Or merchantmen go to leeve Londòn
    To buy ware or to sell;

XIV

'And as oftentimes he greets you well
    As any heart can think,
Or schoolmasters are in any school
    Writing with pen and ink.

XV

'Here is a glove, a glove,' he says,
    'Lined wi' the silver-gris;
Ye're bidden to come to Silver Wood
    To speak with Childe Maurice.

XVI

'And here is a ring, a ring of gold,
    Set wi' the precious stone:
He prays you to come to Silver Wood
    And ask the leave of none.'—

XVII

'Now peace, now peace, thou little man John,
    For Christ's sake I pray thee!
For gif my lord heard one o' thy words
    Thou must be hangèd hie!'

XVIII

O aye she stampèd with her foot
    And winkèd with her e'e;
But for all that she could say or do
    Forbidden he would not be.

XIX

'It's surely to my bower-woman,
    It cannot be to me!'——
'Nay, I brought it to John Steward's lady,
    And I trow that thou art she.'

XX

Out then spake the wily nurse,
    Wi' the bairn just on her knee:
'If this be come from Childe Maurice
    It's dear welcome to me.'——

XXI

'Thou liest, thou liest, thou wily nurse,
    So loud as I hear thee lie!
I brought it to John Steward's lady,
    And I trow thou be not she.'

XXII

Then up and rose him John Steward,
    And an angry man was he:
'Did I think there was a lord in the world
    My lady loved but me!'

XXIII

He struck the table wi' his foot,
    And kepp'd it with his knee,
Till silver cup and ezar dish
    In flinders they did flee.

XXIV

He call'd unto his horse-keeper,
    ' Make ready you my steed ! '
So did he to his chamberlain,
    ' Go fetch my lady's weed ! '

XXV

O he dress'd himself in the holland smock,
    [The mantle and the snood],
And he cast a lease upon his back,
    And he rode to Silver Wood.

XXVI

And when he came to Silver Wood,
    No body saw he there
But Childe Maurice upon a block
    Combing his yellow hair.

XXVII

Childe Maurice sat in Silver Wood,
    He whistled and he sang :
I think I see the woman come
    That I have lovèd lang.'

XXVIII

But then stood up him Childe Maurice
    His mother to help from horse :
' O alas, alas ! ' says Childe Maurice,
    ' My mother was ne'er so gross ! '

kepp'd] caught.   ezar] ? *for* 'mazer,' maple.   weed] clothing.   lease] leash, thong.

XXIX

'No wonder, no wonder,' John Steward he said,
  ' My lady loved thee well,
For the fairest part of my body
  Is blacker than thy heel.'

XXX

John Steward had a little brown sword
  That hung low down by his knee;
He has cut the head off Childe Maurice
  And the body put on a tree.

XXXI

And he prick'd the head on his sword's point,
  Went singing there beside,
And he rode till he came to the castle
  Whereas his lady ly'ed.

XXXII

And when he came to his lady—
  Look'd o'er the castle-wall—
He threw the head into her lap,
  Saying ' Lady, tak' the ball ! '

XXXIII

Says, ' Dost thou know Childe Maurice' head,
  If that thou dost it see ?
And lap it soft, and kiss it oft,
  For thou loved'st him better than me.'

XXXIV

But when she look'd on Childe Maurice' head
  She ne'er spake words but three :
' I never bare no child but one,
  And you have slain him, trulye.'

    ly'ed] lived.   tak'] take, catch.

CHILDE MAURICE

And she has taken the bloody head
    And kiss'd it, cheek and chin :
' I was once as full o' Childe Maurice
    As the hip is o' the stane.

'I got him in my mother's bower
    Wi' mickle sin and shame ;
I brought him up in the good greenwood
    Under the shower and rain.'

And she has taken her Childe Maurice
    And kiss'd him, mouth and chin :
' O better I love my Childe Maurice
    Than all my royal kin ! '

'Woe be to thee ! ' John Steward he said,
    And a woe, woe man was he ;
· For if you had told me he was your son
    He had never been slain by me.'

Says, 'Wicked be my merry men all,
    I gave meat, drink and cloth !
But could they not have holden me
    When I was in all that wrath ? '

Brown Adam

I

O WHA would wish the wind to blau
    Or the green leaves fa' therewith?
Or wha would wish a lealer love
    Than Brown Adam the Smith?

II

But they hae banish'd Brown Adam,
    Frae father and frae mither;
And they hae banish'd Brown Adam,
    Frae sister and frae brither.

III

And they hae banish'd Brown Adam
    Frae the flow'r o' a' his kin;
And he's biggit a bow'r i' the good green-wood
    Between his ladye and him.

IV

O it fell once upon a day
    Brown Adam he thought long,
And he is to the green-wood
    As fast as he could gang.

V

He has ta'en his bow his arm over,
    His sword intill his han',
And he is to the good green-wood
    To hunt some venison.

VI

O he's shot up, and he's shot down
    The bunting on the breer;
And he's sent it hame to his ladye,
    Bade her be of good cheer.

      biggit] built.   breer] briar.

BROWN ADAM

VII

O he 's shot up, and he 's shot down,
    The linnet on the thorn,
And sent it hame to his ladye,
    Said he'd be hame the morn.

VIII

When he cam' till his lady's bow'r-door
    He stood a little forbye,
And there he heard a fu' fause knight
    Tempting his gay ladye.

IX

O he 's ta'en out a gay gold ring
    Had cost him mony a poun';
'O grant me love for love, ladye,
    And this sall be your own.'—

X

'I lo'e Brown Adam well,' she says,
    'I wot sae does he me;
I wadna gie Brown Adam's love
    For nae fause knight I see.'

XI

Out he has ta'en a purse of gold
    Was a' fu' to the string;
'O grant me love for love, ladye,
    And a' this sall be thine.'—

XII

'I lo'e Brown Adam well,' she says,
    An' I ken sae does he me;
An' I wadna be your light leman
    For mair nor ye could gie.'

XIII

Then out he drew his lang, lang bran',
  And he's flash'd it in her e'en:
'Now grant me love for love, lady,
  Or thro' you this sall gang.'—

XIV

'O,' sighing said that gay ladye,
  'Brown Adam tarries lang!'—
Then up and starts him Brown Adam,
  Says, 'I'm just to your hand.'

XV

He's gar'd him leave his bow, his bow,
  He's gar'd him leave his brand;
He's gar'd him leave a better pledge—
  Four fingers o' his right hand.

49. *Jellon Grame*

I

O JELLON GRAME sat in Silverwood,
  He sharp'd his broadsword lang;
And he has call'd his little foot-page
  An errand for to gang.

II

'Win up, my bonny boy,' he says,
  'As quickly as ye may;
For ye maun gang for Lillie Flower
  Before the break of day.'—

III

The boy has buckled his belt about,
  And through the green-wood ran;
And he came to the ladye's bower
  Before the day did dawn.

JELLON GRAME

IV

'O sleep ye, wake ye, Lillie Flower?
　　The red sun's on the rain;
Ye're bidden come to Silverwood,
　　But I doubt ye'll never win hame.'

V

She hadna ridden a mile, a mile,
　　A mile but barely three,
Ere she came to a new-made grave
　　Beneath a green aik tree.

VI

O then up started Jellon Grame
　　Out of a bush thereby;
'Light down, light down, now, Lillie Flower,
　　For it's here that ye maun lye.'

VII

She lighted aff her milk-white steed,
　　And kneel'd upon her knee;
'O mercy, mercy, Jellon Grame,
　　For I'm no prepared to die!

VIII

'Your bairn, that stirs between my sides,
　　Maun shortly see the light;
But to see it weltering in my blood
　　Would be a piteous sight.'—

IX

'O should I spare your life,' he says,
　　'Until that bairn were born,
Full weel I ken your auld father
　　Would hang me on the morn.'—

JELLON GRAME

X

'O spare my life now, Jellon Grame!
  My father ye needna dread!
I'll keep my babe in gude green-wood,
  Or wi' it I'll beg my bread.'—

XI

He took nae pity on Lillie Flower,
  Though she for life did pray ;
But pierced her through the fair body
  As at his feet she lay.

XII

He felt nae pity for Lillie Flower,
  Where she was lying dead ;
But he felt some for the bonny bairn
  That lay weltering in her bluid.

XIII

Up has he ta'en that bonny boy,
  Given him to nurses nine ;
Three to sleep, and three to wake,
  And three to go between.

XIV

And he bred up that bonny boy,
  Call'd him his sister's son ;
And he thought nae eye could ever see
  The deed that had been done.

XV

O so it fell upon a day,
  When hunting they might be,
They rested them in Silverwood,
  Beneath that green aik tree.

XVI

And many were the green-wood flowers
    Upon that grave that grew,
And marvell'd much that bonny boy
    To see their lovely hue.

XVII

' What 's paler than the primrose wan ?
    What 's redder than the rose ?
What 's fairer than the lilye flower
    On this wee know that grows ? '—

XVIII

O out and answer'd Jellon Grame,
    And he spak hastilie :
' Your mother was a fairer flower,
    And lies beneath this tree.

XIX

' More pale she was, when she sought my grace,
    Than primrose pale and wan ;
And redder than rose her ruddy heart's blood,
    That down my broadsword ran.'—

XX

Wi' that the boy has bent his bow,
    It was baith stout and lang ;
And thro' and thro' him, Jellon Grame,
    He gar'd an arrow gang.

XXI

Says,—' Lie ye there, now, Jellon Grame !
    My malisoun gang you wi' !
The place that my mother lies buried in
    Is far too good for thee.'

wee know] little hillock.

50. *Little Musgrave and Lady Barnard*

O wow for day!
 And, dear, gin it were day!
Gin it were day, and I were away—
 For I ha' na lang time to stay.

I

AS it fell on one holy-day,
 As many be in the year,
When young men and maids together did go
 Their matins and mass to hear,

II

Little Musgrave came to the church-door—
 The priest was at private mass—
But he had more mind of the fair women
 Than he had of Our Lady's grace.

III

The one of them was clad in green,
 Another was clad in pall,
And then came in my Lord Barnard's wife,
 The fairest amongst them all.

IV

She cast an eye on Little Musgrave
 As bright as the summer sun ;
And then bethought him Little Musgrave,
 ' This lady's heart have I won.'

V

Quoth she, ' I have loved thee, Little Musgrave,
 Full long and many a day.'—
' So have I loved you, fair ladye,
 Yet never word durst I say.'—

    pall] fine cloth.

VI

'But I have a bower at Bucklesfordberry,
    Full daintily it is dight;
If thou'lt wend thither, thou Little Musgrave,
    Thou's lig in my arms all night.'

VII

Quoth he, 'I thank thee, fair ladye,
    This kindness thou showest to me;
And whether it be to my weal or woe
    This night I will lodge with thee.'

VIII

With that beheard a little tiny page,
    By his lady's coach as he ran.
Says, 'Although I am my lady's foot-page,
    Yet I am Lord Barnard's man.'

IX

Then he's cast off his hose and shoon,
    Set down his feet and ran,
And where the bridges were broken down
    He bent his bow and swam.

X

'Awake! awake! thou Lord Barnard,
    As thou art a man of life!
Little Musgrave is at Bucklesfordberry
    Along with thy own wedded wife.'—

XI

'If this be true, thou little tiny page,
    This thing thou tellest to me,
Then all the land in Bucklesfordberry
    I freely will give to thee.

lig] lie.

228

XII

'But if it be a lie, thou little tiny page,
  This thing thou tellest to me,
On the highest tree in Bucklesfordberry
  Then hangèd shalt thou be.'

XIII

He callèd up his merry men all:
  'Come saddle me my steed;
This night must I to Bucklesfordberry,
  For I never had greater need.'

XIV

But some they whistled, and some they sung,
  And some they thus could say,
Whenever Lord Barnard's horn it blew:
  'Away, Musgrave, away! . . .

XV

'Methinks I hear the threstle cock,
  Methinks I hear the jay;
Methinks I hear Lord Barnard's horn,
  Away, Musgrave, away!'—

XVI

'Lie still, lie still, thou little Musgrave,
  And huggle me from the cold;
'Tis nothing but a shepherd's boy
  A-driving his sheep to the fold.'

XVII

By this, Lord Barnard came to his door
  And lighted a stone upon;
And he's pull'd out three silver keys,
  And open'd the doors each one.

XVIII

He lifted up the coverlet,
  He lifted up the sheet:
'Dost thou like my bed, Little Musgrave?
  Dost thou find my lady sweet?'—

XIX

'I find her sweet,' quoth Little Musgrave,
  'The more 'tis to my pain;
I would gladly give three hundred pounds
  That I were on yonder plain.'—

XX

'Arise, arise, thou Little Musgrave,
  And put thy clothès on;
It shall ne'er be said in my country
  I have kill'd a naked man.

XXI

'I have two swords in one scabbard,
  They are both sharp and clear;
Take you the best, and I the worst,
  We'll end the matter here.'

XXII

The first stroke Little Musgrave struck,
  He hurt Lord Barnard sore;
The next stroke that Lord Barnard struck,
  Little Musgrave ne'er struck more.

XXIII

With that bespake this fair lady,
  In bed where as she lay:
'Although thou'rt dead, thou Little Musgrave,
  Yet I for thee will pray.

230

XXIV

'And wish well to thy soul will I
  So long as I have life;
So will I not for thee, Barnard,
  Although I'm thy wedded wife.'

XXV

He cut her paps from off her breast;
  Great pity it was to see
That some drops of this lady's heart's blood
  Ran trickling down her knee.

XXVI

'Woe worth you, woe worth, my merry men all,
  You were ne'er born for my good!
Why did you not offer to stay my hand
  When you saw me wax so wood?

XXVII

'For I have slain the fairest lady
  That ever wore woman's weed,
Soe I have slain the fairest lady
  That ever did woman's deed.

XXVIII

'A grave, a grave,' Lord Barnard cried,
  'To put these lovers in!
But lay my lady on the upper hand,
  For she comes of the nobler kin.'

wood] mad, fierce.

I

LORD INGRAM and Childe Vyet
   Were both born in one hall;
Laid both their hearts on one lady;
   The worse did them befall.

II

Lord Ingram woo'd Lady Maisry
   From father and from mother;
Lord Ingram woo'd Lady Maisry
   From sister and from brother;

III

Lord Ingram woo'd Lady Maisry
   With leave of all her kin;
And every one gave full consent,
   But she said ' no ' to him.

IV

Now it fell out, upon a day
   She was dressing of her head,
That in did come her father dear,
   Wearing the gold so red.

V

' Get up now, Lady Maisry,
   Put on your wedding-gown;
For Lord Ingram he will be here,
   Your wedding must be done.'—

VI

' I'd rather be Childe Vyet's wife,
   The white fish for to sell,
Before I were Lord Ingram's wife,
   To wear the silk so well.

VII

'I'd rather be Childe Vyet's wife,
  With him to beg my bread,
Before I were Lord Ingram's wife,
  To wear the gold so red. . . .

VIII

'O where will I get a bonny boy,
  Will win gold to his fee,
And will run unto Childe Vyet
  With this letter from me?'—

IX

'O here I am, the boy,' says one,
  'Will win gold to my fee,
And carry away any letter
  To Childe Vyet from thee.'

X

The first line that Childe Vyet read,
  A grievèd man was he;
The next line that Childe Vyet read,
  A tear blinded his e'e.
'I wonder what ails my one brother,
  He'll not let my love be!

XI

'But I'll send to my brother's bridal—
  The gammons o' the swine—
With four and twenty buck and roe,
  And ten tun of the wine;
And bid my love be blithe and glad,
  And I will follow syne.'

I 3

XII

There was no groom in that castle
  But got a gown of green ;
And all was blithe, and all was glad,
  But Lady Maisry was neen.

XIII

There was no cook in that kitchen
  But got a gown of grey ;
And all was blithe, and all was glad,
  But Lady Maisry was wae.

XIV

O sweetly play'd the merry organs
  Within her mother's bower ;
But dumb stood Lady Maisry,
  And let the tears down pour.

XV

O sweetly play'd the harp so fine
  Within her father's hall ;
But still stood Lady Maisry,
  And let the tears down fall.

XVI

'Tween Mary Kirk and the castle
  Was all spread o'er with garl,
To keep Lady Maisry and her maidens
  From tramping on the marl.

XVII

From Mary Kirk to the castle
  Was spread a cloth of gold,
To keep Lady Maisry and her maidens
  From treading upon the mould.

neen] none, not.   garl]? gravel.

234

LORD INGRAM AND CHILDE VYET

When mass was sung, and bells were rung,
  And all men bound for bed,
Lord Ingram and Lady Maisry
  In one bed they were laid.

When they were laid into one bed,
  It was both soft and warm;
He laid his hand over her side,
  Says, 'I think you are with bairn.'—

'I told you once, so did I twice,
  When ye came for my wooer,
That Childe Vyet, your one brother,
  One night lay in my bower.

'I told you twice, I told you thrice,
  Ere ye came me to wed,
That Childe Vyet, your one brother,
  One night lay in my bed.'—

'O father your bairn on me, Maisry,
  And on no other man;
And I'll gie him to his dowry
  Full fifty ploughs of land.'—

'I will not father my bairn on you,
  Nor on no wrongeous man,
Though ye'd give him to his dowry
  Five thousand ploughs of land.'

XXIV

He has taken out his trusty sword
   And laid it between them tway ;
Says, ' Lie you there, you ill woman,
   A maid for me till day.'

XXV

Then in it came him Childe Vyet,
   Shed back his yellow hair,
And gave Lord Ingram to the heart
   A deep wound and a sair.

XXVI

Then up did start him Lord Ingram
   Shed back his coal-black hair,
And gave Childe Vyet to the heart
   A deep wound and a sair.

XXVII

There was no pity for those two lords,
   In bower where they lay slain ;
But all was for Lady Maisry,
   In bower where she went brain.

XXVIII

Says, ' If I have been an ill woman,
   Alas, and woe is me !
And if I have been an ill woman,
   A good woman I'll be.

XXIX

' Ye'll take from me my silk attire,
   Bring me a palmer's weed ;
And for their sakes the world thoro'
   I'll gang and beg my bread.

brain] mad.

XXX

' If I gang a step for Childe Vyet,
   For Lord Ingram I'll gang three;
All for the honour that he paid
   At Mary Kirk to me.'

52.   *Fair Janet*

I

' YE maun gang to your father, Janet,
   Ye maun gang to him sune;
Ye maun gang to your father, Janet,
   In case that his days are dune.'

II

Janet's awa' to her father
   As fast as she could hie:
' O what's your will wi' me, father?
   O what's your will wi' me?'—

III

' My will wi' you, Fair Janet,' he said,
   ' It is both bed and board;
Some say that ye love Sweet Willie,
   But ye maun wed a French lord.'

IV

Janet's awa to her chamber
   As fast as she could go;
Wha's the first ane that tappèd there,
   But Sweet Willie her jo?

V

' O we maun part this love, Willie,
   That has been lang between;
There's a French lord coming o'er the sea
   To wed me wi' a ring.'—

         jo] sweetheart.

FAIR JANET

VI

'If we maun part this love, Janet,
　　It causeth mickle woe;
If we maun part this love, Janet,
　　It makes me in mourning go.'——

VII

'But ye maun gang to your three sisters,
　　Meg, Marion and Jean;
Tell them to come to Fair Janet,
　　In case that her days are dune.'

VIII

Willie's awa' to his three sisters,
　　Meg, Marion and Jean:
'O haste and gang to Fair Janet,
　　I fear that her days are dune!'

IX

Some drew to them their silken hose,
　　Some drew to them their shoon,
Some drew to them their silk manteils,
　　Their coverings to put on;
And they're awa' to Fair Janet
　　By the hie light o' the moon. . . .

X

'O I have borne this babe, Willie,
　　Wi' mickle toil and pain;
Take hame, take hame your babe, Willie,
　　For nurse I dare be nane.'

XI

He's ta'en his young son in his arms
　　And kiss'd him cheek and chin,
And he's awa' to his mother's bower
　　By the hie light o' the moon.

FAIR JANET

XII

'O open, open, mother!' he says,
  'O open, and let me in!
The rain rains on my yellow hair
  And the dew drops o'er my chin;
And I hae my young son in my arms,—
  I fear that his days are dune.'

XIII

Then with her fingers long and sma'
  She lifted up the pin,
And with her arms sae long and sma'
  Received the baby in.

XIV

'Gae back, gae back now, Sweet Willie,
  And comfort your fair ladye;
For where ye had but ae nourice
  Your young son shall hae three.'

XV

Willie he was scarce awa'
  And Janet put to bed,
When in and came her father dear:
  'Mak' haste, and busk the bride!'—

XVI

'There's a sair pain in my head, father,
  There's a sair pain in my side;
And ill, O ill I am, father,
  This day for to be a bride!'—

XVII

'O ye maun busk this bonny bride,
  And put a gay mantle on;
For she shall wed this auld French lord,
  Gin she should die this morn.'

busk] array.

XVIII

Some put on the gay green robes,
    And some put on the brown ;
But Janet put on the scarlet robes,
    Shone foremost thro' the town.

XIX

And some they mounted the black steed,
    And some mounted the brown ;
But Janet mounted the milk-white steed,
    Rode foremost thro' the town.

XX

'O wha will guide your horse, Janet ?
    O wha will guide him best ? '—
'O wha but Willie, my true-love ?
    He kens I love him best.'

XXI

And when they came to Mary's kirk
    To tie the holy ban',
Fair Janet's colour gaed and came,
    And her cheek look'd pale and wan.

XXII

When dinner it was past and done,
    And dancing to begin,
'O we'll go take the bride's maidens,
    And we'll go fill the ring.'

XXIII

O ben then came the auld French lord,
    Saying, 'Bride, will ye dance wi' me ? '—
'Awa', awa', ye auld French lord !
    Your face I downa see.'

FAIR JANET

XXIV

O ben then came Sweet Willie,
  He came with ane advance:
'O I'll go tak' the bride's maidens,
  And we'll go tak' a dance.'—

XXV

'I've seen ither days wi' you, Willie,
  And so has mony mae,
Ye would hae danced wi' me mysel',
  Let a' my maidens gae.'

XXVI

O ben now came Sweet Willie,
  Saying, 'Bride, will ye dance wi' me?'—
'Ay, by my sooth, and that I will
  Gin my back should break in three.'

XXVII

She hadna danced her o'er the floor,
  She hadna turn'd but thrice,
When she fell doun at Willie's feet,
  And up did never rise.

XXVIII

Willie's ta'en the key of his coffer
  And gi'en it to his man:
'Gae hame, and tell my mother dear
  My horse he has me slain;
And bid her be kind to my young son,
  For father he has nane.'

mae] more.

I

GOD ! let never soe old a man
   Marry soe young a wife
As did old Robin of Portingale !
   He may rue all the days of his life.

II

For the Mayor's daughter of Lin, God wot,
   He chose her to his wife,
And thought to have lived in quietnesse
   With her all the dayes of his life.

III

They had not in their wed-bed laid,
   Scarcely were both on sleepe,
But up she rose, and forth she goes
   To Sir Gyles, and fast can weepe.

IV

Saies, 'Sleepe you, wake you, faire Sir Gyles ?
   Or be you not within ?
[Or hear you not your true love
   That tirleth at the pin ? ']—

V

' But I am waking, sweete,' he said,
   ' Lady, what is your will ? '—
I have unbethought me of a wile
   How my wed lord we shall spill.

VI

' Four and twenty knights,' she sayes,
   ' That dwells about this towne,
E'en four and twenty of my next cozens
   Will help to ding him downe.'

   unbethought] bethought.   ding] smite.

VII

With that beheard his little foot-page,
  Was watering his master's steed;
Soe [sore a hearing it was to him]
  His very heart did bleed.

VIII

He mournèd, sikt, and wept full sore;
  I swear by the Holy Rood
The teares he for his master wept
  Were blent water and bloude.

IX

With that beheard his dear mastèr
  As he in his garden sate;
Sayes, 'Ever alack, my little page,
  What causes thee to weepe?

X

'Hath any one done to thee wronge,
  Any of thy fellowes here?
Or is any of thy good friends dead,
  What makes thee shed such teares?

XI

'Or if it be my head-cookes-man
  Griev'd againe he shall be,
Nor noe man within my house
  Shall doe wrong unto thee.'—

XII

'But it is not your head-cookes-man,
  Nor none of his degree;
But or tomorrow, ere it be noone
  You are deemèd to die.

sikt] sighed.   againe] in return.   deemèd] doomed.

XIII

' And of that thanke your head-stewàrd,
　　And, after, your ladie fair.'——
' If it be true, my little foot-page,
　　Of my land I'll make thee heir.'——

XIV

' If it be not true, my deare master,
　　God let me never thye.'——
' If it be not true, thou little foot-page,
　　A dead corse shalt thou be.'

XV

He callèd down his head-cookes-man
　　In kitchen supper to dress ;
' All and anon, my deere master !
　　Anon at your request ! '——

XVI

[' Let supper be drest, and of the best
　　Let it prepared be]
And call you downe my faire lady,
　　This night to supp with mee.'

XVII

And downe then came that fair lady,
　　'Was clad all in purple and palle ;
The rings that were upon her fingers
　　Cast light thorrow the hall.

XVIII

' What is your will, my owne wed lord,
　　What is your will with mee ? '——
' 'Tis I am sicke, fayre lady,
　　Sore sicke and like to dye.'——

　　　thye] thrive.　　palle] fine cloth.

XIX

'But an you be sicke, my owne wed lord,
　　Soe sore it grieveth mee ;
But my five maidens and my selfe
　　[Will bedd you presentlye].

XX

'And at the waking of your first sleepe
　　You shall have a hott drinke made,
And at the waking of your next sleepe
　　Your sorrowes will have a slake.'

XXI

He put a silk cote on his backe
　　'Was thirteen inches folde,
And put a steele cap upon his head
　　'Was gilded with good red gold.

XXII

And he layd a bright browne sword by his side,
　　And another at his feete,
And full well knew Old Robin then
　　Whether he shold wake or sleepe.

XXIII

And about the middle time of the night
　　Came twenty-four Knights in;
Sir Gyles he was the foremost man,
　　Soe well he knew that ginne.

XXIV

Old Robin with a bright browne sword
　　Sir Gyles' head he did winne,
Soe did he all those twenty-four,
　　Ne'er a one went quicke out [agen] ;

ginne] gin, contrivance, here a door-latch.　　quicke] alive.

XXV

None but one little foot-page
   Crept forth at a window of stone;
And he had two armes when he came in
   And [when he went out he had one].

XXVI

Upp then came that ladie light,
   With torches burning bright;
Shee thought to have brought Sir Gyles a drinke,
   But shee found her owne wed Knight.

XXVII

And the first thing that shee stumbled upon
   Was of Sir Gyles his foote;
Sayes, ' Ever alacke, and woe is me,
   Here lies my sweet hart-roote ! '

XXVIII

And the second thing shee stumbled upon
   Was of Sir Gyles his head;
Sayes, ' Ever alacke, and woe is me,
   Here lyes my true-love deade ! '

XXIX

He cut the papps beside her brest,
   And bade her wish her will;
And he cutt the eares beside her heade,
   And bade her wish on still.

XXX

' Mickle is the men's blood I have spent
   To doe thee and me some good ';
Sayes, ' Ever alacke, my fayre lady,
   I thinke that I was woode ! '

hart-roote] heart-root, dear one.   woode] mad.

XXXI

And he shope the cross on his right sho'lder
　　Of the white flesh and the redd,
And he went him into the Holy Land,
　　Wheras Christ was quicke and deade.

54. *Lord Thomas and Fair Annet*

I

LORD THOMAS and Fair Annet
　Sat all day on a hill;
When night was come, and sun was set,
　　They had not talk'd their fill.

II

Lord Thomas said a word in jest,
　　Fair Annet took it ill:
' I'll never wed a tocherless maid
　　Against my ain friends' will.'—

III

' Gif ye'll not wed a tocherless wife,
　　A wife will ne'er wed ye:
Fare ye well now, Lord Thomas,
　　It's fare ye well a wee.'

IV

O Annet she's gane till her bower,
　　Lord Thomas down the den;
And he's come till his mither's bower
　　By the lee light o' the moon.

shope] shaped, made.　　tocherless] without a dowry.　　lee]
calm, pleasant.

V

'O sleep ye, wake ye, mither?' he says,
   'Or are ye the bower within?'—
'I sleep right aft, I wake right aft;
   What want ye with me, son?

VI

'Where have ye been a' night, Thomas?
   O wow, ye've tarried long!'—
'I have been courtin' Fair Annet,
   And she is frae me gone.

VII

'O rede, O rede, mither,' he says,
   A gude rede gie to me:
O sall I tak' the nut-brown bride,
   And let Fair Annet be?'—

VIII

'The nut-brown bride has gold and gear,
   Fair Annet she's got nane;
And the little beauty Fair Annet has
   O it will soon be gane.

IX

'It's an' ye wed the nut-brown bride,
   I'll heap gold wi' my hand;
But an' ye wed her, Fair Annet,
   I'll straik it wi' a wand.

X

'The nut-brown bride has sheep and kye,
   Fair Annet she's got nane;
Son Thomas, for my benison
   Bring ye the brown bride hame. —

rede] counsel.   straik] stroke, as one might smooth over
the top of a bushel of corn to make it bare measure.

XI

'But alas, alas!' says Lord Thomas,
  O fair is Annet's face!'—
'But what matter for that, son Thomas?
  She has nae ither grace.'—

XII

'Alas, alas!' says Lord Thomas,
  'But white is Annet's hand!'—
'What matter for that, son Thomas?
  She has not a fur' o' land.'—

XIII

'Sheep will die in cots, mither,
  And owsen die in byre;
And what is warldis wealth to me,
  An' I getna my heart's desire?'

XIV

And he has till his sister gane:
  'Now, sister, rede ye me;
O sall I marry the nut-brown bride
  And set Fair Annet free?'—

XV

'I'se rede ye tak' Fair Annet, Thomas,
  And let the brown bride alane,
Lest ye should sigh and say Alas!
  What is this we brought hame?'—

XVI

'No, I will tak' my mither's counsel,
  And marry me out of hand;
And I will tak' the nut-brown bride;
  Fair Annet may leave the land.'

fur'] furrow.   owsen] oxen.

249

XVII

Up then rose Fair Annet's father
    Twa hours or it were day,
And he is gone to Fair Annet,
    To the bower wherein she lay.

XVIII

' Rise up, rise up, Fair Annet,' he says,
    'Put on your silken sheen;
Ye are bidden come to St. Mary's Kirk,
    To see a rich weddìn'.'. . .

XIX

' My maids, gae to my dressing-room
    And dress to me my hair;
Where'er ye laid a plait before
    See ye lay ten times mair.

XX

' My maids gae to my dressing-room
    And dress to me my smock;
The one half is o' the holland fine,
    The other o' needle-work.'

XXI

At yae tett o' her horse's mane
    Was tied a silver bell,
And yae tift o' the norland wind
    It gar'd them a' to knell.

XXII

Four and twenty gay good knights
    Rade by Fair Annet's side,
And four and twenty fair ladies
    As gin she had been a bride.

yae] each.   tett] tuft.   tift] puff, whiff.

LORD THOMAS AND FAIR ANNET

XXIII

And when she came to Mary's Kirk,
   She shimmer'd like the sun;
The belt that was about her waist
   Was a' wi' pearls bedone.

XXIV

And when she came to Mary's Kirk,
   And sat down in the deas,
The cleiding that Fair Annet had on
   Enlighten'd a' that place.

XXV

She sat her by the nut-brown bride,
   And her e'en they were sae clear,
Lord Thomas he clean forgat the bride
   When Fair Annet drew near.

XXVI

He had a rose into his hand,
   He gave it kisses three,
And reaching by the nut-brown bride,
   Laid it on Annet's knee.

XXVII

' O wha is this, my father dear,
   Blinks in Lord Thomas's e'e?'—
' O this Lord Thomas's first true-love
   Before he lovèd thee.'

XXVIII

Up then spake the nut-brown bride—
   She spake wi' mickle spite:
' And where gat ye the rose-water
   That washes thy face so white?'—

bedone] adorned.   deas] daïs, pew.   cleiding] clothing.

LORD THOMAS AND FAIR ANNET

XXIX

'O I did get my rose-water
    Where ye will ne'er get nane,
For I did get that very rose-water
    Into my mither's wame.'

XXX

The bride she drew a long bodkin
    Frae out her gay head-gear,
And strake Fair Annet to the heart,
    That word spak' never mair.

XXXI

'O Christ thee save!' Lord Thomas he said,
    'Methinks thou look'st wondrous wan;
'Thou was used to look with as fresh a colour
    As ever the sun shined on.'

XXXII

'O art thou blind, Lord Thomas?' she said,
    'Or canst thou not very well see?
Or dost thou not see my own heart's blood
    Runs trickling down my knee?'

XXXIII

Lord Thomas he saw Fair Annet was pale,
    And marvellèd what mote be;
But when he saw her dear heart's blood,
    All wood-wroth waxèd he.

XXXIV

He drew his dagger frae his side,
    That was so sharp and meet,
And drave it into the nut-brown bride,
    That fell dead at his feet.

wame] womb.   wood-wroth] mad with rage.

XXXV

'Now stay for me, dear Annet,' he said,
'Now stay, my dear!' he cried;
Then strake the dagger untill his heart,
And fell dead by her side.

55. *Rose the Red and White Lily*

I

O ROSE the Red and White Lilly,
Their mother dear was dead,
And their father married an ill woman
Wish'd them twa little gude.

II

Yet she had twa as fu' fair sons
As e'er brake manis bread;
And Bold Arthur he lo'ed her White Lilly
And Brown Robin Rose the Red.

III

O they hae biggit a bigly tow'r,
And strawn it o'er wi' sand;
There was mair mirth i' these ladies' bow'r
Than in a' their father's land.

IV

But out and spake their step-mither,
At the stair-foot stood she:
'I'm plaguit wi' your troublesome noise!
What makes your melodie?

bigly] commodious, habitable.   makes] means.

253

V

'O Rose the Red, ye sing too loud,
  White Lilly, your voice is strang:
But gin I live and bruik my life,
  I'll gar ye change your sang.'

VI

She's call'd her son, Brown Robin,
  'Come hither, my son, to me;
It fears me sair, my eldest son,
  That ye maun sail the sea.'—

VII

'Gin it fear you sair, my mither dear,
  Your bidding I maun dee;
But be never warse to Rose the Red
  Than ye ha' been to me.'—

VIII

'O haud your tongue, my eldest son,
  For sma' sall be her part;
You'll ne'er get kiss o' her comely mouth,
  Tho' you sh'uld break your heart.'

IX

She's call'd her son, Bold Arthur:
  'Come hither, my son, to me;
It fears me sair, my youngest son,
  That ye maun sail the sea.'—

X

'Gin it fear you sair, my mither dear,
  Your bidding I maun dee;
But be never warse to White Lilly
  Than ye ha' been to me.'—

bruik] brook, enjoy.

XI

' O haud your tongue, my yongest son,
　　For sma' sall be her part ;
You'll ne'er get kiss o' White Lilly's mouth
　　Tho' it break your very heart.'

XII

When Rose the Red and White Lilly
　　Saw their twa loves were gane,
Then stoppit ha' they their loud, loud sang
　　For and the still mournin' :
And their step-mither stood forbye,
　　To hear the maiden's mane.

XIII

Then out it spake her White Lilly :
　　' My sister, we'll be gane ;
Why should we stay in Burnèsdale
　　To waste our youth in pain ? '

XIV

Then cuttit ha' they their green clothing
　　A little below their knee,
And sae ha' they their yellow hair
　　A little abune their bree ;
And they're do'en them to haly chapel,
　　Was christen'd by Our Ladye.

XV

There ha' they changed their ain twa names,
　　Sae far frae ony town ;
And the tane o' them hight Sweet Willy,
　　And the tither Roge the Roun.

mane] moan.　　abune their bree] above their brows.　　hight]
was called.　　Roun] roan, red.

ROSE THE RED AND WHITE LILY

XVI

Between this twa a vow was made,
    And they sware it to fulfil;
That at three blasts o' a bugle-horn
    She'd come her sister till.

XVII

Now Sweet Willy's gane to the Kingis court,
    Her true-love there to see,
And Roge the Roun to good green-wood,
    Brown Robin's man to be.

XVIII

As it fell out upon a day
    They a' did put the stane,
Fu' seven feet ayont them a'
    She gar'd the puttin'-stane gang.

XIX

She lean'd her back against an oak,
    And ga'e a loud Ohone!
Then out it spake him Brown Robin,
    'But that's a woman's moan!'

XX

'O ken ye by my red rose lip?
    Or by my yallow hair?
Or ken ye by my milk-white breast?
    For ye never saw it bare.'

XXI

'I ken no by your red rose lip,
    Nor by your yallow hair;
Nor ken I by your milk-white breast,
    For I never saw it bare;
But come to your bow'r whaever sae likes
    Will find a lady there.'

256

XXII

About the tenth hour of the night
  The lady's bow'r-door was broken ;
And ere the first hour of the night
  The bonny knave-bairn was gotten.

XXIII

When days were gane, and months were run,
  Rose the Red took travailing ;
And sair she cried for a bow'r-woman,
  Her pine to wait upon.

XXIV

Then out it spake him Brown Robin :
  ' Now what needs a' this din ?
For what cou'd any woman do
  But I cou'd do the same ? '—

XXV

' It was never my mither's fashion,
  Nor sall it e'er be mine,
That belted Knights shou'd e'er stand by
  Where ladies dreed their pine.

XXVI

' But tak' ye up my bugle-horn,
  And blaw three blasts for me ;
I've a brither in the Kingis court
  Will come me quickly ti'.'—

XXVII

' O gin ye hae a brither on earth
  That ye love better nor me,
Ye blaw the horn yoursel',' he says,
  ' For ae blast I'll not gie.'

knave-bairn] man-child.   pine] pain.   dreed] endured.

XXVIII

She set the horn untill her mouth,
 And blawn three blasts sae shrill ;
Sweet Willy heard i' the Kingis court,
 And came her quickly till . . .

XXIX

[Word is to the kitchen gane,
 And word is to the ha',
Bold Arthur's lost his little foot-page,
 To the green-wood stown awa'.]

XXX

And word has gane to the Kingis court,
 To the King himsel' [at dine]
'Now, by my fay,' the King can say,
 [' Sweet Willy we maun find.']

XXXI

'Bring me my steed,' then cry'd the King,
 'My bow and arrows keen ;
I'll ride mysel' to good green-wood
 An' see what's to be seen.'

XXXII

'An't please your grace,' says Bold Arthur,
 'My liege I'll gang you wi',
An' try to find my little foot-page
 That's stray'd awa' frae me.'

XXXIII

O they have hunted in good green-wood
 The back but and the rae,
And they've drawn near Brown Robin's bow'r
 About the close of day.

XXXIV

Then out it spak' the King in haste,
   Says, ' Arthur, look an' see
Gin that be no your little foot-page
   That leans against yon tree ? '

XXXV

Bold Arthur took his bugle-horn,
   And blew a blast sae shrill,
Sweet Willy started at the sound
   And ran him quickly till.

XXXVI

' O wanted ye your meat, Willy ?
   Or wanted ye your fee ?
Or get ye ever an angry word,
   That ye ran awa' frae me ?'—

XXXVII

' I wanted nought, my master dear ;
   To me ye aye was good ;
I came but to see my ae brither
   That wons in this green-wood.'

XXXVIII

Then out and spak' the King again,
   Says, ' Bonny boy, tell to me
Who lives into yon bigly bow'r,
   Stands by yon green oak-tree ? '

XXXIX

' O pardon me,' says Sweet Willy,
   My liege, I daurna tell ;
And I pray you go no near that bow'r,
   For fear they do you fell.'—

      wons] dwells.   fell] kill.

XL

'O haud your tongue, my bonny boy,
    For I winna be said nay;
But I will gang that bow'r within,
    Betide me weal or wae.'

XLI

They've lighted off their milk-white steeds,
    And saftly enter'd in;
And then they saw her, Rose the Red,
    Nursing her bonny young son.

XLII

'Now, by the rood,' the King could say,
    'This is a comely sight;
I trow, instead of a forrester,
    This is a lady bright!'

XLIII

Then out it spake White Lilly
    And fell down on her knee:
'O pardon us, my gracious liege,
    An' our story I'll tell to thee.

XLIV

'Our father was a wealthy lord,
    That wonn'd in Barnèsdale;
But we had a wicked step-mother,
    That wrought us mickle bale.

XLV

'Yet she had twa as fu' fair sons
    As ever the sun did see;
An' the tane o' them lo'ed my sister dear,
    An' the tother said he lo'ed me.'

bale] harm.

XLVI

Then out and spak' him Bold Arthur,
   As by the King he stood,
'Now, this should be my White Lilly,
   An' that should be Rose the Red!'

XLVII

Then in it came him Brown Robin
   Frae hunting o' the deer,
But whan he saw the King was there,
   He started back for fear.

XLVIII

The King has ta'en him by the hand
   And bade him naething dread;
Says, 'Ye maun leave the good green-wood,
   Come to the court wi' speed.'

XLIX

Then up he took Brown Robin's son,
   And set him on his knee;
Says, 'Gin ye live to wield a bran',
   My bowman ye sall be.'

L

The King he sent for robes o' green,
   And girdles o' shining gold;
He gart the ladies be array'd
   Most comely to behold.

LI

They've doen them unto Mary Kirk,
   And there gat fair weddìng,
And whan the news spread o'er the lan',
   For joy the bells did ring.

LII

Then out it spak' her Rose the Red,
 And a hearty laugh laugh'd she;
'I wonder what would our step-dame say,
 Gin she this sight did see!'

56.   *Leesome Brand*

or, The Sheath and the Knife

I

'THERE is a feast in your father's house,
 The broom blooms bonnie and sae it is fair—
It becomes you and me to be very douce,
And we'll never gang down to the broom nae mair.'

II

But it is talk'd all over [the land],
'Lady Marget's plighted to Leesome Brand.'

III

He's done him to her father's stable
And tane twa steeds baith wicht and able:

IV

Ane for him, and another for her
To carry them baith wi' might and virr.

V

When they had ridden about six mile,
Lady Marget then began to fail.

VI

'O gin I had but a gude midwife
Here this day to save my life!

douce] quiet. wicht] sturdy. virr] vigour.
262

LEESOME BRAND

VII

'Ye'll take your arrow and your bow
And ye will hunt the deer and roe.

VIII

'But be sure ye touch not the milk-white hynde,
For she is o' the woman-kind.'

IX

He took sic pleasure in deer and rae
Till he forgot his ladye gay.

X

Till by it came that milk-white hynde,
And then he mind on his ladye syne.

XI

He heard her gie a loud, loud cry,
He shot his bow, and he let her lie.

XII

When he saw she was lying still,
He threw down his bow and came running her till;

XIII

But he found his ladye lying dead,
Likewise her young son at her head.

XIV

He's houkit a grave, long, large and wide,
He's buried his auld son doun by her side.

XV

It was nae wonder his heart was sair
When he shool'd the mools on her yellow hair.

XVI

His mother lay owre her castle wa';
There was music and minstrels and dancing and a'.

---

her till] to her.   houkit] dug.   auld] eldest, first-born.
shool'd] shovelled.   mools] mould.

LEESOME BRAND

XVII

[She said as she look'd owre] dale and down,
'My son comes merrilie to the toun.'—

XVIII

'Seek nae minstrels to play in your room,
Your son comes sorry to the toun.

XIX

'O I hae lost my gowden knife;
I rather had lost my ain sweet life!

XX

'And I hae lost a far better thing,
The gilded sheath that it was in.'—

XXI

'Are there nae gowdsmiths here in Fife
Can make to you anither knife?

XXII

'Are there nae sheath-makers in the land
Can make a sheath to Leesome Brand?'—

XXIII

'There are nae gowdsmiths here in Fife
Can make to me sic a gowden knife;

XXIV

'Nor nae sheath-makers in the land
Can make to me sic a sheath again.

XXV

'For I've lost my lady I loved sae dear,
The broom blooms bonnie and sae it is fair—
Likewise the son she did me bear,
And we'll never gang doun to the broom nae mair.'

57

Babylon
or, The Bonnie Banks o' Fordie

I

THERE where three ladies live in a bower—
Eh, wow, bonnie!
And they went out to pull a flower
On the bonnie banks o' Fordie.

II

They hadna pu'ed a flower but ane,
When up started to them a banisht man.

III

He's ta'en the first sister by her hand,
And he's turn'd her round and made her stand.

IV

'It's whether will ye be a rank robber's wife,
Or will ye die by my wee pen-knife?'

V

'It's I'll not be a rank robber's wife,
But I'll rather die by your wee pen-knife.'

VI

He's killed this may, and he's laid her by,
For to bear the red rose company.

VII

He's ta'en the second ane by the hand,
And he's turn'd her round and made her stand.

VIII

'It's whether will ye be a rank robber's wife,
Or will ye die by my wee pen-knife?'

IX

'It's I'll not be a rank robber's wife,
But I'll rather die by your wee pen-knife.'

K 3

BABYLON

X
He's killed this may, and he's laid her by,
For to bear the red rose company.

XI
He's taken the youngest ane by the hand,
And he's turn'd her round and made her stand.

XII
Says, 'Will ye be a rank robber's wife,
Or will ye die by my wee pen-knife?'

XIII
'It's I'll not be a rank robber's wife,
Nor will I die by your wee pen-knife.

XIV
'For in this wood a brother I hae;
And gin ye kill me, it's he'll kill thee.'

XV
'What's thy brother's name? come tell to me.'
'My brother's name is Baby Lon.'

XVI
'O sister, sister, what have I done!
O have I done this ill to thee!

XVII
'O since I've done this evil deed,
Good sall never be my meed.'

XVIII
He's taken out his wee pen-knife,
   Eh, wow, bonnie!
And he's twyn'd himsel' o' his ain sweet life
   On the bonnie banks o' Fordie.

twyned] taken away, bereaved.

58

Prince Robert

I

PRINCE Robert has wedded a gay ladye,
   He has wedded her with a ring;
Prince Robert has wedded a gay ladye,
   But he daur na bring her hame.

II

'Your blessing, your blessing, my mother dear,
   Your blessing now grant to me!'—
'Instead of a blessing ye sall have my curse,
   And you'll get nae blessing frae me.'

III

She has call'd upon her waiting-maid,
   To fill her a glass of wine;
She has called upon her fause steward,
   To put rank poison in.

IV

She has put it to her roudès lip,
   And to her roudès chin;
She has put it to her fause, fause mouth,
   But the never a drop gaed in.

V

He has put it to his bonny mouth,
   And to his bonny chin,
He's put it to his cherry lip,
   And sae fast the rank poison ran in.

VI

'O ye hae poison'd your ae son, mother,
   Your ae son and your heir;
O ye hae poisoned your ae son, mother,
   And sons you'll never hae mair.

roudès] hag-like.

VII

'O where will I get a little boy,
    That will win hose and shoon,
To rin sae fast to Darlinton,
    And bid Fair Eleanor come?'

VIII

Then up and spake a little boy,
    That wad win hose and shoon,
'O I'll away to Darlinton,
    And bid Fair Eleanor come.'

IX

O he has run to Darlinton,
    And tirlèd at the pin;
And wha was sae ready as Eleanor's sel'
    To let the bonny boy in?

X

'Your gude-mother's made ye a rare dinour,
    She's made it baith gude and fine;
Your gude-mother's made ye a gay dinour,
    And ye maun come till her and dine.'

XI

It's twenty lang miles to Sillertoun town,
    The langest that ever were gane;
But the steed it was wight, and the ladye was light,
    And she cam' linkin' in.

XII

But when she came to Sillertoun town,
    And into Sillertoun ha',
The torches were burning, the ladies were mourning,
    And they were weeping a'.

# PRINCE ROBERT

XIII

'O where is now my wedded lord,
  And where now can he be?
O where is now my wedded lord?
  For him I canna see.'—

XIV

'Your wedded lord is dead,' she says,
  'And just gane to be laid in the clay;
Your wedded lord is dead,' she says,
  'And just gane to be buried the day.

XV

'Ye'se get nane o' his gowd, ye'se get nane o' his gear,
  Ye'se get nae thing frae me;
Ye'se na get an inch o' his gude broad land,
  Tho' your heart suld burst in three.'

XVI

'I want nane o' his gowd, I want nane o' his gear,
  I want nae land frae thee;
But I'll hae the rings that's on his finger,
  For them he did promise to me.'

XVII

'Ye'se na get the rings that's on his finger,
  Ye'se na get them frae me;
Ye'se na get the rings that's on his finger,
  An' your heart suld burst in three.'

XVIII

She's turn'd her back unto the wa',
  And her face unto a rock,
And there, before the mother's face,
  Her very heart it broke.

269

59

Young Andrew

I

AS I was cast in my first sleepe,
  A dreadfull draught in my mind I drew,
For I was dreamèd of a young man,
    Some men callèd him Yonge Andrew.

II

The moone shone bright, and it cast a fayre light:
  ' Welcome,' says she, ' my honey, my sweete !
For I have loved thee this seven long yeare,
    And our chance it was we co'ld never meete.'

III

Then he tooke her in his armès two,
  And kissèd her both cheeke and chin,
And twise or thrise he kissèd this may
    Before they two did part in twin.

IV

' Faire maid I cannot do as I wo'ld ;
  [Yet what I can will I pleasure thee]
Goe home and fett thy father's red gold,
    And I'le goe to the church and marry thee.'

V

This ladye is gone to her father's hall,
  And well she knew where his red gold [lain],
And counted forth five hundred pound,
    Besides all other jewels and chaines :

VI

And brought it all to Younge Andrew,
  It was well counted upon his knee :
Then he tooke her by the lilye-white hand
    And led her up to an hill sae hie.

draught] picture.   may] maid.   fett] fetch.

VII

She had on a gowne of blacke velvett,
  (A pityfull sight after ye shall see)
'Put off thy clothes, bonny wenche,' he sayes,
  'For no foot further thou'st gang with mee.

VIII

But then she put off her gowne of velvett,
  With many a salt teare from her e'e,
And in a kirtle of fine breaden silke
  She stood before Yonge Andrew's e'e.

IX

Sayes, 'O put off thy kirtle of silke,
  For some and all shall goe with mee;
Unto my owne lady I must it beare,
  Whom I must needs love better than thee!'

X

Then she put off her kirtle of silke,
  With many a salt teare still from her e'e;
In a petticoate of scarlett redd
  She stood before Yonge Andrew's e'e.

XI

Sayes, 'O put off thy petticoate,
  For some and all shall goe with mee;
Unto my owne ladye I will it beare,
  That dwells soe far in a strange countrye.'

XII

But then she put off her petticoate,
  With many a salt teare still from her e'e,
And in a smocke of brave white silk
  She stood before Yonge Andrew's e'e.

breaden] braided.

YOUNG ANDREW

XIII

Sayes, ' O put off thy smocke of silke,
  For some and all shall goe with me ;
Unto my owne ladye I will it beare,
  That dwells soe far in a strange countrye.'—

XIV

Sayes, ' O remember, Yonge Andrew,
  Once of a woman you were borne ;
And for the birth that Marye bore
  I pray you let my smocke be upon ! '—

XV

Sayes, ' Yes, fayre ladye I know it well,
  Once of a woman I was borne ;
Yet for noe birth that Marye bore
  Thy smocke shall not be left upon.'

XVI

But then she put off her headgeare fine—
  She had billaments worth a hundred pound—
The hayre was upon that bonny wench' head
  Cover'd her bodye downe to the ground.

XVII

Then he pull'd forth a Scottish brand,
  And held it there in his owne right hand ;
Sayes, ' Whether wilt dye upon my sword's point,
  Or thou wilt goe naked home againe ? '—

XVIII

' Life is sweet,' then, ' Sir,' said she,
  ' Therefore I pray you leave me with mine ;
Before I wo'ld dye on your sword's point
  I had rather goe naked home againe.

billaments] habiliments.

YOUNG ANDREW

XIX

'My father,' she sayes, 'is a right guod earle
As any remaines in his owne countrye;
Gif ever he doe your bodye take,
You are sure to flower a gallow-tree.

XX

'And I have seven brethren,' she sayes,
'And they are all hardy men and bold;
Gif ever they doe your bodye take
You'll never again gang quicke over molde.'—.

XXI

'If your father be a right good earle
As any remaines in his owne countrye,
Tush! he shall never my bodye take,
I'll gang soe fast and over the sea.

XXII

'If you have seven brethren,' he sayes,
'If they be never soe hardy and bold,
Tush! they shall never my bodye take,
I'll gang soe fast over Scottish molde.'

XXIII

This ladye is gone to her father's hall,
Where every body their rest did take;
For but the Earle which was her father
Lay wakin' for his deere daughter's sake.

XXIV

'But who is that,' her father can say—
'Who is 't soe privily knows the pinn?'
'It 's Helen, your owne deere daughter, father,
I pray you rise and lett me in!

273

XXV

[' I pray you, pray you, lett me in ! '—]
  ' Noe, by my hood ! ' quoth her father then ;
' My house thou'st never come within,
  Without I had my red gold againe.'

XXVI

' Nay, nay, your gold is gone, father,
  [Yet I pray you rise and let me in ! ']
' Then naked thou came into this world,
  And naked thou shalt return againe.'

XXVII

' Nay, God forgave His death, father,
  And soe I hope you will doe mee.'
' Away, away, thou cursèd woman !
  Pray God an ill death thou may dee ! '

XXVIII

I' the morning, when her father got upp,
  A pittyful sight there he might see ;
His owne deere daughter was dead, without clothes,—
  And this was the end of that bonny ladye.

XXIX

But let us leave talking of this ladye
  And talke some more of Yonge Andrew :
For false he was to this bonny ladye—
  More pitty that he had not beene true !

XXX

He was not gone in the forest a mile,
  Or half a mile into the heart of Wales,
But a shee-wolfe caught him by such a wyle
  That hee must come to tell noe more tales.

XXXI

And now Yonge Andrew he is dead,
  But he never was buryèd under molde;
And there as the wolfe devourèd him
  There lyès all this great Earle's gold.

60. *The Gay Goshawk*

I

'O WELL 's me o' my gay goss-hawk,
    That he can speak and flee!
He'll carry a letter to my love,
  Bring back another to me.'—

II

'O how can I your true-love ken,
  Or how can I her know?
Whan frae her mouth I never heard couth,
  Nor wi' my eyes her saw.'—

III

'O well sall ye my true-love ken,
  As soon as you her see;
For, of a' the flow'rs in fair England,
  The fairest flow'r is she.

IV

'At even at my love's bower-door
  There grows a bowing birk,
An' sit ye down and sing thereon,
  As she gangs to the kirk.

couth] word.

THE GAY GOSHAWK

V

‘ An’ four-and-twenty ladies fair
　　Will wash and go to kirk,
But well shall ye my true-love ken,
　　For she wears gowd on her skirt.

VI

‘ An’ four-and-twenty gay ladies
　　Will to the mass repair,
But well sall ye my true-love ken,
　　For she wears gowd on her hair.’

VII

O even at that lady’s bower-door
　　There grows a bowing birk,
An’ he set down and sang thereon,
　　As she gaed to the kirk.

VIII

‘ O eet and drink, my marys a’,
　　The wine flows you among,
Till I gang to my shot-window,
　　An’ hear yon bonny bird’s song.

IX

‘ Sing on, sing on, my bonny bird,
　　The song ye sang the streen,
For I ken by your sweet singin’
　　You’re frae my true-love sen.’

X

O first he sang a merry song,
　　An’ then he sang a grave,
An’ then he peck’d his feathers gray,
　　To her the letter gave.

marys] maidens.　　　　shot-window] here = bow-window.
the streen] yestreen.

XI

'Ha, there's a letter frae your love,
  He says he sent you three ;
He canna wait your luve langer,
  But for your sake he'll dee.

XII

'He bids you write a letter to him ;
  He says he's sent you five ;
He canna wait your luve langer,
  Tho' you're the fairest alive.'—

XIII

'Ye bid him bake his bridal-bread,
  And brew his bridal-ale,
An' I'll meet him in fair Scotland
  Lang, lang or it be stale.'

XIV

She's doen her to her father dear
  Fa'n low down on her knee :
'A boon, a boon, my father dear
  I pray you, grant it me !'—

XV

'Ask on, ask on, my daughter,
  An' granted it sall be ;
Except ae squire in fair Scotland,
  An' him you sall never see.'—

XVI

'The only boon, my father dear,
  That I do crave of thee,
Is, gin I die in southin lands,
  In Scotland to bury me.

THE GAY GOSHAWK

XVII

' An' the firstin kirk that ye come till,
  Ye gar the bells be rung,
An' the nextin kirk that ye come till,
  Ye gar the mass be sung.

XVIII

' An' the thirdin kirk that ye come till,
  You deal gold for my sake,
An' the fourthin kirk that ye come till,
  You tarry there till night.'

XIX

She is doen her to her bigly bow'r,
  As fast as she could fare,
An' she has tane a sleepy draught,
  That she had mixt wi' care.

XX

She's laid her down upon her bed,
  An' soon she's fa'n asleep,
And soon o'er every tender limb
  Cauld death began to creep.

XXI

Whan night was flown, an' day was come,
  Nae ane that did her see
But thought she was as surely dead
  As ony lady cou'd be.

XXII

Her father an' her brothers dear
  Gar'd make to her a bier ;
The tae half was o' guid red gold,
  The tither o' silver clear.

bigly] commodious.

THE GAY GOSHAWK

Her mither an' her sisters fair
  Gar'd work for her a sark ;
The tae half was o' cambrick fine,
  The tither o' needle wark.

XXIV

The firstin kirk that they came till,
  They gar'd the bells be rung,
An' the nextin kirk that they came till,
  They gar'd the mess be sung.

XXV

The thirdin kirk that they came till,
  They dealt gold for her sake,
An' the fourthin kirk that they came till,
  Lo, there they met her make !

XXVI

' Lay down, lay down the bigly bier,
  Lat me the dead look on ! '—
Wi' cherry cheeks and ruby lips
  She lay and smil'd on him.

XXVII

' O ae sheave o' your bread, true-love,
  An' ae glass o' your wine !
For I hae fasted for your sake
  These fully days is nine.

XXVIII

' Gang hame, gang hame, my seven bold brothers,
  Gang hame and sound your horn ;
An' ye may boast in southin lands
  Your sister 's play'd you scorn ! '

make] mate, lover.   sheave] slice.

I

'WILLIE, Willie, what makes you sae sad?'
   And the sun shines over the valleys and a'—
'I lie sairly sick for the love of a maid.'
   Amang the blue flowers and the yellow and a'.

II

'O Willie, my son, I'll learn you a wile,
How this pretty fair maid ye may beguile.

III

'Ye maun lie doun just as ye were dead,
And tak' your windin'-sheet round your head.

IV

'Ye maun gie the bellman his bell-groat,
To ring your dead-bell at your lover's yett.'

V

Willie lay doun just as he war dead,
And took his windin'-sheet round his head.

VI

He gied the bellman his bell-groat
To ring his dead-bell at his lover's yett.

VII

'O wha is this that is dead, I hear?'—
'O wha but Willie that lo'ed ye sae dear?'

VIII

She is hame to her father's ain bour:
'I'll gang to yon lyke-wake ae single hour.'—

IX

'Ye maun tak' with you your brither John;
It's not meet for maidens to venture alone.'—

    yett] gate.   lyke-wake] corpse-watching.

X

'I'll not tak' with me my brither John,
But I'll gang along myself all alone.'

XI

It's when she cam' to her true lovers yett,
She dealt the red gold round for his sak'.

XII

It's when she came to her true lover's bed
She lifted the sheet to look at the dead.

XIII

He's ta'en her hand sae meek and sae sma',
[And ca'd her his wife before them a'].

XIV

'Fair maid, ye cam' without horse or boy,
But I'll send you home with a merry convoy.'

62. Fair Margaret and Sweet William

I

AS it fell out on a long summer's day,
   Two lovers they sat on a hill:
They sat together that long summer's day,
   And could not talk their fill.

II

'I see no harm by you, Margaret,
   Nor you see none by me;
Before to-morrow eight o'clock
   A rich wedding shall you see.'

III

Fair Margaret sat in her bower-window
   Combing her yellow hair,
She saw Sweet William and his brown bride
   Unto the church draw near.

281

IV

Then down she laid her ivory comb,
    And up she bound her hair;
She went out from her bower alive
    But alive never more came there.

V

When day was gone, and night was come,
    And all men fast asleep,
Came in the ghost of fair Margaret,
    And stood at William's feet.

VI

' How like ye the lady, Sweet William,
    That lies in your arms asleep?
God give you joy of your gay bride-bed,
    And me of my winding-sheet ! '

VII

When night was gone, and day was come,
    And all men waked from sleep,
His lady said to Sweet William,
    ' My dear, I have cause to weep :

VIII

' I dream'd a dream, Sweet William,
    That seldom comes to good :
My bower was fill'd with wild-wood swine,
    And our bride-bed full of blood.'

IX

He callèd up his merry men all,
    By one, by two, by three.
Saying, ' I'll away to Fair Margaret's bower,
    With the leave of my ladye.'

282

X

And when he came to Fair Margaret's bower
  He knockèd at the ring ;
And who so ready as her seven brothers
  To rise and let him in ?

XI

' O, is she in the parlour ? ' he said,
  ' Or is she in the hall ?
Or is she in the long chamber
  Amongst her merry maids all ? '—

XII

' No, she 's not in the parlour,' they said,
  ' Nor she 's not in the hall :
But she is in the long chamber,
  Laid out against the wall.'—

XIII

He turnèd up the covering-sheet,
  And look'd upon the dead.
' Methinks her lips are pale and wan,
  She has lost her cherry red.'

XIV

With that bespake the seven brothers,
  Making a piteous moan :
' You may go kiss your jolly brown bride,
  And let our sister alone.'—

XV

' If I do kiss my jolly brown bride,
  I do but what is right ;
For I made no vow to your sister dear,
  By day nor yet by night.

XVI

'Deal on, deal on, my merry men all,
    Deal on your cake and wine !
For whatever is dealt at her funeral to-day
    Shall be dealt to-morrow at mine.'

XVII

Fair Margaret died on the over night,
    Sweet William died on the morrow :
Fair Margaret died for pure, pure love,
    Sweet William died for sorrow.

XVIII

Go with your right to Newcastle,
    And come with your left side home ;
There you will see these two lovers
    Lie printed on one stone.

63.   *The Twa Brothers*

I

THERE were twa brethren in the North,
    They went to school thegither ;
The one unto the other said,
    'Will you try a warsle, brither ? '

II

They warsled up, they warsled down,
    Till Sir John fell to the ground,
And there was a knife in Sir Willie's pouch
    Gied him a deadly wound.

warsle] wrestle.

THE TWA BROTHERS

III

'Tak' aff, tak' aff my holland sark,
  Rive it frae gare to gare,
And stap it in my bleeding wound—
  'Twill aiblins bleed nae mair.'

IV

He's pu'it aff his holland sark,
  Rave it frae gare to gare,
And stapt it in his bleeding wound—
  But aye it bled the mair.

V

'O tak' now aff my green cleiding
  And row me saftly in,
And carry me up to Chester kirk,
  Whar the grass grows fair and green.

VI

'But what will ye say to your father dear
  When ye gae home at e'en?'—
'I'll say ye're lying at Chester kirk,
  Whar the grass grows fair and green.'—

VII

'O no, O no, when he speers for me
  Saying, "William, whar is John?"
Ye'll say ye left me at Chester school
  Leaving the school alone.'

VIII

He's ta'en him up upo' his back,
  And borne him hence away,
And carried him to Chester kirk,
  And laid him in the clay.

rive] tear.   gare] gore.   aiblins] perhaps.
cleiding] clothing.   row] wrap.   speers] asks.

IX

But when he sat in his father's chair,
   He grew baith pale and wan :
' O what blude 's that upon your brow ?
   And whar is your brither John ? '—

X

' O John 's awa' to Chester school,
   A scholar he'll return ;
He bade me tell his father dear
   About him no' to mourn.

XI

' And it is the blude o' my gude grey steed ;
   He wadna hunt for me.'—
' O thy steed's blude was ne'er so red,
   Nor ne'er so dear to me !

XII

' And whaten blude's that upon your dirk ?
   Dear Willie, tell to me.'—
' It is the blude o' my ae brither
   And dule and wae is me ! '—

XIII

' O what sall I say to your mither ?
   Dear Willie, tell to me.'—
' I'll saddle my steed and awa' I'll ride,
   To dwell in some far countrie.'—

XIV

' O when will ye come hame again ?
   Dear Willie, tell to me ! '—
' When the sun and moon dance on yon green :
   And that will never be ! '

The Cruel Brother

I

THERE were three ladies play'd at the ba',
  With a hey ho! and a lily gay!
By came a knight and he woo'd them a'
  As the primrose spreads so sweetly.
    Sing Annet, and Marret, and fair Maisrie,
    As the dew hangs i' the wood, gay ladie!

II

The first ane she was clad in red:
'O lady fair, Will you be my bride?'

III

The midmost ane was clad in green:
'O lady fair, will you be my queen?'

IV

The youngest o' them was clad in white:
'O lady fair, be my heart's delight!'—

V

'Sir knight ere ye my favour win,
Ye maun get consent frae a' my kin.

VI

'Ye maun go ask my father, the King:
Sae maun ye ask my mither, the Queen.

VII

'Sae maun ye ask my sister Anne,
And dinna forget my brother John.'

VIII

He has sought her from her father, the King
And sae did he her mither, the Queen.

THE CRUEL BROTHER

IX

He has sought her from her sister Anne:
But he has forgot her brither John.

X

Now when the wedding day was come,
The knight would take his bonny bride home.

XI

And many a lord and many a knight
Came to behold that ladie bright.

XII

And there was nae man that did her see
But wish'd himself bridegroom to be.

XIII

Her father led her down the stair,
And her mither dear she kiss'd her there.

XIV

Her sister Anne led her thro' the close,
And her brother John set her on her horse.

XV

She lean'd her o'er the saddle-bow,
To give him a kiss ere she did go.

XVI

He has ta'en a knife, baith lang and sharp,
And stabb'd that bonny bride to the heart.

XVII

She hadna ridden half thro' the town,
Until her heart's blude stain'd her gown.

XVIII

'Ride saftly up,' said the best young man;
'I think our bride come hooly on.'

hooly] slowly, softly.

XIX

' Ride up, ride up,' said the second man ;
' I think our bride looks pale and wan.'

XX

Up then comes the gay bridegroom,
And straight unto the bride he came.

XXI

' Does your side-saddle sit awry ?
Or does your steed [go heavily] ? '—

XXII

' O lead me gently over yon stile,
For there would I sit and bleed awhile.

XXIII

' O lead me gently up yon hill,
For there would I sit and make my will.'—

XXIV

' O what will you leave to your father dear ? '—
' The milk-white steed that brought me here.'—

XXV

' What will you leave to your mother dear ? '—
' My wedding shift that I do wear.'— .

XXVI

' What will you leave to your sister Anne ? '—
' My silken snood and my golden fan.'—

XXVII

' What will you leave to your brother John ? '—
With a hay ho ! and a lily gay !
' The gallows-tree to hang him on.'
And the primrose spreads so sweetly.
Sing Annet, and Marret, and fair Maisrie,
And the dew hangs i' the wood, gay ladie !

I

'WHY does your brand sae drop wi' blude,
      Edward, Edward?
Why does your brand sae drop wi' blude,
      And why sae sad gang ye, O?'—
'O I hae kill'd my hawk sae gude,
      Mither, mither;
O I hae kill'd my hawk sae gude,
      And I had nae mair but he, O.'

II

'Your hawk's blude was never sae red,
      Edward, Edward;
Your hawk's blude was never sae red,
      My dear son, I tell thee, O.'—
'O I hae kill'd my red-roan steed,
      Mither, mither;
O I hae kill'd my red-roan steed,
      That erst was sae fair and free, O.'

III

'Your steed was auld, and ye hae got mair,
      Edward, Edward;
Your steed was auld, and ye hae got mair;
      Some other dule ye dree, O.'—
'O I hae kill'd my father dear,
      Mither, mither;
O I hae kill'd my father dear,
      Alas, and wae is me, O!'

dule ye dree] grief you suffer.

290

EDWARD, EDWARD

IV

'And whatten penance will ye dree for that,
    Edward, Edward?
Whatten penance will ye dree for that?
    My dear son, now tell me, O.'—
'I'll set my feet in yonder boat,
    Mither, mither;
I'll set my feet in yonder boat,
    And I'll fare over the sea, O.'

V

'And what will ye do wi' your tow'rs and your ha',
    Edward, Edward?
And what will ye do wi' your tow'rs and your ha',
    That were sae fair to see, O?'—
'I'll let them stand till they doun fa',
    Mither, mither;
I'll let them stand till they doun fa',
    For here never mair maun I be, O.'

VI

'And what will ye leave to your bairns and your wife,
    Edward, Edward?
And what will ye leave to your bairns and your wife,
    When ye gang owre the sea, O?'—
'The warld's room: let them beg through life,
    Mither, mither;
The warld's room: let them beg through life;
    For them never mair will I see, O.'

VII

'And what will ye leave to your ain mither dear,
    Edward, Edward?
And what will ye leave to your ain mither dear,
    My dear son, now tell me, O?'—

'The curse of hell frae me sall ye bear,
    Mither, mither;
The curse of hell frae me sall ye bear:
    Sic counsels ye gave to me, O!'

66: *Lord Randal*

I

'O WHERE hae ye been, Lord Randal, my son?
    O where hae ye been, my handsome young man?'—
'I hae been to the wild wood; mother, make my bed
    soon,
For I'm weary wi' hunting, and fain wald lie down.'

II

'Where gat ye your dinner, Lord Randal, my son?
Where gat ye your dinner, my handsome young man?'—
'I dined wi' my true-love; mother, make my bed soon,
For I'm weary wi' hunting, and fain wald lie down.'

III

'What gat ye to your dinner, Lord Randal, my son?
What gat ye to your dinner, my handsome young man?'—
'I gat eels boil'd in broo'; mother, make my bed soon,
For I'm weary wi' hunting, and fain wald lie down.'

IV

'What became of your bloodhounds, Lord Randal, my son?
What became of your bloodhounds, my handsome young
    man?'—
'O they swell'd and they died; mother, make my bed soon,
For I'm weary wi' hunting, and fain wald lie down.'

V

'O I fear ye are poison'd, Lord Randal, my son!
O I fear ye are poison'd, my handsome young man!'—
'O yes! I am poison'd; mother, make my bed soon,
For I'm sick at the heart, and I fain wald lie down.'

The Twa Corbies

(SCOTTISH VERSION)

I

AS I was walking all alane,
I heard twa corbies making a mane:
The tane unto the tither did say,
'Whar sall we gang and dine the day?'

II

'—In behint yon auld fail dyke
I wot there lies a new-slain knight;
And naebody kens that he lies there
But his hawk, his hound, and his lady fair.

III

'His hound is to the hunting gane,
His hawk to fetch the wild-fowl hame,
His lady's ta'en anither mate,
So we may mak' our dinner sweet.

IV

'Ye'll sit on his white hause-bane,
And I'll pike out his bonny blue e'en:
Wi' ae lock o' his gowden hair
We'll theek our nest when it grows bare.

V

'Mony a one for him maks mane,
But nane sall ken whar he is gane:
O'er his white banes, when they are bare,
The wind sall blaw for evermair.'

corbies] ravens.   fail] turf.   hause] neck.   theek]
thatch.

293

I

THERE were three ravens sat on a tree,
They were as black as they might be.

II

The one of them said to his make,
' Where shall we our breakfast take ? '

III

' Down in yonder greenè field
There lies a knight slain under his shield ;

IV

' His hounds they lie down at his feet,
So well do they their master keep ;

V

' His hawks they flie so eagerly,
There 's no fowl dare come him nigh.

VI

' Down there comes a fallow doe
As great with young as she might goe.

VII

' She lift up his bloudy head
And kist his wounds that were so red.

VIII

' She gat him up upon her back
And carried him to earthen lake.

IX

' She buried him before the prime,
She was dead herself ere evensong time.

X

' God send every gentleman
Such hounds, such hawks, and such a leman ! '

make] mate.

BOOK III

69.   *The Nut-Brown Maid*

I

He.   *BE it right or wrong, these men among*
            On women do complain;
      Affirming this, how that it is
          A labour spent in vain
      To love them wele; for never a dele
          They love a man again:
      For let a man do what he can
          Their favour to attain,
      Yet if a new to them pursue,
          Their first true lover than
      Laboureth for naught; for from her thought
          He is a banished man.

II

She.   *I say not nay, but that all day*
           It is both written and said
       That woman's faith is, as who saith,
           All utterly decay'd:
       But nevertheless, right good witnèss
           In this case might be laid
       That they love true and continùe:
           Record the Nut-brown Maid,
       Which, when her love came her to prove,
           To her to make his moan,
       Would not depart; for in her heart
           She loved but him alone.

never a dele] never a bit.   than] then.

III

He.   *Then between us let us discuss*
    What was all the manere
    Between them two : we will also
    Tell all the pain in fere
    That she was in.   Now I begin,
    So that ye me answere :
    Wherefore all ye that present be,
    I pray you, give an ear.
    I am the Knight.   I come by night,
    As secret as I can,
    Saying, Alas ! thus standeth the case,
    I am a banished man.

IV

She.   *And I your will for to fulfil*
    In this will not refuse ;
    Trusting to show, in wordès few,
    That men have an ill use—
    To their own shame—women to blame,
    And causeless them accuse.
    Therefore to you I answer now,
    All women to excuse :
    Mine own heart dear, with you what cheer?
    I pray you, tell anone ;
    For, in my mind, of all mankind
    I love but you alone.

V

He.   It standeth so : a deed is do
    Whereof great harm shall **grow** :
    My destiny is for to die
    A shameful death, I trow ;

      in fere] in company, together.

296

Or else to flee. The t' one must be.
  None other way I know
But to withdraw as an outlàw,
  And take me to my bow.
Wherefore adieu, mine own heart true!
  None other rede I can:
For I must to the green-wood go,
  Alone, a banished man.

VI

She. O Lord, what is this worldis bliss,
    That changeth as the moon!
  My summer's day in lusty May
    Is darked before the noon.
  I hear you say, farewell: Nay, nay,
    We dèpart not so soon.
  Why say ye so? whither will ye go?
    Alas! what have ye done?
  All my welfàre to sorrow and care
    Should change, if ye were gone:
  For, in my mind, of all mankind
    I love but you alone.

VII

He. I can believe it shall you grieve,
    And somewhat you distrain;
  But afterward, your painès hard
    Within a day or twain
  Shall soon aslake; and ye shall take
    Comfort to you again.
  Why should ye ought? for, to make thought,
    Your labour were in vain.

rede I can] counsel I know.   distrain] distress.

And thus I do; and pray you to,
    As hartèly as I can:
For I must to the green-wood go,
    Alone, a banished man.

VIII

She. Now, sith that ye have showed to me
    The secret of your mind,
I shall be plain to you again,
    Like as ye shall me find.
Sith it is so that ye will go,
    I will not live behind.
Shall never be said the Nut-brown Maid
    Was to her love unkind.
Make you readỳ, for so am I,
    Although it were anone:
For, in my mind, of all mankind
    I love but you alone.

IX

He. Yet I you rede to take good heed
    What men will think and say:
Of young, of old, it shall be told
    That ye be gone away
Your wanton will for to fulfil,
    In green-wood you to play;
And that ye might for your delight
    No longer make delay.
Rather than ye should thus for me
    Be called an ill womàn
Yet would I to the green-wood go,
    Alone, a banished man.

THE NUT-BROWN MAID

X

She. Though it be sung of old and young
     That I should be to blame,
  Theirs be the charge that speak so large
     In hurting of my name:
  For I will prove that faithful love
     It is devoid of shame;
  In your distress and heaviness
     To part with you the same:
  And sure all tho that do not so
     True lovers are they none:
  For, in my mind, of all mankind
     I love but you alone.

XI

He. I counsel you, Remember how
     It is no maiden's law
  Nothing to doubt, but to run out
     To wood with an outlàw.
  For ye must there in your hand bear
     A bow readỳ to draw;
  And as a thief thus must you live
     Ever in dread and awe;
  Whereby to you great harm might grow:
     Yet had I liever than
  That I had to the green-wood go,
     Alone, a banished man.

XII

She. I think not nay but as ye say;
     It is no maiden's lore;
  But love may make me for your sake,
     As I have said before,

part with] share with.   tho] those.

To come on foot, to hunt and shoot,
   To get us meat and store;
For so that I your company
   May have, I ask no more.
From which to part it maketh my heart
   As cold as any stone;
For, in my mind, of all mankind
   I love but you alone.

XIII

He.   For an outlàw this is the law,
   That men him take and bind:
Without pitie, hangèd to be,
   And waver with the wind.
If I had need (as God forbede!)
   What socours could ye find?
Forsooth, I trow, you and your bow
   For fear would draw behind.
And no mervail; for little avail
   Were in your counsel than:
Wherefore I'll to the green-wood go,
   Alone, a banished man.

XIV

She.   Right well know ye that women be
   But feeble for to fight;
No womanhede it is, indeed,
   To be bold as a knight:
Yet in such fear if that ye were
   With enemies day and night,
I would withstand, with bow in hand,
   To grieve them as I might,

And you to save; as women have
   From death men many one:
For, in my mind, of all mankind
   I love but you alone.

XV

He. Yet take good hede; for ever I drede
     That ye could not sustain
The thorny ways, the deep vallèys,
   The snow, the frost, the rain,
The cold, the heat; for dry or wete,
   We must lodge on the plain;
And, us above, no other roof
   But a brake bush or twain:
Which soon should grieve you, I believe;
   And ye would gladly than
That I had to the green-wood go,
   Alone, a banished man.

XVI

She. Sith I have here been partynere
     With you of joy and bliss,
I must alsò part of your woe
   Endure, as reason is:
Yet I am sure of one pleasùre,
   And shortly it is this—
That where ye be, me seemeth, pardé,
   I could not fare amiss.
Without more speech I you beseech
   That we were shortly gone;
For, in my mind, of all mankind
   I love but you alone.

XVII

He. If ye go thyder, ye must consider,
  When ye have lust to dine,
 There shall no meat be for to gete,
  Nether bere, ale, ne wine,
 Ne shetès clean, to lie between,
  Made of the thread and twine;
 None other house, but leaves and boughs,
  To cover your head and mine.
 Lo, mine heart sweet, this ill diète
  Should make you pale and wan:
 Wherefore I'll to the green-wood go,
  Alone, a banished man.

XVIII

She. Among the wild deer such an archère,
  As men say that ye be,
 Ne may not fail of good vitayle
  Where is so great plentè:
 And water clear of the rivere
  Shall be full sweet to me;
 With which in hele I shall right wele
  Endure, as ye shall see;
 And, or we go, a bed or two
  I can provide anone;
 For, in my mind, of all mankind
  I love but you alone.

XIX

He. Lo yet, before, ye must do more,
  If ye will go with me:
 As, cut your hair up by your ear,
  Your kirtle by the knee;

hele] health.

302

With bow in hand for to withstand
    Your enemies, if need be:
And this same night, before daylight,
    To woodward will I flee.
If that ye will all this fulfil,
    Do it shortly as ye can:
Else will I to the green-wood go,
    Alone, a banished man.

XX

She.   I shall as now do more for you
    Than 'longeth to womanhede;
To short my hair, a bow to bear,
    To shoot in time of need.
O my sweet mother! before all other
    For you I have most drede!
But now, adieu! I must ensue
    Where fortune doth me lead.
All this make ye: Now let us flee;
    The day cometh fast upon:
For, in my mind, of all mankind
    I love but you alone.

XXI

He.   Nay, nay, not so; ye shall not go,
    And I shall tell you why—
Your appetite is to be light
    Of love, I well espy:
For, right as ye have said to me,
    In likewise hardily
Ye would answere whosoever it were,
    In way of company:

It is said of old, Soon hot, soon cold;
  And so is a womàn :
Wherefore I to the wood will go,
  Alone, a banished man.

XXII

She. If ye take heed, it is no need
  Such words to say to me ;
For oft ye prayed, and long assayed,
  Or I loved you, pardè :
And though that I of ancestry
  A baron's daughter be,
Yet have you proved how I you loved,
  A squire of low degree ;
And ever shall, whatso befall,
  To die therefore anone ;
For, in my mind, of all mankind
  I love but you alone.

XXIII

He. A baron's child to be beguiled,
  It were a cursèd deed !
To be felàw with an outlaw—
  Almighty God forbede !
Yet better were the poor squyere
  Alone to forest yede
Than ye shall say another day
  That by my cursèd rede
Ye were betrayed. Wherefore, good maid,
  The best rede that I can,
Is, that I to the green-wood go,
  Alone, a banished man.

yede] went.

THE NUT-BROWN MAID

XXIV

She. Whatever befall, I never shall
    Of this thing be upbraid:
But if ye go, and leave me so,
    Then have ye me betrayed.
Remember you wele, how that ye dele;
    For if ye, as ye said,
Be so unkind to leave behind
    Your love, the Nut-brown Maid,
Trust me truly that I shall die
    Soon after ye be gone:
For, in my mind, of all mankind
    I love but you alone.

XXV

He. If that ye went, ye should repent;
    For in the forest now
I have purveyed me of a maid
    Whom I love more than you:
Another more fair than ever ye were
    I dare it well avow;
And of you both each should be wroth
    With other, as I trow:
It were mine ease to live in peace;
    So will I, if I can:
Wherefore I to the wood will go,
    Alone, a banished man.

XXVI

She. Though in the wood I understood
    Ye had a paramour,
All this may nought remove my thought,
    But that I will be your':

305

And she shall find me soft and kind
    And courteis every hour;
Glad to fulfil all that she will
    Command me, to my power:
For had ye, lo, an hundred mo,
    Yet would I be that one:
For, in my mind, of all mankind
    I love but you alone.

XXVII

He. Mine own dear love, I see the prove
    That ye be kind and true;
Of maid, of wife, in all my life,
    The best that ever I knew.
Be merry and glad; be no more sad;
    The case is changèd new;
For it were ruth that for your truth
    Ye should have cause to rue.
Be not dismayed, whatsoever I said
    To you when I began;
I will not to the green-wood go;
    I am no banished man.

XXVIII

She. These tidings be more glad to me
    Than to be made a queen,
If I were sure they should endure;
    But it is often seen
When men will break promise they speak
    The wordis on the splene.
Ye shape some wile me to beguile,
    And steal from me, I ween:

        on the splene] in haste.

306

Then were the case worse than it was,
    And I more wo-begone:
For, in my mind, of all mankind
    I love but you alone.

XXIX

He. Ye shall not nede further to drede:
    I will not disparàge
You (God defend), sith you descend
    Of so great a linàge.
Now understand: to Westmoreland,
    Which is my heritage,
I will you bring; and with a ring,
    By way of marriàge
I will you take, and lady make,
    As shortly as I can:
Thus have you won an Earle's son,
    And not a banished man.

XXX

Here may ye see that women be
    In love meek, kind, and stable;
Let never man reprove them than,
    Or call them variable;
But rather pray God that we may
    To them be comfortable;
Which sometime proveth such as He loveth,
    If they be charitable.
For sith men would that women should
    Be meek to them each one;
Much more ought they to God obey,
    And serve but Him alone.

Fause Foodrage

I

KING EASTER has courted her for her lands,
King Wester for her fee,
King Honour for her comely face,
And for her fair bodie.

II

They had not been four months married,
As I have heard them tell,
Until the nobles of the land
Against them did rebel.

III

And they cast kevils them amang,
And kevils them between ;
And they cast kevils them amang,
Wha suld gae kill the king.

IV

O, some said yea, and some said nay,
Their words did not agree ;
Till up and got him, Fause Foodrage,
And swore it suld be he.

V

When bells were rung, and mass was sung,
And a' men bound to bed,
King Honour and his gay ladye
In a high chamber were laid.

kevils] lots.

FAUSE FOODRAGE

VI

Then up and raise him, Fause Foodrage,
  When a' were fast asleep,
And slew the porter in his lodge,
  That watch and ward did keep.

VII

O four-and-twenty silver keys
  Hang hie upon a pin ;
And aye, as ae door he did unlock,
  He has fasten'd it him behin'.

VIII

Then up and raise him, King Honour,
  Says—' What means a' this din ?
Or what 's the matter, Fause Foodrage,
  Or wha has loot you in ? '—

IX

' O ye my errand weel sall learn,
  Before that I depart.'—
Then drew a knife, baith lang and sharp,
  And pierced him to the heart.

X

Then up and got the Queen hersell,
  And fell low down on her knee,
' O spare my life, now, Fause Foodrage !
  For I never injured thee.

XI

' O spare my life, now, Fause Foodrage !
  Until I lighter be !
And see gin it be lad or lass,
  King Honour has left me wi'.'—

309

FAUSE FOODRAGE

XII

' O gin it be a lass,' he says,
  ' Weel nursèd it sall be ;
But gin it be a lad bairn,
  He sall be hangèd hie.

XIII

' I winna spare for his tender age,
  Nor yet for his hie hie kin ;
But soon as e'er he born is,
  He sall mount the gallows pin.'——

XIV

O four-and-twenty valiant knights
  Were set the Queen to guard ;
And four stood aye at her bour door,
  To keep both watch and ward.

XV

But when the time drew near an end,
  That she suld lighter be,
She cast about to find a wile,
  To set her body free.

XVI

O she has birled these merry young men
  With the ale but and the wine,
Until they were a' deadly drunk
  As any wild-wood swine.

XVII

' O narrow, narrow is this window,
  And big, big am I grown ! '——
Yet through the might of Our Ladye,
  Out at it she is gone.

FAUSE FOODRAGE

XVIII

She wander'd up, she wander'd down,
  She wander'd out and in ;
And, at last, into the very swine's stythe
  The Queen brought forth a son.

XIX

Then they cast kevils them amang,
  Which suld gae seek the Queen ;
And the kevil fell upon Wise William,
  And he sent his wife for him.

XX

O when she saw Wise William's wife,
  The Queen fell on her knee :
'Win up, win up, madam !' she says :
  'What needs this courtesie ? '—

XXI

'O out o' this I winna rise,
  Till a boon ye grant to me ;
To change your lass for this lad bairn,
  King Honour left me wi'.

XXII

'And ye maun learn my gay goss-hawk
  Right weel to breast a steed ;
And I sall learn your turtle dow
  As weel to write and read.

XXIII

'And ye maun learn my gay goss-hawk
  To wield both bow and brand ;
And I sall learn your turtle dow
  To lay gowd wi' her hand.

dow] dove.   lay gowd] embroider in gold.

XXIV

' At kirk and market when we meet,
 We'll dare make nae avowe,
But—" Dame, how does my gay goss-hawk ? "
 " Madame, how does my dow ? " '

XXV

When days were gane, and years came on,
 Wise William he thought lang ;
And he has ta'en King Honour's son
 A-hunting for to gang.

XXVI

It sae fell out, at this hunting,
 Upon a simmer's day,
That they came by a fair castell,
 Stood on a sunny brae.

XXVII

' O dinna ye see that bonny castell,
 Wi' halls and towers sae fair ?
Gin ilka man had back his ain,
 Of it you suld be heir.'—

XXVIII

' How I suld be heir of that castell,
 In sooth, I canna see ;
For it belangs to Fause Foodrage,
 And he is na kin to me.'—

XXIX

' O gin ye suld kill him, Fause Foodrage,
 You would do but what was right ;
For I wot he kill'd your father dear,
 Or ever ye saw the light.

FAUSE FOODRAGE

XXX

'And gin ye suld kill him, Fause Foodrage,
   There is no man durst you blame;
For he keeps your mother a prisoner,
   And she darna take ye hame.'—

XXXI

The boy stared wild like a gray goss-hawk;
   Says—'What may a' this mean?'—
'My boy, ye are King Honour's son,
   And your mother 's our lawful Queen.'—

XXXII

'O gin I be King Honour's son,
   By Our Ladye I swear,
This night I will that traitor slay,
   And relieve my mother dear!'—

XXXIII

He has set his bent bow to his breast,
   And leaped the castell wa';
And soon he has seized on Fause Foodrage,
   Wha loud for help 'gan ca'.

XXXIV

'O haud your tongue, now, Fause Foodrage,
   Frae me ye shanna flee!'—
Syne pierced him through the fause, fause heart,
   And set his mother free.

XXXV

And he has rewarded Wise William
   Wi' the best half of his land;
And sae has he the turtle dow,
   Wi' the truth o' his right hand.

313

I

IT was a knight in Scotland born,
  Follow, my love, come over the strand—
Was taken prisoner and left forlorn,
    Even by the good Earl of Northumberland.

II

Then was he cast in prison strong,
  Follow, my love, come over the strand—
Where he could not walk nor lie along,
    Even by the good Earl of Northumberland.

III

And as in sorrow thus he lay,
  Follow, my love, come over the strand—
The Earl's sweet daughter walk'd that way,
    And she the faire flower of Northumberland.

IV

And loud to her this knight did crie,
  Follow, my love, come over the strand—
The salt teares standing in his eye,
    And she the faire flower of Northumberland.

V

'Faire lady,' he said, 'take pity on me,
  Follow, my love, come over the strand—
And let me not in prison dee,
    And you the faire flower of Northumberland.'—

VI

'Faire sir, how should I take pity on thee?
  Follow, my love, come over the strand—
Thou being a foe to our countrie,
    And I the faire flower of Northumberland.'

dee] die.

314

VII

'Faire lady, I am no foe,' he said,
 Follow, my love, come over the strand—
'Through thy sweet love here was I stay'd,
 For thee, the faire flower of Northumberland.'—

VIII

'Why shouldst thou come here for love of me,
 Follow, my love, come over the strand—
Having wife and children in thy countrie?
 —And I the faire flower of Northumberland.'—

IX

'I swear by the blessèd Trinitie,
 Follow, my love, come over the strand—
I have no wife nor children, I,
 But I'll make you my ladye in faire Scotland.

X

'I swear by Him that was crown'd with thorn,
 Follow, my love, come over the strand—
That I never had wife since the day I was born,
 But I live a free lord in faire Scotland.'—

XI

She stole from her father's pillow the key,
 Follow, my love, come over the strand—
And soon out of prison she's set him free
 To wend with her into faire Scotland.

XII

Likewise much gold she got by sleight,
 Follow, my love, come over the strand—
And all to help this forlorne knight
 To wend from her father to faire Scotland.

XIII

She 's led him down to her father's stable,
Follow, my love, come over the strand—
And she 's stolen two steeds both wight and able,
To carry them on to faire Scotland.

XIV

They rode till they came to a water clear,
Follow, my love, come over the strand—
' Good Sir, how should I follow you here,
And I the faire flower of Northumberland ?

XV

' The water is rough and wonderful steepe,
Follow, my love, come over the strand—
And on my saddle I shall not keepe,
And I the faire flower of Northumberland.'—

XVI

' Fear not the ford, faire lady,' quoth he,
Follow, my love, come over the strand—
' For long I cannot stay for thee,
And thou the faire flower of Northumberland.'

XVII

From top to toe all wet was she :
Follow, my love, come over the strand—
' This have I done for love of thee,
And I the faire flower of Northumberland.'

XVIII

They rode till they came to a Scottish moss,
Follow, my love, come over the strand—
He bade her light off from her father's horse,
Says, ' Go, get you back to Northumberland.

wight] sturdy.

XIX

'For I have a wife and children five,
  Follow, my love, come over the strand—
In Edenborrow they be alive,
  So get thee home to Northumberland.'—

XX

'Have pity on me as I had it on thee !
  Follow, my love, come over the strand—
A cook in your kitchen I will be,
  Even I, the faire flower of Northumberland.

XXI

'Or take me by the body so meek,
  Follow, my love, come over the strand—
And throw me in the water so deep,
  For I darena go back to Northumberland.'

XXII

He turn'd him around and he thought of a plan,
  Follow, my love, come over the strand—
He bought an old horse and he hired an old man
  To carry her back to Northumberland.

XXIII

When she came thro' her father's ha',
  Follow, my love, come over the strand—
She louted her low amongst them a',
  She was the faire flower of Northumberland.

XXIV

Down came her father, he saw her and smiled,
  Follow, my love, come over the strand—
'You arena the first the false Scots have beguiled,
  And ye're aye welcome back to Northumberland !'

louted] bowed.

I

A FAIR maid sat in her bower-door,
    Wringing her lily hands,
And by it came a sprightly youth,
    Fast tripping o'er the strands.

II

'Where gang ye, young John,' she says,
    'Sae early in the day?
It gars me think, by your fast trip,
    Your journey's far away.'

III

He turn'd about wi' a surly look,
    And said, 'What's that to thee?
I'm gaen to see a lovely maid,
    Mair fairer far than ye.'—

IV

'Now hae ye play'd me this, fause love,
    In simmer, 'mid the flowers?
I shall repay ye back again,
    In winter, 'mid the showers.

V

'But again, dear love, and again, dear love,
    Will ye not turn again?
For as ye look to other women,
    Sall I to other men.'—

VI

'Go make your choice of whom you please,
    For I my choice will have;
I've chosen a maid more fair than thee,
    I never will deceive.'

VII

She 's kilted up her claithing fine,
  And after him gaed she;
But aye he said, ' Ye'll turn again,
  Nae farther gang wi' me.'—

VIII

' But again, dear love, and again, dear love,
  Will ye ne'er love me again?
Alas, for loving you sae well,
  And you nae me again!'

IX

The firstan town that they cam' till,
  He bought her brooch and ring;
And aye he bade her turn again,
  And nae farther gang wi' him.

X

' But again, dear love, and again, dear love,
  Will ye ne'er love me again?
Alas, for loving you sae well,
  And you nae me again!'

XI

The nextan town that they cam' till,
  He bought her muff and gloves;
But aye he bade her turn again,
  And choose some other loves.

XII

' But again, dear love, and again, dear love,
  Will ye ne'er love me again?
Alas, for loving you sae well,
  And you nae me again!'

319

XIII

The nextan town that they cam' till,
　　His heart it grew mair fain,
And he was as deep in love wi' her
　　As she was ower again.

XIV

The nextan town that they cam' till,
　　He bought her wedding gown,
And made her lady of ha's and bowers,
　　Into sweet Berwick town.

73. *Lady Maisry*

I

THE young lords o' the north country
　　Have all a-wooing gone,
To win the love of Lady Maisry,
　　But o' them she wou'd hae none.

II

O they hae courted Lady Maisry
　　Wi' a' kin kind of things ;
An' they hae sought her Lady Maisry
　　Wi' brooches an' wi' rings.

III

An' they ha' sought her Lady Maisry
　　Frae father and frae mother ;
An' they ha' sought her Lady Maisry
　　Frae sister an' frae brother.

IV

An' they ha' follow'd her Lady Maisry
   Thro' chamber an' thro' ha';
But a' that they cou'd say to her,
   Her answer still was Na.

V

'O haud your tongues, young men,' she says,
   ' An' think nae mair o' me;
For I've gi'en my love to an English lord,
   An' think nae mair o' me.'

VI

Her father's kitchy-boy heard that,
   An ill death may he dee!
An' he is on to her brother,
   As fast as gang cou'd he.

VII

'O is my father an' my mother well,
   But an' my brothers three?
Gin my sister Lady Maisry be well,
   There 's naething can ail me.'—

VIII

'Your father an' your mother is well,
   But an' your brothers three;
Your sister Lady Maisry 's well,
   So big wi' bairn gangs she.'

IX

' Gin this be true you tell to me,
   My malison light on thee!
But gin it be a lie you tell,
   You sal be hangit hie.'

LADY MAISRY

X

He 's done him to his sister's bow'r,
 Wi' meikle doole an' care ;
An' there he saw her Lady Maisry
 Kaiming her yellow hair.

XI

' O wha is aught that bairn,' he says,
 ' That ye sae big are wi' ?
And gin ye winna own the truth,
 This moment ye sall dee.'

XII

She turn'd her right and roun' about,
 An' the kame fell frae her han' ;
A trembling seiz'd her fair body,
 An' her rosy cheek grew wan.

XIII

' O pardon me, my brother dear,
 An' the truth I'll tell to thee ;
My bairn it is to Lord William,
 An' he is betroth'd to me.'—

XIV

' O cou'd na ye gotten dukes, or lords,
 Intill your ain country,
That ye draw up wi' an English dog,
 To bring this shame on me ?

XV

' But ye maun gi' up the English lord,
 Whan your young babe is born ;
For, gin you keep by him an hour langer,
 Your life sall be forlorn.'—

aught] owed. forlorn] lost to you.

322

XVI

'I will gi' up this English blood,
　Till my young babe be born;
But the never a day nor hour langer,
　Tho' my life should be forlorn.'—

XVII

'O whare is a' my merry young men,
　Whom I gi' meat and fee,
To pu' the thistle and the thorn,
　To burn this woman wi'?'—

XVIII

She turn'd her head on her left shoulder,
　Saw her girdle hang on a tree;
'O God bless them wha gave me that,
　They'll never give more to me.

XIX

'O whare will I get a bonny boy,
　To help me in my need,
To rin wi' haste to Lord William,
　And bid him come wi' speed?'—

XX

O out it spake a bonny boy,
　Stood by her brother's side:
'O I would run your errand, lady,
　O'er a' the world sae wide.

XXI

'Aft have I run your errands, lady,
　Whan blawn baith win' and weet;
But now I'll rin your errand, lady,
　Wi' saut tears on my cheek.'

LADY MAISRY

O whan he came to broken briggs,
    He bent his bow and swam,
An' whan he came to the green grass growin',
    He slack'd his shoone and ran.

O whan he came to Lord William's gates,
    He baed na to chap or ca',
But set his bent bow till his breast,
    An' lightly lap' the wa' ;
An', or the porter was at the gate,
    The boy was i' the ha'.

' O is my biggins broken, boy ?
    Or is my towers won ?
Or is my lady lighter yet,
    Of a dear daughter or son ?' —

' Your biggin is na broken, sir,
    Nor is your towers won ;
But the fairest lady in a' the land
    For you this day maun burn.'—

' O saddle me the black, the black,
    Or saddle me the brown ;
O saddle me the swiftest steed
    That ever rade frae a town ! '

bred] abode, tarried.   chap] knock.   biggins] buildings.

LADY MAISRY

XXVII

Or he was near a mile awa',
  She heard his wild horse sneeze:
'Mend up the fire, my false brother,
  It 's na come to my knees.'

XXVIII

O whan he lighted at the gate,
  She heard his bridle ring;
'Mend up the fire, my false brother,
  It 's far yet frae my chin.

XXIX

'Mend up the fire to me, brother,
  Mend up the fire to me;
For I see him comin' hard an' fast,
  Will soon mend it up to thee.

XXX

'O gin my hands had been loose, Willy,
  Sae hard as they are boun',
I would have turn'd me frae the gleed,
  And casten out your young son.'—

XXXI

'O I'll gar burn for you, Maisry,
  Your father an' your mother;
An' I'll gar burn for you, Maisry,
  Your sister an' your brother.

XXXII

'An' I'll gar burn for you, Maisry,
  The chief of a' your kin;
An' the last bonfire that I come to,
  Mysel' I will cast in.'

gleed] glowing fire, embers.

74

Bonny Bee Ho'm

I

BY Arthur's Dale as late I went
　　I heard a heavy moan;
I heard a ladie lamenting sair,
　　And ay she cried ' Ohone !

II

' Ohone, alas ! what shall I do,
　　Tormented night and day !
I never loved a love but ane,
　　And now he 's gone away.

III

' But I will do for my true-love
　　What ladies wou'd think sair ;
For seven year shall come and go
　　Ere a kaim gang in my hair.

IV

' There shall neither a shoe gang on my foot,
　　Nor a kaim gang in my hair,
Nor e'er a coal nor candle-light
　　Shine in my bower nae mair.'

V

She thought her love had been on the sea,
　　Fast sailing to Bee Ho'm ;
But he was in a quiet cham'er,
　　Hearing his ladie's moan.

VI

' Be husht, be husht, my ladie dear,
　　I pray thee mourn not so ;
For I am deep sworn on a book
　　To Bee Ho'm for to go.'

kaim] comb.　　　cham'er] chamber.

BONNY BEE HO'M

VII

She has gien him a chain of the beaten gowd,
    And a ring with a ruby stone :
' As lang as this chain your body binds,
    Your blude can never be drawn.

VIII

' But gin this ring shou'd fade or fail,
    Or the stone shou'd change its hue,
Be sure your love is dead and gone,
    Or she has proved untrue.'

IX

He had no been at Bonny Bee Ho'm
    A twelve month and a day,
Till, looking on his gay gowd ring,
    The stone grew dark and gray.

X

' O ye take my riches to Bee Ho'm,
    And deal them presentlie,
To the young that canna, the auld that maunna,
    And the blind that does not see.

XI

' Fight on, fight on, my merry men all !
    With you I'll fight no more ;
But I will gang to some holy place
    And pray to the King of Glore.'

Glore] Glory.

327

75

Sir Patrick Spens

1. *The Sailing.*

I

THE king sits in Dunfermline town
　　Drinking the blude-red wine;
' O whare will I get a skeely skipper
　　To sail this new ship o' mine?'

II

O up and spak an eldern knight,
　　Sat at the king's right knee:
' Sir Patrick Spens is the best sailor
　　That ever sail'd the sea.'

III

Our king has written a braid letter,
　　And seal'd it with his hand,
And sent it to Sir Patrick Spens,
　　Was walking on the strand.

IV

' To Noroway, to Noroway,
　　To Noroway o'er the faem;
The king's daughter o' Noroway,
　　'Tis thou must bring her hame.'

V

The first word that Sir Patrick read
　　So loud, loud laugh'd he;
The neist word that Sir Patrick read
　　The tear blinded his e'e.

VI

' O wha is this has done this deed
　　And tauld the king o' me,
To send us out, at this time o' year,
　　To sail upon the sea?

　　　　skeely] skilful.

SIR PATRICK SPENS

VII

'Be it wind, be it weet, be it hail, be it sleet,
  Our ship must sail the faem ;
The king's daughter o' Noroway,
  'Tis we must fetch her hame.'

VIII

They hoysed their sails on Monenday morn
  Wi' a' the speed they may ;
They hae landed in Noroway
  Upon a Wodensday.

II. *The Return.*

IX

'Mak ready, mak ready, my merry men a' !
  Our gude ship sails the morn.'—
'Now ever alack, my master dear,
  I fear a deadly storm.

X

'I saw the new moon late yestreen
  Wi' the auld moon in her arm ;
And if we gang to sea, master,
  I fear we'll come to harm.'

XI

They hadna sail'd a league, a league,
  A league but barely three,
When the lift grew dark, and the wind blew loud,
  And gurly grew the sea.

lift] sky.

M 3

XII

The ankers brak, and the topmast lap,
    It was sic a deadly storm :
And the waves cam owre the broken ship
    Till a' her sides were torn.

XIII

' O where will I get a gude sailor
    To tak' my helm in hand,
Till I get up to the tall topmast
    To see if I can spy land ? '—

XIV

' O here am I, a sailor gude,
    To tak' the helm in hand,
Till you go up to the tall topmast,
    But I fear you'll ne'er spy land.'

XV

He hadna gane a step, a step,
    A step but barely ane,
When a bolt flew out of our goodly ship,
    And the saut sea it came in.

XVI

' Go fetch a web o' the silken claith,
    Another o' the twine,
And wap them into our ship's side,
    And let nae the sea come in.'

XVII

They fetch d a web o' the silken claith,
    Another o' the twine,
And they wapp'd them round that gude ship's side,
    But still the sea came in.

      lap] sprang.   wap] wrap.

SIR PATRICK SPENS

XVIII

O laith, laith were our gude Scots lords
  To wet their cork-heel'd shoon ;
But lang or a' the play was play'd
  They wat their hats aboon.

XIX

And mony was the feather bed
  That flatter'd on the faem ;
And mony was the gude lord's son
  That never mair cam hame.

XX

O lang, lang may the ladies sit,
  Wi' their fans into their hand,
Before they see Sir Patrick Spens
  Come sailing to the strand !

XXI

And lang, lang may the maidens sit
  Wi' their gowd kames in their hair,
A-waiting for their ain dear loves !
  For them they'll see nae mair.

XXII

Half-owre, half-owre to Aberdour,
  'Tis fifty fathoms deep ;
And there lies gude Sir Patrick Spens,
  Wi' the Scots lords at his feet !

flatter'd] tossed afloat.   kames] combs.

The Lord of Lorn

I

IT was the worthy Lord of Lorn,
He was a lord of high degree;
And he has set his one young son
    To school, to learn civility.

II

He learn'd more learning in one day
    Than other children did in three;
And then bespake the schoolmaster,
    Unto the heir of Lorn said he:

III

'In faith thou are the honestest boy
    That ere I blinkt on with mine e'e;
I think thou be some easterling born,
    The Holy Ghost it is with thee.'

IV

He said he was no easterling born,
    The child thus answer'd courteouslye:
'My father he is the Lord of Lorn,
    And I his one young son, perdie.'

V

The schoolmaster turn'd round about,
    His angry mind he could not 'swage;
He marvell'd the child could speak so wise,
    He being of so tender age.

VI

He girt the saddle to the steed,
    A golden bridle done him upon;
He took his leave of his schoolfellows,
    And home this Child of Lorn has gone.

THE LORD OF LORN

VII

And when he came to his father dear
    He kneelèd down upon his knee:
'God's blessing, father, I would ask,
    If Christ would grant you to give it me.'—

VIII

'Now God thee bless, my son, my heir,
    His servant in heaven that thou may be!
What tidings hast thou brought me, child?
    Thou art comen home so hastilye.'—

IX

'Good tidings, father, I have you brought,
    Good tidings I hope it is to thee;
There's never a book in all Scotland
    But I can read it truëlye.'

X

A joyèd man his father was
    All in the place where he did stand:
'My son, thou shalt go into France,
    To learn the speeches of ilka land.'

XI

'Who shall go with him?' said his lady;
    'Husband, we have no more but he.'—
'Madam,' he saith, 'my hend steward,
    For he hath been true to you and me.'

XII

She call'd the steward to an account,
    A thousand pound she gave him anon;
Says, 'Steward, I'll give thee as mickle more
    If thou be as good to my one son.'—

hend] courteous.

333

XIII

' If I be false unto my young lord,
　Then God be the like to me indeed ! '
—So now to France they both are gone,
　And the God [of Heaven] be their good speed !

XIV

Over the sea into France land
　They had not been three weeks to an end,
But meat and drink the child got none,
　Nor penny of money in purse to spend.

XV

The child ran to a river's side ;
　He was fain to drink the water thin ;
And after follow'd the false steward
　To drown the bonny boy therein.

XVI

' But nay, by Mary ! ' said the child,
　He askèd mercy pitifullye ;
' Good Steward, let me have my life,
　And all I have I will give to thee ! '

XVII

Mercy to him the steward did take,
　And pull'd the child out o'er the brim
But, ever alack, the more pitye !
　He took his clothing even from him.

XVIII

Says, ' Do thou me off that velvet gown,
　The crimson hose beneath thy knee,
And do me off thy cordinant shoon
　That are buckled with the gold so free.

cordinant] of Cordovan leather.

334

XIX

'Do thou me off thy satin doublèt,
  Thy shirtband wrought wi' glisterin' gold,
And do me off thy golden chain
  About thy neck with many a fold.

XX

'And do me off thy velvet hat,
  With feather in it that is so fine ;
And all unto thy silken shirt,
  That's work'd with many a golden seam.'

XXI

But when the child was naked stript,
  With skin as white as the lily-flow'r,
He might, for his body and his bewtie,
  Have been a princess' paramour.

XXII

He put him in an old kelter coat,
  And hose of the same above the knee,
And he bade him go to a shepherd's house,
  To tend sheep on a lonely lee.

XXIII

The child said, 'What shall be my name ?
  Prithee, good Steward, tell to me.'—
'Thy name shall be Poor Disaware,
  To tend sheep on a lonely lee.'

XXIV

The child came to the shepherd's house—
  O Lord ! he weepèd pitifullye—
Says, 'Do you not want a servant-boy,
  To tend your sheep on a lonely lee ?'

kelter] of undyed wool.

335

XXV

'I have no child,' the shepherd said,
 'My boy, thou'st tarry and dwell with me;
My living, my house, but and my goods,
 I'll make thee heir of them all, perdie.'

XXVI

And then bespake the shepherd's wife
 Unto the child so tenderlye:
'Thou must take the sheep and go to the field,
 And tend them upon the lonely lee.'

XXVII

Now let us leave talk of the child
 That is tending sheep on the lonely lee,
And we'll talk more of the false steward,
 Of him and of his treacherye.

XXVIII

He bought himself a suit of apparel
 That any lord might a-seem'd to worn;
He went a-wooing to the Duke's daughter,
 And call'd himself the Lord of Lorn.

XXIX

The Duke he welcomed the [brisk] young lord
 With three baked stags and the Rhenish wine:
If he had wist him the false steward,
 With the devil he'd have bade him dine.

XXX

But when they were at supper set
 With dainty delicates that was there,
The Duke said, 'If thou'lt wed my daughter
 I'll give thee a thousand pound a year.'

THE LORD OF LORN

XXXI

Then hand in hand the steward her took,
  And plight that lady his troth alone,
That she should be his married wife,
  And he would make her the Lady of Lorn.

XXXII

The lady would see the roebuck run
  Up hills and dales and the forest free,
When she was 'ware of a shepherd's boy
  Was tending sheep on a lonely lee.

XXXIII

And ever he sigh'd and made his moan
  [Unto himself] most pitifullye,
'My father is the Lord of Lorn,
  And knows not what's become of me!'

XXXIV

O then bespake the lady gay
  And to her maid she spake anon,
'Go fetch me hither yon shepherd's boy:
  I'll know why he doth make his moan.'

XXXV

But when he came to that lady fair
  He fell down low upon his knee;
He was [of birth and] so brought up
  He needed not to learn courtesye.

XXXVI

'What is thy name?   Where wast thou born?
  For whose sake makest thou this moan?'—
'I am Poor Disaware, in Scotland born,
  And I mourn one dead these years agone.'—

337

XXXVII

‘ Tell me [of Scotland], thou bonny child,
  Tell me the truth and do not lee :
Knowest thou there the young Lord of Lorn ?
  He is come into France a-wooing of me.’—

XXXVIII

‘ Yes, that I do, madam,’ he said,
  ‘ I know that lord, yea, verilye ;
The Lord of Lorn is a worthy lord,
  If he were at home in his own countrye.’—

XXXIX

‘ Wilt leave thy sheep, thou bonny child,
  And come in service unto me ? ’—
‘ [I thank you, madam]; yea, forsooth,
  And at your bidding I will be.’

XL

When the steward look’d upon the child
  He ’gan bewrail him villainouslye :
‘ Where wast thou born, thou vagabone ?
  Thou art a thief, I will prove thee.’

XLI

‘ Ha’ done ! ha’ done ! ’ said the lady gay,
  ‘ Peace, Lord of Lorn, I do pray thee !
Without you bear him more good will,
  No favour will you get of me.’

XLII

O then bespake the false steward,
  ‘ Believe me or no, I tell to thee,
At Aberdonie, beyond the seas,
  His father robbèd thousands three.’

bewrail] rail at.

THE LORD OF LORN

But then bespake the Duke of France
   (The child was pleasant to his e'e),
Says, ' Boy, if thou love horses well,
   My groom of stables thou shalt be.'

The child applied his office so well
   Till that twelve months drew to an end ;
He was so courteous and so true
   That every man became his friend.

He led a gelding forth one morning,
   To water him at the water so free—
The gelding up, and with his head
   He hit the child above the e'e.

' Woe worth thee, gelding ! ' said the child,
   ' Woe worth the mare that foalèd thee !
Thou little knowest the Lord of Lorn :
   Thou'st stricken a lord of high degree.'

The lady was in her garden green,
   And heard the child that made this moan :
All weeping [straight] she ran to him
   And left her maidens all alone.

' Sing on thy song, thou stable groom,
   I will release thee of thy pain.'—
' Nay, lady, I have made an oath ;
   I dare not tell my tale again.'—

XLIX

' Sing on thy song, then, to thy gelding,
  And so thy oath shall savèd be.'—
But when he told his horse the tale,
  O the lady wept full tenderlye.

L

She sent in for her father the Duke:
  ' O sick I am, and like to dee !
Put off my wedding, father,' she said,
  ' For the love of God, these monthës three.'

LI

The lady she did write à letter
  Full speedily with her own hand ;
She has sent it to the Lord of Lorn
  Wheras he dwelt in fair Scotland.

LII

When the Lord of Lorn had read the letter
  His lady wept, Lord ! bitterlye ;
' Peace, Lady of Lorn, for Christ his love !
  And wroken upon him I will be.'

LIII

The old lord call'd up his merry men,
  And all that he gave cloth and fee,
With seven lords to ride beside him,
  And into the land of France rides he.

LIV

The wind was good, and they did sail
  Five hundred men into France land,
Till they were 'ware of the Heir of Lorn,
  Stood with a porter's staff in 's hand.

wroken] revenged.

LV

The lords then cast their hats into air,
    The serving-men fell on their knee.
' What fools be yonder,' said the steward,
    ' That makes the porter courtesye ? '

LVI

' Thou 'rt a false thief,' said the Lord of Lorn,
    ' [This child, thy master] to betray ! '
And they set the castle round about,
    A swallow could not have flown away.

LVII

And when they had taken the false steward,
    By the law of France all hastilye
A quest of lords there chosen was
    That judged this traitor he must dee.

LVIII

First they took him and hang'd him half,
    And then they lat him down anon,
And quarter'd and put him in boiling lead,
    And there he was sodden, breast and bone.

LIX

O then bespake the Lord of Lorn,
    With many other lordës mo,
' Sir Duke, if you be as willing as we,
    We'll have a marriage before we go.'

LX

But then bespake the Duke of France,
    Unto the Child of Lorn right there :
Says, ' Heir of Lorn, if thou'lt marry my daughter,
    I'll mend thy living a thousand a year.'

341

LXI

But then bespake that Child of Lorn,
  And answer'd the Duke right merrilye:
' I had rather have her with a ring of gold
  Than all the gold you can proffer to me.'

77. *Edom o' Gordon*

I

IT fell about the Martinmas,
  When the wind blew shrill and cauld,
Said Edom o' Gordon to his men,
  ' We maun draw to a hauld.

II

' And what a hauld sall we draw to,
  My merry men and me?
We will gae to the house o' the Rodes,
  To see that fair ladye.'

III

The lady stood on her castle wa',
  Beheld baith dale and down;
There she was 'ware of a host of men
  Cam' riding towards the town.

IV

' O see ye not, my merry men a',
  O see ye not what I see?
Methinks I see a host of men;
  I marvel wha they be.'

hauld] place of shelter.   town] stead.

EDOM O' GORDON

V

She ween'd it had been her lovely lord,
    As he cam riding hame;
It was the traitor, Edom o' Gordon,
    Wha reck'd nae sin nor shame.

VI

She had nae sooner buskit hersell,
    And putten on her gown,
But Edom o' Gordon an' his men
    Were round about the town.

VII

They had nae sooner supper set,
    Nae sooner said the grace,
But Edom o' Gordon an' his men
    Were lighted about the place.

VIII

The lady ran up to her tower-head,
    Sae fast as she could hie,
To see if by her fair speeches
    She could wi' him agree.

IX

' Come doun to me, ye lady gay,
    Come doun, come doun to me;
This night sall ye lig within mine arms,
    To-morrow my bride sall be.'—

X

' I winna come down, ye fals Gordon,
    I winna come down to thee;
I winna forsake my ain dear lord,
    That is sae far frae me.'—

buskit] attired.

EDOM O' GORDON

XI

'Gie owre your house, ye lady fair,
    Gie owre your house to me ;
Or I sall brenn yoursel therein,
    But and your babies three.'—

XII

'I winna gie owre, ye fals Gordon,
    To nae sic traitor as yee ;
And if ye brenn my ain dear babes,
    My lord sall mak ye dree.

XIII

'Now reach my pistol, Glaud, my man,
    And charge ye weel my gun ;
For, but an I pierce that bluidy butcher,
    My babes, we been undone ! '

XIV

She stood upon her castle wa',
    And let twa bullets flee :
She miss'd that bluidy butcher's heart,
    And only razed his knee.

XV

'Set fire to the house ! ' quo' fals Gordon,
    All wud wi' dule and ire :
'Fals lady, ye sall rue this deid
    As ye brenn in the fire ! '—

XVI

'Wae worth, wae worth ye, Jock, my man !
    I paid ye weel your fee ;
Why pu' ye out the grund-wa' stane,
    Lets in the reek to me ?

dree] suffer.   wud] mad.   grund-wa'] ground-wall.

EDOM O' GORDON

' And e'en wae worth ye, Jock, my man!
    I paid ye weel your hire;
Why pu' ye out the grund-wa' stane,
    To me lets in the fire?'—

' Ye paid me weel my hire, ladye,
    Ye paid me weel my fee:
But now I'm Edom o' Gordon's man,
    Maun either do or dee.'

O then bespake her little son,
    Sat on the nurse's knee:
Says, ' Mither dear, gie owre this house,
    For the reek it smithers me.'—

' I wad gie a' my gowd, my bairn,
    Sae wad I a' my fee,
For ae blast o' the western wind,
    To blaw the reek frae thee.'

O then bespake her dochter dear—
    She was baith jimp and sma':
' O row me in a pair o' sheets,
    And tow me owre the wa'!'

They row'd her in a pair o' sheets,
    And tow'd her owre the wa';
But on the point o' Gordon's spear
    She gat a deadly fa'.

jimp] slender, trim.   row] wrap.

XXIII

O bonnie, bonnie was her mouth,
    And cherry were her cheiks,
And clear, clear was her yellow hair,
    Whereon the red blood dreips.

XXIV

Then wi' his spear he turn'd her owre ;
    O gin her face was wane !
He said, ' Ye are the first that e'er
    I wish'd alive again.'

XXV

He turn'd her owre and owre again ;
    O gin her skin was white !
' I might hae spared that bonnie face
    To hae been some man's delight.

XXVI

' Busk and boun, my merry men a',
    For ill dooms I do guess ;
I canna look in that bonnie face
    As it lies on the grass.'—

XXVII

' Wha looks to freits, my master dear,
    It 's freits will follow them ;
Let it ne'er be said that Edom o' Gordon
    Was daunted by a dame.'

XXVIII

But when the lady saw the fire
    Come flaming owre her head,
She wept, and kiss'd her children twain,
    Says, ' Bairns, we been but dead.'

Busk and boun] trim up and prepare to go.   freits] ill omens.

XXIX

The Gordon then his bugle blew,
    And said, ' Awa', awa' !
This house o' the Rodes is a' in a flame ;
    I hauld it time to ga'.'

XXX

And this way lookit her ain dear lord,
    As he cam owre the lea ;
He saw his castle a' in a lowe,
    As far as he could see.

XXXI

Then sair, O sair, his mind misgave,
    And all his heart was wae :
' Put on, put on, my wighty men,
    Sae fast as ye can gae.

XXXII

' Put on, put on, my wighty men,
    Sae fast as ye can drie !
For he that 's hindmost o' the thrang
    Sall ne'er get good o' me.'

XXXIII

Then some they rade, and some they ran,
    Out-owre the grass and bent ;
But ere the foremost could win up,
    Baith lady and babes were brent.

XXXIV

And after the Gordon he is gane,
    Sae fast as he might drie ;
And soon i' the Gordon's foul heart's blude
    He 's wroken his dear ladye.

lowe] flame.   wighty] sturdy, active.   wroken] avenged.

78

Lamkin

I

I T 's Lamkin was a mason good
As ever built wi' stane ;
He built Lord Wearie's castle,
But payment got he nane.

II

'O pay me, Lord Wearie,
Come, pay to me my fee.'—
'I canna pay you, Lamkin,
For I maun gang o'er the sea.'—

III

'O pay me now, Lord Wearie,
Come, pay me out o' hand.'—
'I canna pay you, Lamkin,
Unless I sell my land.'—

IV

'O gin ye winna pay me,
I here sall mak' a vow,
Before that ye come hame again,
Ye sall hae cause to rue.'

V

Lord Wearie got a bonny ship,
To sail the saut sea faem ;
Bade his lady weel the castle keep,
Ay till he should come hame.

VI

'Gae bar the doors,' the lady said,
'Gae well the windows pin ;
And what care I for Lamkin
Or any of his gang ?'

LAMKIN

VII

But the nourice was a fause limmer
  As e'er hung on a tree;
She laid a plot wi' Lamkin,
  Whan her lord was o'er the sea.

VIII

She laid a plot wi' Lamkin,
  When the servants were awa',
Loot him in at a little shot-window,
  And brought him to the ha'.

IX

' O whare 's a' the men o' this house,
  That ca' me the Lamkin ? '—
' They're at the barn-well thrashing ;
  'Twill be lang ere they come in.'—

X

' And whare 's the women o' this house,
  That ca' me the Lamkin ? '—
' They're at the far well washing ;
  'Twill be lang ere they come in.'—

XI

' And whare 's the bairns o' this house,
  That ca' me the Lamkin ? '—
' They're at the school reading ;
  'Twill be night or they come hame.'—

XII

' O whare 's the lady o' this house,
  That ca's me the Lamkin ? '—
' She 's up in her bower sewing,
  But we soon can bring her down.

limmer] wretch, jade.   shot-window] a window opening on
a hinge.

LAMKIN

XIII

Then Lamkin 's tane a sharp knife,
    That hung down by his gare,
And he has gi'en the bonny babe
    A deep wound and a sair.

XIV

Then Lamkin he rockèd,
    And the fause nourice sang,
Till frae ilka bore o' the cradle
    The red blood out sprang.

XV

Then out it spak' the lady,
    As she stood on the stair:
'What ails my bairn, nourice,
    That he 's greeting sae sair?

XVI

'O still my bairn, nourice,
    O still him wi' the pap!'—
'He winna still, lady,
    For this nor for that.'—

XVII

'O still my bairn, nourice,
    O still him wi' the wand!'—·
'He winna still, lady,
    For a' his father's land.'—

XVIII

'O still my bairn, nourice,
    O still him wi' the bell!'—
'He winna still, lady,
    Till ye come down yoursel'.'—

gare] a seam of the skirt.   bore] hole, crevice.   greeting]
wailing, crying.

LAMKIN

O the firsten step she steppit,
  She steppit on a stane;
But the neisten step she steppit,
  She met him Lamkin.

XX

O mercy, mercy, Lamkin,
  Hae mercy upon me!
Though you hae ta'en my young son's life,
  Ye may let mysel' be.'—

XXI

' O sall I kill her, nourice,
  Or sall I lat her be?'—
'O kill her, kill her, Lamkin,
  For she ne'er was good to me.'—

XXII

' O scour the bason, nourice,
  And mak' it fair and clean,
For to keep this lady's heart's blood,
  For she's come o' noble kin.'—

XXIII

' There need nae bason, Lamkin,
  Lat it run through the floor;
What better is the heart's blood
  O' the rich than o' the poor?'

XXIV

But ere three months were at an end,
  Lord Wearie came again;
But dowie, dowie was his heart
  When first he came hame.

dowie] heavy, sorrowful.

LAMKIN

'O wha's blood is this,' he says,
  'That lies in the cham'er?'—
'It is your lady's heart's blood;
  'Tis as clear as the lamer.'—

'And wha's blood is this,' he says,
  'That lies in my ha'?'—
'It is your young son's heart's blood;
  'Tis the clearest ava'.'

O sweetly sang the black-bird
  That sat upon the tree;
But sairer grat Lamkin,
  When he was condemn'd to dee.

And bonny sang the mavis
  Out o' the thorny brake;
But sairer grat the nourice,
  When she was tied to the stake.

cham'er] chamber.   lamer] amber.   ava'] of all.

79

Hugh of Lincoln

and The Jew's Daughter

I

A' THE boys of merry Lincoln
   Were playing at the ba',
And by it came him sweet Sir Hugh,
  And he play'd o'er them a'.

II

He kick'd the ba' with his right foot,
  And catch'd it wi' his knee,
And thro'-and-thro' the Jew's window
  He gar'd the bonny ba' flee.

III

He's doen him to the Jew's castell,
  And walk'd it round about;
And there he saw the Jew's daughter
  At the window looking out.

IV

'Throw down the ba', ye Jew's daughter,
  Throw down the ba' to me!'——
'Never a bit,' says the Jew's daughter,
  'Till up to me come ye.'——

V

'How will I come up? How can I come up?
  How can I come up to thee?
I winna come up, I darena come up,
  Without my play-feres three.'

VI

She's ta'en her to the Jew's garden,
  Where the grass grew long and green,
She's pu'd an apple red and white
  To wyle the pretty boy in.

ba'] ball, football.   doen] betaken.   play-feres] playfellows.

HUGH OF LINCOLN

She's wyled him in through ae dark door,
    And sae has she through nine;
She's laid him on a dressing table,
    And stickit him like a swine.

And first came out the thick, thick blood,
    And syne came out the thin,
And syne came out the bonny heart's blood;
    There was no more within.

She's row'd him in a cake o' lead,
    Bade him lie still and sleep;
She's thrown him into Our Lady's draw-well,
    Was fifty fathom deep.

When bells were rung, and mass was sung,
    And a' the bairns came hame,
Then every lady had hame her son,
    But Lady Helen had nane.

She's ta'en her mantle her about,
    Her coffer by the hand,
And she's gone out to seek her son,
    And wander'd o'er the land.

She's doen her to the Jew's castell
    Where a' were fast asleep;
Cries, ' Bonnie Sir Hugh, O pretty Sir Hugh,
    I pray you to me speak ! '

row'd] wrapped.

354

HUGH OF LINCOLN

XIII

She near'd Our Lady's deep draw-well,
  And fell down on her knee :
'Where'er ye be, my sweet Sir Hugh,
  I pray you speak to me ! '—

XIV

' O the lead is wondrous heavy, mother,
  The well is wondrous deep ;
The little penknife sticks in my throat,
  And I downa to ye speak.

XV

' Gae hame, gae hame, my mither dear,
  Prepare my winding sheet,
And at the back o' merry Lincoln
  The morn I will you meet.'

XVI

Now Lady Helen is gane hame,
  Made him a winding sheet,
And at the back o' merry Lincoln
  The dead corpse did her meet.

XVII

And a' the bells o' merry Lincoln
  Without men's hands were rung ;
And a' the books o' merry Lincoln
  Were read without man's tongue ;
And never was such a burial
  Sin' Adam's day begun.

downa] cannot, have not the force to.

I

THE bonny heir, and the well-faur'd heir,
   The weary heir o' Linne—
Yonder he stands at his father's yetts,
   And naebody bids him in.

II

'O see for he gangs, and see for he stands,
   The unthrifty heir o' Linne!
O see for he stands on the cauld causey,
   And nane bids him come in!'

III

His father and mother were dead him fro',
   And so was the head o' his kin;
To the cards and dice that he did run,
   Did neither cease nor blin.

IV

To drink the wine that was so clear
   With all he would mak' merrye;
And then bespake him John o' the Scales,
   To the heir of Linne said he:

V

'How doest thou, thou Lord of Linne
   Doest want or gold or fee?
Wilt thou not sell thy lands so broad
   To such a good fellow as me?'

VI

He told the gold upon the board,
   Wanted never a bare pennye:
'The gold is thine, the land is mine,
   The heir of Linne I will be.'

well-faur'd] well-favoured.   yetts] gates.   causey] causeway,
pavement.   blin] stint, check.

VII

'Here 's gold enow,' saith the heir of Linne,
   'For me and my companye.'
He drank the wine that was so clear,
   And with all he made merrye.

VIII

Within three quarters of a year
   His gold it waxèd thin;
His merry men were from him gone,
   Bade him, 'To the de'il ye'se gang!'

IX

'Now well-a-day!' said the heir of Linne,
   'I have left not one pennye.
God be with my father!' he said,
   'On his land he lived merrilye.'

X

His nourice at her window look'd,
   Beholding dale and down,
And she beheld this distress'd young man
   Come walking to the town.

XI

'O see for he gangs, and see for he stands,
   The weary heir o' Linne!
O see for he stands on the cauld causey,
   And nane bids him come in!'—

XII

'Sing owre again that sang, nourice,
   The sang ye sung just now.'—
'I never sung a sang i' my life
   But I would sing owre to you.

357

XIII

'Come here, come here, Willy,' she said,
    'And rest yoursel' wi' me;
I hae seen you in better days,
    And in jovial companye.'—

XIV

'Gie me a sheave o' your bread, nourice,
    And a bottle o' your wine,
And I will pay it you owre again
    When I am Lord of Linne.'—

XV

'Ye'se get a sheave o' my bread, Willy,
    And a bottle o' my wine;
But ye'll pay me when the seas gang dry,
    For ye'll ne'er be Lord o' Linne.'

XVI

Then he turn'd him right and round about,
    As will a woman's son,
And aff he set and bent his way
    And cam' to the house o' Linne.

XVII

But when he cam' to that castle,
    They were set down to dine;
A score of nobles there he saw,
    Sat drinking at their wine.

XVIII

Then some bade gie him beef and fish,
    And some but bane and fin,
And some bade gie him naething at a',
    But let the palmer gang.

sheave] slice.

THE HEIR OF LINNE

Then out it speaks him John o' Scales,
  A saucy word spak' he :
' Put round the cup, give the beggar a sup,
  Let him fare on his way.'

Then out it speaks Sir Ned Magnew,
  Ane o' young Willy's kin :
' This youth was ance a sprightly boy
  As ever lived in Linne.'

He turn'd him right and round about,
  As will a woman's son,
Then minded him on a little wee key
  That his mother left to him.

His mother left him this little wee key
  A little before she deed ;
And bade him keep this little wee key
  Till he was in maist need.

Then forth he went, these nobles left
  All drinking in the room ;
Wi' walking rod intill his hand
  He walk'd the castle roun' :

Till that he found a little door,
  And therein slipp'd the key ;
And there he found three chests in fere
  Of the red and the white monie.

in fere] together.

THE HEIR OF LINNE

XXV

Back then through the nobles a'
  He went and did not blin,
Until he cam' where John o' the Scales
  Was seated [at the wine].

XXVI

Then out and spake it John o' Scales,
  He spake wi' mock and jeer :
'I'd gie a seat to the Lord o' Linne
  If sae be that he were here.

XXVII

'When the lands o' Linne a-selling were
  A' men said they were free ;
I will sell them twenty pound better cheap
  Nor ever I bought of thee.'—

XXVIII

'I tak' ye to witness, nobles a' !
  —He cast him a God's pennye—
'I will buy them twenty pound better cheap
  Nor ever he bought of me.'

XXIX

He's done him to the gaming-table,
  For it stood fair and clean ;
And there he's tould as much rich gold
  As free'd the lands o' Linne.

XXX

He told the gold there over the board,
  Wanted never a broad pennye ;
'The gold is thine, the land is mine,
  Lord o' Linne again I'll be.'

God's pennye] earnest or luck-penny.

XXXI

'Well-a-day!' said John o' the Scales' wife,
  'Well-a-day, and woe is me!
Yesterday I was the Lady o' Linne,
  And now I'm a naebodye!'

XXXII

But 'Fare thee well,' said the heir of Linne,
  'Now John o' the Scales!' said he:
'A curse light on me if ever again
  My lands be in jeopardye!'

81. *Fair Mary of Wallington*

I

WHEN we were silly sisters seven,
  —Sisters were so fair,—
Five of us were brave knights' wives,
  And died in childbed lair.

II

Up then spake Fair Mary,
  Marry wou'd she nane;
If ever she came in man's bed,
  The same gate wad she gang.

III

'Make no vows, Fair Mary,
  For fear they broken be;
Here's been the Knight of Wallington,
  Asking good will of thee.'—

lair] lying-in.   gate] way.

IV

'If here's been the knight, mother,
　　Asking good will of me,
Within three quarters of a year
　　You may come bury me.'

V

But when she came to Wallington,
　　And into Wallington hall,
There she spy'd her [lord's] mother,
　　Walking about the wall.

VI

'You're welcome, welcome, daughter dear,
　　To thy castle and thy bowers.'—
'I thank you kindly, mother,
　　I hope they'll soon be yours.'

VII

She had not been in Wallington
　　Three quarters and a day,
Till upon the ground she could not walk,
　　She was a weary prey.

VIII

She had not been in Wallington
　　Three quarters and a night,
Till on the ground she could not walk,
　　She was a weary wight.

IX

'Is there ne'er a boy into this town,
　　Who'll win him hose and shoon,
That will run to fair Paddington,
　　And bid my mother come?'

X

Up then spake a little boy,
  Near unto her a-kin :
' Full oft I have your errands gone,
  But now I will it run.'

XI

Then she call'd her waiting-maid
  To bring up bread and wine :
' Eat and drink, my bonny boy,
  Thou'll ne'er eat more of mine.

XII

' Give my respects to my mother,
  She sits in her chair of stone,
And ask her how she likes the news,
  Of seven to have but one ?

XIII

' Give my respects to my mother,
  As she sits in her chair of oak,
And bid her come to my sickening,
  Or my merry lake-wake.

XIV

' Give my love to my brothers
  William, Ralph, and John,
And to my sister Betty fair,
  And to her white as bone :

XV

' And bid her keep her maidenhead,
  Be sure [to keep it lang :]
For if e'er she come into man's bed,
  The same gate will she gang.'

lake-wake] lyke-wake, corpse-watching.

FAIR MARY OF WALLINGTON

XVI

Away this little boy is gone,
    As fast as he could run;
When he came where brigs were broke,
    He laid him down and swum.

XVII

When he saw the lady, he said,
    ' Lord may your keeper be ! '—
' What news, my pretty boy,
    Hast thou to tell to me ? '—

XVIII

' Your daughter Mary orders me,
    As you sit in a chair of stone,
To ask you how you like the news,
    Of seven to have but one ?

XIX

' Your daughter gives you her commands,
    As you sit in a chair of oak,
And bids you come to her sickening,
    Or her merry lake-wake.

XX

' She gives command to her brothers
    William, Ralph, and John,
[And] to her sister Betty fair,
    And to her white as bone.

XXI

' She bids her keep her maidenhead,
    Be sure [to keep it lang :]
For if e'er she come into man's bed,
    The same gate will she gang.'

364

XXII

She kickt the table with her foot,
    She kickt it with her knee,
The silver plate into the fire,
    So far she made it flee.

XXIII

Then she call'd her waiting-maid
    To bring her riding-hood,
So did she on her stable-groom
    To bring her riding-steed.

XXIV

' Go saddle to me the black, the black,
    Go saddle to me the brown,
Go saddle to me the swiftest steed
    That e'er rid to Wallington ! '

XXV

When they came to Wallington,
    And into Wallington hall,
There she spy'd her son Fenwick,
    Walking about the wall.

XXVI

' God save you, my dearest son,
    Lord may your keeper be !
Tell me where is my daughter fair,
    That used to walk with thee ? '

XXVII

He turn'd his head him round about,
    The tears did fill his e'e :
' 'Tis a month,' he said, ' since Fair Mary
    Took her chambers from me.'

FAIR MARY OF WALLINGTON

XXVIII

She went on [to her daughter's chamber];
And there were in the hall
Four and twenty ladies,
Letting the tears down fall.

XXIX

Her daughter had a scope into
Her cheek and eke her chin,
All to keep in her dear life
Till her dear mother came.

XXX

'Come take the rings off my fingers,
The skin it is so white,
And give them to my mother dear,
For she was all the wyte.

XXXI

'Come take the rings off my fingers,
The veins they are so red,
Give them to Sir William Fenwick,
I'm sure his heart will bleed.'

XXXII

Then she took out a razor
That was both sharp and fine,
And out of her left side she has taken
The heir of Wallington.

XXXIII

There is a race in Wallington,
And that I rue full sare;
Tho' the cradle it be full spread up,
The bride-bed is left bare.

scope] bandage, gag.   wyte] blame, cause of trouble.

Young Waters

I

ABOUT Yule, when the wind blew cule,
  And the round tables began,
O there is come to our King's court
  Mony a well-favor'd man.

II

The Queen luikt owre the castle-wa'
  Beheld baith dale and down,
And there she saw Young Waters
  Come riding to the town.

III

His footmen they did rin before,
  His horsemen rade behind;
Ane mantel of the burning gowd
  Did keip him frae the wind.

IV

Gowden-graith'd his horse before,
  And siller-shod behind;
The horse Young Waters rade upon
  Was fleeter than the wind.

V

Out then spak' a wylie lord,
  Unto the Queen said he:
'O tell me wha 's the fairest face
  Rides in the company?'—

VI

'I've sene lord, and I've sene laird,
  And knights of high degree,
Bot a fairer face than Young Waters'
  Mine eyne did never see.'

  graith'd] harnessed.

VII

Out then spake the jealous King,
  And an angry man was he :
' O if he had bin twice as fair,
  You micht have excepted me.

VIII

You're neither laird nor lord,' she says,
  ' But the King that wears the crown ;
There is not a knight in fair Scotland
  But to thee maun bow down.'

IX

For a' that she cou'd do or say,
  Appeas'd he wad nae bee,
But for the words which she had said,
  Young Waters he maun dee.

X

They hae ta'en Young Waters,
  And put fetters to his feet ;
They hae ta'en Young Waters, and
  Thrown him in dungeon deep.

XI

' Aft have I ridden thro' Stirling town,
  In the wind but and the weet ;
But I neir rade thro' Stirling town
  Wi' fetters at my feet.

XII

' Aft have I ridden thro' Stirling town,
  In the wind but and the rain ;
But I neir rade thro' Stirling town
  Neir to return again.'

YOUNG WATERS

XIII

They hae ta'en to the heiding-hill
  His young son in his craddle;
And they hae ta'en to the heiding-hill
  His horse but and his saddle.

XIV

They hae ta'en to the heiding-hill
  His lady fair to see;
And for the words the Queen had spoke
  Young Waters he did dee.

83.   *The Queen's Marie*

I

MARIE HAMILTON's to the kirk gane,
  Wi' ribbons in her hair;
The King thought mair o' Marie Hamilton
  Than ony that were there.

II

Marie Hamilton's to the kirk gane
  Wi' ribbons on her breast;
The King thought mair o' Marie Hamilton
  Than he listen'd to the priest.

III

Marie Hamilton's to the kirk gane,
  Wi' gloves upon her hands;
The King thought mair o' Marie Hamilton
  Than the Queen and a' her lands.

heiding-hill] beheading mound.

THE QUEEN'S MARIE

IV

She hadna been about the King's court
  A month, but barely ane,
Till she was beloved by a' the King's court,
  And the King the only man.

V

She hadna been about the King's court
  A month, but barely three,
Till frae the King's court Marie Hamilton,
  Marie Hamilton durstna be.

VI

The King is to the Abbey gane,
  To pu' the Abbey tree,
To scale the babe frae Marie's heart;
  But the thing it wadna be.

VII

O she has row'd it in her apron,
  And set it on the sea—
'Gae sink ye or swim ye, bonny babe,
  Ye'se get nae mair o' me.'

VIII

Word is to the kitchen gane,
  And word is to the ha',
And word is to the noble room
  Amang the ladies a',
That Marie Hamilton's brought to bed,
  And the bonny babe's miss'd and awa'.

scale] drive away, get rid of.   row'd] wrapped.
370

THE QUEEN'S MARIE

IX

Scarcely had she lain down again,
　　And scarcely fa'en asleep,
When up and started our gude Queen
　　Just at her bed-feet;
Saying—'Marie Hamilton, where's your babe?
　　For I am sure I heard it greet.'—

X

'O no, O no, my noble Queen!
　　Think no sic thing to be;
'Twas but a stitch into my side,
　　And sair it troubles me!'—

XI

'Get up, get up, Marie Hamilton:
　　Get up and follow me;
For I am going to Edinburgh town,
　　A rich wedding for to see.'

XII

O slowly, slowly rase she up,
　　And slowly put she on;
And slowly rade she out the way
　　Wi' mony a weary groan.

XIII

The Queen was clad in scarlet,
　　Her merry maids all in green;
And every town that they cam to,
　　They took Marie for the Queen.

XIV

'Ride hooly, hooly, gentlemen,
　　Ride hooly now wi' me!
For never, I am sure, a wearier burd
　　Rade in your companie.'

　　greet] wail, cry.　　hooly] gently.

XV

But little wist Marie Hamilton,
    When she rade on the brown,
That she was gaen to Edinburgh town,
    And a' to be put down.

XVI

'Why weep ye sae, ye burgess wives,
    Why look ye sae on me?
O I am going to Edinburgh town,
    A rich wedding to see.'

XVII

When she gaed up the tolbooth stairs,
    The corks frae her heels did flee;
And lang or e'er she cam down again,
    She was condemn'd to die.

XVIII

When she cam to the Netherbow port,
    She laugh'd loud laughters three;
But when she came to the gallows foot
    The tears blinded her e'e.

XIX

'Yestreen the Queen had four Maries,
    The night she'll hae but three;
There was Marie Seaton, and Marie Beaton,
    And Marie Carmichael, and me.

XX

'O often have I dress'd my Queen,
    And put gowd upon her hair;
But now I've gotten for my reward
    The gallows to be my share.

THE QUEEN'S MARIE

' Often have I dress'd my Queen
   And often made her bed ;
But now I've gotten for my reward
   The gallows tree to tread.

XXII

' I charge ye all, ye mariners,
   When ye sail owre the faem,
Let neither my father nor mother get wit
   But that I'm coming hame.

XXIII

' I charge ye all, ye mariners,
   That sail upon the sea,
That neither my father nor mother get wit
   The dog's death I'm to die.

XXIV

' For if my father and mother got wit,
   And my bold brethren three,
O mickle wad be the gude red blude
   This day wad be spilt for me !

XXV

' O little did my mother ken,
   The day she cradled me,
The lands I was to travel in
   Or the death I was to die ! '

I

ETTRICK Forest is a fair forest,
  In it grows many a seemly tree;
There's hart and hind, and dae and rae,
  And of a' wild beasts great plentie.

II

There's a castle, bigg'd wi' lime and stane;
  O gif it stands not pleasantlie!
In the fore-front o' that castle fair,
  Twa unicorns are bra' to see;
There's the picture of a knight, and a lady bright,
  And the green hollin abune their bree.

III

There an Outlaw keeps five hundred men,
  He keeps a royal companie;
His merry men are a' in ae livery clad,
  O' the Lincoln green sae gay to see;
He and his lady in purple clad,
  O gin they live not royallie!

IV

Word is gane to our noble King,
  In Edinburgh where that he lay,
That there was an Outlaw in Ettrick Forest,
  Counted him nought, nor his courtrie gay.

V

' I make a vow,' then the gude King said,
  ' Unto the Man that dear bought me,
I'se either be King of Ettrick Forest,
  Or King of Scotland that Outlaw 's be! '

bigg'd] built. hollin] holly. bree] brow. courtrie] courtiers.

THE OUTLAW MURRAY

VI

Then spake the Earl hight Hamilton,
    And to the noble King said he,
' My sovereign prince, some counsel take,
    First at your nobles, syne at me.

VII

' I rede ye, send yon braw Outlaw till,
    And see gif your man come will he:
Desire him come and be your man,
    And hold of you yon forest free.

VIII

' Gif he refuses to do that,
    We'll conquess baith his lands and he!
Or else we'll throw his castle down,
    And mak' a widow o' his gay ladye.'

IX

The King call'd on a gentleman,
    James Boyd (the Earl of Arran his brother was he);
When James he came before the King,
    He kneel'd before him on his knee.

X

' Welcome, James Boyd!' said our noble King,
    ' A message ye maun gang for me:
Ye maun hie to Ettrick Forest,
    To yon Outlàw, where dwelleth he.

XI

' Ask him of whom he holds his lands,
    Or man wha may his master be,
And desire him come and be my man,
    And hold of me yon forest free.

rede] advise.

XII

' To Edinburgh to come and gang,
  A safe warrànt I sall him gie ;
And gif he refuses to do that,
  We'll conquess baith his lands and he.

XIII

' Thou mayst vow I'll cast his castle down,
  And mak' a widow o' his gay ladye ;
I'll hang his merry men, pair by pair,
  In ony frith where I may them see.'

XIV

James Boyd took his leave o' the noble King,
  To Ettrick Forest fair cam' he ;
Down Birkendale Brae when that he cam',
  He saw the fair forest wi' his e'e.

XV

Baith dae and rae, and hart and hin',
  And of a' wild beasts great plentie ;
He heard the bows that boldly ring,
  And arrows whidderand him near by.

XVI

Of that fair castle he got a sight ;
  The like he ne'er saw wi' his e'e !
On the fore-front o' that castle fair,
  Twa unicorns were bra' to see ;
The picture of a knight, and lady bright,
  And the green hollin abune their bree.

XVII

Thereat he spyed five hundred men,
  Shooting with bows on Newark Lee ;
They were a' in ae livery clad,
  O' the Lincoln green sae gay to see.

frith] wood.   whidderand] whizzing.

XVIII

His men were a' clad in the green,
　The knight was armèd cap-a-pie,
With a bended bow, on a milkwhite steed;
　And I wot they rank'd right bonnilie.

XIX

Thereby Boyd kend he was master man,
　And servèd him in his ain degree:
'God mote thee save, brave Outlaw Murray!
　Thy ladye, and all thy chivalrie!'—
'Marry, thou's welcome, gentleman,
　Some king's messenger thou seems to be.'—

XX

'The King of Scotland sent me here,
　And, gude Outlàw, I am sent to thee;
I wad wot of whom ye hold your lands,
　Or man wha may thy master be?'—

XXI

'Thir lands are mine,' the Outlaw said;
　'I own nae king in Christentie;
Frae Soudron I this forest wan,
　When the King nor his knights were not to see.'—

XXII

'He desires you'll come to Edinburgh,
　And hauld of him this forest free;
And, gif ye refuse to do this thing,
　He'll conquess baith thy lands and thee.
He hath vow'd to cast thy castle down,
　And mak' a widow o' thy gay ladye;

Soudron] Southron, English.

377

XXIII

'He'll hang thy merry men, pair by pair,
  In ony frith where he may them find.'—
'Ay, by my troth!' the Outlaw said,
  'Than wad I think me far behind.

XXIV

'Ere the King my fair country get,
  This land that 's nativest to me,
Mony o' his nobles sall be cauld,
  Their ladies sall be right wearie.'

XXV

Then spak' his lady, fair of face :
  She said, ' 'Twere without consent of me,
That an outlaw suld come before a King ;
  I am right rad of treasonrie.
Bid him be gude to his lords at hame,
  For Edinburgh my lord sall never see.'

XXVI

James Boyd took his leave o' the Outlaw keen,
  To Edinboro' boun' is he ;
When James he cam' before the King,
  He kneelèd lowly on his knee.

XXVII

'Welcome, James Boyd!' said our noble King,
  'What forest is Ettrick Forest free?'—
'Ettrick Forest is the fairest forest
  That ever man saw wi' his e'e.

XXVIII

'There 's the dae, the rae, the hart, the hin',
  And of a' wild beasts great plentie ;
There 's a pretty castle of lime and stane,
  O gif it stands not pleasantlie !

rad] afraid.

378

XXIX

'There's in the fore-front o' that castle
  Twa unicorns, sae bra' to see;
There's the picture of a knight, and a lady bright,
  Wi' the green hollìn abune their bree.

XXX

' There the Outlaw keeps five hundred men,
  He keeps a royal companie;
His merry men in ae livery clad,
  O' the Lincoln green sae gay to see:
He and his lady in purple clad;
  O gin they live not royallie!

XXXI

' He says, yon forest is his ain;
  He wan it frae the Soudronie;
Sae as he wan it, sae will he keep it,
  Contrair all kings in Christentie.'—

XXXII

' Gar warn me Perthshire, and Angus baith,
  Fife, up and down, and Lothians three,
And graith my horse!' said our noble King,
  ' For to Ettrick Forest hie will I me.'

XXXIII

Then word is gane the Outlaw till,
  In Ettrick Forest, where dwelleth he,
That the King was comand to Ettrick Forest,
  To conquess baith his lands and he.

XXXIV

' I mak' a vow,' the Outlaw said,
  ' I mak' a vow, and that trulie:
Were there but three men to tak' my part,
  Yon King's coming full dear suld be!'

graith] harness.

XXXV

Then messengers he callèd forth,
  And bade them hie them speedilye :
' Ane of ye gae to Halliday,
  The Laird of the Corehead is he.

XXXVI

' He certain is my sister's son ;
  Bid him come quick and succour me ;
The King comes on for Ettrick Forest,
  And landless men we a' will be.'—

XXXVII

' What news ? what news ? ' said Halliday,
  ' Man, frae thy master unto me ? '—
' Not as ye would ; seeking your aid ;
  The King 's his mortal enemie.'—

XXXVIII

' Ay, by my troth ! ' said Halliday,
  ' Even for that it repenteth me ;
For gif he lose fair Ettrick Forest,
  He'll tak' fair Moffatdale frae me.

XXXIX

' I'll meet him wi' five hundred men,
  And surely mair, if mae may be ;
And before he gets the forest fair,
  We a' will die on Newark Lee ! '

XL

The Outlaw call'd a messenger,
  And bid him hie him speedilye
To Andrew Murray of Cockpool :
  ' That man 's a dear cousin to me ;
Desire him come and mak' me aid
  With a' the power that he may be.'

THE OUTLAW MURRAY

XLI

'It stands me hard,' Andrew Murray said,
  'Judge gif it stand na hard wi' me;
To enter against a king wi' crown,
  And set my lands in jeopardie!
Yet, if I come not on the day,
  Surely at night he sall me see.'

XLII

To Sir James Murray of Traquair,
  A message came right speedilie:
'What news? what news?' James Murray said,
  'Man, frae thy master unto me?'—

XLIII

'What needs I tell? for weel ye ken
  The King's his mortal enemie;
And now he is coming to Ettrick Forest,
  And landless men ye a' will be.'

XLIV

'And, by my troth,' James Murray said,
  'Wi' that Outlaw will I live and dee;
The King has gifted my lands lang syne—
  It cannot be nae warse wi' me.'

XLV

The King was comand thro' Cadden Ford,
  And full five thousand men was he;
They saw the dark forest them before,
  They thought it awsome for to see.

XLVI

Then spak' the Earl hight Hamilton,
  And to the noble King said he,
'My sovereign prince, some counsel tak',
  First at your nobles, syne at me.

XLVII

' Desire him meet thee at Permanscore,
  And bring four in his companie ;
Five earls sall gang yoursell before,
  Gude cause that you suld honour'd be.

XLVIII

' And, gif he refuses to do that,
  With fire and sword we'll follow thee ;
There sall never a Murray, after him,
  Hold land in Ettrick Forest free.'

XLIX

The King then call'd a gentleman,
  Royal banner-bearer there was he,
James Hope Pringle of Torsonse by name ;
  He cam' and kneel'd upon his knee.

L

' Welcome, James Pringle of Torsonse !
  A message ye maun gae for me :
Ye maun gae to yon Outlaw Murray,
  Surely where boldly bideth he.

LI

' Bid him meet me at Permanscore,
  And bring four in his companie ;
Five earls sall come mysell before,
  Gude reason I suld honour'd be.

LII

' And gif he refuses to do that,
  Bid him look for nae good o' me ;
There sall never a Murray, after him,
  Have land in Ettrick Forest free.'

LIII

James cam' before the Outlaw keen,
    And servèd him in his ain degree.—
' Welcome, James Pringle of Torsonse !
    What message frae the King to me ?'—

LIV

' He bids ye meet him at Permanscore,
    And bring four in your company ;
Five earls sall gang himsell before,
    Nae mair in number will he be.

LV

' And gif you refuse to do that,
    (I freely here upgive wi' thee,)
He'll cast your bonny castle down,
    And mak' a widow o' your gay ladye.
There will never a Murray, after thysell,
    Have land in Ettrick Forest free.'—

LVI

' It stands me hard,' the Outlaw said,
    ' Judge gif it stands na hard wi' me :
What reck o' the losing of mysell ?—
    But a' my offspring after me !

LVII

' Auld Halliday, young Halliday,
    Ye sall be twa to gang wi' me ;
Andrew Murray, and Sir James Murray,
    We'll be nae mae in companie.'

LVIII

When that they cam' before the King,
    They fell before him on their knee :
' Grant mercy, mercy, noble King !
    E'en for his sake that dyed on tree.'

LIX

' Siccan like mercy sall ye have;
   On gallows ye sall hangit be ! '——
' Over God's forbode,' quoth the Outlaw then,
   'I hope your grace will better be!
Else, ere you come to Edinburgh port,
   I trow thin guarded sall ye be.

LX

Thir lands of Ettrick Forest fair,
   I wan them from the enemie ;
Like as I wan them, sae will I keep them,
   Contrair a' kings in Christentie.'

LXI

All the nobles the King about,
   Said pity it were to see him dee.
' Yet grant me mercy, sovereign prince,
   Extend your favour unto me !

LXII

' I'll give thee the keys of my castell,
   Wi' the blessing o' my gay ladye,
Gin thou'lt make me sheriff of this forest,
   And a' my offspring after me.'——

LXIII

' Wilt thou give me the keys of thy castell,
   Wi' the blessing of thy gay ladye ?
I'se make thee sheriff of Ettrick Forest,
   Surely while upward grows the tree ;
If you be not traitor to the King,
   Forfaulted sall thou never be.'

siccan] such.   Forfaulted] forfeited.

LXIV

'But, Prince, what sall come o' my men?
    When I gae back, traitor they'll ca' me.
I had rather lose my life and land,
    Ere my merry men rebukèd me.'—

LXV

'Will your merry men amend their lives,
    An' a' their pardons I grant thee?
Now, name thy lands where'er they lie,
    And here I render them to thee.'—

LXVI

'Fair Philiphaugh is mine by right,
    And Lewinshope still mine shall be;
Newark, Foulshiells, and Tinnès baith,
    My bow and arrow purchased me.

LXVII

'And I have native steads to me,
    The Newark Lee and Hanginshaw;
I have mony steads in Ettrick Forest,
    But them by name I dinna knaw.'

LXVIII

The keys of the castle he gave the King,
    Wi' the blessing o' his fair ladye;
He was made sheriff of Ettrick Forest,
    Surely while upward grows the tree;
And if he was na traitor to the King,
    Forfaulted he suld never be.

LXIX

Wha ever heard, in ony times,
    Siccan an outlaw in his degree
Sic favour get before a King,
    As did Outlaw Murray of the forest free?

Glenlogie

I

FOUR-AND-TWENTY nobles rade to the King's ha',
But bonny Glenlogie was the flow'r o' them a'.

II

Lady Jeanie Melville cam' trippin' down the stair;
When she saw Glenlogie her hairt it grew sair.

III

She call'd to the footman that ran by his side:
Says, 'What is your lord's name, an' where does he bide?'—

IV

'His name is Glenlogie when he is from home:
He 's of the gay Gordons, his name it is John.'—

V

'Glenlogie, Glenlogie, an you will prove kind,
My love is laid on you; I am tellin' my mind.'—

VI

He turn'd about lightly, as the Gordons do a';
Says, 'I thank you, Lady Jeanie, but I'm promised awa'.'

VII

She call'd on her maidens her bed for to make,
Her rings from her fingers she did them a' break.

VIII

'Where will I get a bonny boy, to win hose and shoon,
To go to Glenlogie and bid Logie come?'

IX

When Glenlogie got the letter, amang noblemen,
'I wonder,' said Glenlogie, 'what does young women mean?

GLENLOGIE

X

' I wonder i' the warld what women see at me,
That bonny Jeanie Melville for my sake shou'd dee ?

XI

' O what is my lineage, or what is my make,
That bonny Jeanie Melville shou'd dee for my sake ?

XII

' Go saddle my black horse, go saddle him soon,
Till I ride to Bethelnie, to see Lady Jean ! '

XIII

When he came to Bethelnie, he rade round about,
And he saw Jeanie's father at the window look out.

XIV

When he came to the gateway, small mirth was there ;
But was weepin' and wailin', a' tearin' their hair.

XV

O pale and wan look'd she when Glenlogie came ben,
But red ruddy grew she whene'er he sat down.

XVI

' Turn round Jeanie Melville, turn round to this side,
And I'll be the bridegroom, and you'll be the bride ! '

XVII

O 'twas a merry weddin', and the portion down told,
Of bonny Jeanie Melville, scarce sixteen years old !

I

'O BRENT's your brow, my Lady Elspat;
    O gowden yellow is your hair !
Of a' the maids o' fair Scotland
    There's nane like Lady Elspat fair.'

II

' Perform your vows,' she says, ' Sweet William ;
    The vows which ye ha' made to me ;
And at the back o' my mither's castle
    This night I'll surely meet wi' thee.'

III

But wae be to her brother's page,
    Wha heard the words this twa did say !
He's tauld them to her lady mither,
    Wha wrought Sweet William mickle wae.

IV

For she's ta'en him, Sweet William,
    And she's gar'd bind him wi's bow-string.
Till the red blood o' his fair body
    Frae ilka nail o' his hand did spring.

V

O it fell ance upon a time
    That the Lord Justice came to town ;
Out she has ta'en him, Sweet William,
    Brought him before the Lord Justice boun'.

VI

' And what is the crime now, madame,' he says,
    ' Has been committed by this young man ? '—
' O he has broken my bonny castle,
    That was well biggit wi' lime and stane.

brent] straight, smooth.   biggit] built.

388

VII

'And he has broken my bonny coffers,
  That was well bandit wi' aiken ban';
And he has stolen my rich jewels;
  I wot he has them every ane.'

VIII

Then out it spak' her Lady Elspat
  As she sat by the Lord Justice' knee:
'Now ye hae tauld your tale, mither,
  I pray, Lord Justice, you'll now hear me.

IX

'He hasna broken her bonny castle,
  That was well biggit wi' lime and stane;
Nor has he stolen her rich jewels,
  For I wot she has them every one.

X

'But tho' he was my first true love,
  And tho' I had sworn to be his bride,
'Cause he had not a great estate
  She would this way our loves divide.'

XI

Then out it spak' the Lord Justice
  (I wot the tear was in his e'e):
'I see nae fault in this young man;
  Sae loose his bands, and set him free.

XII

'Tak' back your love now, Lady Elspat,
  And my best blessing you baith upon!
For gin he be your first true love,
  He is my eldest sister's son.

bandit] bound.   aiken] oaken.

XIII

'There is a steed within my stable
 Cost me baith gowd and white monèy ;
Ye'se get as mickle o' my free land
 As he'll ride about in a summer's day.'

87.   *Jamie Douglas*

I

I WAS a lady of high renown
 As ever lived in the north countrie ;
I was a lady of high renown
 When the Earl Douglas luvèd me.

II

And when we came through Glasgow toun,
 We were a comely sight to see ;
My gude lord in the black velvèt,
 And I mysel' in cramasie.

III

But when we came to Douglas toun,
 We were a fine sight to behold :
My gude lord in the cramasie
 And I mysel' in the shining gold.

IV

And when that my auld son was born
 And set upon his nurse's knee,
I was happy a woman as e'er was born,
 And my gude lord he luvèd me.

cramasie] crimson.   auld] eldest.

JAMIE DOUGLAS

V

But O an my young son was born
    And set upon his nurse's knee
And I mysel' were dead and gane,
    For a maid again I'll never be!

VI

There cam' a man into this house,
    And Jamie Lockhart was his name,
And it was told to my gude lord
    That I was owre in love wi' him.

VII

O wae be unto thee, Blackwòod,
    And ae an ill death may ye dee!
For ye was the first and foremost man
    That parted my gude lord and me.

VIII

I sent a word to my gude lord,
    'Come down, and sit, and dine wi' me,
And I'll set thee on a chair of gowd,
    And a siller towel on thy knee.'—

IX

'When cockle-shells turn silver bells,
    And mussell grow on every tree,
When frost and snow turns fire to burn,
    Then I'll sit down and dine wi' thee.'

X

When that my father he had word
    That my gude lord had forsaken me,
He sent a fifty brisk dragoons
    To fetch me home to my ain countrie.

JAMIE DOUGLAS

XI

'Fare thee well, my Jamie Douglas!
    Fare thee well, ever dear to me!
But O, an my young babe were born
    And set upon some nourice' knee!

XII

'And fare thee well, my pretty palace!
    And fare ye well, my children three!
God grant your father grace to be kind,
    More kind to you than he was to me!'

XIII

Then slowly, slowly rase I up,
    But quickly, quickly he cam' doun,
And when he saw me sit in my coach,
    He made his drums and trumpets sound.

XIV

When we cam' in by Edinbro' town,
    My father and mother they met me
Wi' trumpets soundin' on every side;
    But it was nae music at a' to me.

XV

'Now hau'd your comfort my father dear,
    And mother your weeping let abee!
I'll never lye in another man's arms
    Since my dear lord has forsaken me.'

XVI

It's very true, and it's aft-times said,
    The hawk will flie far far frae her nest:
And a' the warld may plainly see
    They are far frae me that I luve best.

JAMIE DOUGLAS

Lament
of Barbara, Marchioness of Douglas

XVII

O waly, waly, up the bank,
    And waly, waly, doun the brae,
And waly, waly, yon burn-side,
    Where I and my Love wont to gae!

XVIII

I lean'd my back unto an aik,
    I thocht it was a trustie tree;
But first it bow'd and syne it brak—
    Sae my true love did lichtlie me.

XIX

O waly, waly, gin love be bonnie
    A little time while it is new!
But when 'tis auld it waxeth cauld,
    And fades awa' like morning dew.

XX

O wherefore should I busk my heid,
    Or wherefore should I kame my hair?
For my true Love has me forsook,
    And says he'll never lo'e me mair.

XXI

Now Arthur's Seat sall be my bed,
    The sheets sall ne'er be 'filed by me;
Saint Anton's well sall be my drink;
    Since my true Love has forsaken me.

XXII

Marti'mas wind, when wilt thou blaw,
    And shake the green leaves aff the tree?
O gentle Death, when wilt thou come?
    For of my life I am wearìe.

    lichtlie] slight, treat with disrespect.

JAMIE DOUGLAS

XXIII

'Tis not the frost, that freezes fell,
  Nor blawing snaw's inclemencie,
'Tis not sic cauld that makes me cry;
  But my Love's heart grown cauld to me.

XXIV

When we cam' in by Glasgow toun,
  We were a comely sicht to see;
My Love was clad in the black velvèt,
  And I mysel' in cramasie.

XXV

But had I wist, before I kist,
  That love had been sae ill to win,
I had lock'd my heart in a case o' gowd,
  And pinn'd it wi' a siller pin.

XXVI

And O! if my young babe were born,
  And set upon the nurse's knee;
And I mysel' were dead and gane,
  And the green grass growing over me!

Katharine Johnstone

I

THERE was a may, and a weel-far'd may,
  Lived high up in yon glen ;
Her name was Katharine Johnstone
  She was courted by mony men.

II

Doun cam' the Laird o' Lamington
  Out frae the North Countrie,
All for to court this pretty may,
  Her bridegroom for to be.

III

He tell'd na her father, he tell'd na her mither,
  He tell'd na ane o' her kin,
But he tell'd the bonnie lass hersel'
  An' her consent did win.

IV

But up then cam' Lord Faughanwood
  Out frae the English Border,
And for to court this pretty may,
  A' mounted in good order.

V

He's tell'd her father, he's tell'd her mither,
  And a' the lave o' her kin ;
But he's tell'd na the bonny lass hersel'
  Till on her weddin'-e'en.

VI

She's sent unto her first fere love,
  Gin he would come to see,
And Lamington has sent back word
  Weel answer'd should she be.

weel-far'd] well-favoured.   lave] rest.   fere] mate.

VII

Then he has sent a messenger
    Right quietly thro' the land,
For four-and-twenty armèd men
    To ride at his command.

VIII

The bridegroom from a high window
    Beheld baith dale and down,
And there he spied her first fere love
    Cam' riding to the toun.

IX

She scoffèd and she scornèd him
    Upon her weddin'-day,
And said it was the Fairy Court
    He saw in sic array!

X

When a' were at the dinner set,
    Drinking the blude-red wine,
In cam' the Laird o' Lamington
    The bridegroom 'should hae been.

XI

' O come ye here to fight, young lord?
    Or come ye here to play?
Or come ye here to drink good wine
    Upon the weddin'-day?'—

XII

' I come na here to fight,' he said
    ' I come na here to play;
I'll but lead a dance wi' the bonny bride,
    And mount and go my way.'

396

XIII

There was a glass of the blude-red wine
  Was fill'd them up between,
But aye she drank to Lamington,
  Wha her true love had been.

XIV

He's ta'en her by the milk-white hand,
  And by the grass-green sleeve;
He's mounted her high behind himsel',
  At her kin he's spier'd nae leave.

XV

There were four-and-twenty bonny boys
  A' clad in the Johnstone grey,
They swore they would tak' the bride again
  By the strong hand, if they may.

XVI

It's up, it's up the Cowden bank,
  It's down the Cowden brae;
The bride she gar'd the trumpet sound
  'It is a weel-won play!'

XVII

The blude ran down by Cowden bank
  And down by Cowden brae,
But aye she gar'd the trumpet sound
  'It's a' fair play!'

XVIII

'My blessing on your heart, sweet thing!
  Wae to your wilfu' will!
Sae mony a gallant gentleman's blood
  This day as ye've gar'd spill.'

spier'd] asked.

XIX

But a' you lords of fair England,
　　If you be English born,
Come never to Scotland to seek a wife
　　Or else ye'll get the scorn.

XX

They'll haik ye up, and settle ye by,
　　Until your weddin'-day ;
Then gie ye frogs instead o' fish,
　　And do ye foul, foul play.

89.　　　*Johnie Armstrong*

I

SUM speiks of lords, sum speiks of lairds,
　　And sick lyke men of hie degrie ;
Of a gentleman I sing a sang,
　　Sum tyme called Laird of Gilnockie.

II

The King he wrytes a luving letter,
　　With his ain hand sae tenderly,
And he hath sent it to Johnie Armstrang,
　　To cum and speik with him speedily.

III

The Eliots and Armstrangs did convene ;
　　They were a gallant cumpanie—
' We'll ride and meit our lawful King,
　　And bring him safe to Gilnockie.'

haik ye up] hold you in suspense.　　　settle ye by] keep you
waiting aside.

398

JOHNIE ARMSTRONG

IV

'Make kinnen and capon ready, then,
   And venison in great plentie;
We'll wellcum here our royal King;
   I hope he'll dine at Gilnockie!'—

V

They ran their horse on the Langholme howm,
   And brak their spears wi' mickle main;
The ladies lukit frae their loft windows—
   'God bring our men weel hame agen!'

VI

When Johnie cam' before the King,
   Wi' a' his men sae brave to see,
The King he movit his bonnet to him;
   He ween'd he was King as weel as he.

VII

'May I find grace, my sovereign liege,
   Grace for my loyal men and me?
For my name it is Johnie Armstrang,
   And a subject of yours, my liege,' said he.

VIII

'Away, away, thou traitor strang!
   Out o' my sight soon mayst thou be!
I grantit never a traitor's life,
   And now I'll not begin wi' thee.'—

IX

'Grant me my life, my liege, my King!
   And a bonny gift I'll gie to thee:
Full four-and-twenty milk-white steids,
   Were a' foal'd in ae yeir to me.

kinnen] rabbits.

399

X

' I'll gie thee a' these milk-white steids,
   That prance and nicker at a speir;
And as mickle gude Inglish gilt,
   As four o' their braid backs dow bear.'—

XI

' Away, away, thou traitor strang!
   Out o' my sight soon mayst thou be!
I grantit never a traitor's life,
   And now I'll not begin wi' thee!'—

XII

' Grant me my life, my liege, my King!
   And a bonny gift I'll gie to thee:
Gude four-and-twenty ganging mills,
   That gang thro' a' the yeir to me.

XIII

'These four-and-twenty mills complete
   Sall gang for thee thro' a' the yeir;
And as mickle of gude reid wheit,
   As a' thair happers dow to bear.'—

XIV

' Away, away, thou traitor strang!
   Out o' my sight soon mayst thou be!
I grantit never a traitor's life,
   And now I'll not begin wi' thee.'—

XV

' Grant me my life, my liege, my King!
   And a great great gift I'll gie to thee:
Bauld four-and-twenty sisters' sons,
   Sall for thee fetch, tho' a' should flee!'—

nicker] neigh.   gilt] gold.   dow] are able to.   ganging]
going.   happers] mill-hoppers.

JOHNIE ARMSTRONG

XVI

'Away, away, thou traitor strang !
  Out o' my sight soon mayst thou be !
I grantit never a traitor's life,
  And now I'll not begin wi' thee.'—

XVII

'Grant me my life, my liege, my King !
  And a brave gift I'll gie to thee :
All between heir and Newcastle town
  Sall pay their yeirly rent to thee.'—

XVIII

'Away, away, thou traitor strang !
  Out o' my sight soon mayst thou be !
I grantit never a traitor's life,
  And now I'll not begin wi' thee.'—

XIX

'Ye lied, ye lied, now, King,' he says,
  'Altho' a King and Prince ye be !
For I've luved naething in my life,
  I weel dare say it, but honesty :

XX

'Save a fat horse, and a fair woman,
  Twa bonny dogs to kill a deir ;
But England suld have found me meal and mault,
  Gif I had lived this hundred yeir !

XXI

'She suld have found me meal and mault,
  And beef and mutton in a' plentie ;
But never a Scots wyfe could have said
  That e'er I skaith'd her a puir flee.

skaith'd] hurt, wronged.

XXII

' To seik het water beneith cauld ice,
   Surely it is a greit folie—
I have asked grace at a graceless face,
   But there is nane for my men and me !

XXIII

' But had I kenn'd ere I cam' frae hame,
   How thou unkind wadst been to me !
I wad have keepit the Border side,
   In spite of all thy force and thee.

XXIV

' Wist England's King that I was ta'en,
   O gin a blythe man he wad be !
For anes I slew his sister's son,
   And on his breist bane brak a trie.'

XXV

John wore a girdle about his middle,
   Imbroider'd owre wi' burning gold,
Bespangled wi' the same metal,
   Maist beautiful was to behold.

XXVI

There hung nine targats at Johnie's hat,
   And ilk ane worth three hundred pound—
' What wants that knave that a King suld have,
   But the sword of honour and the crown ?

XXVII

' O where got thou these targats, Johnie,
   That blink sae brawlie abune thy brie ? '—
' I gat them in the field fechting,
   Where, cruel King, thou durst not be.

targats] round ornaments.   blink sae brawlie] glance so
bravely.   brie] brow.

JOHNIE ARMSTRONG

XXVIII

' Had I my horse, and harness gude,
    And riding as I wont to be,
It suld have been tauld this hundred yeir,
    The meeting of my King and me !

XXIX

' God be with thee, Kirsty, my brother,
    Lang live thou Laird of Mangertoun !
Lang mayst thou live on the Border syde,
    Ere thou see thy brother ride up and doun !

XXX

' And God be with thee, Kirsty, my son,
    Where thou sits on thy nurse's knee !
But an thou live this hundred yeir,
    Thy father's better thou'lt never be.

XXXI

' Farewell ! my bonny Gilnock hall,
    Where on Esk side thou standest stout !
Gif I had lived but seven yeirs mair,
    I wad hae gilt thee round about.'

XXXII

John murder'd was at Carlinrigg,
    And all his gallant companie ;
But Scotland's heart was ne'er sae wae,
    To see sae mony brave men die—

XXXIII

Because they saved their country deir
    Frae Englishmen !   Nane were sa bauld,
Whyle Johnie lived on the Border syde,
    Nane of them durst cum neir his hauld.

I

WILLIE stands in his stable door,
   And clapping at his steed,
And over his white fingers
   His nose began to bleed.

II

' Gie corn unto my horse, mither,
   Gie meat unto my man ;
For I maun gang to Margaret's bour
   Before the nicht comes on.'—

III

' O bide at hame this nicht, Willie,
   This ae bare nicht wi' me :
The bestan bed in a' my house
   Sall be well made to thee.

IV

' O bide at hame this nicht, Willie,
   This ae bare nicht wi' me :
The bestan bird in a' the roost
   At your supper, son, sall be.'—

V

' A' your beds and a' your roosts
   I value not a pin ;
But I sall gae to my love's gates
   This nicht, gif I can win.'—

VI

' O stay at home, my son Willie,
   The wind blaws cauld an' sour ;
The nicht will be baith mirk and late
   Before ye reach her bour.'—

CLYDE WATER

'O though the nicht were ever sae dark,
  Or the wind blew never sae cauld,
I will be in my Margaret's bour
  Before twa hours be tald.'—

VIII

'O an ye gang to Margaret's bour
  Sae sair against my will,
I' the deepest pot o' Clyde's water
  My malison ye'se feel.'

IX

As he rade owre yon high high hill,
  And doun yon dowie den,
The roaring that was in Clyde's water
  Wad fley'd five hundred men.

X

His heart was warm, his pride was up,
  Sweet Willie kentna fear;
But yet his mither's malison
  Aye soundit in his ear.

XI

'O spare, O spare me, Clyde's water!
  Your stream rins wondrous strang:
Mak' me your wrack as I come back,
  But spare me as I gang!'

XII

Then he rade in, and further in,
  And he swam to an' fro,
Until he's grippit a hazel bush
  That brung him to the brow.

malison] curse.   dowie] dismal, gloomy.   fley'd]
frightened.

405

XIII

Then he is on to Margaret's bour,
    And tirlèd at the pin ;
But doors were steek'd and windows barr'd,
    And nane wad let him in.

XIV

' O open the door to me, Marg'ret !
    O open and let me in !
For my boots are fu' o' Clyde's water
    And the rain rins owre my chin.'—

XV

' I darena open the door to you,
    Nor darena let you in ;
For my mither she is fast asleep,
    And I maun mak' nae din.'—

XVI

' O hae ye ne'er a stable ?' he says,
    ' Or hae ye ne'er a barn ?
Or hae ye ne'er a wild-goose house
    Where I might rest till morn ?'—

XVII

' My barn it is fu' o' corn,' she says,
    ' My stable is fu' o' hay ;
My house is fu' o' merry young men ;
    They winna remove till day.'—

XVIII

' O fare ye weel then, May Marg'ret,
    Sin' better may na be !
I've gotten my mither's malison
    This nicht, coming to thee.'

XIX

He 's mounted on his coal-black steed,
  —O but his heart was wae !
But ere he came to Clyde's water
  'Twas half up owre the brae.

XX

' An hey, Willie ! an hoa, Willie !
  Winna ye turn agen ? '
But aye the louder that she cried
  He rade agenst the win'.

XXI

As he rade owre yon high high hill,
  And doun yon dowie den,
The roaring that was in Clyde's water
  Wad fley'd a thousand men.

XXII

Then he rade in, and farther in,
  Till he cam' to the chine ;
The rushing that was in Clyde's water
  Took Willie's riding-cane.

XXIII

He lean'd him owre his saddle-bow
  To catch the rod by force ;
The rushing that was in Clyde's water
  Took Willie frae his horse.

XXIV

' O how can I turn my horse's head ?
  How can I learn to sowm ?
I 've gotten my mither's malison,
  And it 's here that I maun drown ! '

sowm] swim.

407

CLYDE WATER

XXV

O he swam high, and he swam low,
   And he swam to and fro,
But he couldna spy the hazel-bush
   Wad bring him to the brow.

XXVI

He's sunk and he never rase agen
   Into the pot sae deep . . .
And up it waken'd May Margaret
   Out o' her drowsie sleep.

XXVII

'Come hither, come here, my mither dear,
   Read me this dreary dream;
I dream'd my Willie was at our gates,
   And nane wad let him in.'—

XXVIII

'Lie still, lie still now, my Meggie:
   Lie still and tak' your rest;
Sin' your true-love was at your gates
   It's but twa quarters past.'—

XXIX

Nimbly, nimbly rase she up,
   And nimbly put she on;
And the higher that the lady cried,
   The louder blew the win'.

XXX

The firstan step that she stept in,
   She steppit to the queet:
'Ohon, alas!' said that lady,
   This water's wondrous deep.'

queet] ankle.

408

XXXI

The neistan step that she stept in,
　　She waded to the knee ;
Says she, ' I cou'd wade farther in,
　　If I my love cou'd see.'

XXXII

The neistan step that she wade in,
　　She waded to the chin ;
The deepest pot in Clyde's water
　　She got sweet Willie in.

XXXIII

' Ye've had a cruel mither, Willie !
　　And I have had anither ;
But we sall sleep in Clyde's water
　　Like sister an' like brither.'

91. *Young Benjie*

I

OF a' the maids o' fair Scotland,
　　The fairest was Marjorie ;
And young Benjie was her ae true love,
　　And a dear true-love was he.

II

And wow ! but they were lovers dear,
　　And loved fu' constantlie ;
But ay the mair when they fell out,
　　The sairer was their plea.

plea] quarrel.

409

YOUNG BENJIE

III

And they hae quarrell'd on a day,
  Till Marjorie's heart grew wae,
And she said she'd chuse another luve,
  And let young Benjie gae.

IV

And he was stout, and proud-hertèd,
  And thought o't bitterlie,
And he's gaen by the wan moon-light,
  To meet his Marjorie.

V

'O open, open, my true love!
  O open, and let me in!'—
I dare na open, young Benjie,
  My three brothers are within.—

VI

'Ye lied, ye lied, my bonny burd,
  Sae loud's I hear ye lie;
As I came by the Lowden banks,
  They bade gude e'en to me.

VII

'But fare ye weel, my ae fause love,
  That I hae loved sae lang!
It sets ye chuse another love,
  And let young Benjie gang.'

VIII

Then Marjorie turned her round about,
  The tear blinding her e'e,
'I darena, darena let thee in,
  But I'll come down to thee.'

sets] befits.

YOUNG BENJIE

IX

Then saft she smiled, and said to him,
  'O what ill hae I done?'
He took her in his armis twa,
  And threw her o'er the linn.

X

The stream was strang, the maid was stout,
  And laith laith to be dang;
But, ere she wan the Lowden banks,
  Her fair colour was wan.

XI

Then up bespak her eldest brother,
  'O see na ye what I see?'
And out then spak her second brother,
  'It's our sister Marjorie!'

XII

Out then spak her eldest brother,
  'O how shall we her ken?'
And out then spak her youngest brother,
  'There's a honey mark on her chin.'

XIII

Then they've ta'en up the comely corpse,
  And laid it on the grund:
'O wha has killed our ae sister,
  And how can he be found?

XIV

'The night it is her low lykewake,
  The morn her burial day,
And we maun watch at mirk midnight,
  And hear what she will say.'

linn] stream.   dang] overcome.   lykewake] corpse-watching.

YOUNG BENJIE

XV

Wi' doors ajar, and candle-light,
    And torches burning clear,
The streikit corpse, till still midnight,
    They waked, but naething hear.

XVI

About the middle o' the night,
    The cocks began to craw,
And at the dead hour o' the night,
    The corpse began to thraw.

XVII

' O wha has done the wrang, sister,
    Or dared the deadly sin ?
Wha was sae stout, and feared nae dout,
    As thraw ye o'er the linn ? '—

XVIII

' Young Benjie was the first ae man,
    I laid my love upon ;
He was sae stout and proud-hearted,
    He threw me o'er the linn.'—

XIX

' Sall we young Benjie head, sister,
    Sall we young Benjie hang,
Or sall we pike out his twa gray e'en,
    And punish him ere he gang ? '—

XX

' Ye mauna Benjie head, brothers,
    Ye mauna Benjie hang,
But ye maun pike out his twa gray e'en,
    And punish him ere he gang.

streikit] stretched out.   thraw] twist, writhe.
412

XXI

'Tie a green gravat round his neck,
  And lead him out and in,
And the best ae servant about your house,
  To wait young Benjie on.

XXII

'And ay, at every seven years' end,
  Ye'll tak him to the linn ;
For that 's the penance he maun drie,
  To scug his deadly sin.'

92. *Annan Water*

I

ANNAN water 's wading deep,
  And my love Annie 's wondrous bonny;
And I am laith she suld weet her feet,
  Because I love her best of ony.

II

'Gar saddle me the bonny black,
  Gar saddle sune, and make him ready :
For I will down the Gatehope-Slack,
  And all to see my bonny ladye.'

III

He has loupen on the bonny black,
  He stirr'd him wi' the spur right sairly ;
But, or he wan the Gatehope-Slack,
  I think the steed was wae and weary.

gravat] cravat, collar.   drie] endure.   scug] screen, expiate.

IV

He has loupen on the bonny grey,
  He rade the right gate and the ready ;
I trow he would neither stint nor stay,
  For he was seeking his bonny ladye.

V

O he has ridden o'er field and fell,
  Through muir and moss, and mony a mire :
His spurs o' steel were sair to bide,
  And frae her fore-feet flew the fire.

VI

' Now, bonny grey, now play your part !
  Gin ye be the steed that wins my deary,
Wi' corn and hay ye'se be fed for aye,
  And never spur sall make you wearie.'

VII

The grey was a mare, and a right good mare ;
  But when she wan the Annan water,
She couldna hae ridden a furlong mair,
  Had a thousand merks been wadded at her.

VIII

' O boatman, boatman, put off your boat !
  Put off your boat for gowden money !
I cross the drumly stream the night,
  Or never mair I see my honey.'—

IX

' O I was sworn sae late yestreen,
  And not by ae aith, but by many ;
And for a' the gowd in fair Scotland,
  I dare na take ye through to Annie.'—

gate] way.   wadded] wagered.   drumly] turbid.
414

X

The side was stey, and the bottom deep,
    Frae bank to brae the water pouring ;
And the bonny grey mare did sweat for fear,
    For she heard the water-kelpy roaring.

XI

O he has pu'd aff his dapperpy coat,
    The silver buttons glancèd bonny ;
The waistcoat bursted aff his breast,
    He was sae full of melancholy.

XII

He has ta'en the ford at that stream tail ;
    I wot he swam both strong and steady,
But the stream was broad, and his strength did fail,
    And he never saw his bonny ladye !

XIII

O wae betide the frush saugh wand !
    And wae betide the bush of brier !
It brake into my true love's hand,
    When his strength did fail, and his limbs did tire.

XIV

' And wae betide ye, Annan Water,
    This night that ye are a drumlie river !
For over thee I'll build a bridge,
    That ye never more true love may sever.'—

stey] steep.   water-kelpy] water-sprite.   dapperpy]
diapered.   frush] brittle.   saugh] willow.

93. *Rare Willy drowned in Yarrow*

I

'WILLY's rare, and Willy's fair,
  And Willy's wondrous bonny;
And Willy heght to marry me,
  Gin e'er he marryd ony.

II

'Yestreen I made my bed fu' braid,
  The night I'll make it narrow,
For a' the live-long winter's night
  I lie twin'd of my marrow.

III

'O came you by yon water-side?
  Pu'd you the rose or lilly?
Or came you by yon meadow green?
  Or saw you my sweet Willy?'

IV

She sought him east, she sought him west,
  She sought him braid and narrow;
Sine, in the clifting of a craig,
  She found him drown'd in Yarrow.

heght] promised.   twin'd] deprived.   marrow] mate.
clifting] cleft.

416

94. *The Duke of Gordon's Daughter*

I

THE Duke of Gordon had three daughters,
  Elizabeth, Marg'ret and Jean ;
They would not stay in bonny Castle Gordon,
  But they went to bonny Aberdeen.

II

They had not been in bonny Aberdeen
  A twelvemonth and a day,
Lady Jean fell in love with Captain Ogilvie
  And awa' with him she would gae.

III

Word came to the Duke of Gordon,
  In the chamber where he lay,
Lady Jean was in love with Captain Ogilvie,
  And from him she would not stay.

IV

'Go saddle to me the black horse,
  And you'll ride on the grey,
And I will gang to bonny Aberdeen
  Forthwith to bring her away.'

V

They were not a mile from Aberdeen,
  A mile but only one,
Till he met with his two daughters,
  But awa' was Lady Jean.

VI

' Where is your sister, maidens ?
  Where is your sister now ?
Say, what is become of your sister,
  That she is not walking with you ? '

VII

'O pardon us, honour'd father,
  O pardon us !' they did say ;
'Lady Jean is wed with Captain Ogilvie,
  And from him she will not stay.'

VIII

[Then an angry man the Duke rade on]
  Till he came to bonny Aberdeen,
And there did he see brave Captain Ogilvie
  A-training of his men on the green.

IX

'O woe be to thee, thou Captain Ogilvie !
  And an ill death thou shalt dee.
For taking to thee my daughter Jean
  High hangit shalt thou be.'

X

The Duke has written a broad letter,
  To the King [with his own han' ;]
It was to hang Captain Ogilvie
  If ever he hang'd a man.

XI

'I will not hang Captain Ogilvie
  For no lord that I see ;
But I'll gar him put off the broad scarlèt,
  And put on the single liverỳ.'

XII

Now word came to Captain Ogilvie,
  In the chamber where he lay,
To cast off the gold lace and scarlet,
  And put on the single liverỳ.

single livery] private's uniform.

XIII

'If this be for bonny Jeanie Gordon,
　This penance I can take wi';
If this be for dear Jeanie Gordon,
　All this and mair will I dree.'

XIV

Lady Jeanie had not been married
　A year but only three,
Till she had a babe upon every arm
　And another upon her knee.

XV

'O but I'm weary of wand'rin'!
　O but my fortune is bad!
It sets not the Duke of Gordon's daughter
　To follow a soldier lad.

XVI

'O but I'm weary, weary wand'rin'!
　O but I think it lang!
It sets not the Duke of Gordon's daughter
　To follow a single man.

XVII

'O hold thy tongue, Jeanie Gordon,
　O hold thy tongue, my lamb!
For once I was a noble captain,
　Now for thy sake a single man.'

XVIII

But when they came to the Highland hills,
　Cold was the frost and snow;
Lady Jean's shoes they were all torn,
　No farther could she go.

　　　　dree] endure.

XIX

'Now woe to the hills and the mountains !
   Woe to the wind and the rain !
My feet is sair wi' going barefoot :
   No farther can I gang.

XX

' O were I in the glens o' Foudlen,
   Where hunting I have been,
I would go to bonny Castle Gordon,
   There I'd get hose and sheen ! '

XXI

When they came to bonny Castle Gordon,
   And standing on the green,
The porter out with loud loud shout,
   ' O here comes our Lady Jean ! '—

XXII

' You are welcome, bonny Jeanie Gordon,
   You are dear welcome to me ;
You are welcome, dear Jeanie Gordon,
   But awa' with your Ogilvie ! '

XXIII

Over-seas now went the Captain,
   As a soldier under command ;
But a message soon follow'd after,
   To come home for to heir his land.

XXIV

' O what does this mean ? ' says the Captain ;
   ' Where's my brother's children three ? '—
' They are a' o' them dead and buried :
   Come home, pretty Captain Ogilvie ! '

sheen] shoes.

XXV

'Then hoist up your sail,' says the Captain,
  'And we'll hie back owre the sea;
And I'll gae to bonny Castle Gordon,
  There my dear Jeanie to see.'

XXVI

He came to bonny Castle Gordon,
  And upon the green stood he:
The porter out with a loud loud shout,
  'Here comes our Captain Ogilvie!'—

XXVII

'You're welcome, pretty Captain Ogilvie,
  Your fortune's advanced, I hear;
No stranger can come to my castle
  That I do love so dear.'—

XXVIII

'Put up your hat, Duke of Gordon;
  Let it fa' not from your head.
It never set the noble Duke of Gordon
  To bow to a single soldier lad.

XXIX

'Sir, the last time I was at your Castle,
  You would not let me in;
Now I'm come for my wife and children,
  No friendship else I claim.'

XXX

Down the stair Lady Jean came tripping,
  With the saut tear in her e'e;
She had a babe in every arm,
  And another at her knee.

XXXI

The Captain took her straight in his arms,
　—O a happy man was he!—
Saying, 'Welcome, bonny Jeanie Gordon,
　My Countess o' Cumberland to be!'

95.　*The Bonny Earl of Murray*

I

YE Highlands and ye Lawlands,
　O where hae ye been?
They hae slain the Earl of Murray,
　And hae laid him on the green.

II

Now wae be to thee, Huntley!
　And whairfore did ye sae!
I bade you bring him wi' you,
　But forbade you him to slay.

III

He was a braw gallant,
　And he rid at the ring;
And the bonny Earl of Murray,
　O he might hae been a king!

IV

He was a braw gallant,
　And he play'd at the ba';
And the bonny Earl of Murray
　Was the flower amang them a'!

422

V

He was a braw gallant,
  And he play'd at the gluve;
And the bonny Earl of Murray,
  O he was the Queen's luve!

VI

O lang will his Lady
  Look owre the Castle Downe,
Ere she see the Earl of Murray
  Come sounding through the town!

96. *Bonny George Campbell*

I

HIE upon Hielands,
  And laigh upon Tay,
Bonny George Campbell
  Rade out on a day:
Saddled and bridled,
  Sae gallant to see,
Hame cam' his gude horse,
  But never cam' he.

II

Down ran his auld mither,
  Greetin' fu' sair;
Out ran his bonny bride,
  Reaving her hair;
'My meadow lies green,
  And my corn is unshorn,
My barn is to bigg,
  And my babe is unborn.'

laigh] low.   greeting] crying, lamenting.   Reaving] tearing.
bigg] build.

III

Saddled and bridled
And booted rade he ;
A plume in his helmet,
A sword at his knee ;
But toom cam' his saddle
A' bluidy to see,
O hame cam' his gude horse,
But never cam' he !

toom] empty.

BOOK IV

97.   *Judas*

I

HIT wes upon a Scere-thorsday
     that ure loverd aros ;
Ful milde were the wordès
     he spec to Judas.

II

' Judas, thou most to Jurselem,
     oure mete for to bugge ;
Thritti platen of selver
     thou bere up othi rugge.

III

' Thou comest fer ithe brode stret,
     fer ithe brode strete,
Summe of thine tunesmen
     ther thou meist i-mete.'

IV

Imette wid is soster,
     the swikele wimon :
' Judas, thou were wrthè
     me stende the wid ston,
For the false prophete
     that tou bilevest upon.'

Scere-thorsday] Thursday before Easter.   ure loverd] our lord
bugge] buy.   platen] plates, i. e. coins, pieces.   rugge]
ridge, back.   tunesmen] townsmen.   Imette] being met.
swikele] treacherous.   wrthe] worthy.   me stende, &c.]
men stoned thee.

P 3   425

V

' Be stille, leve soster,
  thin herte the to-breke !
Wiste min loverd Crist,
  ful wel he wolde be wreke.'

98. *St. Stephen and King Herod*

I

SAINT STEPHEN was a clerk
In King Herod's hall,
And servèd him of bread and cloth
  As every king befall.

II

Stephen out of kitchen came
  With boar's head on hand,
He saw a star was fair and bright
  Over Bethlehem stand.

III

He cast adown the boar's head
  And went into the hall ;
' I forsake thee, Herod,
  And thy workès all.

IV

' I forsake thee, King Herod,
  And thy workès all,
There is a child in Bethlehem born
  Is better than we all.'—

leve] dear.   wreke] avenged.

426

V

' What aileth thee, Stephen ?
    What is thee befall ?
Lacketh thee either meat or drink
    In King Herod's hall ? '—

VI

' Lacketh me neither meat ne drink
    In King Herod's hall ;
There is a child in Bethlehem born
    Is better than we all.'—

VII

' What aileth thee, Stephen ?
    Art wode or 'ginnest to brede ?
Lacketh thee either gold or fee,
    Or any rich weed ? '—

VIII

' Lacketh me neither gold ne fee
    Ne none rich weed ;
There is a child in Bethlehem born
    Shall helpen us at our need.'—

IX

' That is all so sooth, Stephen,
    All so sooth, I-wys,
As this capon crowè shall
    That li'th here in my dish.'

X

That word was not so soon said,
    That word in that hall,
The capon crew *Christus natus est*
    Among the lordès all.

wode] mad.   brede] become (mad).   weed] clothing.

XI

'Risit up, my tormentors,
    By two and all by one,
And leadit Stephen out of this town,
    And stonit him with stone.'

XII

Tooken they Stephen
    And stoned him in the way;
And therefore is his even
    On Christe's own day.

99. *The Maid and the Palmer*

I

THE maid she went to the well to washe,
Dew fell off her lily-white fleshe.

II

White she washte, and white she rong,
White she hang'd on the hazel wand.

III

There came an old palmer by the way,
Says, 'God speed thee well, thou fair may.'

IV

'Has tow either cup or can,
To give an old palmer drink therein?'

V

Says, 'I have neither cup nor can,
To give an old palmer drink therein.'

Risit, leadit, stonit] imperatives.   rong] wrung.

VI

' But an thy leman come from Rome,
Cups and cans thou wilt find soon.'

VII

She swore by God and good Saint John
Leman she had never none.

VIII

Says, ' Peace, fair maid, you are forsworne,
Ninè children you have borne.

IX

' Three were buryed under thy bed's head,
Other three under thy brewing lead.

X

' Other three play on yon greene ;
Count, maid, and there be nine.'—

XI

' But I hope you are the good old man
That all the world beleeves upon.

XII

' Old palmer, I pray thee,
Penaunce that thou wilt give to me.'—

XIII

' Penaunce I can give thee none
But seven year to be a stepping-stone.

XIV

Other seven a clapper in a bell,
Other seven to lead an ape in hell.

XV

When thou hast thy penaunce done,
Then thou'st come a mayden home.'

leman] lover.   lead] vat.

I

LULLY, *lulley! lully, lulley!*
The faucon hath borne my make away!

II

He bare him up, he bare him down,
He bare him into an orchard brown.

III

In that orchard there was an halle,
That was hangèd with purple and pall.

IV

And in that hall there was a bed,
It was hangèd with gold sa red.

V

And in that bed there li'th a knight,
His woundès bleeding day and night.

VI

At that bed's foot there li'th a hound,
Licking the blood as it runs down.

VII

By that bed-side kneeleth a may,
And she weepeth both night and day.

VIII

And at that bed's head standeth a stone,
Corpus Christi written thereon.

IX

Lully, lulley! lully, lulley!
The faucon hath borne my make away.

make] mate.   pall] fine cloth.   may] maiden.
430

I

JOSEPH was an old man,
And an old man was he,
When he wedded Mary
In the land of Galilee.

II

Joseph and Mary walk'd
Through an orchard good,
Where was cherries and berries
So red as any blood.

III

Joseph and Mary walk'd
Through an orchard green,
Where was berries and cherries
As thick as might be seen.

IV

O then bespoke Mary,
So meek and so mild,
'Pluck me one cherry, Joseph,
For I am with child.'

V

O then bespoke Joseph
With words so unkind,
'Let him pluck thee a cherry
That brought thee with child.'

VI

O then bespoke the babe
Within his mother's womb,
'Bow down then the tallest tree
For my mother to have some.'

431

THE CHERRY-TREE CAROL

VII

Then bow'd down the highest tree
Unto his mother's hand :
Then she cried, ' See, Joseph,
I have cherries at command ! '

VIII

O then bespake Joseph—
' I have done Mary wrong;
But cheer up, my dearest,
And be not cast down.

IX

' O eat your cherries, Mary,
O eat your cherries now ;
O eat your cherries, Mary,
That grow upon the bough.'

X

Then Mary pluck'd a cherry
As red as the blood ;
Then Mary went home
With her heavy load.

ii

XI

As Joseph was a-walking,
He heard an angel sing :
' This night shall be born
Our heavenly King.

XII

' He neither shall be born
In housen nor in hall,
Nor in the place of Paradise,
But in an ox's stall.

place] palace.

XIII

'He neither shall be clothèd
    In purple nor in pall,
But all in fair linen,
    As were babies all.

XIV

'He neither shall be rock'd
    In silver nor in gold,
But in a wooden cradle
    That rocks on the mould.

XV

'He neither shall be christen'd
    In white wine nor red,
But with fair spring water
    With which we were christenèd.

iii

XVI

Then Mary took her young son
    And set him on her knee ;
'I pray thee now, dear child,
    Tell how this world shall be.'—

XVII

'O I shall be as dead, mother,
    As the stones in the wall ;
O the stones in the street, mother,
    Shall mourn for me all.

XVIII

'And upon a Wednesday
    My vow I will make,
And upon Good Friday
    My death I will take.

pall] fine cloth.

XIX

' Upon Easter-day, mother,
   My uprising shall be ;
O the sun and the moon, mother,
   Shall both rise with me ! '

102. *The Carnal and the Crane*

I

AS I pass'd by a river side,
   And there as I did reign,
In argument I chanced to hear
   A Carnal and a Crane.

II

The Carnal said unto the Crane,
   ' If all the world should turn,
Before we had the Father,
   But now we have the Son !

III

' From whence does the Son come ?
   From where and from what place ? '—
He said, ' In a manger,
   Between an ox and an ass ! '

IV

' I pray thee,' said the Carnal,
   ' Tell me before thou go'st,
Was not the mother of Jesus
   Conceived by the Holy Ghost ? '—

Carnal] crow.   reign] run.

434

V

'She was the purest Virgin,
  And the cleanest from sin ;
She was the handmaid of our Lord,
  And mother of our King.'—

VI

'Where is the golden cradle
  That Christ was rockèd in?
Where are the silken sheets
  That Jesus was wrapt in?'—

VII

'A manger was the cradle
  That Christ was rockèd in ;
The provender the asses left
  So sweetly he slept on.

VIII

'There was a star in the West land,
  So bright did it appear
Into King Herod's chamber,
  And where King Herod were.

IX

'The Wise Men soon espied it,
  And told the king on high,
A princely babe was born that night
  No king could e'er destroy.

X

'If this be true, King Herod said,
  As thou tellest unto me,
This roasted cock that lies in the dish
  Shall crow full fences three.

fences] times.

XI

' The cock soon freshly feathered was
   By the work of God's own hand,
And then three fences crowèd he
   In the dish where he did stand.

XII

' Rise up, rise up, you merry men all,
   See that you ready be,
All children under two years old
   Now slain they all shall be.

XIII

' Then Jesus, ah ! and Joseph,
   And Mary, that was so pure,
They travelled into Egypt,
   As you shall find it sure.

XIV

' And when they came to Egypt's land,
   Amongst those fierce wild beasts,
Mary, she being weary,
   Must needs sit down to rest.

XV

' Come sit thee down, says Jesus,
   Come sit thee down by me,
And thou shalt see how these wild beasts
   Do come and worship me.

XVI

' First came the lovely lion,
   Which Jesu's grace did spring,
And of the wild beasts in the field,
   The lion shall be the king.

XVII

' We'll choose our virtuous princes,
  Of birth and high degree,
In every sundry nation,
  Where'er we come and see.

XVIII

' Then Jesus, ah ! and Joseph,
  And Mary, that was unknown,
They travelled by a husbandman,
  Just while his seed was sown.

XIX

' God speed thee, man ! said Jesus,
  Go fetch thy ox and wain,
And carry home thy corn again,
  Which thou this day hast sown.

XX

' The husbandman fell on his knees,
  Even before his face ;
Long time hast thou been looked for,
  But now thou art come at last.

XXI

' And I myself do now believe
  Thy name is Jesus called ;
Redeemer of mankind thou art,
  Though undeserving all.

XXII

' The truth, man, thou hast spoken,
  Of it thou may'st be sure,
For I must lose my precious blood
  For thee and thousands more.

XXIII

' If any one should come this way,
  And inquire for me alone,
Tell them that Jesus passèd by,
  As thou thy seed did sow.

XXIV

' After that there came King Herod,
  With his train so furiously,
Inquiring of the husbandman,
  Whether Jesus passèd by.

XXV

' Why, the truth it must be spoke,
  And the truth it must be known,
For Jesus passèd by this way
  When my seed was sown.

XXVI

' But now I have it reapen,
  And some laid on my wain,
Ready to fetch and carry
  Into my barn again.

XXVII

' Turn back, says the Captain,
  Your labour and mine's in vain,
It's full three-quarters of a year
  Since he his seed has sown.

XXVIII

' So Herod was deceivèd
  By the work of God's own hand,
And further he proceeded
  Into the Holy Land.

XXIX

'There's thousands of children young,
   Which for his sake did die,—
Do not forbid those little ones,
   And do not them deny.

XXX

'The truth now I have spoken,
   And the truth now I have shown
Even the blessed Virgin,
   She's now brought forth a Son.'

103.   *Jolly Wat*

Can I not sing but 'Hoy',
Whan the joly shepard made so much joy?

I

THE shepard upon a hill he sat;
   He had on him his tabard and his hat,
His tarbox, his pipe, and his flagat;
His name was callèd Joly Joly Wat,
      For he was a gud herdés boy.
            Ut hoy!
   For in his pipe he made so much joy.

II

The shepard upon a hill was laid;
His dog unto his girdell was taid;
He had not slept but a litill braid,
But '*Gloria in excelsis*' was to him said.
            Ut hoy!
   For in his pipe he made so much joy.

tabard] short coat.   flagat] flask.   taid] tied.
braid] time.

439

III

The shepard on a hill he stode ;
Round about him his shepe they yode ;
He put his hond under his hode,
He saw a star as rede as blode.
　　　　Ut hoy !
　　For in his pipe he made so much joy.

IV

The shepard said anon right,
' I will go see yon ferly sight,
Whereas the angel singeth on hight,
And the star that shineth so bright.'
　　　　Ut hoy !
　　For in his pipe he made so much joy.

V

' Now farewell, Mall, and also Will !
For my love go ye all still
Unto I cum again you till,
And evermore, Will, ring well thy bell.'
　　　　Ut hoy !
　　For in his pipe he made so much joy.

VI

' Now must I go there Crist was born ;
Farewell ! I cum again to-morn.
Dog, kepe well my shepe fro the corn,
And warn well "Warroke" when I blow my horn ! '
　　　　Ut hoy !
　　For in his pipe he made so much joy.

yode] went.　　　hode] hood.　　　ferly] marvellous.
440

JOLLY WAT

VII

Whan Wat to Bedlem cumen was,
He swet, he had gone faster than a pace;
He found Jesu in a simpell place,
Betwen an ox but and an asse.
        Ut hoy!
  For in his pipe he made so much joy.

VIII

'Jesu, I offer to thee here my pipe,
My skirt, my tar-box, and my scrip;
Home to my felowes now will I skip,
And also look unto my shepe.'
        Ut hoy!
  For in his pipe he made so much joy.

IX

'Now farewell, mine owne herdesman Wat!'—
'Yea, for God, lady, even so I hat;
Lull well Jesu in thy lap,
And farewell, Joseph, with thy round cap!'
        Ut hoy!
  For in his pipe he made so much joy.

X

'Now may I well both hope and sing,
For I have bene at Cristes bering;
Home to my felowes now will I fling.
Crist of heven to his bliss us bring!'
        Ut hoy!
  For in his pipe he made so much joy.

hat] = am hight, called.

I

AS I sat under a sycamore tree,
  —A sycamore tree, a sycamore tree,
I looked me out upon the sea
    On Christ's Sunday at morn.

II

I saw three ships a-sailing there,
  —A-sailing there, a-sailing there,
Jesu, Mary and Joseph they bare
    On Christ's Sunday at morn.

III

Joseph did whistle and Mary did sing,
  —Mary did sing, Mary did sing,
And all the bells on earth did ring
    For joy our Lord was born.

IV

O they sail'd in to Bethlehem !
  —To Bethlehem, to Bethlehem ;
Saint Michael was the sterèsman,
    Saint John sate in the horn.

V

And all the bells on earth did ring
  —On earth did ring, on earth did ring :
'Welcome be thou Heaven's King,
    On Christ's Sunday at morn ! '

horn] prow.

I

THE first good joy our Mary had,
  It was the joy of one,
To see her own Son Jesus
  To suck at her breast bone ;
To suck at her breast bone, good man,
    And blessed may he be,
      Both Father, Son, and Holy Ghost,
        To all eternity.

II

The next good joy our Mary had,
  It was the joy of two,
To see her own son Jesus
  To make the lame to go ;
To make the lame to go, good man, &c.

III

The next good joy our Mary had,
  It was the joy of three ;
To see her own Son Jesus
  To make the blind to see ;
To make the blind to see, good man, &c.

IV

The next good joy our Mary had,
  It was the joy of four,
To see her own Son Jesus
  To read the Bible o'er ;
To read the Bible o'er, good man, &c.

THE TWELVE GOOD JOYS

V

The next good joy our Mary had,
　It was the joy of five,
To see her own son Jesus
　　To raise the dead alive ;
To raise the dead alive, good man, &c.

VI

The next good joy our Mary had,
　It was the joy of six,
To see her own Son Jesus
　　To wear the crucifix ;
To wear the crucifix, good man, &c.

VII

The next good joy our Mary had,
　It was the joy of seven,
To see her own Son Jesus
　　To wear the crown of Heaven ;
To wear the crown of Heaven, good man, &c.

VIII

The next good joy our Mary had,
　It was the joy of eight,
To see our blessed Saviour
　　Turn darkness into light ;
Turn darkness into light, good man, &c.

IX

The next good joy our Mary had,
　It was the joy of nine,
To see our blessèd Saviour
　　Turn water into wine ;
Turn water into wine, good man, &c.

444

THE TWELVE GOOD JOYS

X

The next good joy our Mary had,
    It was the joy of ten,
To see our blessed Saviour
    To write without a pen;
To write without a pen, good man, &c.

XI

The next good joy our Mary had,
    It was the joy of eleven,
To see our blessed Saviour
    To show the gates of Heaven;
To show the gates of Heaven, good man, &c.

XII

The next good joy our Mary had,
    It was the joy of twelve,
To see our blessed Saviour
    Shut close the gates of hell;
Shut close the gates of hell, good man,
        And blessed may he be,
           Both Father, Son, and Holy Ghost,
             To all eternity.

445

I

THE Angel Gabriel from God
   Was sent to Galilee,
Unto a Virgin fair and free,
   Whose name was called Mary:
And when the Angel thither came,
   He fell down on his knee,
And looking up in the Virgin's face,
   He said, ' All hail, Mary ! '
     Then, sing we all, both great and small,
       Noël, Noël, Noël ;
     We may rejoice to hear the voice
       Of the Angel Gabriel.

II

Mary anon looked him upon,
   And said, ' Sir, what are ye ?
I marvel much at these tidings
   Which thou hast brought to me.
Married I am unto an old man,
   As the lot fell unto me ;
Therefore, I pray, depart away,
   For I stand in doubt of thee.'
          Then, sing, &c.

III

' Mary,' he said, ' be not afraid,
   But do believe in me :
The power of the Holy Ghost
   Shall overshadow thee ;

446

THE ANGEL GABRIEL

Thou shalt conceive without any grief,
    As the Lord told unto me ;
God's own dear Son from Heaven shall come,
    And shall be born of thee.'
                Then, sing, &c.

IV

This came to pass as God's will was,
    Even as the Angel told.
About midnight an Angel bright
    Came to the Shepherds' fold,
And told them then both where and when
    Born was the child, our Lord,
And all along this was their song,
    ' All glory be given to God.'
                Then, sing, &c.

V

Good people all, both great and small,
    The which do hear my voice,
With one accord let's praise the Lord,
    And in our hearts rejoice ;
Like sister and brother, let's love one another
    Whilst we our lives do spend,
Whilst we have space let's pray for grace,
    And so let my Carol end.
                Then, sing, &c.

I

NOW is Christëmas y-come,
  Father and Son together in one,
Holy Ghost us be on
        In fere-a ;
      God send us a good New Year-a !

II

I would you sing, for and I might,
Of a Child is fair in sight ;
His mother him bare this endris night
        So still-a,
      And as it was his will-a.

III

There came three Kings from Galilee
Into Bethlehem, that fair citie,
To seek to Him that e'er should be
        By right-a
      Lord and king and knight-a.

IV

As they came forth with their off'ring,
They met with Herod that moody king ;
He askèd them of their coming
        This tide-a,
      And this to them he said-a.

V

' Of whence be ye, you Kingès three ? '—
' Of the East, as you may see,
To seek to Him that should ever be
        By right-a
      Lord and king and knight-a.'—

In fere] in company.   endris] last.

THE THREE KINGS

VI

' When you at this Child have been,
Come you home this way again ;
Tell me the sight that you have seen ;
      I pray-a,
    Go you none other way-a.'

VII

They took their leave both old and ying
Then of Herod that moody king ;
They went forth with their offering
      By light-a
    Of the star that shone so bright-a.

VIII

Till they came into the place
Where Jesu and his mother was ;
Offer'd they up with great solace
      In fere-a
    Gold, incense and myrrh-a.

IX

When they had their offering made
As the Holy Ghost them bade,
Then they were both merry and glad
      And light-a ;
    It was a good fair sight-a.

X

Anon, as on their way they went,
The Father of heaven an angel sent
To these three kings that made present
      This tide-a,
    And this to them he said-a :—

      ying] young.

THE THREE KINGS

XI

' My Lord hath warn'd you every one
By Herod king you go not home,
For an you do he will you slone
         And 'stroy-a,
    And hurt you wonderly-a.'

XII

So forth they went another way
Through the might of God his lay,
As the angel to them did say,
         Full right-a ;
    It was a good fair sight-a.

XIII

When they came home to their countrie,
Glad and blithe they were all three
Of the sight that they had see ;
         By dene-a
    The company was clean-a.

XIV

Kneel we now here a-down ;
Pray we in good devotion
To the King of great renown,
         Of grace-a
    In heaven to have a place-a.

slone] slay.   lay] law.   By dene] at once, or all together.

The Innocents

I

MARK this song, for it is true,
For it is true as clerkès tell:
In old time strange things came to pass,
Great wonder and great marvel was
    In Israel.

II

There was one Octavian,
Octavian of Rome Emperour,
As bookès old doe specify,
Of all the wide world truëly
    He was lord and governour.

III

The Jews that time lackèd a king,
They lackèd a king to guide them well,
The Emperour of power and might,
Chose one Herod against all right,
    In Israel.

IV

This Herod then was King of Jews
Was King of Jews, and he no Jew.
Forsooth he was a Paynim born,
Wherefore on faith it may be sworn
    He reignèd King untrue.

V

By prophecy one Isaï,
One Isaï at least did tell
A child should come (wondrous news)
That should be born true King of Jews
    In Israel.

THE INNOCENTS

VI

This Herod knew one born should be,
One born should be of true linàge,
That should be right heritour;
For he but by the Emperour
    Was made by usurpage.

VII

Wherefore of thought this King Herod,
This King Herod in great fear fell,
For all the days most in his mirth,
Ever he fearèd Christ his birth
    In Israel.

VIII

The time came it pleasèd God,
It pleasèd God so to come to pass,
For man's soul indeed
His blessed Son was born with speed
    As his will was.

IX

Tidings came to King Herod,
To King Herod, and did him tell,
That one born forsooth is he,
Which lord and king of all shall be
    In Israel.

X

Herod then raged as he were wode,
As he were wode of this tidìng,
And sent for all his scribès sure,
Yet would he not trust the Scripture,
    Nor of their counselling.

wode] mad.

452

THE INNOCENTS

XI

Then this was the conclusion,
The conclusion of his counsèl ;
To send unto his knights anon
To slay the children every one
    In Israel.

XII

This cruel king this tyranny,
This tyranny did put in ure ;
Between a day and years two
All men-children he did slew,
    Of Christ for to be sure.

XIII

Yet Herod miss'd his cruel prey,
His cruel prey as was God's will ;
Joseph with Mary then did flee ;
With Christ to Egypt gone was she
    From Israel.

XIV

All the while these tyrànts,
These tyrànts would not convert,
But innocents ying
That lay sucking,
    They thrust to the heart.

XV

This Herod sought the children ying,
The children ying, with courage fell,
But in doing this vengeànce
His own son was slain by chance
    In Israel.

ure] practice.   ying] young.

THE INNOCENTS

XVI

Alace ! I think the mothers were woe,
The mothers were woe, it was great skill :
What motherly pain
To see them slain
        In cradles lying still !

XVII

But God Himself hath them elect,
Hath them elect, in heaven to dwell :
For they were bathèd in their blood,
For their Baptism forsooth it stood
        In Israel.

XVIII

Alace ! again what hearts had they,
What hearts had they those babes to kill !
With swords when they them caught,
In cradles they lay and laught,
        And never thought ill.

        skill] reason.

I

AS it fell out upon a day,
Rich Dives he made a feast,
And he invited all his friends
   And gentry of the best.

II

Then Lazarus laid him down and down,
   And down at Dives' door;
' Some meat, some drink, brother Dives,
   Bestow upon the poor ! '—

III

' Thou art none of my brother, Lazarus,
   That lies begging at my door;
No meat nor drink will I give thee,
   Nor bestow upon the poor.'

IV

Then Lazarus laid him down and down,
   And down at Dives' wall,
' Some meat, some drink, brother Dives,
   Or with hunger starve I shall ! '—

V

' Thou art none of my brother, Lazarus,
   That lies begging at my wall;
No meat nor drink will I give thee,
   But with hunger starve you shall.'

VI

Then Lazarus laid him down and down,
   And down at Dives' gate :
' Some meat, some drink, brother Dives,
   For Jesus Christ his sake ! '—

VII

' Thou art none of my brother, Lazarus,
    That lies begging at my gate ;
No meat nor drink will I give thee,
    For Jesus Christ his sake.'

VIII

Then Dives sent out his merry men,
    To whip poor Lazarus away ;
They had no power to strike a stroke,
    But flung their whips away.

IX

Then Dives sent out his hungry dogs,
    To bite him as he lay ;
They had no power to bite at all,
    But lickèd his sores away.

X

As it fell out upon a day,
    Poor Lazarus sicken'd and died ;
Then came two angels out of heaven
    His soul therein to guide.

XI

' Rise up, rise up, brother Lazarus,
    And go along with me ;
For you've a place prepared in heaven,
    To sit on an angel's knee.'

XII

As it fell out upon a day,
    Rich Dives sicken'd and died ;
Then came two serpents out of hell,
    His soul therein to guide.

DIVES AND LAZARUS

' Rise up, rise up, brother Dives,
  And go with us to see
A dismal place, prepared in hell,
  To sit on a serpent's knee.'

Then Dives look'd up with his eyes,
  And saw poor Lazarus blest :
' Give me one drop of water, brother Lazarus,
  To quench my flaming thirst.

' Oh had I as many years to abide
  As there are blades of grass,
Then there would be an end, but now
  Hell's pains will ne'er be past !

' Oh was I now but alive again,
  The space of one half hour !
Oh that I had my peace secure !
  Then the devil should have no power.'

I

AS it fell out one May morning,
  And upon one bright holiday,
Sweet Jesus asked of his dear mother,
  If he might go to play.

II

' To play, to play, sweet Jesus shall go,
  And to play pray get you gone ;
And let me hear of no complaint
  At night when you come home.'

III

Sweet Jesus went down to yonder town,
  As far as the Holy Well,
And there did see as fine children
  As any tongue can tell.

IV

He said, ' God bless you every one,
  And your bodies Christ save and see :
Little children, shall I play with you,
  And you shall play with me ? '

V

But they made answer to him, ' No :
  They were lords and ladies all ;
And he was but a maiden's child,
  Born in an ox's stall.'

VI

Sweet Jesus turnèd him around,
  And he neither laughed nor smiled,
But the tears came trickling from his eyes
  To be but a maiden's child.

THE HOLY WELL

Sweet Jesus turnèd him about,
   To his mother's dear home went he,
And said, ' I have been in yonder town,
   As far as you can see.

' I have been down in yonder town
   As far as the Holy Well,
There did I meet as fine children
   As any tongue can tell.

' I bid God bless them every one,
   And their bodies Christ save and see :
Little children, shall I play with you,
   And you shall play with me ?

' But they made answer to me, No :
   They were lords and ladies all ;
And I was but a maiden's child,
   Born in an ox's stall.'—

' Though you are but a maiden's child,
   Born in an ox's stall,
Thou art the Christ, the King of heaven,
   And the Saviour of them all.

' Sweet Jesus, go down to yonder town
   As far as the Holy Well,
And take away those sinful souls,
   And dip them deep in hell.'

XIII

'Nay, nay,' sweet Jesus said,
'Nay, nay, that may not be ;
For there are too many sinful souls
Crying out for the help of me.'

111.   *The Seven Virgins*

I

ALL under the leaves and the leaves of life
I met with virgins seven,
And one of them was Mary mild,
Our Lord's mother of Heaven.

II

'O what are you seeking, you seven fair maids,
All under the leaves of life ?
Come tell, come tell, what seek you
All under the leaves of life ?'

III

'We're seeking for no leaves, Thomas,
But for a friend of thine ;
We're seeking for sweet Jesus Christ,
To be our guide and thine.'

IV

'Go down, go down, to yonder town,
And sit in the gallery,
And there you'll see sweet Jesus Christ
Nail'd to a big yew-tree.'

V

So down they went to yonder town
As fast as foot could fall,
And many a grievous bitter tear
From the virgins' eyes did fall.

THE SEVEN VIRGINS

VI

'O peace, Mother, O peace, Mother,
 Your weeping doth me grieve :
I must suffer this,' He said,
 ' For Adam and for Eve.

VII

'O Mother, take you John Evangelist
 All for to be your son,
And he will comfort you sometimes,
 Mother, as I have done.'

VIII

'O come, thou John Evangelist,
 Thou'rt welcome unto me ;
But more welcome my own dear Son,
 Whom I nursed on my knee.'

IX

Then He laid his head on His right shoulder,
 Seeing death it struck Him nigh—
' The Holy Ghost be with your soul,
 I die, Mother dear, I die.'

X

O the rose, the gentle rose,
 And the fennel that grows so green !
God give us grace in every place
 To pray for our king and queen.

XI

Furthermore for our enemies all
 Our prayers they should be strong :
Amen, good Lord ; your charity
 Is the ending of my song.

PART II

BOOK V

112.   *Robyn and Gandelyn*

I

I HERDE a carpyng of a clerk,
   Al at yone wodes ende,
Of gode Robyn and Gandeleyn ;
   Was ther non other thynge.
Robynn lyth in grene wode bowndyn.

II

Stronge thevys wern tho chylderin none,
   But bowmen gode and hende ;
He wentyn to wode to getyn hem fleych,
   If God wold it hem sende.

III

Al day wentyn tho chylderin two,
   And fleych fowndyn he non,
Til it were ageyn evyn ;
   The chylderin wold gon hom.

IV

Half an honderid of fat falyf der
   He comyn ayon,
And alle he wern fayr and fat i-now,
   But markyd was ther non :
'Be dere God,' seyde gode Robyn,
   'Hereof we shul have on.'

carpyng] talking, tale.   hende] gracious, courteous.   He]
they.   ageyn evyn] towards evening.   He comyn ayon]
came over against them, in their path.   on] one.

462

ROBYN AND GANDELYN

v

Robyn bent his joly bowe,
    Ther in he set a flo;
The fattest der of alle
    The herte he clef a to.

vi

He hadde not the der i-flawe,
    Ne half out of the hyde,
There cam a schrewde arwe out of the west,
    That felde Robertes pryde.

vii

Gandeleyn lokyd hym est and west,
    Be every syde:
' Hoo hat myn mayster slayin?
    Ho hat don this dede?
Shal I never out of grene wode go
    Til I se his sydis blede.'

viii

Gandeleyn lokyd hym est and west,
    And sowt under the sunne;
He saw a lytil boy,
    He clepyn Wrennok of Donne.

ix

A good bowe in his hond,
    A brod arwe ther-ine,
And fowre and twenti goode arwys,
    Trusyd in a thrumme:
' Be war the, war the, Gandeleyn,
    Her-of thu shalt han summe!

flo] arrow.   a to] in two.   i-flawe] flayed.   schrewde]
sharp.   He clepyn] whom they call.   Trusyd] trussed,
bound up.   thrumme] end of a warp.

ROBYN AND GANDELYN

X

'Be war the, war the, Gandeleyn,
 Her of thu gyst plenté!'—
'Ever on for an other,' seyde Gandeleyn;
 'Mysaunter have he shal fle.

XI

'Qwer-at shal our marke be?'
 Seyde Gandeleyn.—
'Everyche at otheris herte,'
 Seyde Wrennok ageyn.

XII

'Ho shal yeve the ferste schote?'
 Seyde Gandeleyn.
'And I shul yeve the on be-forn,'
 Seyde Wrennok ageyn.

XIII

Wrennok schette a ful good schote,
 And he schet not to hye;
Throw the sanchothis of his bryk;
 It towcyhd neyther thye.

XIV

'Now hast thu yovyn me on be-forn,'
 Al thus to Wrennok seyde he,
'And throw the myyt of our lady
 A bettere I shal yeve the.'

XV

Gandeleyn bent his goode bowe,
 And set ther-in a flo;
He schet throw his grene certyl,
 His herte he clef on too.

gyst] gettest.   Mysaunter] misadventure.   Ho] who.
yeve] give.   sanchothis] fork.   bryk] breeches.   yovyn
me on] given me one.   certyl] kirtle.

464

XVI

'Now shalt thu never yelpe, Wrennok,
  At ale ne at wyn,
That thu hast slawe goode Robyn,
  And his knave Gandeleyn.

XVII

'Now shalt thu never yelpe, Wrennok,
  At wyn ne at ale,
That thu hast slawe goode Robyn,
  And Gandeleyn his knave.'
  Robyn lyth in grene wode bowndyn.

113. *The Birth of Robin Hood*

I

O WILLIE's large o' limb and lith,
    And come o' high degree,
And he is gane to Earl Richard,
    To serve for meat and fee.

II

Earl Richard had but ae daughter,
    Fair as a lily-flower,
And they made up their love-contract
    Like proper paramour.

III

It fell upon a simmer's nicht,
    Whan the leaves were fair and green,
That Willie met his gay ladie
    Intil the wood alane.

IV

'O narrow is my gown, Willie,
    That wont to be sae wide ;
And gane is a' my fair colour,
    That wont to be my pride.

yelpe] brag.   lith] joint.

465

V

' But gin my father should get word
    What 's past between us twa,
Before that he should eat or drink,
    He'd hang you o'er that wa'.

VI

' But ye'll come to my bower, Willie,
    Just as the sun gaes down,
And kep me in your arms twa,
    And latna me fa' down.'

VII

O whan the sun was now gane down,
    He 's doen him till her bower,
And there, by the lee licht o' the moon,
    Her window she lookit o'er.

VIII

Intill a robe o' red scarlèt
    She lap, fearless o' harm ;
And Willie was large o' lith and limb,
    And keppit her in his arm.

IX

And they've gane to the gude green-wood,
    And, ere the night was deen,
She 's born to him a bonny young son,
    Amang the leaves sae green.

X

Whan night was gane, and day was come,
    And the sun began to peep,
Up and raise the Earl Richard
    Out o' his drowsy sleep.

kep] catch.

466

XI

He 's ca'd upon his merry young men,
  By ane, by twa, and by three :
' O what 's come o' my daughter dear,
  That she 's nae come to me ?

XII

' I dreamt a dreary dream last night,
  God grant it come to gude !
I dreamt I saw my daughter dear
  Drown in the saut sea flood.

XIII

' But gin my daughter be dead or sick,
  Or yet be stown awa',
I mak a vow, and I'll keep it true,
  I'll hang ye ane and a' ! '

XIV

They sought her back, they sought her fore,
  They sought her up and down ;
They got her in the gude green-wood,
  Nursing her bonny young son.

XV

He took the bonny boy in his arms,
  And kist him tenderlie ;
Says, 'Though I would your father hang,
  Your mother 's dear to me.'

XVI

He kist him o'er and o'er again :
  ' My grandson I thee claim,
And Robin Hood in gude green-wood,
  And that shall be your name.'

XVII

And mony ane sings o' grass, o' grass,
    And mony ane sings o' corn,
And mony ane sings o' Robin Hood
    Kens little whare he was born.

XVIII

It wasna in the ha', the ha',
    Nor in the painted bower;
But it was in the gude green-wood,
    Amang the lily-flower.

114. *Adam Bell, Clym of the Clough, and William of Cloudesley*

Fytte the First

I

MERY it was in the grene foreste
    Amonge the levès grene,
Wheras men hunt east and west
    Wyth bowes and arrowes kene;

II

To raise the dere out of theyr denne;
    Suche sightes hath ofte bene sene;
As by thre yemen of the north countrey,
    By them it is I meane.

III

The one of them hight Adam Bell,
    The other Clym of the Clough,
The thyrd was Wyllyam of Cloudesley,
    An archer good ynough.

Clym of the Clough] Clement of the Clift.

468

IV

They were outlaw'd for venyson,
  These yemen everych-one ;
They swore them brethren upon a day,
  To Englyshe-wood for to gone.

V

Now lith and lysten, gentylmen,
  That of myrthes loveth to here :
Two of them were single men,
  The third had a wedded fere.

VI

Wyllyam was the wedded man,
  Muche more then was hys care :
He sayde to hys brethren upon a day,
  To Carleile he would fare ;

VII

For to speke with fayre Alyce his wife,
  And with hys chyldren thre.
'By my trouth,' sayde Adam Bel,
  'Not by the counsell of me :

VIII

'For if ye go to Carleile, brother,
  And from thys wylde wode wende,
If that the Justice may you take,
  Your lyfe were at an ende.'—

IX

'If that I come not to-morowe, brother,
  By pryme to you agayne,
Truste you then that I am taken,
  Or else that I am slayne.'

Englyshe-wood] Inglewood, near Carlisle.   lith] hearken.
fere] mate.   pryme] six in the morning.

ADAM BELL,

X

He toke his leave of hys brethren two,
    And to Carleile he is gon :
There he knock'd at his owne windòwe
    Shortlye and anone.

XI

' Wher be you, fayre Alyce,' he sayd,
    ' My wife and chyldren three ?
Lyghtly let in thyne owne husbànde,
    Wyllyam of Cloudesley.' —

XII

' Alas ! ' then sayde fayre Alyce,
    And syghèd wonderous sore,
' Thys place hath ben besette for you
    Thys halfè yere and more.' —

XIII

' Now am I here,' sayde Cloudesley,
    ' I would that in I were.
Now fetche us meate and drynke ynoughe,
    And let us make good chere.'

XIV

She fetchèd hym meate and drynke plentye,
    Lyke a true wedded wyfe ;
And pleasèd hym with that she had,
    Whom she loved as her lyfe.

XV

There lay an old wyfe in that place,
    A lytle besyde the fyre,
Whych Wyllyam had found of charytye
    More than seven yere.

        found] provided for.

XVI

Up she rose, and forth shee goes,
    Evel mote shee speede therfore !
For shee had sett no foote on ground
    In seven yere before.

XVII

She went unto the Justice Hall,
    As fast as she could hye :
' Thys night,' shee sayd, ' is come to town
    Wyllyam of Cloudeslyè.'

XVIII

Thereof the Justice was full fayne,
    And so was the Shirife also :
' Thou shalt not trauaile hither, dame, for nought,
    Thy meed thou shalt have or thou go.'

XIX

They gave to her a ryght good goune,
    Of scarlate, [and of graine] :
She toke the gyft, and home she wente,
    And couchèd her doune agayne.

XX

They raysed the towne of mery Carleile
    In all the haste they can ;
And came thronging to Wyllyam's house,
    As fast as they might gone.

XXI

There they besette that good yeman
    Round about on every syde :
Wyllyam hearde great noyse of folkes,
    That thither-ward fast hyed.

fayne] rejoiced.

471

XXII

Alyce opened a backe wyndowe,
  And lokèd all aboute ;
She was ware of the Justice and Shirife bothe,
  Wyth a full great route.

XXIII

' Alas ! treason ! ' cryed Alyce,
  ' Ever wo may thou be !
Goe into my chamber, my husband,' she sayd,
  ' Swete Wyllyam of Cloudesley.'

XXIV

He toke hys sword and hys buckler,
  Hys bow and hys chyldren thre,
And wente into hys strongest chamber,
  Where he thought surest to be.

XXV

Fayre Alyce, like a lover true,
  Took a polaxe in her hande :
Said, ' He shall dye that cometh in
  Thys dore, whyle I may stand.'

XXVI

Cloudesley bente a wel good bowe,
  That was of a trusty tre,
He smot the Justice on the brest,
  That hys arowe brast in three.

XXVII

' God's curse on his harte,' saide Wyllyam,
  ' Thys day thy cote dyd on !
If it had ben no better then myne,
  It had gone nere thy bone.'—

XXVIII

' Yelde the Cloudesley,' sayd the Justice,
 ' And thy bowe and thy arrowes the fro.'—
' God's curse on hys hart,' sayd fair Alyce,
 ' That my husband councelleth so ! '—

XXIX

' Set fyre on the house,' saide the Sherife,
 ' Syth it wyll no better be,
And brenne we therin Wyllyam,' he saide,
 ' Hys wyfe and chyldren thre.'

XXX

They fyred the house in many a place,
 The fyre flew up on hye :
' Alas ! ' then cryèd fayre Alyce,
 ' I see we here shall dye.'

XXXI

Wyllyam openyd a backe wyndowe,
 That was in hys chamber hie,
And there with sheetes he did let downe
 His wyfe and children three.

XXXII

' Have you here my treasure,' sayde Wyllyam,
 ' My wyfe and my chyldren thre :
For Christès love do them no harme,
 But wreke you all on me.'

XXXIII

Wyllyam shot so wonderous well,
 Tyll hys arrowes were all agoe,
And the fyre so fast upon hym fell,
 That hys bowstryng brent in two.

ADAM BELL,

XXXIV

The sparkles brent and fell upon
　Good Wyllyam of Cloudesley:
Than was he a wofull man, and sayde,
　'Thys is a cowardes death to me.

XXXV

'Leever had I,' sayde Wyllyam,
　'With my sworde in the route to renne,
Then here among myne enemyes wode
　Thus cruelly to bren.'

XXXVI

He toke hys sword and hys buckler,
　And among them all he ran,
Where the people were most in prece,
　He smot downe many a man.

XXXVII

There myght no man abyde hys stroakes,
　So fersly on them he ran:
Then they threw windowes and dores on him,
　And so toke that good yemàn.

XXXVIII

There they hym bounde both hand and fote,
　And in a deepe dungeon him cast:
'Now Cloudesley,' sayd the Justice,
　'Thou shalt be hangèd in hast.'

XXXIX

'A payre of new gallowes,' sayd the Sherife,
　Now shal I for thee make;'
And the gates of Carleile shal be shutte:
　No man shal come in therat.

wode] wild, savage.　　prece] press, crowd.

CLYM OF THE CLOUGH, ETC.

XL

' Then shall not helpe Clym of the Clough,
  Nor yet shall Adam Bell,
Though they came with a thousand mo,
  Nor all the devels in hell.'

XLI

Early in the mornynge the Justice uprose,
  To the gates first can he gone,
And commaunded to be shut full close
  Lightilè everych-one.

XLII

Then went he to the markett place,
  As fast as he coulde hye;
There a payre of new gallowes he set up
  Besyde the pyllorye.

XLIII

A lytle boy among them asked,
  What meanèd that gallow-tre?
They sayde to hange a good yemàn,
  Called Wyllyam of Cloudeslèy.

XLIV

That lytle boye was the towne swyne-heard,
  And kept fayre Alyce's swyne;
Oft he had seene Wyllyam in the wodde,
  And geven hym there to dyne.

XLV

He went out att a crevis of the wall,
  And lightly to the woode dyd gone;
There met he with these wight yemen
  Shortly and anone.

475

XLVI

'Alas!' then sayde the lytle boye,
  'Ye tary here all too longe;
Cloudeslee is taken, and dampned to death,
  And readye for to honge.'

XLVII

'Alas!' then sayd good Adam Bell,
  'That ever we saw thys daye!
He had better have tarryed with us,
  So ofte as we dyd him praye.

XLVIII

'He myght have dwelt in grene foreste,
  Under the shadowes greene,
And have kepte both hym and us att reste,
  Out of all trouble and teene.'

XLIX

Adam bent a ryght good bow,
  A great hart sone hee had slayne:
'Take that, chylde, to thy dynner,
  And bryng me myne arrowe agayne.'

L

'Now go we hence,' sayed these wight yeomen,
  'Tarry we no longer here;
We shall hym borowe by God his grace,
  Though we buy itt full dere.'

LI

To Carleile wente these bold yemen,
  All in a mornyng of maye.—
Here is a Fyt of Cloudesley,
  And another is for to saye.

dampned] condemned.   teene] sorrow.   borowe]
ransom, redeem.

476

Fytte the Second

LII

And when they came to mery Carleile,
  In a fayre mornyng tyde,
They founde the gates shut them untyll
  About on every syde.

LIII

' Alas ! ' then sayd good Adam Bell,
  ' That ever we were made men !
These gates be shut so wonderly well,
  We may not come therein.'

LIV

Then bespake him Clym of the Clough,
  ' With a wyle we wyl us in bryng ;
Let us say we be messengers,
  Streyght comen from our King.'

LV

Adam said, ' I have a letter written,
  Now let us wysely werke,
We wyl saye we have the Kyngè's seale ;
  I holde the porter no clerke.'

LVI

Then Adam Bell bete on the gates
  With strokès great and stronge :
The porter herde such a noyse therat.
  And to the gates he thronge.

LVII

' Who is there now,' sayd the porter,
  ' That maketh all thys knockinge ?'—
' We be two messengers,' quoth Clym of the Clough,
  ' Be come ryght from our Kynge.'—

thronge] hastened.

LVIII

'We have a letter,' sayd Adam Bell,
　'To the Justice we must it brynge;
Let us in our message to do,
　That we were agayne to the Kynge.'—

LIX

'Here commeth none in,' sayd the porter,
　'By hym that dyed on a tre,
Tyll a false thefe be hangèd,
　Called Wyllyam of Cloudesley.'

LX

Then spake the good yeman, Clym of the Clough,
　And swore by Mary fre,
'And if that we stande long wythout,
　Lyke a thefe hangèd shalt thou be.

LXI

'Lo! here we have got the Kynge's seale:
　What, lordane, art thou wode?'
The porter wende it had ben so,
　And lyghtly dyd off hys hode.

LXII

'Welcome is my lordes seale,' he saide;
　'For that ye shall come in.'
He opened the gate right shortlye:
　An evyl openyng for him!

LXIII

'Now are we in,' sayde Adam Bell,
　'Wherof we are full faine;
But Christ he knowes, that harowed hell,
　How we shall come out agayne.'

lordane] dolt.　　wode] mad.　　wende] weened, thought.
478

LXIV

'Had we the keys,' said Clym of the Clough,
  'Ryght wel then shoulde we spede,
Then might we come out wel ynough
  When we se tyme and nede.'

LXV

They callèd the porter to counsell,
  And wrang his necke in two,
And caste hym in a depe dungeon,
  And toke hys keys hym fro.

LXVI

'Now am I porter,' sayd Adam Bell,
  'Se, brother, the keys are here!
The worst porter to merry Carleile
  That ye had thys hundred yere.

LXVII

'And now wyll we our bowès bend,
  Into the towne wyll we go,
For to delyver our dere brothèr,
  That lyeth in care and wo.'

LXVIII

Then they bent theyr good yew bowes,
  And lokèd theyr stringes were round,
The market-place of mery Carleile
  They beset in that stound.

LXIX

And, as they lokèd them besyde,
  A paire of new galowes they see,
And the Justice with a quest of swerers,
  That judged Cloudesley hangèd to be.

round] i. e. not frayed.   stound] time.   swerers] swearers, jurymen.

LXX

And Cloudesley lay redy in a cart,
    Fast bound both fote and hand ;
And a stronge rope about hys necke,
    All readye for to be hang'd.

LXXI

The Justice called to him a ladde,
    Cloudesley's clothes shold hee have,
To take the measure of that yeman,
    Thereafter to make hys grave.

LXXII

' I have sene as great mervaile,' said Cloudesley,
    ' As betweyne thys and pryme,
He that maketh a grave for mee,
    Hymselfe may lye therin.'

LXXIII

' Thou speakest proudlye,' said the Justice,
    ' I will thee hange with my hande.'
Full wel herd this his brethren two,
    There styll as they dyd stande.

LXXIV

Then Cloudesley cast his eyen asyde
    And saw hys brethren stande
At a corner of the market place,
    With theyr good bowes bent in theyr hand.

LXXV

' I se comfort,' sayd Cloudesley ;
    ' Yet hope I well to fare ;
If I might have my handes at wyll,
    Ryght lytell wolde I care.'

LXXVI

Then bespake good Adam Bell
    To Clym of the Clough so fre,
' Brother, se you marke the Justyce wel ;
    Lo ! yonder you may him se :

LXXVII

' And at the Sheryfe shote I wyll
    Strongly wyth an arrowe kene.'—
A better shote in mery Carleile
    Thys seven yere was not sene.

LXXVIII

They loosed their arrowes both at once,
    Of no man had they drede ;
The one hyt the Justice, the other the Sheryfe,
    That both theyr sides gan blede.

LXXIX

All men voyded, that them stode nye,
    When the Justice fell to the grounde,
And the Sheryfe fell nye hym by ;
    Eyther had his deathes wounde.

LXXX

All the citezeyns fast gan flye,
    They durst no longer abyde :
There lyghtly they losèd Cloudesley,
    Where he with ropes lay tyde.

LXXXI

Wyllyam start to an officer of the towne,
    Hys axe out hys hand he wronge,
On echè syde he smote them downe,
    Hym thought he taryed to long.

voyded] gave room, ran off.

LXXXII

Wyllyam sayde to hys brethren two,
  ' Thys daye let us lyve and die,
If e'er you have nede, as I have now,
  The same you shall finde by me.'

LXXXIII

They shot so well in that tyde
  (Theyr stringes were of silke ful sure)
That they kept the stretes on every side ;
  That batayle did long endure.

LXXXIV

They fought together as brethren true,
  Lyke hardy men and bolde,
Many a man to the ground they threw,
  And many a herte made colde.

LXXXV

But when their arrowes were all gon,
  Men presyd to them full fast,
They drew theyr swordès then anone,
  And theyr bowès from them cast.

LXXXVI

They went lyghtlye on theyr way,
  Wyth swordes and bucklers round ;
By that it was mydd of the day,
  They had made many a wound.

LXXXVII

There was many an out-horne in Carleile blowen,
  And the belles backwarde dyd ryng ;
Many a woman sayde, Alas !
  And many theyr handes dyd wryng.

out-horne] a horn blown to call citizens to help the law.
482

LXXXVIII

The Mayre of Carleile forth com was,
 Wyth hym a ful great route :
These thre yemen dred hym full sore,
 For theyr lyvès stode in doute.

LXXXIX

The Mayre came armèd a full great pace,
 With a polaxe in hys hande ;
Many a strong man wyth him was,
 There in that stowre to stande.

XC

The Mayre smot at Cloudesley with his byll,
 Hys buckler he brast in two,
Full many a yeman with great yll,
 ' Alas ! Treason ! ' they cryed for wo.
' Kepe well the gatès fast we wyll,
 That these traytours therout not go.'

XCI

But al for nought was that they wrought,
 For so fast they downe were layde,
Tyll they all thre, that so manfully fought
 Were gotten without, at a braide.

XCII

' Have here your keys,' sayd Adam Bell,
 ' Myne office I here forsake ;
And yf you do by my counsell
 A new porter do ye make.'

XCIII

He threw theyr keys there at theyr hedes,
 And bad them well to thryve,
And all that letteth any good yeman
 To come and comfort his wyfe.

stowre] press of fight. braide] sudden spring. letteth]
hindereth.

XCIV

Thus be these good yeman gon to the wode
    As lyghtly as lefe on lynde ;
They laughe and be mery in theyr mode,
    Theyr enemyes were farre behynd.

XCV

When they came to Inglyswode,
    Under theyr trysty tre,
There they found bowès full good,
    And arrowès great plentye.

XCVI

' So God me help,' sayd Adam Bell,
    And Clym of the Clough so fre,
' I would we were in mery Carleile,
    Before that fayre meynye.'

XCVII

They set them downe, and made good chere,
    And eate and dranke full well.—
A second Fyt of the wightye yeomen :
    Another I wyll you tell.

Fytte the Third.

XCVIII

As they sat in Inglyswode,
    Under theyr trysty tre,
They thought they herd a woman wepe,
    But her they mought not se.

XCIX

Sore syghèd there fayre Alyce, and sayd,
    ' That ever I sawe thys day !
For nowe is my dere husband slayne :
    Alas ! and wel-a-waye !

lynde] linden.   meynye] company.   trysty tre] trysting tree.
484

C

'Myght I have spoken wyth hys dere brethren
    Or with eyther of them twayne,
To show to them what him befell,
    My hart were out of payne.'

CI

Cloudesley walked a lytle beside,
    Looked under the grene wood lynde,
He was ware of his wife and chyldren three,
    Full wo in herte and mynde.

CII

'Welcome, wyfe,' then sayde Wyllyam,
    'Under this trysty tre:
I had wende yesterday, by swete saynt John,
    Thou sholdest me never have se.'—

CIII

'Now well is me that ye be here,
    My harte is out of wo.'—
'Dame,' he sayde, 'be mery of chere,
    And thanke my brethren two.'

CIV

'Herof to speake,' said Adam Bell,
    'I-wis it is no bote:
The meate, that we must supp withall,
    It runneth yet fast on fote.'

CV

Then went they downe into a launde.
    These noble archars all thre;
Eche of them slew a hart of greece,
    The best they cold there se.

launde] forest-park.   of greece] of grease, fat.

CVI

' Have here the best, Alyce, my wyfe,'
  Sayde Wyllyam of Cloudesley ;
' By cause ye so bouldly stode me by
  When I was slayne full nye.'

CVII

Then wente they to theyr suppere
  Wyth such meate as they had ;
And thankèd God of theyr fortune :
  They were both mery and glad.

CVIII

And when that they had suppèd well,
  Certayne withouten lease,
Cloudesley sayd, ' We wyll to our Kynge,
  To get us a charter of peace.

CIX

' Alyce shal be at sojournyng
  In a nunnery here besyde ;
My tow sonnes shall wyth her go,
  And there they shall abyde.

CX

' My eldest son shall go wyth me ;
  For hym have I no care :
And he shall bring you worde agayn,
  How that we do fare.'

CXI

Thus be these wightmen to London gone
  As fast as they myght hye,
Tyll they came to the Kynge's pallàce,
  Where they woulde needès be.

lease] lying.   tow] two.   wightmen] stout fellows.
486

CXII

And whan they came to the Kynge's courte,
    Unto the pallace gate,
Of no man wold they aske no leave,
    But boldly went in therat.

CXIII

They presyd prestly into the hall,
    Of no man had they dreade :
The porter came after, and dyd them call,
    And with them began to chyde.

CXIV

The usher sayde, ' Yemen, what wold ye have?
    I pray you tell to me.
You myght thus make offycers shent :
    Good syrs, of whence be ye ? '—

CXV

' Syr, we be outlawes of the forest,
    Certayne withouten lease ;
And hether we be come to the Kyng,
    To get us a charter of peace.'

CXVI

And whan they came before our Kynge,
    As it was the lawe of the lande,
They kneled downe without lettyng,
    And eche held up his hand.

CXVII

They sayd, ' Lord, we beseche you here
    That ye wyll graunt us grace ;
For we have slayne your fat falowe dere
    In many a sondry place.'

presyd prestly] pressed quickly.   shent] ruined.   lettyng] delay.

CXVIII

' What be your names,' then said our Kynge,
  ' Anone that you tell me?'—
They sayd, 'Adam Bell, Clym of the Clough,
  And Wyllyam of Cloudesley.'—

CXIX

' Be ye those theves,' then sayd our Kynge,
  ' That men have tolde of to me?
Here to God I make an avowe,
  Ye shal be hangèd al thre.

CXX

' Ye shal be dead without mercy,
  As I am Kynge of this lande.'
He commanded his officers everich-one,
  Fast on them to lay hande.

CXXI

There they toke these good yemen,
  And arested them al thre:
' So may I thryve,' sayd Adam Bell,
  ' Thys game lyketh not me!

CXXII

' But, good lorde, we beseche you then,
  That yee graunt us grace,
Insomuche as we be to you comen,
  Or else we may fro you passe,

CXXIII

' With such weapons as we have here,
  Tyll we be out of your place;
And yf we lyve this hundred yere,
  We wyll aske you no grace.'

488

CXXIV

' Ye speake proudly,' sayd the Kynge ;
　' Ye shall be hangèd all thre.'
' That were great pitye,' then sayd the Quene,
　' If any grace myght be.

CXXV

' My lorde, whan I came fyrst into this lande
　To be your wedded wyfe,
The fyrst boone that I wold aske,
　Ye would graunt it me belyfe :

CXXVI

' And I asked you never none tyll now ;
　Therefore, lorde, graunt it me ! '—
' Now aske it, madam,' sayd the Kynge,
　' And graunted it shal be.'—

CXXVII

' Then, good my lord, I you beseche,
　These yemen graunt ye me.'—
' Madame, ye myght have asked a boone
　That shuld have been worth them thre.

CXXVIII

' Ye myght have askèd towres and townes,
　Parkes and forestes plentye.'—
' None soe pleasant to my pay,' shee sayd ;
　' Nor none so lefe to me.'—

CXXIX

' Madame, sith it is your desyre,
　Your askyng graunted shal be ;
But I had lever have geven you
　Good market-townès thre.'

belyfe] straightway.　　　pay] satisfaction.　　lefe] dear.

CXXX

The Quenè was a glad woman,
  And sayde, 'Lord, gramarcy!
I dare and undertake for them
  That true men shal they be.

CXXXI

'But good lord, speke som mery word,
  That comfort they may se.'—
'I graunt you grace,' then sayd our Kynge;
  'Washe, felows, and to meate go ye.'

CXXXII

They had not setten but a whyle,
  Certayne without lesynge,
There came messengers out of the north
  With letters to our Kynge.

CXXXIII

And whan they came before the Kynge,
  They knelt downe on theyr kne;
And sayd, 'Lord, your officers grete you well,
  Of Carleile in the north countrè.'

CXXXIV

'How fareth my Justice,' sayd the Kynge,
  'And my Sheryfe also?'—
'Syr, they be slayne, without leasynge,
  And many an officer mo.'—

CXXXV

'Who hath them slayne,' sayd the Kynge,
  'Anone that thou tell me.'—
'Adam Bell, and Clym of the Clough,
  And Wyllyam of Cloudesley.'—

490

CXXXVI

' Alas for rewth ! ' then sayd our Kynge :
  ' My herte is wonderous sore ;
I had lever than a thousande pounde,
  I had knowne of thys before ;

CXXXVII

' For I have y-graunted them grace,
  And that forthynketh me :
But had I knowne all thys before,
  They had been hangèd all thre.'

CXXXVIII

The Kyng hee opened the letter anone,
  Himselfe he red it thro,
And founde how these outlàwes had slain
  Thre hundred men and mo :

CXXXIX

Fyrst the Justice, and the Sheryfe,
  And the Mayre of Carleile towne ;
Of all the constables and catchipolles
  Alyve were scant left one :

CXL

The baylyes, and the bedyls both,
  And the sergeauntes of the law,
And forty fosters of the fe,
  These outlawes had y-slaw ;

CXLI

And broke his parks, and slayne his dere ;
  Of all they chose the best ;
So perèlous out-lawes as they were
  Walked not by easte nor west.

forthynketh] repenteth.   fosters of the fe] foresters of the
lordship.

CXLII

When the Kynge this letter had red,
  In hys herte he syghèd sore :
' Take up the tables,' anone he bad,
  ' For I may eat no more.'

CXLIII

The Kynge callèd hys best archars
  To the buttes wyth hym to go :
' I wyll se these felowes shote,' he sayd,
  ' In the north have wrought this wo.'

CXLIV

The Kynge's bowmen buske them blyve,
  And the Quene's archers also ;
So dyd these thre wyght yemen ;
  With them they thought to go.

CXLV

There twyse or thryse they shote about
  For to assay theyr hande ;
There was no shote these yemen shot,
  That any prycke myght stand.

CXLVI

Then spake Wyllyam of Cloudesley :
  ' By God that for me dyed,
I hold hym never no good archar,
  That shoteth at buttes so wyde.'—

CXLVII

' At what a butte now wold ye shote,
  I pray thee tell to me ? '—
' Nay, syr,' he sayd, ' at such a butte
  As men use in my countrè.'

---

buttes] targets.   buske them] busked, made them **ready**.
blyve] = belyfe *supra*, straightway.   prycke] mark.

CXLVIII

Wyllyam wente into a fyeld,
    And with him his two brethren :
There they set up two hasell roddes
    Twenty score paces betwene.

CXLIX

' I hold him an archar,' said Cloudesley,
    ' That yonder wande cleveth in two,'—
' Here is none suche,' sayd the Kynge,
    ' Nor no man can so do.'

CL

' I shall assaye, syr,' sayd Cloudesley,
    ' Or that I farther go.'
Cloudesley with a bearyng arowe
    Clave the wand in two.

CLI

' Thou art the best archer,' then said the Kynge,
    ' Forsothe that ever I se.'—
' And yet for your love,' sayd Wyllyam,
    ' I wyll do more maystery.

CLII

' I have a sonne is seven yere olde,
    He is to me full deare ;
I wyll hym tye unto a stake :
    All shall se, that be here ;

CLIII

' And lay an apple upon hys head,
    And go syxe score paces hym fro,
And I my selfe with a brode arow
    Shall cleve the apple in two.'

bearyng arowe] a long arrow, tapered to carry far.

CLIV

'Now hastè the,' then sayd the Kynge,
    'By hym that dyed on a tre,
But yf thou do not, as thou hest sayde,
    Hangèd shalt thou be.

CLV

'An thou touche his head or gowne,
    In syght that men may se,
By all the sayntes that be in heaven,
    I shall hange you all thre !'

CLVI

'That I have promised,' said Wyllyam,
    'That I wyll never forsake.'
And there even before the Kynge
    In the earth he drove a stake :

CLVII

And bound thereto his eldest sonne,
    And bad hym stand styll thereat ;
And turned the childè's face him fro,
    Because he should not start.

CLVIII

An apple upon his head he set,
    And then his bowe he bent :
Syxe score paces they were out-met,
    And thether Cloudesley went

CLIX

There he drew out a fayr brode arrowe,
    —Hys bowe was great and longe,—
He set that arrowe in his bowe,
    That was both styffe and stronge.

out-met] measured out.

494

CLX

He prayèd the people, that was there,
    That they all styll wold stand,
' For he that shoteth for such a wager,
    Behoveth a stedfast hand.'

CLXI

Muche people prayèd for Cloudesley,
    That his lyfe savèd myght be,
And whan he made hym redy to shote,
    There was many weeping e'e.

CLXII

But Cloudesley clefte the apple in two,
    That many a man it se;
' Over God's forbode,' sayde the Kynge,
    ' That thou shold shote at me !'

CLXIII

' I geve thee eightene pence a day,
    And my bowè shalt thou bere,
And over all the north countrè
    I make the chyfe rydère.'

CLXIV

' And I thyrtene pence,' said the Quene,
    ' By God, and by my fay;
Come feche thy payment when thou wylt,
    No man shall say the nay.

CLXV

' Wyllyam, I make the a gentleman
    Of clothyng, and of fe:
And thy brethren yemen of my chambre,
    For they are so semely to se.

rydère] ranger.

495

CLXVI

'Your sonne, for he is tendre of age,
  Of my wyne-seller he shall be;
And when he commeth to mans estate,
  Better avaunced shall he be.

CLXVII

'And, Wyllyam, bring me your wife,' said the Quene,
  'Me longeth her sore to se:
She shall be my chefe gentlewoman,
  To governe my nurserye.'

CLXVIII

The yemen thanked them all courteously,
  And sayd, 'To Rome wyl we wend,
Of all the synnes, that we have done,
  To be assoyld at his hand.'

CLXIX

So forth be gone these good yemèn,
  As fast as they might hye;
And after came and dwell'd with the Kynge,
  And dyed good men all thre.

CLXX

Thus endeth the lyves of these good yemèn;
  God send them eternall blysse;
And all, that with a hand-bowe shoteth:
  That of heven they may never mysse!

A Little Geste of Robin Hood and his Meiny

The First Fytte

How Robin Hood befriended a poor Knight, Sir Richard
at the Lee

I

LITHE and listen, Gentlemen,
　That be of free-born blood :
I shall you tell of a good yeoman,
　His name was Robin Hood.

II

Robin was a proud outlaw,
　The while he walked on ground ;
So courteous an outlaw as he was one
　Was never none y-found.

III

Robin stood in Barnèsdale,
　And leaned him to a tree ;
And by him stood Little John,
　A good yeoman was he.

IV

And also did good Scathèlock,
　And Much, the miller's son ;
There was none inch of his body,
　But it was worth a groom.

V

Then bespake him Little John
　All unto Robin Hood :
' Master, an ye would dine betimes
　It would do you much good.'

Meiny] retinue.　　Lithe] hearken.　　Barnèsdale] a forest
region between Pontefract and Doncaster.　　groom] man.

VI

Then bespake him good Robin :
　' To dine I have no lest,
Till that I have some bold baron,
　Or some uncouth guest,

VII

' Till that I have some bold baron
　That may pay for the best,
Or else some knight, or some squièr
　That dwelleth here by West.'

VIII

A good mannèr then had Robin ;
　In land where that he were,
Every day ere he would dine
　Three masses would he hear :

IX

The one in worship of the Father,
　The other of the Holy Ghost,
The third was of Our dear Lady
　That he loved alder-most.

X

Robin loved our dear Lady ;
　For doubt of deadly sin
Would he no company do harm
　That woman was therein.

XI

' Master,' then said Little John,
　' An we our board shall spread,
Tell us whither we shall go,
　And what life we shall lead ;

lest] lust, desire.　　　uncouth] unknown, strange.　　　were]
might be.　　　alder] of all.　　　doubt] fear.
498

XII

'Where we shall take, where we shall leave,
  Where we shall abide behind,
Where we shall rob, where we shall reave,
  Where we shall beat and bind.'

XIII

'Thereof no force,' then said Robin;
  'We shall do well enow;
But look ye do no husband harm
  That tilleth with his plough.

XIV

'No more ye shall no good yeoman
  That walketh by green-wood shaw;
Nor yet no knight nor no squièr
  That will be a good fellaw.

XV

'These bishops and these archbishops,
  Ye shall them beat and bind;
The High Sheriff of Nottingham,
  Him hold ye in your mind.'

XVI

'This word shall be held,' said Little John,
  'This lesson we shall lere;
It is far days; God send us a guest,
  That we were at our dinnere.'

XVII

'Take thy good bow,' said Robin Hood,
  'Let Much wend with thee,
And so shall William Scathèlock,
  And no man abide with me;

reave] plunder.   force] matter, account.   husband]
husbandman.   shaw] grove.   lere] learn.   far days]
late in the day.

499

XVIII

'And walk ye up unto the Sayles,
  And so to Watling Street,
And wait after some uncouth guest;
  Upchance ye may them meet.

XIX

'Be he an earl, or any baron,
  Abbot, or any knight,
Bring ye him to lodge with me;
  His dinner shall be dight.'

XX

Then went they up unto the Sayles,
  Those yeoman allè three;
They lookèd east, they lookèd west,
  They mightè no man see.

XXI

But as they looked in Barnèsdale,
  By a dernè street,
Then came a knight a-riding up;
  Full soon they gan him meet.

XXII

All dreary then was his semblaunt,
  And little was his pride;
His one foot in the stirrup stood,
  The other wavèd beside.

the Sayles] a small farm near Pontefract.   Watling Street]
the great North road.   Upchance] perchance.   dight]
prepared.   dernè] hidden, retired.   street] road.
semblaunt] aspect.

500

XXIII

His hood hang'd in his eyen two ;
    He rode in simple array ;
A sorrier man than he was one
    Rode never in summer day.

XXIV

Little John was full courteous,
    And set him on his knee ;
' Welcome be ye, gentle Knight,
    Welcome are ye to me.

XXV

' Welcome be thou to greenè wood.
    Hendè Knight and free ;
My master hath abiden you fasting
    Sir, all these hourès three.'

XXVI

' Who is thy master ? ' said the Knight.
    John said, ' Robin Hood.'
' He is a good yeoman,' said the Knight,
    ' Of him I have heard much good.

XXVII

' I grant,' he said, ' with you to wend,
    My brethren, all in fere ;
My purpose was to have dined to-day
    At Blyth or Doncastere.'

XXVIII

Forth then went this gentle Knight,
    With a careful cheer ;
The tears out of his eyen ran,
    And fell down by his leer.

And set him, &c.] and knelt down.   Hendè] gracious.
fere] company.   Blyth] near E. Retford.   careful
cheer] sad countenance.   leer] cheek.

XXIX

They brought him to the lodgè door ;
  When Robin gan him see,
Full courteously did off his hood,
  And set him on his knee.

XXX

' Welcome, Sir Knight,' then said Robin,
  ' Welcome art thou to me ;
I have abiden you fasting, sir,
  All these hourès three.'

XXXI

Then answerèd the gentle Knight,
  With wordès fair and free ;
' God thee savè, good Robin,
  And all thy fair meinèe.'

XXXII

They washèd together and wipèd both,
  And set to their dinnere ;
Bread and wine they had enough,
  And numbles of the deer.

XXXIII

Swans and pheasants they had full good,
  And fowls of the rivere ;
There failèd none so little a bird
  That ever was bred on brere.

XXXIV

' Do gladly, Sir Knight,' said Robin.
  ' Gramerci, sir,' said he ;
' Such a dinner had I not
  Of all these weekès three.

numbles] inwards, tripe.   brere] briar.

502

xxxv

'If I come again, Robin,
  Here by this country,
As good a dinner I shall thee make
  As thou hast made to me.'

xxxvi

'Gramerci, Knight,' said Robin Hood;
  'My dinner when I have,
I was never so greedy, by dear-worth God,
  My dinner for to crave.

xxxvii

'But pray ere ye wend,' said Robin Hood;
  'Me thinketh it is good right;
It was never the manner, by dear-worth God,
  A yeoman to pay for a knight.'

xxxviii

'I have nought in my coffers,' said the Knight,
  'That I may proffer for shame:'
'Little John, go look,' said Robin Hood,
  'Nor let not for no blame.'

xxxix

'Tell me truth,' said Robin Hood,
  'So God have part of thee.'—
'I have no more than ten shillings,
  So God have part of me.'

xl

'If thou hast no more,' said Robin,
  'I will not one penny;
And if thou need of any more,
  More shall I lendè thee.

dear-worth] precious.   let] desist.   **have part of
thee**] side with thee, aid thee.

XLI

'Go now forth, Little John,
  The truthè tell thou me ;
If there be no more but ten shillings,
  No penny that I see.'

XLII

Little John his mantle spread
  Full fair upon the ground,
And there he found in the Knight's coffer
  But even half a pound.

XLIII

Little John let it lie full still,
  And went to his master low ;
'What tidings, John?' said Robin Hood.—
  'Sir, the Knight is true enow.'

XLIV

'Fill of the best wine,' said Robin,
  'The Knight shall begin ;
Muchè wonder thinketh me
  Thy clothing is so thin.

XLV

'Tell me one word,' said Robin,
  'And counsel shall it be ;
I trow thou wert made a knight of force,
  Or else of yeomanry.

XLVI

'Or else thou hast been a sorry husband,
  And lived in stroke and strife ;
An okerer, or a lecher,
  With wrong hast led thy life.'

counsel] secret.   of force] by force.   of yeomanry]
from the yeoman class.   a sorry husband] a wretched manager.
okerer] usurer.   lecher] an unchaste man.

XLVII

' I am none of those,' said the Knight,
  ' By Him that made me ;
An hundred winter here before
  Mine anc'tors knights have be.

XLVIII

' But oft it hath befal'n, Robin,
  A man hath been disgrate ;
But God, that sitteth in heaven above,
  May amend his state.

XLIX

' Within these two years, Robin,' he said,
  ' My neighbours well it kenn'd,
Four hundred pounds of good money
  Full well then might I spend.

L

' Now have I no good,' said the Knight,
  ' God hath shapen such an end,
But my children and my wife,
  Till God it may amend.'

LI

' In what manner,' then said Robin,
  ' Hast thou lorn thy richess ? '
' For my great folly,' he said,
  ' And for my kindeness.

LII

' I had a son forsooth, Robin,
  That should have been mine heir ;
When he was twenty winter old
  In field would joust full fair.

---

disgrate] fallen in fortune.   kenn'd] knew.   lorn] lost.

LIII

'He slew a knight of Lancashire,
  And a squièr bold ;
For to save him in his right
  My goods are set and sold.

LIV

'My lands are set to wed, Robin,
  Until a certain day,
To a rich Abbot here beside
  Of St. Mary's Abbèy.'

LV

'What is the sum ? ' said Robin Hood ;
  'The truthè tell thou me ; '
'Sir,' he said, 'four hundred pound ;
  The Abbot told it me.'

LVI

'An thou lose thy land,' said Robin Hood,
  'What shall fall of thee ? '—
'Hastily I will me busk
  Over the saltè sea,

LVII

'And see where Christ was quick and dead,
  On the mount of Calvary ;
Farewell, friend, and have good day ;
  It may no better be.'

LVIII

Tears fell out of his eyen two ;
  He would have gone his way ;
'Farewell, friends, and have good day,
  I have no more to pay.'

set to wed] put to pledge, mortgaged.   told] counted.
fall of] become of.   busk] make ready to go.

LIX

'Where be thy friends,' said Robin Hood.
  'Sir, never one will me know;
While I was rich enough at home
  Great boast then would they blow.

LX

'And now they run away from me,
  As beastès in a raw;
They takè no more heed of me
  Than they me never saw.'

LXI

For ruth then weptè Little John,
  Scathèlock and Much in fere;
'Fill of the best wine,' said Robin,
  'For here is a simple cheer.

LXII

'Hast thou any friends,' said Robin Hood,
  'Thy borrows that will be?'
'I havè none,' then said the Knight,
  'But Him that died on tree!'

LXIII

'Do way thy japès,' said Robin,
  'Thereof will I right none;
Ween'st thou I would have God to borrow,
  Peter, Paul or John?

LXIV

'Nay, by Him that madè me,
  And shope both sun and moon,
Find better borrow,' said Robin,
  'Or money get'st thou none.'

raw] row.   borrows] sureties.   Do way thy japès] away
with thy jests.   to] for.   shope] created.

LXV

'I have none other,' said the Knight,
   'The soothè for to say,
But if it be Our dear Lady;
   She fail'd never ere this day.'

LXVI

'By dear-worth God,' said Robin Hood,
   'To seek all England thorough,
Yet found I never to my pay
   A muchè better borrow.

LXVII

'Come now forth, Little John,
   And go to my treasurỳ,
And bringè me four hundred pound,
   And look well told it be.'

LXVIII

Forth then wentè Little John,
   And Scathèlock went before;
He told him out four hundred pound
   By eight and twenty score.

LXIX

'Is this well told?' said Little Much;
   John said, 'What grieveth thee?
It is alms to help a gentle knight
   That is fal'n in poverty.'

LXX

'Master,' then said Little John,
   'His clothing is full thin;
Ye must give the Knight a livery
   To lap his body therein.

But if] unless.   lap] wrap.

LXXI

' For ye have scarlet and green, master,
    And many a rich array ;
There is no merchant in merry England
    So rich, I dare well say.'—

LXXII

' Take him three yards of each colour,
    And look well mete it be.'—
Little John took no measùre
    But his bowè-tree.

LXXIII

And at every handful that he met
    He leapèd o'er feet three ;
' What devilkin's draper,' said Little Much,
    ' Thinkest thou for to be ? '

LXXIV

Scathèlock stood full still and laughed,
    And said, ' He meteth right.
John may give him good measure,
    For it costeth him but light.'

LXXV

' Master,' then said Little John
    All unto Robin Hood,
' Ye must give the Knight a horse
    To lead home all this good.'

LXXVI

' Take him a grey courser,' said Robin,
    ' And a saddle new ;
He is Our Lady's messenger ;
    God grant that he be true ! '

mete] meted, measured.   met] measured.

LXXVII

'And a good palfrey,' said Little Much,
  'To maintain him in his right ;'
'And a pair of boots,' said Scathèlock,
  'For he is a gentle knight.'

LXXVIII

'What shalt thou give him, Little John ?'—
  'Sir, a pair of gilt spurs clean,
To pray for all this company ;
  God bring him out of teen.'

LXXIX

'When shall my day be,' said the Knight,
  'Sir, an your willè be ?'—
'This day twelve moneth,' said Robin,
  'Under this green-wood tree.

LXXX

'It were great shamè,' said Robin,
  'A knight alone to ride,
Withoutè squire, yeoman, or page,
  To walkè by his side.

LXXXI

'I shall thee lend Little John, my man,
  For he shall be thy knave ;
In a yeoman's stead he may thee stand,
  If thou great needè have.'

palfrey] a saddle-horse.   teen] trouble.   knave] servant.

The Second Fytte

How the Knight paid his Creditors against their will

LXXXII

Now is the Knight gone on his way ;
  This game him thought full good ;
When he looked on Barnèsdale,
  He blessèd Robin Hood.

LXXXIII

And when he thought on Barnèsdale,
  On Scathelock, Much, and John,
He blessèd them for a company
  The best he ever in come.

LXXXIV

' Then spake that gentle Knight,
  To Little John gan he say,
' To-morrow I must to York town
  To Saint Mary's Abbèy ;

LXXXV

' And to the Abbot of that place
  Four hundred pound must pay ;
But I be there upon this night
  My land is lost for aye.'

LXXXVI

The Abbot said to his Convènt,
  Where he stood on ground,
' This day twelve moneth came a knight,
  And borrowed four hundred pound.

come] came.   But] unless.

511

LXXXVII

'He borrowèd four hundred pound
    Upon his land and fee ;
But he come this ilkè day
    Disherited shall he be.'

LXXXVIII

'It is full early,' said the Prior,
    'The day is not yet far gone ;
I had liever pay an hundred pound,
    And lay it down anon.

LXXXIX

'The Knight is far beyond the sea,
    In England is his right,
And suffereth hunger and cold
    And many a sorry night.

XC

'It were great pity,' said the Prior,
    'So to have his land ;
An ye be so light of your conscience,
    Ye do him muchè shand.'

XCI

'Thou art ever in my beard,' said the Abbot,
    'By God and Saint Richard !'
With that came in a fat-headed monk,
    The Highè Cellarèr.

XCII

'He is dead or hangèd,' said the monk,
    'By Him that bought me dear,
And we shall have to spend in this place
    Four hundred pound by year.'

fee] property.   ilkè] same.   shand] shame.   in my
beard] contradicting, or thwarting me.

XCIII

The Abbot and the High Cellarer
    Started forth full bold,
The High Justice of Engèland
    The Abbot there did hold.

XCIV

The High Justice and many mo
    Had taken into their hand
Wholly all the Knightès debt,
    To put that Knight to shand.

XCV

They deemèd the Knight wonder sore,
    The Abbot and his meinèe :
'But he come this ilkè day,
    Disherited shall he be.'

XCVI

'He will not come yet,' said the Justice,
    'I dare well undertake.'
But in sorry timè for them all
    The Knight came to the gate.

XCVII

Then bespake that gentle Knight
    Until his meinèe :
'Now put on your simple weeds
    That ye brought from the sea.'

XCVIII

They putten on their simple weeds,
    They came to the gates anon ;
The Porter was ready himself,
    And welcomed them every one.

deemèd] judged.   wonder sore] monstrous severely.
Until] unto.

XCIX

'Welcome, Sir Knight,' said the Porter,
  'My lord to meat is he,
And so is many a gentle man,
  For the love of thee.'

C

The Porter swore a full great oath:
  'By Him that madè me,
Here be the bestè corsèd horse
  That ever yet I see.

CI

'Lead them into the stable,' he said,
  'That easèd might they be';
'They shall not come therein,' said the Knight,
  'By Him that died on tree.'

CII

Lordès were to meat y-set
  In that Abbot's hall;
The Knight went forth and kneelèd down
  And salued them great and small.

CIII

'Do gladly, Sir Abbot,' said the Knight,
  'I am come to hold my day.'
The first word that the Abbot spake,
  'Hast thou brought me my pay?'

CIV

'Not one penny,' said the Knight,
  'By Him that makèd me':
'Thou art a shrewd debtor,' said the Abbot;
  'Sir Justice, drink to me!'

corsèd] bodied.   salued] saluted.   shrewd] cursed.

CV

' What doest thou here,' said the Abbot,
   ' But thou hadst brought thy pay ? '
' Alack is me,' then said the Knight,
   ' To pray of a longer day ! '

CVI

' Thy day is broke,' said the Justice,
   ' Land gettest thou none.'—
' Now, good Sir Justice, be my friend,
   And fend me of my fone ! '

CVII

' I am held with the Abbot,' said the Justice,
   ' Both with cloth and fee.'—
' Now, good Sir Sheriff, be my friend ! '
   ' Nay, nay, not I,' said he.

CVIII

' Now, good Sir Abbot, be my friend,
   For thy courtesy,
And hold my landès in thy hand
   Till I have made thee gree

CIX

' And I will be thy true servànt
   And truly servè thee,
Till ye have four hundred pound
   Of money good and free.'

CX

The Abbot sware a full great oath,
   ' By Him that died on tree,
Get thy landès where thou mayst,
   For thou gettest none of me ! '

But] if not.   fend] defend.   fone] foes.   gree] satisfaction.

CXI

' By dear-worth God,' then said the Knight,
   ' That all this worldè wrought,
But I have my land again,
   Full dear it shall be bought.

CXII

' God, that was of a maiden born,
   Give us well to speed !
For it is good to assay a friend
   Ere that a man have need.'

CXIII

The Abbot loathly on him gan look,
   And villainously him gan call ;
' Out,' he said, ' thou falsè Knight,
   Speed thee out of my hall !

CXIV

' Thou liest,' said the gentle Knight.
   ' Abbot, in thy hall ;
Falsè Knight was I never,
   By God that made us all.'

CXV

Up then stood that gentle Knight,
   To the Abbot said he,
' To suffer a knight to kneel so long,
   Thou canst no courtesy.

CXVI

' In joustès and in tournaments
   Full far then have I be,
And put myself as far in press
   As any that ever I see.'

But I have] unless I have.   canst] knowest.   put myself . . .
in press] adventured myself.

CXVII

'What will ye give more,' said the Justice,
  'An the Knight shall make a release?
And ellès dare I safely swear
  Ye hold never your land in peace.'

CXVIII

'An hundred pound,' said the Abbot;
  The Justice said, 'Give him two;'
'Nay, by God,' said the Knight,
  'Ye get not my land so.

CXIX

'Though ye would give a thousand more,
  Yet were ye never the nigher;
Shall there never be mine heir
  Abbot, Justice, nor Friar.'

CXX

He started to a board anon,
  Till a table round,
And here he shook out of a bag
  Even four hundred pound.

CXXI

'Have here thy gold, Sir Abbot,' he said,
  'Which that thou lentest me;
Hadst thou been courteous at my coming,
  I would have rewarded thee.'

CXXII

The Abbot sat still, and ate no more,
  For all his royal fare;
He cast his head on his shoulder,
  And fast began to stare.

release] quittance.　　ellès] else.

CXXIII

'Take me my gold again,' he said,
  'Sir Justice, that I took thee.'—
'Not a penny,' said the Justice,
  'By Him that died on tree.'—

CXXIV

'Sir Abbot, and ye men of law,
  Now have I held my day;
Now shall I have my land again,
  For aught that you can say.'

CXXV

The Knight out started of the door,
  Away was all his care,
And on he put his good clothing,
  The other he left there.

CXXVI

He went him forth full merry singing,
  As men have told in tale;
His Lady met him at the gate,
  At home in Uttersdale.

CXXVII

'Welcome, my lord,' said his Lady;
  'Sir, lost is all your good?'—
'Be merry, damè,' said the Knight,
  'And pray for Robin Hood,

CXXVIII

'That ever his soulè be in bliss:
  He help me out of teen;
Ne had not been his kindèness,
  Beggars had we been.

Take] give.   Ne had not been] had it not been for.

CXXIX

The Abbot and I accorded be,
  He is servèd of his pay ;
The goodè yeoman lent it me,
  As I came by the way.'

CXXX

This Knight then dwellèd fair at home,
  The soothè for to say,
Till he had got four hundred pound,
  All ready for to pay.

CXXXI

He purvey'd him an hundred bows,
  The stringès well y-dight,
An hundred sheaf of arrows good,
  The heads burnish'd full bright ;

CXXXII

And every arrow an ellè long,
  With peacock well y-dight,
Y-notchèd all with white silvèr ;
  It was a seemly sight.

CXXXIII

He purvey'd him an hundred men,
  Well harness'd in that stead,
And himself in that samè suit,
  And clothed in white and red.

CXXXIV

He bare a lancegay in his hand,
  And a man led his mail,
And roden with a lightè song
  Unto Barnèsdale.

With peacock . . . y-dight] fitted with peacock feathers.
lancegay] a javelin-lance.   his mail] his bag or trunk.   roden]
they rode.

CXXXV

As he went at a bridge there was a wrestling,
 And there tarrièd was he,
And there was all the best yeomen,
 Of all the west countrỳ.

CXXXVI

A full fair game there was upset,
 A white bull up y-pight ;
A great courser with saddle and bridle,
 With gold burnish'd full bright ;

CXXXVII

A pair of gloves, a red gold ring,
 A pipe of wine, in good fay :
What man beareth him best, i-wis,
 The prize shall bear away.

CXXXVIII

There was a yeoman in that place,
 And best worthy was he,
And for he was far and frembd bestad,
 I-slain he should have be.

CXXXIX

The Knight had ruth of this yeoman.
 In place where that he stood,
He said that yeoman should have no harm,
 For love of Robin Hood.

CXL

The Knight pressèd into the place,
 An hundred followed him free,
With bows bent, and arrows sharp,
 For to shende that company.

y-pight] placed, fixed. far and frembd bestad] in the plight
of one from far and a stranger. shende] shame.

They shoulder'd all, and made him room,
  To wete what he would say,
He took the yeoman by the hand
  And gave him all the play ;

He gave him five mark for his wine,
  There it lay on the mould,
And bade it should be set a-broach,
  Drink who so would.

Thus long tarried this gentle Knight,
  Till that play was done . .
So long abode Robin fasting,
  Three hours after the noon.

The Third Fytte

How Little John robbed the Sheriff of Nottingham and
delivered him into Robin Hood's hands

Lithe and listen, gentlemen,
  All that now be here,
Of Little John, that was the Knight's man,
  Good mirth shall ye hear.

It was upon a merry day,
  That young men would go shete ;
Little John fet his bow anon,
  And said he would them meet.

wete] know.   shete] shoot.   fet] fetched.

CXLVI

Three times Little John shot about,
   And alway cleft the wand,
The proud Sheriff of Nottingham
   By the marks gan stand.

CXLVII

The Sheriff swore a full great oath,
   ' By Him that died on a tree,
This man is the best archèr
   That yet saw I me.

CXLVIII

' Say me now, wight young man,
   What is now thy name ?
In what country were thou born,
   And where is thy woning wane ? '—

CXLIX

' In Holderness I was bore,
   I-wis, all of my dame,
Men call me Reynold Greenleaf,
   When I am at hame.'—

CL

' Say me, Reynold Greenleaf,
   Wilt thou dwell with me ?
And every year I will thee give
   Twenty mark to thy fee.'—

CLI

' I have a master,' said Little John,
   ' A courteous knight is he
May ye get leave of him,
   The better may it be.'

wight] strong, brave.   woning wane] usual dwelling-place.
I-wis] assuredly.

CLII

The Sheriff got Little John
  Twelve months of the Knight,
Therefore he gave him right anon
  A good horse and a wight.

CLIII

Now is Little John the Sheriff's man,
  He give us well to speed,
But alway thought Little John
  To quit him well his meed.

CLIV

' Now so God me help,' said Little John,
  ' And by my true lewtè,
I shall be the worst servant to him
  That ever yet had he.'

CLV

It befell upon a Wednesday,
  The Sheriff on hunting was gone,
And Little John lay in his bed,
  And was forgotten at home.

CLVI

Therefore he was fasting
  Till it was past the noon.
' Good sir steward, I pray thee,
  Give me to dine,' said Little John.

CLVII

' It is too long for Greenleaf,
  Fasting so long to be ;
Therefore I pray thee, steward,
  My dinner give thou me.'

meed] reward.   lewtè] loyalty.

CLVIII

'Shalt thou never eat nor drink,' said the steward,
  'Till my lord be come to town.'
'I make mine avow to God,' said Little John,
  'I had liefer to crack thy crown.'

CLIX

The butler was full uncourteous,
  There he stood on floor,
He started to the buttery,
  And shut fast the door.

CLX

Little John gave the butler such a rap,
  His back yede nigh in two:
Tho' he lived an hundred winter,
  The worse he should go.

CLXI

He spurn'd the door with his foot,
  It went up well and fine,
And there he made a large livery
  Both of ale and wine.

CLXII

'Sith ye will not dine,' said Little John,
  'I shall give you to drink,
And though ye live an hundred winter,
  On Little John ye shall think.'

CLXIII

Little John ate, and Little John drank,
  The while that he wolde.
The Sheriff had in his kitchen a cook,
  A stout man and a bold.

yede] went.   livery] allowance of food.   Sith] since.

CLXIV

' I make mine avow to God,' said the cook,
  ' Thou art a shrewd hind,
In an household to dwell,
  For to ask thus to dine.'

CLXV

And there he lent Little John,
  Good strokès three.
' I make mine avow,' said Little John,
  ' These strokes liketh well me.

CLXVI

' Thou art a bold man and an hardy,
  And so thinketh me ;
And or I pass from this place,
  Assay'd better shalt thou be.'

CLXVII

Little John drew a good sword,
  The cook took another in hand ;
They thought nothing for to flee,
  But stiffly for to stand.

CLXVIII

There they fought sore together,
  Two mile way and more,
Might neither other harm done,
  The mountenance of an hour.

CLXIX

' I make mine avow to God,' said Little John,
  ' And by my true lewtè,
Thou art one of the best swordsmen
  That ever yet saw I me.

hind] knave, servant.   lent] gave.   mountenance]
extent, space.

CLXX

' Couldest thou shoot as well in a bow,
　To green-wood thou shouldest with me,
And two times in the year thy clothing
　I-changèd should be ;

CLXXI

' And every year of Robin Hood
　Twenty mark to thy fee.'—
' Put up thy sword,' said the cook,
　' And fellows will we be.'

CLXXII

Then he fette to Little John
　The numbles of a doe,
Good bread and full good wine,
　They ate and drank thereto.

CLXXIII

And when they had drunken well,
　Their troths together they plight,
That they would be with Robin
　That ilk same day at night.

CLXXIV

They did them to the treasure-house,
　As fast as they might gone,
The locks that were of good steel
　They broke them every one ;

CLXXV

They took away the silver vessel,
　And all that they might get,
Pieces, masars, and spoons,
　Would they none forget ;

fette] fetched.　　　　　masars] maple-bowls.

CLXXVI

Also they took the good pence,
    Three hundred pound and three ;
And did them straight to Robin Hood,
    Under the green-wood tree.

CLXXVII

' God thee save, my dear master,
    And Christ thee save and see ! '
And then said Robin to Little John,
    ' Welcome might thou be ;

CLXXVIII

' And also be that fair yeoman
    Thou bringest there with thee.
What tidings from Nottingham
    Little John, tell thou me ?'—

CLXXIX

' Well thee greeteth the proud Sheriff,
    And send thee here by me
His cook and his silver vessel,
    And three hundred pound and three.'—

CLXXX

' I make mine avow to God,' said Robin,
    ' And to the Trinity,
It was never by his good will,
    This good is come to me.'

CLXXXI

Little John him there bethought,
    On a shrewèd wile,
Five mile in the forest he ran,
    Him happèd at his will.

527

CLXXXII

Then he met the proud Sheriff,
  Hunting with hound and horn,
Little John cou'd his courtesy,
  And kneelèd him beforn :

CLXXXIII

'God thee save, my dear master,
  And Christ thee save and see ! '—
'Reynold Greenleaf,' said the Sheriff,
  'Where hast thou now be ?'—

CLXXXIV

'I have been in this forest,
  A fair sight can I see,
It was one of the fairest sights
  That ever yet saw I me ;

CLXXXV

'Yonder I see a right fair hart,
  His colour is of green,
Seven score of deer upon an herd
  Be with him all bedene ;

CLXXXVI

'His tyndès are so sharp, master,
  Of sixty and well mo,
That I durst not shoot for dread
  Lest they would me sloo.'

CLXXXVII

'I make mine avow to God,' said the Sheriff,
  'That sight would I fain see.'
'Busk you thitherward, my dear master,
  Anon, and wend with me.'

cou'd] knew.   bedene] in company, together.   tyndès]
tines, antlers.   sloo] slay.

528

CLXXXVIII

The Sheriff rode, and Little John
    Of foot he was full smart,
And when they came afore Robin:
    'Lo, here is the master hart!'

CLXXXIX

Still stood the proud Sheriff,
    A sorry man was he:
'Woe worth thee, Reynold Greenleaf!
    Thou hast now betrayèd me.'

CXC

'I make mine avow to God,' said Little John,
    'Master, ye be to blame,
I was mis-served of my dinner,
    When I was with you at hame.'

CXCI

Soon he was to supper set,
    And servèd with silver white;
And when the Sheriff saw his vessel,
    For sorrow he might not eat.

CXCII

'Make good cheer,' said Robin Hood,
    'Sheriff, for charity!
And for the love of Little John,
    Thy life is granted to thee.'

CXCIII

When they had suppèd well,
    The day was all agone,
Robin commanded Little John
    To draw off his hosen and shoon,

CXCIV

His kirtle and his courtepy,
   That was furrèd well fine,
And take him a green mantèl,
   To lap his body therein.

CXCV

Robin commanded his wight young men,
   Under the green-wood tree,
They shall lie in that same sort;
   That the Sheriff might them see.

CXCVI

All night lay that proud Sheriff,
   In his breech and in his shirt,
No wonder it was in green-wood,
   Tho' his sides do smerte.

CXCVII

'Make glad cheer,' said Robin Hood,
   'Sheriff, for charity!
For this is our ordèr, i-wis,
   Under the green-wood tree.'

CXCVIII

'This is harder order,' said the Sheriff,
   'Than any anchor or frere;
For all the gold in merry England
   I would not long dwell here.'

CXCIX

'All these twelve months,' said Robin
   'Thou shalt dwell with me;
I shall thee teach, proud Sheriff,
   An outlaw for to be.'

courtepy] a short coat or cloak.   lap] wrap.   smerte] smart.
anchor] hermit.   frere] friar.

CC

'Or I here another night lie,' said the Sheriff,
    'Robin, now I pray thee,
Smite off my head rather to-morne,
    And I forgive it thee.

CCI

'Let me go,' then said the Sheriff,
    'For saint Charity!
And I will be thy best friend
    That ever yet had thee.'

CCII

'Thou shalt swear me an oath,' said Robin,
    'On my bright brand,
Thou shalt never await me scathe,
    By water nor by land.

CCIII

'And if thou find any of my men,
    By night or by day,
Upon thine oath thou shalt swear,
    To help them that thou may.'

CCIV

Now has the Sheriff i-sworn his oath,
    And home he began to gone,
He was as full of green-wood
    As ever was hip of stone.

to-morne] to-morrow.   brand] sword   await] plan, plot.
scathe] harm.   hip] the fruit of the wild rose.

The Fourth Fytte

How Robin Hood was repaid his Loan

CCV

The Sheriff dwelled in Nottingham,
    He was fain that he was gone ;
And Robin and his merry men
    Went to wood anon.

CCVI

' Go we to dinner,' said Little John :
    Robin Hood said ' Nay ;
For I fear Our Lady be wroth with me,
    For she sent me not my pay.'

CCVII

' Have no doubt, master,' said Little John ;
    ' Yet is not the sun at rest ;
For I dare say and safely swear,
    The Knight is true and trest.'

CCVIII

' Take thy bow in hande,' said Robin,
    ' Let Much wend with thee,
And so shall William Scathèlock.
    And no man abide with me.

CCIX

' And walk ye up unto the Sayles,
    And so to Watling Street,
And wait after some uncouth guest,
    Upchance ye may them meet.

trest] trusty.

CCX

' Whether he be a messenger,
  Or a man that mirthès can,
Of my good he shall have some,
  If he be a poorè man.'

CCXI

Forth then started Little John,
  Half in tray and teen,
And girt him with a full good sword,
  Under a mantle of green.

CCXII

They wenten up unto the Sayles,
  Those yeomen allè three;
They lookèd east, they lookèd west,
  They mightè no man see.

CCXIII

But as they looked in Barnèsdale,
  By the highè-way,
Then were they ware of a Black Monk,
  Upon a good palfrèy.

CCXIV

Then bespake him Little John,
  To Muchè gan he say:
' I dare well lay my life to wed,
  That Monk hath brought our pay.

CCXV

' Make glad cheer,' said Little John,
  ' And dress your bows of yew,
And look your hearts be seker and sad,
  Your strings trusty and true.

that mirthès can] that can crack a joke.   tray and teen] grief
and trouble.   a Black Monk] a Benedictine.   wed] wager.
seker and sad] sure and steady.

CCXVI

'The Monk hath two and fifty men,
    And seven somers strong ;
There rideth no bishop in this land
    So royally along.

CCXVII

'Bretheren,' said Little John,
    'Here are no more but three ;
But we bring them to dinnèr,
    Our master we dare not see.

CCXVIII

'Bend your bows,' said Little John,
    'Make all yon press to stand ;
The foremost Monk, his life and death
    Is closèd in my hand.

CCXIX

'Abide, churl Monk!' said Little John,
    'No further that thou wend ;
If thou dost, by dear-worth God,
    Thy death is in my hend.

CCXX

'And evil thrift upon thy head,
    Right under thy hat's band !
For thou hast made our master wroth,
    He is so lang fastand.'

CCXXI

'Who is your master ?' said the Monk.—
    Little John said, 'Robin Hood.'—
'He is a strong thief,' said the Monk,
    'Of him I never heard good.'

somers] pack-horses.   But] unless.   press] crowd.
hend] hands.   thrift] thriving, luck.

CCXXII

'Thou liest,' then said Little John,
    'And that shall ruè thee;
He is a yeoman of the forest,
    To dine he hath bidden thee.'

CCXXIII

Much was ready with a bolt,
    Rathely and anon,
He set the Monk to-fore the breast
    To the ground that he gan gon.

CCXXIV

Of two and fifty wight yeomen
    There abode not one,
Save a little page and a groom
    To lead the somers on.

CCXXV

They brought the Monk to the lodgè door,
    Whether he were loath or lief,
For to speak with Robin Hood,
    Maugre in his teeth.

CCXXVI

Robin did a-down his hood,
    The Monk when that he see;
The Monk was not so courteous,
    His hood he lettè be.

CCXXVII

'He is a churl, by dear-worth God,'
    Then said Little John.
'Thereof no force,' said Robin Hood,
    'For courtesy can be none.'

bolt] a blunt arrow.   Rathely] quickly.   set ... to-fore]
hit upon.   gan gon] did go.   lief] glad.   Maugre
in his teeth] in spite of him.   no force] no matter.

535

CCXXVIII

' How many men,' said Robin Hood,
  ' Haddè this Monk, Johan ? '—
' Fifty and two when that we met,
  But many of them be gane.'

CCXXIX

' Let blow a horn,' said Robin Hood,
  ' That fellowship may us know.'—
Seven score of wight yeomen
  Came pricking on a row.

CCXXX

Each of them had a good mantèl
  Of scarlet and of ray ;
All they came to good Robin,
  To wit what he would say.

CCXXXI

They made the Monk to wash and wipe,
  And sit at his dinnere,
Robin Hood and Little John
  They served him both in fere.

CCXXXII

' Do gladly, Monk,' said Robin Hood ;
  ' Gramerci, sir,' said he.
' Where is your Abbey, when you are at home,
  And who is your avowè ? '

CCXXXIII

' Saint Mary's Abbey,' said the Monk,
  ' Though I be simple here.'—
' In what office ? ' said Robin ;
  ' Sir, the High Cellerèr.'

ray] striped cloth.   avowè] founder, patron.

CCXXXIV

'Ye be the more welcome,' said Robin,
  'So ever mote I the:
Fill of the best wine,' said Robin,
  'This Monk shall drink to me.

CCXXXV

'But I have great marvel,' said Robin,
  'Of all this longè day;
I dread Our Lady be wroth with me,
  She sent me not my pay.'

CCXXXVI

'Have no doubt, master,' said Little John,
  'Ye have no need, I say,
This Monk hath brought it, I dare well swear,
  For he is of her Abbèy.'

CCXXXVII

'And she was a borrow,' said Robin,
  'Between a Knight and me,
Of a little money that I him lent,
  Under the green-wood tree.

CCXXXVIII

'And if thou hast that silver brought,
  I pray thee let me see;
And I shall helpè thee eftsoons,
  If thou have need to me.'

CCXXXIX

The Monk swore a full great oath,
  With a sorry cheer,
'Of the borrowhood thou speak'st to me
  Heard I never ere.'—

So . . . mote I the] so may I prosper.   eftsoons] soon.
borrowhood] surety.

CCXL

' I makè mine avow to God,
  Monk, thou art to blame ;
For God is held a righteous Man,
  And so is eke his Dame.

CCXLI

' Thou toldest with thine ownè tongue,
  Thou mayst not sayè naye,
How thou art her servant,
  And servest her every day.

CCXLII

' And thou art made her messenger,
  My money for to pay ;
Therefore I can thee morè thank
  Thou art come at thy day.

CCXLIII

' What is in your coffers ?' said Robin,
  ' Truthè tell thou me.'—
' Sir,' he saidè, ' twenty mark,
  All so mote I the.'

CCXLIV

' If there be no more,' said Robin,
  ' I will not one pennỳ ;
If thou hast myster of any more,
  More I shall lend to thee.

CCXLV

' And if I find more,' said Robin,
  ' I-wis thou shalt it forgone ;
For of thy spending-silver, Monk,
  Thereof will I right none.

Dame] Mother.   mark] 13*s*. 4*d*.   myster] need.
538

CCXLVI

' Go now forth, Little John,
  The truthè tell thou me ;
If there be no more but twenty mark,
  No penny that I see.'

CCXLVII

Little John spread his mantle down,
  As he had done before,
And he told out of the Monkès mail
  Eight hundred pound and more.

CCXLVIII

Little John let it lie full still,
  And went to his master in haste ;
' Sir,' he said, ' the Monk is true enough,
  Our Lady hath doubled your cast ! '—

CCXLIX

' I makè mine avow to God,
  Monk, what told I thee ?
Our Lady is the truest woman
  That ever found I me.

CCL

' By dear-worth God,' said Robin Hood,
  ' To seek all England thorough,
Yet found I never to my pay
  A muchè better borrow.

CCLI

' Fill of the best wine,' said Robin,
  ' And greet thy Lady hend,
And if she have need to Robin Hood
  She shall him find a friend.

cast] throw, as in dice.　　　hend] gracious.

CCLII

' And if she need any more silvèr,
  Come thou again to me,
And, by this token she hath me sent,
  She shall have suchè three.'

CCLIII

The Monk was going to Londonward,
  There to hold great moot,
The Knight that rode so high on horse,
  To bring him under foot.

CCLIV

' Whither be ye away ? ' said Robin.—
  ' Sir, to manors in this londe,
To reckon with our revès,
  That have done much wrong.'—

CCLV

'Come now forth, Little John,
  And hearken to my tale,
A better yeoman I know none,
  To seek a Monkès mail.'

CCLVI

' How much is in yon other forcèr ?
  The soothè must we see : '
' By our Lady,' then said the Monk,
  ' That were no courtesy,

CCLVII

' A man to biddè to dinnèr,
  And sith him beat and bind.'—
' It is our old manner,' said Robin,
  ' To leave but little behind.'

moot] meeting, assembly.　　seek] search.　　mail] wallet,
bag.　　forcèr] coffer, strong-box.　　sith] then.

CCLVIII

The Monk took the horse with spur,
  No longer would he abide ;
' Ask to drink,' then said Robin,
  ' Ere that ye further ride.'

CCLIX

' Nay, 'fore God,' then said the Monk,
  ' Me rueth I came so near ;
For better cheap I might have dined
  In Blyth or Doncastere.'

CCLX

' Greet well your Abbot,' said Robin,
  ' And your prior, I you pray,
And bid him send me such a Monk
  To dinner every day ! '

CCLXI

Now lettè we that Monk be still,
  And speak we of that Knight :
Yet he came to hold his day,
  The while that it was light.

CCLXII

He did him straight to Barnèsdale,
  Under the green-wood tree,
And he found there Robin Hood,
  And all his merry meinèe.

CCLXIII

The Knight lit down off his good palfrèy,
  Robin when he gan see ;
Courteously he did a-down his hood,
  And set him on his knee.

For better cheap] more cheaply.

541

CCLXIV

'God thee savè, Robin Hood,
  And all this company ! '—
'Welcome be thou, gentle Knight,
  Right welcome unto me.'

CCLXV

Then bespake him Robin Hood
  To that Knight so free :
'What need driveth thee to greenè-wood ?
  I pray, sir Knight, tell me.

CCLXVI

'And welcome be thou, gentle Knight,
  Why hast thou been so long ? '—
'For the Abbot and the High Justice
  Would have had my land with wrong.'

CCLXVII

'Hast thou thy land again ?' said Robin ;
  'Truthè tell thou me.'—
'Yea, 'fore God,' said the Knight,
  'That thank I God and thee.

CCLXVIII

'But take no grief I have been so long ;
  I came by a wrestèling,
And there I holp a poor yeoman,
  With wrong was put behind.'

CCLXIX

'Nay, 'fore God,' said Robin Hood,
  'Sir Knight, that thank I thee ;
What man that helpeth a good yeoman,
  His friend I willè be.'

CCLXX

' Have here four hundred pound,' said the Knight,
  ' The which ye lent to me ;
And here is also twenty mark
  For your courtesy.'

CCLXXI

' Nay, 'fore God,' said Robin Hood,
  ' Thou brook it well for aye ;
For Our Lady, by her Cellarèr,
  Hath sent to me my pay.

CCLXXII

' And if I would it twicè take
  A shame it were to me ;
But truly now, thou gentle Knight,
  Welcome art thou to me.'

CCLXXIII

When Robin Hood had told his tale,
  He laugh'd and made good cheer.
' By my truthè,' said the Knight,
  ' Your money is ready here.'

CCLXXIV

' Brook it well,' said Robin Hood,
  ' Thou gentle Knight so free ;
And welcome be thou, gentle Knight,
  Under my trystell-tree !

CCLXXV

' But what shall these bows do,' said Robin,
  ' And these arrows feather'd free ?'—
' With your will,' then said the Knight,
  ' A poor present to thee.'—

brook] enjoy, use.

CCLXXVI

'Come now forth, Little John,
 And go to my treasurỳ,
And bring me thence four hundred pound;
 The Monk overtold it me.

CCLXXVII

' Have here four hundred pound,
 Thou gentle Knight and true,
And buy thee horse and harness good,
 And giltè spurs all new.

CCLXXVIII

' And if thou fail any spending,
 Come to Robin Hood,
And by my troth thou shalt none fail,
 While I have any good.

CCLXXIX

' And brook well thy four hundred pound,
 Which I lent to thee,
And make thyself no more so bare,
 By the counsel of me.'

CCLXXX

Thus then holp him good Robin,
 The Knight all of his care :
God, that sitt'st in heaven high,
 Grant us well to fare !

overtold] counted over.

ROBIN HOOD AND HIS MEINY

The Fifth Fytte

How at Archery in Nottingham Robin Hood was treacherously
attacked, but escaped into Sir Richard's Castle

CCLXXXI

Now hath the Knight his leave i-take,
  And went him on his way ;
Robin Hood and his merry men
  Dwelt still full many a day.

CCLXXXII

Lithe and listen, Gentlemen,
  And hearken what I shall say,
How the proud Sheriff of Nottingham,
  Did cry a full fair play ;

CCLXXXIII

That all the best archers of the North
  Should come upon a day,
' And he that shooteth alder-best
  The game shall bear away.

CCLXXXIV

' He that shooteth alder-best,
  Furthest, fair, and law,
At a pair of fynly butts,
  Under the green-wood shaw,

CCLXXXV

' A right good arrow he shall have,
  The shaft of silver white,
The head and feathers of rich red gold,
  In England is none like.'

---

alder-best] best of all.   law] low.   fynly] goodly.

CCLXXXVI
This then heardè good Robin,
  Under his trystell-tree :
'Make you ready, ye wight young men ;
  That shooting will I see.

CCLXXXVII
'Busk you, my merry young men,
  Ye shall go with me ;
And I will wete the Sheriff's faith,
  True an if he be.

CCLXXXVIII
When they had their bows i-bent,
  Their tackles feather'd free,
Seven score of wight young men
  Stood by Robin's knee.

CCLXXXIX
When they came to Nottingham,
  The butts were fair and long ;
Many was the bold archèr
  That shot with bowè strong.

CCXC
'There shall but six shoot with me,
  The other shall keep my heed,
And stand with good bowès bent
  That I be not deceived.'

CCXCI
The fourth outlaw his bow gan bend,
  And that was Robin Hood,
And that beheld the proud Sheriff,
  All by the butt he stood.

    wete] know.   tackles] arrows.

CCXCII

Thrice Robin shot about,
    And alway he sliced the wand,
And so did good Gilbert,
    With the white hand.

CCXCIII

Little John and good Scathelock
    Were archers good and free ;
Little Much and good Reynold,
    The worst would they not be.

CCXCIV

When they haddè shot about,
    These archers fair and good,
Evermore was the best,
    For soothè, Robin Hood.

CCXCV

Him was deliver'd the good arròw,
    For best worthy was he ;
He took the gift so courteously,
    To greenè-wood would he.

CCXCVI

They crièd out on Robin Hood
    And great horns gan they blow :
' Woe worth thee, treason ! ' said Robin,
    ' Full evil thou art to know.

CCXCVII

' And woe be thee, thou proud Sheriff,
    Thus gladding thy guest ;
Otherwise thou behotè me
    In yonder wild forèst.

worth thee] be to thee.   behotè] didst promise.

CCXCVIII

'But had I thee in greenè-wood,
    Under my trystell-tree,
Thou shouldest leave me a better wed
    Than thy true lewtè.'

CCXCIX

Full many a bowè there was bent,
    And arrows let they glide ;
Many a kirtle there was rent,
    And hurt full many a side.

CCC

The outlaws' shottè was so strong
    That no man might them drive,
And the proudè Sheriff's men
    They fled away full blive.

CCCI

Robin saw the bushment broke,
    In green-wood he would be ;
Many an arrow there was shot
    Among that company.

CCCII

Little John was hurt full sore,
    With an arrow in his knee,
That he might neither go nor ride ;
    It was full great pity.

CCCIII

'Master,' then said Little John,
    ' If ever thou lovest me,
And for that ilk Lordès love,
    That died upon a tree,

wed] pledge, security.   blive] quickly.   bushment]
ambush.

548

CCCIV

' And for the meeds of my service,
  That I have servèd thee,
Let never the proud Sheriff
  Alive now findè me ;

CCCV

' But take out thy brown sword,
  And smite all off my head
And give me wounds dead and wide,
  No life on me be left.'

CCCVI

' I would not that,' said Robin,
  ' John, that thou were slawe,
For all the gold in merry England,
  Though it lay now on a rawe.'

CCCVII

' God forbid,' said little Much,
  ' That died on a tree,
That thou shouldest, Little John,
  Part our company.'

CCCVIII

Up Robin took him on his back,
  And bare him well a mile ;
Many a time he laid him down,
  And shot another while.

CCCIX

Then was there a fair castèll,
  A little within the wood ;
Double-ditch'd it was about,
  And wallèd, by the rood.

meeds] wages.   dead] certain, sure.   rawe] row.

CCCX

And there dwelt that gentle Knight,
    Sir Richard at the Lee,
That Robin haddè lent his good,
    Under the green-wood tree.

CCCXI

In he took good Robin,
    And all his company :
' Welcome be thou, Robin Hood,
    Welcome art thou to me ;

CCCXII

' And much I thank thee of thy comfort,
    And of thy courtesy,
And of thy great kindness,
    Under the green-wood tree ;

CCCXIII

' I love no man in all this world
    So much as I do thee ;
For all the proud Sheriff of Nottingham,
    Right here shalt thou be.

CCCXIV

' Shut the gates and draw the bridge,
    And let no man come in,
And arm you well, and make you ready,
    And to the walls ye win.

CCCXV

' For one thing, Robin, I thee behote,
    I swear by Saint Quintìn,
These twelve days thou wonest with me,
    To sup, eat, and dine.'

win] go, attain.   behote] promise.   wonest] dwellest.

550

CCCXVI

Boards were laid, and cloths spread,
  Readily and anon ;
Robin Hood and his merry men
  To meat gan they gone.

The Sixth Fytte

How Sir Richard was cast by the Sheriff into Prison, and
rescued by Robin Hood

CCCXVII

Lithe and listen, Gentlemen,
  And hearken to my song ;
How the proud Sheriff of Nottingham
  And men of armès strong

CCCXVIII

Full fast came to the High Sheriff,
  The country up to rout,
And they beset the Knight's castell,
  The wallès all about.

CCCXIX

The proudè Sheriff loud gan cry,
  And said, ' Thou traitor Knight,
Thou keep'st here the King's enemies,
  Against the law and right.'—

CCCXX

' Sir, I will avow that I have done,
  The deeds that here be dight,
Upon all the lands that I have,
  As I am a true knight.

up to rout] to assemble in a band, to call to arms.   dight]
done, performed.

551

CCCXXI

'Wend forth, sirs, on your way,
 And doth no more to me,
Till ye wit our King his will
 What he will say to thee.'

CCCXXII

The Sheriff thus had his answère,
 Without any leasing ;
Forth he yede to London town,
 All for to tell our King.

CCCXXIII

There he told him of that Knight,
 And eke of Robin Hood,
And also of the bold archers
 That were so noble and good.

CCCXXIV

'He would avow that he had done,
 To maintain the outlaws strong,
He would be lord, and set you at nought,
 In all the north londe.'

CCCXXV

'I will be at Nottingham,' said our King,
 'Within this fortènight,
And take I willè Robin Hood,
 And so I will that Knight.

CCCXXVI

'Go home, thou proud Sheriff,
 And do as I bid thee,
And ordain good archers enough,
 Of all the wide countrey.'

leasing] lying.   yede] went.

CCCXXVII

The Sheriff had his leave i-take,
  And went him on his way ;
And Robin Hood to green-wood went
  Upon a certain day ;

CCCXXVIII

And Little John was whole of the arrow,
  That shot was in his knee,
And did him straight to Robin Hood,
  Under the green-wood tree.

CCCXXIX

Robin Hood walked in the forest
  Under the leavès green ;
The proud Sheriff of Nottingham
  Thereof he had great teen.

CCCXXX

The Sheriff there fail'd of Robin Hood,
  He might not have his prey ;
Then he awaited this gentle Knight,
  Both by night and day.

CCCXXXI

Ever he waited that gentle Knight,
  Sir Richard at the Lee,
As he went hawking by the river-side,
  And let his hawkès flee.

CCCXXXII

Took he there this gentle Knight,
  With men of armès strong,
And led him to Nottingham-ward,
  Bound both foot and hond.

whole] healed.

CCCXXXIII

The Sheriff swore a full great oath,
　　By Him that died on a tree,
He had liefer than an hundred pound,
　　That Robin Hood had he.

CCCXXXIV

This heard the Knightès wife,
　　A fair lady and a free ;
She set her on a good palfrey,
　　To green-wood anon rode she.

CCCXXXV

When she came in the forèst,
　　Under the green-wood tree,
Found she there Robin Hood
　　And all his fair meinèe.

CCCXXXVI

' God thee save, thou good Robin,
　　And all thy company ;
For Ourè dearè Lady's sake,
　　A boon grant thou me !

CCCXXXVII

' Let thou never my wedded Lord
　　Shamefully slayen be ;
He is fast bound at Nottingham,
　　For the love of thee.'

CCCXXXVIII

Anon then said good Robin,
　　To that lady free,
' What man hath your lord i-take ? '—
　　' The proud Sheriff,' then said she.

CCCXXXIX

'The proud Sheriff hath him i-take
  Forsooth as I thee say ;
He is not yet three miles,
  Passèd on his way.'

CCCXL

Up then started good Robin
  As a man that had been wood ;
'Buskè you, my merry men,
  For Him that died on rood !

CCCXLI

'And he that this sorròw forsaketh,
  By Him that died on a tree,
And by Him that all things maketh,
  No longer shall dwell with me.'

CCCXLII

Soon there were good bows y-bent,
  More than seven score ;
Hedge nor ditch they sparèd none
  That was them before.

CCCXLIII

'I make mine avow to God,' said Robin,
  'The Knight would I fain see,
And if I may him takè,
  I-quit then shall he be.'

CCCXLIV

And when they came to Nottingham,
  They walkèd in the street ;
And with the proud Sheriff i-wis
  Soonè gan they meet.

  wood] furious, mad.

CCCXLV

' Abide, thou proud Sheriff,' he said,
   ' Abide, and speak with me ;
Of some tidings of our King
   I would fain hear of thee.

CCCXLVI

'This seven year, by dear-worthy God,
   Ne yede I so fast on foot,
I make mine avow to God, thou proud Sheriff,
   It is not for thy good.'

CCCXLVII

Robin bent a full good bow,
   An arrow he drew at will ;
He hit so the proud Sheriff,
   On the ground he lay full still.

CCCXLVIII

And or he might up arise,
   On his feet to stand,
He smote off the Sheriff's head,
   With his bright brand.

CCCXLIX

' Lie thou there, thou proud Sheriff ;
   Evil mote thou thrive :
There might no man to thee trust
   The while thou wert alive.'

CCCL

His men drew out their brightè swords
   That were so sharp and keen,
And laiden on the Sheriff's men,
   And drave them down bidene.

bidene] together.

CCCLI

Robin started to the Knight,
    And cut in two his band,
And took him in his hand a bow,
    And bade him by him stand.

CCCLII

' Leave thy horsè thee behind,
    And learnè for to ren ;
Thou shalt with me to greenè-wood,
    Through mire, moss, and fen.

CCCLIII

' Thou shalt with me to greenè-wood,
    Without any leasing,
Till that I have got us grace
    Of Edward, our comely King.'

The Seventh Fytte

How the King rode out to punish Robin Hood, and how
he was entertained

CCCLIV

The King came to Nottingham,
    With knights in great array,
For to take that gentle Knight
    And Robin, if he may.

CCCLV

He askèd men of that country
    After Robin Hood,
And eke after that gentle Knight
    That was so bold and good.

took] gave.   ren] run.

CCCLVI

When they had him told the case
  Our King understood their tale,
And he seizèd in his hand
  The Knightès landès all.

CCCLVII

All the pass of Lancashire
  He went both far and near,
Till he came to Plompton Park,
  He fail'd many of his deer.

CCCLVIII

There our King was wont to see
  Herdès many one,
He could unneth find one deer
  That bare any good horn.

CCCLIX

The King was wonder wroth withall,
  And swore by the Trinity,
' I would I haddè Robin Hood,
  With eyes I might him see.

CCCLX

' And he that would smite off the Knightès head,
  And bring it unto me
He shall have the Knightès lands,
  Sir Richard at the Lee.

CCCLXI

' I give it him with my chartèr,
  And seal it with my hand,
To have and hold for evermore
  In all merry England.'

pass] limits, extent.   There] where.   unneth] scarcely.
558

CCCLXII

Then bespake a fair old Knight
  That was true in his fay :
' Ah ! my liegè lord the King,
  One word I shall you say.

CCCLXIII

' There is no man in this country
  May have the Knightès lands,
While Robin Hood may ride or go,
  And bear a bow in his hands.

CCCLXIV

' That he ne shall not lose his head,
  The best ball in his hood ;
Give it no man, my lord the King,
  That ye will any good.'

CCCLXV

Half a year dwelt our comely King
  In Nottingham, and more ;
Could he not hear of Robin Hood,
  In what country he wore.

CCCLXVI

But alway wentè good Robin
  By halk and eke by hill,
And alway slew the Kingès deer,
  And wielded them at will.

CCCLXVII

Then bespake a proud forstèr,
  That stood by our Kingès knee :
' If ye will see good Robin Hood,
  Ye must do after me.

fay] faith.   That ye will] to whom you wish.   halk]
nook, hiding-place.   forstèr] forester.

CCCLXVIII

' Take five of the bestè knights
 That be in yourè lede,
And walkè down by yon Abbèy,
 And get you monkès weed.

CCCLXIX

' And I will be your leadès-man,
 And leadè you the way,
And ere ye come to Nottingham,
 Mine head then dare I lay

CCCLXX

' That ye shall meet with good Robin,
 Alive if that he be ;
Ere ye come to Nottingham
 With eyes ye shall him see.'

CCCLXXI

Full hastily our King was dight,
 So were his knightès five,
Each of them in monkès weed,
 And hasted thither blive.

CCCLXXII

Our King was great above his cowl,
 A broad hat on his crown,
Right as he were abbot-like,
 They rode into the town.

CCCLXXIII

Stiff boots our King had on,
 Forsooth as I you say ;
Singing he rode to the greenè-wood,
 The convent was clothed in gray.

lede] following, retinue. leadès-man] guide. convent]
company of monks.

CCCLXXIV

His mail-horse and his great somèrs
　　Followed our King behind,
Till they came to greenè-wood
　　A mile under the lind.

CCCLXXV

There they met with good Robin,
　　Standing on the way,
And so did many a bold archèr,
　　For sooth as I you say.

CCCLXXVI

Robin took the Kingè's horse
　　Hastily in that stide,
And said, ' Sir Abbot, by your leave,
　　A while ye must abide.

CCCLXXVII

' We be yeomen of this forèst
　　Under the green-wood tree ;
We livè by our Kingès deer,
　　None other shift have we.

CCCLXXVIII

' And ye have churches and rentès both
　　And gold full great plentỳ ;
Give us some of your spending,　*
　　For saintè charity.'

CCCLXXIX

Then bespake our comely King,
　　Anon then saidè he,
' I have brought no more to greenè-wood
　　But forty pound with me.

mail-horse] baggage-horse.　　lind] linden, lime tree.　　stide]
stead, place.

CCCLXXX

' I have lain at Nottingham
   This fortnight with our King,
And spent I have full muchè good
   On many a great lording.

CCCLXXXI

' And I have but forty pound,
   No more I have with me :
But if I had an hundred pound,
   I vouch it half on thee.'

CCCLXXXII

Robin took the forty pound,
   And departed it in twain ;
Halfen-deal he gave his men,
   And bade them be full fain.

CCCLXXXIII

Full courteously Robin gan say,
   ' Sir, this for your spending !
We shall meet another day.'—
   ' Gramerci ! ' said our King.

CCCLXXXIV

' But well thee greeteth Edward our King,
   And sent to thee his seal,
And biddeth thee come to Nottingham,
   Both to meat and meal.'

CCCLXXXV

He took out the broadè targe,
   And soon he let him see ;
Robin could his courtesy,
   And set him on his knee.

lording] gentleman.   Halfen-deal] half.   targe]
disk (seal).

CCCLXXXVI
' I love no man in all the world
    So well as I do my King;
Welcome is my lordès seal ;
    And, Monk, for thy tiding.

CCCLXXXVII
' Sir Abbot, for thy tidings,
    To-day thou shalt dine with me,
For the lovè of my King,
    Under my trystell-tree.'

CCCLXXXVIII
Forth he led our comely King
    Full fairè by the hand ;
Many a deer there was slain,
    They were full fast dightànd.

CCCLXXXIX
Robin took a full great horn,
    And loudè he gan blow ;
Seven score of wight young men
    Came ready on a row.

CCCXC
All they kneelèd on their knee
    Full fair before Robin ;
The King said himself until,
    And swore by Saint Austìn,

CCCXCI
' Here is a wonder seemly sight ;
    Me thinketh, by God's pine,
His men are more at his bidding
    Than my men be at mine.'

dightànd] making preparations.   pine] pain, passion.

CCCXCII

Full hastily was their dinner dight,
　　And thereto gan they gon ;
They servèd our King with all their might,
　　Both Robin and Little John.

CCCXCIII

Anon before our King was set
　　The fattè venisoun,
The good white bread, the good red wine,
　　Thereto fine ale and brown.

CCCXCIV

' Make good cheer,' said Robin Hood,
　　' Abbot, for charity,
And for this ilkè tiding, Sir,
　　Blessed mote thou be.

CCCXCV

' Now shalt thou see what life we lead,
　　Ere thou hennès wend ;
Then thou mayst inform our King,
　　When ye together lend.'

CCCXCVI

Up they started all in haste,
　　Their bows were smartly bent ;
Our King was never so aghast,
　　He weened to have been shent.

CCCXCVII

Two yards there were up set,
　　Thereto gan they gang ;
By fifty paces, our King said,
　　The markès were too lang.

hennès] hence.　　　　lend] dwell.　　　shent] put to shame,
hurt.　　　yards] rods.

CCCXCVIII

On every side a rose garlànd,
   They shot under the line :
' Who fails of the garland,' said Robin,
   ' His tackle he shall tine,

CCCXCIX

' And yield it unto his mastèr,
   Be it never so fine ;
For no man will I spare,' he said,
   ' So drink I ale or wine ;

CCCC

' And bear a buffet on his head
   I-wis aright all bare : '
And all that fell to Robin's lot
   He smote them wonder sair.

CCCCI

Twice Robin shot about,
   And ever he cleft the wand,
And so did eke the good Gilbèrt
   With the white hand.

CCCCII

Little John and good Scathèlock,
   For nothing would they spare ;
When they fail'd of the garlànd
   Robin smote them sair.

CCCCIII

At the last shot that Robin shot,
   For all his friendès fare,
Yet he fail'd of the garlànd
   Three fingers and mair.

tine] forfeit.

565

CCCCIV

Then bespake him good Gilbèrt,
  And thus he gan him say:
' Master,' he said, ' your tackle is lost,
  Stand forth and take your pay.'

CCCCV

' If it be so,' said Robin Hood,
  ' That may no better be,
Sir Abbot, I deliver thee mine arrow,
  I pray thee, serve thou me.'

CCCCVI

' It falls not for mine order,' said our King,
  ' Robin, by thy leave,
For to smite no good yeomàn,
  For doubt I should him grieve.'

CCCCVII

' Smite on boldly,' said Robin,
  ' I give thee largè leave.'
Anon our King with that same word
  He folded up his sleeve,

CCCCVIII

And such a buffet he gave Robin,
  To ground he yede full near:
' I make mine avow to God,' said Robin,
  ' Thou art a stalwart frere.

CCCCIX

' There is pith in thine arm,' said Robin,
  ' I trow thou canst well shoot.'
Thus our King and Robin Hood
  Together then they met.

falls] is proper.   frere] friar.

CCCCX

Robin beheld our comely King
    Wistly in the face,
So did Sir Richard at the Lea,
    And knelt down in that place.

CCCCXI

And so did all the wild outlàws,
    When they saw them kneel :
' My lord the King of Engèland,
    Now I know you weel ! '

CCCCXII

' Mercy then, Robin,' said our King,
    ' Under your trystell-tree,
Of thy goodness and thy grace,
    For my men and me ! '

CCCCXIII

' Yes, 'fore God,' said Robin Hood,
    ' And also God me save !
I ask mercy, my lord the King,
    And for my men I crave.'

CCCCXIV

' Yes, 'fore God,' then said our King,
    ' And thereto sent I me,
With that thou leave the greenè-wood,
    And all thy company ;

CCCCXV

' And come home, sir, unto my court,
    And there dwell with me.'—
' I make mine avow to God,' said Robin,
    ' And right so shall it be.

567

CCCCXVI

'I will come unto your court,
  Your service for to see,
And bringè with me of my men
  Seven score and three.

CCCCXVII

'But me like well your service,
  I will come again full soon,
And shooten at the dunnè deer,
  As I am wont to doon.'

The Eighth Fytte

How Robin Hood lived a while at the King's Court, but
returned to the Green-wood

CCCCXVIII

'Hast thou any green cloth?' said our King,
  'That thou wilt sell now to me?'—
'Yea, 'fore God,' said Robin,
  'Thirty yards and three.'

CCCCXIX

'Robin,' said our King,
  'Now pray I thee,
To sell me some of that cloth,
  To me and my meinèe.'

CCCCXX

'Yes, 'fore God,' then said Robin,
  'Or else I were a fool;
Another day ye will me clothe,
  I trow, against the Yule.'

But me like] unless I like.

ROBIN HOOD AND HIS MEINY

CCCCXXI

The King cast off his coat then,
    A green garment he did on,
And every knight had so, i-wis,
    They clothèd them full soon.

CCCCXXII

When they were clothed in Lincoln green,
    They cast away their gray.
'Now we shall to Nottingham,'
    All thus our king gan say.

CCCCXXIII

Their bows bent and forth they went,
    Shooting all in fere,
Toward the town of Nottingham,
    Outlaws as they were.

CCCCXXIV

Our King and Robin rode together
    Forsooth as I you say,
And they shot pluck-buffet,
    As they went by the way;

CCCCXXV

And many a buffet our King won,
    Of Robin Hood that day:
And nothing spared good Robin
    Our King in his pay.

CCCCXXVI

'So God me help,' said our King,
    'Thy game is nought to lere,
I should not get a shot of thee,
    Though I shot all this year.'

pluck-buffet] 'app. a competition between archers, in which he who missed or failed "caught" a buffet from his competitor' (*N.E.D.*).   lere] learn.

CCCCXXVII

All the people of Nottingham
  They stood and beheld,
They saw nothing but mantles of green
  That cover'd all the felde ;

CCCCXXVIII

Then every man to other gan say,
  ' I dread our King be slone ;
Come Robin Hood to the town, i-wis,
  On life he leaveth not one.'

CCCCXXIX

Full hastily they began to flee,
  Both yeoman and knaves,
The old wives that might evil go,
  They hippèd on their staves.

CCCCXXX

The King laughed full fast,
  And commanded them again ;
When they saw our comely King,
  I-wis they were full fain.

CCCCXXXI

They ate and drank, and made them glad,
  And sang with notès high.
Then bespake our comely King
  To Sir Richard at the Lee :

CCCCXXXII

He gave him there his land again,
  A good man he bade him be.
Robin thanked our comely King,
  And set him on his knee.

hippèd] hopped, limped.

CCCCXXXIII

Robin had dwelt in the Kingès court
    But twelvè months and three,
That he had spent an hundred pound,
    And all his mennès fee.

CCCCXXXIV

In every place where Robin came,
    Evermore he laid down
Both for knightès and for squires,
    To get him great renown.

CCCCXXXV

By then the year was all agone
    He had no man but twain,
Little John and good Scathèlock
    With him all for to gane.

CCCCXXXVI

Robin saw the young men shoot
    Full far upon a day ;
' Alas ! ' then said good Robin Hood,
    ' My wealth is went away.

CCCCXXXVII

' Sometime I was an archer good,
    A stiff and eke a strong ;
I was counted the best archèr
    That was in merry Englond.

CCCCXXXVIII

' Alas ! ' then said good Robin Hood,
    ' Alas and well-a-way !
If I dwell longer with the King.
    Sorrow will me slay.'

laid down] spent money.   By then] by the time that.

CCCCXXXIX

Forth then wentè Robin Hood
　　Till he came to our King:
' My lord the King of Engèland,
　　Grant me mine asking!

CCCCXL

' I made a chapel in Barnèsdale
　　That seemly is to see,
It is of Mary Magdalen,
　　And thereto would I be.

CCCCXLI

' I might never in this seven night
　　No timè sleep nor wink,
Neither all these seven days
　　Neither eat nor drink.

CCCCXLII

' Me longeth sore to Barnèsdale,
　　I may not be therefro;
Barefoot and woolward I have hight
　　Thither for to go.'

CCCCXLIII

' If it be so,' then said our King,
　　' It may no better be;
Seven night I give thee leave,
　　No longer, to dwell from me.'

CCCCXLIV

' Gramerci, lord,' then said Robin,
　　And set him on his knee:
He took his leave full courteously,
　　To green-wood then went he.

therefro] turned from it.　　woolward] in a rough woollen
shirt (as penance).　　hight] promised.

CCCCXLV

When he came to greenè-wood
  In a merry mornìng,
There he heard the notès small
  Of birds merry singìng.

CCCCXLVI

'It is far gone,' said Robin Hood,
  'That I was latest here;
Me list a little for to shoot
  At the dunnè deer.'

CCCCXLVII

Robin slew a full great hart;
  His horn then gan he blow,
That all the outlaws of that forèst
  That horn they couldè know,

CCCCXLVIII

And them together gatherèd
  In a little throw;
Seven score of wight young men
  Came ready on a row,

CCCCXLIX

And fairè didden off their hoods,
  And set them on their knee:
'Welcome,' they said, 'our dear mastèr,
  Under this green-wood tree!'

CCCCL

Robin dwelt in greenè-wood
  Twenty year and two;
For all dread of Edward our King,
  Again would he not go.

Me list] it pleases me.   throw] interval of time.   Again] back.

CCCCLI

Yet he was beguiled, i-wis,
    Through a wicked woman,
The prioress of Kirksley,
    That nigh was of his kin,

CCCCLII

For the love of a knight,
    Sir Roger of Doncastèr,
That was her own special ;
    Full evil might they fare !

CCCCLIII

They took together their counsel
    Robin Hood for to sle,
And how they might best do that deed,
    His banis for to be.

CCCCLIV

Then bespake good Robin,
    In place where as he stood,
' To-morrow I must to Kirksley,
    Craftily to be letten blood.'

CCCCLV

Sir Roger [and the prioress
    A springe for him did] lay,
And there they betray'd good Robin Hood,
    Through their falsè play.

CCCCLVI

Christ have mercy on his soul,
    That died upon the rood !
For he was a good outlàw,
    And did poor men much good.

banis] bane, destruction.   craftily] skilfully.   springe] trap.

116. *Robin Hood and Guy of Gisborne*

I

WHEN shaws beene sheene, and shradds full fayre,
　　And leves both large and longe,
Itt is merrye walking in the fayre forrèst
　　To heare the small birds' songe.

II

The woodweele sang, and wold not cease,
　　[Sitting upon the spraye,
Soe lowde, he wakened Robin Hood,
　　In the grenewood where he lay.

III

'Now by my faye,' sayd jollye Robìn,
　　'A sweaven I had this night;
I dreamt me of two wight yemen,
　　That fast with me can fight.]

IV

'Methought they did mee beate and binde,
　　And tooke my bow mee fro;
If I be Robin alive in this lande,
　　I'll be wroken on them towe.'

V

'Sweavens are swift, Master,' quoth John,
　　'As the wind that blowes ore a hill;
For if itt be never so loude this night,
　　To-morrow itt may be still.'

shaws] woods.　　　sheene] bright.　　　shradds] coppices (?).
woodweele] woodlark, thrush (?).　　sweaven] dream.　　wight]
sturdy.　　wroken] revenged.

575

VI

'Buske yee, bowne yee, my merry men all,
    And John shall goe with mee,
For I'le goe seeke yond wight yemen,
    In grenewood where they bee.

VII

They cast on them their gownes of grene,
    [And tooke theyr bowes each one ;
And all away to the grene forrèst]
    A shooting forth are gone ;

VIII

Until they came to the merry grenewood,
    Where they had gladdest bee,
There were they ware of a wight yemàn,
    His body lean'd to a tree.

IX

A sword and a dagger he wore by his side,
    Of manye a man the bane ;
And he was clad in his capull-hyde
    Topp and tayll and mayne.

X

'Stand you still, Master,' quoth Little John,
    'Under this trusty tree,
And I will go to yond wight yeoman
    To know his meaning trulye.'

XI

'A ! John, by me thou settest noe store,
    And that 's a farley finde.
How offt send I my men beffore,
    And tarry my selfe behinde ?

Buske] dress.   bowne] get ready.   capull-hyde] horse-
hide.   farley] wondrous strange.

XII

'It is noe cunning a knave to ken,
  An a man but heare him speake ;
An itt were not for bursting of my bowe,
  John, I wold thy head breake.'

XIII

As often wordes they breeden bale,
  So they parted Robin and John :
And John is gone to Barnèsdale ;
  The gates he knoweth eche one.

XIV

But when he came to Barnèsdale,
  Great heavinesse there hee hadd,
For he found two of his owne fellòwes
  Were slaine both in a slade.

XV

And Scarlette à-foote he flyinge was
  Fast over stocke and stone,
For the Sheriffe with seven score men
  . Fast after him is gone.

XVI

'Yet one shoote I'le shoote,' quoth Little John,
  'With Christ his might and mayne ;
I'le make yond fellow that flyes soe fast,
  To stopp he shall be fayne.'

XVII

Then John bent up his good yewe-bowe
  And fettl'd him to shoote :
The bow was made of a tender boughe,
  And fell downe to his foote.

gates] ways, paths.   slade] hollow.   fettl'd] prepared.

XVIII

'Woe worth thee, wicked wood,' sayd John,
  'That ere thou grew on a tree !
For now this day thou art my bale,
  My boote when thou shold bee.'

XIX

His shoote it was but loosely shott,
  Yet it flewe not in vaine,
For itt met one of the Sherriff's men,
  Good William à Trent was slaine.

XX

It had bene better of William à Trent
  To have hangèd upon a gallòw,
Than to be that day in the grene-wood
  To meet Little John's arrowe.

XXI

But as it is said, when men be mett
  Fyve can doe more than three,
The Sheriffe hath taken Little John,
  And bound him fast to a tree.

XXII

'Thou shalt be drawen by dale and downe,
  And hangèd hye on a hill.'—
'But thou mayst fayle,' quoth Little John,
  'If itt be Christ his will.'

XXIII

Let us leave talking of Little John,
  And thinke of Robin Hood,
How he is gone to the wight yemàn,
  Where under the leaves he stood.

boote] help.

XXIV

'Good morrowe, good fellowe,' sayd Robin so fayre,
  ' Good morrowe, good fellow,' quoth he :
' Methinkes by this bowe thou beares in thy hande
  A good archere thou sholdst bee.'

XXV

' I am wilfull of my waye,' quo' the yeman,
  ' And of my morning tyde.'
' I'le lead thee through the wood,' sayd Robin ;
  ' Good fellow, I'le be thy guide.'

XXVI

' I seeke an outlàwe,' the straunger sayd,
  ' Men call him Robin Hood ;
Rather I'ld meet with that proud outlàwe,
  Than fortye pound of go'd.'—

XXVII

' If you two met, it wold be seene
  Whether were better man :
But let us under the levès grene
  Some other pastime plan.

XXVIII

' Let us some other masteryes make
  Among the woods so even,
Wee may chance meet with Robin Hood
  Here att some unsett steven.'

XXIX

They cutt them downe two summer shroggs,
  That grew both under a breere,
And sett them threescore rood in twinne
  To shoot the prickes y-fere

wilfull] astray.	tyde] time of day.	masteryes] trials of
skill.	unsett steven] time not appointed.	shroggs] shrubs.
threescore rood in twinne] sixty rods apart.		prickes] marks.

XXX

' Leade on, good fellowe,' quoth Robin Hood,
  ' Leade on, I doe bidd thee.'——
' Nay by my faith, good fellowe,' hee sayd,
  ' My leader thou shalt bee.'

XXXI

The first good shoot that Robin led,
  He mist but an inch it fro' :
The yeoman he was an archer good,
  But he cold ne'er shoote soe.

XXXII

The second shoote had the wight yemàn,
  He shote within the garlànde :
But Robin he shott far better than hee,
  For he clave the good pricke wande.

XXXIII

' God's blessing upon thy heart ! ' he sayd ;
  ' Good fellowe, thy shooting is goode ;
For an thy hart be as good as thy hand,
  Thou wert better than Robin Hood.'

XXXIV

' Now tell me thy name, good fellowe,' sayd he.
  ' Under the leaves of lyne.'——
' Nay by my faith,' quoth good Robìn,
  ' Till thou have told me thine.'

XXXV

' I dwell by dale and downe,' quoth hee,
  ' And Robin to take I'me sworne ;
And when I am callèd by my right name
  I am Guy of good Gisborne.'——

lyne] linden.

XXXVI

'My dwelling is in this wood,' sayes Robin,
  'By thee I set right nought:
I am Robin Hood of Barnèsdale,
  Whom thou so long hast sought.'

XXXVII

He that had neither beene kithe nor kin,
  Might have seene a full fayre sight,
To see how together these yemen went
  With blades both browne and bright:

XXXVIII

To see how these yemen together they fought
  Two howres of a summer's day:
Yett neither Sir Guy nor Robin Hood
  Them fettled to flye away.

XXXIX

Robin was reachles on a roote,
  And stumbled at that tyde;
And Guy was quick and nimble with-all,
  And hitt him o'er the left side.

XL

'Ah deere Lady!' sayd Robin Hood,
  'That art both mother and may,
I think it was never man's destinye
  To dye before his day.'

XLI

Robin thought on Our Ladye deere,
  And soone leapt up againe,
And strait he came with an aukward stroke,
  And he Sir Guy hath slayne.

reachles on] reckless, careless of.   may] maid.   aukward]
back-handed.

XLII

He took Sir Guy's head by the hayre,
    And stickèd itt on his bowes end:
' Thou hast been traytor all thy liffe,
    Which thing must have an ende.'

XLIII

Robin pulled forth an Irish kniffe,
    And nicked Sir Guy in the face,
That he was never on woman born,
    Cold tell whose head it was.

XLIV

Saies, ' Lye there, lye there, good Sir Guy,
    And with me be not wrothe ;
If thou have had the worse strokes at my hand,
    Thou shalt have the better clothe.'

XLV

Robin did off his gowne of greene,
    And on Sir Guy did it throwe,
And hee put on that capull-hyde,
    That clad him topp to toe.

XLVI

' The bowe, the arrowes, and litle horne,
    Now with me I will beare ;
For I will away to Barnèsdale,
    To see how my men doe fare.'

XLVII

Robin sett Guy's horne to his mouth,
    A loud blast in it he did blow.
That beheard the Sheriffe of Nottingham,
    As he leaned under a lowe.

capull-hyde] horse-hide.   lowe] hillock.

XLVIII

'Hearken! hearken!' sayd the Sheriffe,
　'I heare now tydings good,
For yonder I heare Sir Guy's horne blowe,
　And he hath slaine Robin Hood.

XLIX

'Yonder I heare Sir Guy's horne blowe,
　Itt blowes soe well in tyde,
And yonder comes that wight yemàn,
　Cladd in his capull-hyde.

L

'Come hyther, come hyther, thou good Sir Guy,
　Aske what thou wilt of mee.'—
'O I will none of thy gold,' sayd Robin,
　'Nor I will none of thy fee:

LI

'But now I have slaine the master,' he sayes,
　'Let me go strike the knave;
This is all the rewarde I aske;
　Nor noe other will I have.'

LII

'Thou art a madman,' said the Sheriffe,
　'Thou sholdest have had a knight's fee:
But seeing thy asking hath beene so bad,
　Well granted it shall be.'

LIII

When Little John heard his master speake,
　Well knewe he it was his steven:
'Now shall I be looset,' quoth Little John,
　With Christ his might in heaven.'

steven] voice.

583

LIV

Robin hee hyed him to Little John,
  He thought to loose him belive;
The Sheriffe and all his companye
  Fast after him did drive.

LV

' Stand abacke! stand abacke!' sayd Robin Hood;
  ' Why draw you mee soe neere?
Itt was never the use in our countrye,
  One's shrift another shold heere.'

LVI

But Robin pull'd forth an Irysh kniffe,
  And losed John hand and foote,
And gave him Sir Guy's bow into his hand,
  And bade it be his boote.

LVII

Then John he took Guy's bow in his hand,
  His boltes and arrowes eche one:
When the Sheriffe saw Little John bend his bow,
  He fettled him to be gone.

LVIII

Towards his house in Nottingham towne
  He fled full fast away;
And soe did all his companye:
  Not one behind wold stay.

LIX

But he cold neither goe soe fast,
  Nor away soe fast cold runne,
But Little John with an arrowe soe broad,
  Did cleave his herte in twinne.

belive] straightway.

584

I

IN somer, when the shawes be sheyne,
  And leves be large and long,
Hit is full mery in feyre foreste
    To here the foulys song :

II

To se the dere draw to the dale,
  And leve the hillès hee,
And shadow hem in the levès grene,
    Under the grene-wode tre.

III

Hit befel on Whitsontide,
  Erly in a May mornyng,
The Son up feyre can shyne,
    And the briddis mery can syng.

IV

' This is a mery mornyng,' seid Litull John,
  ' Be Hym that dyed on tre ;
A more mery man then I am one
    Lyves not in Cristiantë.

V

' Pluk up thi hert, my dere mayster,'
  Litull John can sey,
' And thynk hit is a full fayre tyme
    In a mornyng of May.'

VI

' Ye, on thyng greves me,' seid Robyn,
  ' And does my hert mych woo ;
That I may not no solem day
    To mas nor matyns goo.

shawes] woods.   sheyne] bright, beautiful.

VII

'Hit is a fourtnet and more,' seid he,
  'Syn I my Savyour see;
To day wil I to Notyngham,' seid Robyn,
  'With the myght of mylde Marye.'

VIII

Than spake Moche, the mylner son,—
  Ever more wel hym betyde!
'Take twelve of thi wyght yemèn,
  Well weppynd, be thi side.
Such on wolde thi selfe slon,
  That twelve dar not abyde.'

IX

'Of all my mery men,' seid Robyn,
  'Be my feith I wil non have,
But Litull John shall beyre my bow,
  Til that me list to drawe.'

X

'Thou shall beyre thin own,' seid Litull John,
  'Maister, and I wyl beyre myne,
And we well shete a peny,' seid Litull John,
  'Under the grene-wode lyne.'

XI

'I wil not shete a peny,' seyd Robyn Hode,
  'In feith, Litull John, with the,
But ever for on as thou shetis,' seide Robyn,
  'In feith I holde the thre.'

---

wyght yemèn] sturdy yeomen.   slon] slay.   shete a peny]
shoot for a penny.   lyne] linden.   holde] wager.

ROBIN HOOD AND THE MONK

XII

Thus shet thei forth, these yemen two,
   Bothe at buske and brome,
Til Litull John wan of his maister
   Five shillings to hose and shone.

XIII

A ferly strife fel them betwene,
   As they went bi the wey ;
Litull John seid he had won five shillings,
   And Robyn Hode seid schortly nay.

XIV

With that Robyn Hode lyed Litull John,
   And smote hym with his hande ;
Litull John waxèd wroth therwith,
   And pull'd out his bright bronde.

XV

' Were thou not my maister,' seid Litull John,
   ' Thou shuldis be hit ful sore ;
Get the a man wher thou wilt,
   For thou getis me no more.'

XVI

Then Robyn goes to Notyngham,
   Hym selfe mornyng allone,
And Litull John to mery Scherwode,
   The pathes he knew ilkone.

XVII

Whan Robyn came to Notyngham,
   Sertenly withouten layn,
He prayed to God and myld Mary
   To bryng hym out save agayn.

buske] bush.   ferly] wondrous, strange.   lyed] gave the lie to.   ilkone] each one.   layn] concealment.

XVIII

He gos in to Seynt Mary chirch,
  And kneled down before the rode ;
Alle that e'er were the church within
  Beheld wel Robyn Hode.

XIX

Beside hym stod a gret-hedid munke,
  I pray to God woo he be !
Fful sone he knew gode Robyn,
  As sone as he hym se.

XX

Out at the durre he ran,
  Fful sone and anon ;
Alle the yatis of Notyngham
  He made to be sparred euerychon.

XXI

' Rise up,' he seid, ' thou prowde Schereff,
  Buske the and make the bowne ;
I have spyèd the Kynggis felon,
  Fforsothe he is in this town.

XXII

' I have spyèd the false felon,
  As he stondis at his masse ;
Hit is long of the,' seide the munke
  ' And ever he fro us passe.

XXIII

' This traytur name is Robyn Hode,
  Under the grene-wode lynde ;
He robbyt me onys of a hundred pouna,
  Hit shalle never out of my mynde.'

yatis] gates.　　　sparred] barred.　　　Buske] get ready.
bowne] bound, ready.　　long of] along of, i. e. thy fault.

XXIV

Up then rose this prowde Shereff,
    And radly made hym yare ;
Many was the moder son
    To the kyrk with hym can fare.

XXV

In at the durres thei throly thrast,
    With stavès ful gode wone ;
' Alas, alas ! ' seid Robyn Hode,
    ' Now mysse I Litull John.'

XXVI

But Robyn toke out a two-hond sworde,
    That hangit down be his kne ;
Ther as the Schereff and his men stode thyckust,
    Thethurwarde wolde he.

XXVII

Thryes thorowout them he ran then,
    Forsothe as I yow sey,
And woundyt mony a moder son,
    And twelve he slew that day.

XXVIII

His sworde upon the Schereff hed
    Sertanly he brake in two ;
' The smyth that the made,' seid Robyn,
    ' I pray to God wyrke hym woo !

XXIX

' Ffor now am I weppynlesse,' seid Robyn,
    ' Alasse ! agayn my wylle ;
But if I may fle these traytors fro,
    I wot thei wil me kyll.'

---

radly] quickly.   yare] ready.   throly thrast] pressed
stubbornly.   gode wone] good number, plenty.   But if] unless.

XXX

Robyn into the churchë ran,
 Throout hem everilkon . . .
[Then word is gone to his yemen
 In grene-wode wher they wone.]

XXXI

Sum fel in swonyng as thei were dede,
 And lay stil as any stone;
Non of theym were in her mynde
 But only Litull John.

XXXII

'Let be your rule,' seid Litull John,
 'Ffor his luf that dyed on tre;
Ye that shulde be dughty men,
 Het is gret shame to se.

XXXIII

'Oure maister has bene hard bystode
 And yet scapyd away;
Pluk up your hertis, and leve this mone,
 And harkyn what I shal say.

XXXIV

'He has seruyd Oure Lady many a day,
 And yet wil, securly;
Therfor I trust in hir specialy
 No wyckud deth shal he dye.

XXXV

'Therfor be glad,' seid Litull John,
 'And let this mournyng be;
And I shal be the munkis gyde,
 With the myght of mylde Mary.'

wone] dwelt. rule] 'taking on,' lamenting. dughty]
doughty. mone] moan. gyde] be the guide = take charge of.

XXXVI

[Than spake Moche, the mylner son,]
  'We will go but we two.'—
'An I mete hym,' seid Litull John,
  [I trust to wyrke hym woo.]

XXXVII

'Loke that ye kepe wel owre tristil-tre,
  Under the levys smale,
And spare non of this venyson,
  That gose in thys vale.'

XXXVIII

Fforthe then went these yemen two,
  Litull John and Moche on fere,
And lokid on Moch' emys hows,—
  The hye-way lay full nere.

XXXIX

Litull John stode at a wyndow in the mornyng,
  And lokid forth at a stage ;
He was war wher the munke came ridyng,
  And with hym a litul page.

XL

'Be my feith,' seid Litull John to Moch,
  'I can the tel tithyngus gode ;
I se wher the monke cumys rydyng,
  I know hym be his wyde hode.'

XLI

They went in to the way, these yemen bothe,
  As curtes men and hende ;
Thei spyrred tithyngus at the munke,
  As they hade bene his frende.

tristil-tre] trysting-tree, rendezvous.　　smale] small.　　on
fere] in company.　　emys hows] uncle's house.　　at a stage]
on an upper floor.　　tithyngus] tidings.　　hende] civil.
spyrred] spiered, inquired.

XLII

'Ffro whens come ye?' seid Litull John,
 'Tel us tithyngus, I yow pray,
Off a false owtlay, callid Robyn Hode,
 Was takyn yisterday.

XLIII

'He robbyt me and my felowes bothe
 Of twenti marke in serten ;
If that false owtlay be takyn,
 Ffor sothe we wolde be fayn.'

XLIV

'So did he me,' seid the munke,
 'Of a hundred pound and more ;
I layde furst hande hym apon,
 Ye may thonke me therfore.'

XLV

'I pray God thanke you,' seid Litull John,
 'And we wil when we may ;
We wil go with you, with your leve,
 And bryng yow on your way.

XLVI

'Ffor Robyn Hode hase many a wilde felow,
 I tell you in certen ;
If thei wist ye rode this way,
 In feith ye shulde be slayn.'

XLVII

As thei went talking be the way,
 The munke and Litull John,
John toke the munkis horse be the hede,
 Fful sone and anon.

XLVIII

John toke the munkis horse be the hed,
    Fforsothe as I yow say ;
So did Much the litull page,
    Ffor he shulde not scape away.

XLIX

Be the golett of the hode
    John pulled the munkè down ;
John was nothyng of hym agast,
    He lete hym falle on his crown.

L

Litull John was sore agrevyd,
    And drew owt his swerde in hye ;
This munkè saw he shulde be ded,
    Lowd mercy can he crye.

LI

' He was my maister,' seid Litull John,
    ' That thou hase browght in bale ;
Shalle thou never cum at our Kyng,
    Ffor to telle hym tale.'

LII

John smote of the munkis hed,
    No longer wolde he dwell ;
So did Moch the litull page,
    Ffor ferd lest he wolde tell.

LIII

Ther thei beryèd hem bothe,
    In nouther mosse nor lyng,
And Litull John and Much in fere
    Bare the letturs to oure Kyng.

golett] gullet, throat.   of hym agast] alarmed about him.
hye] haste.   bale] harm.   ferd] fear.

LIV

[Whan John came unto oure Kyng]
   He knelid down on his kne :
God yow save, my legè lorde,
   Jhesus yow save and se !

LV

'God yow save, my legè Kyng ! '
   To speke John was full bolde ;
He gaf hym the letturs in his hond,
   The Kyng did hit unfold.

LVI

The Kyng red the letturs anon,
   And seid, So mot I the,
Ther was never yoman in mery Inglond
   I longut so sore to se.

LVII

' Wher is the munke that these shuld have brought ? '
   Ourè Kyng can say :
' Be my trouth,' seid Litull John,
   ' He dyed after the way.'

LVIII

The Kyng gaf Moch and Litull John
   Twenti pound in sertan,
And made theim yemen of the crown,
   And bade theim go agayn.

LIX

He gaf John the seel in hand,
   The Sheref for to bere,
To bryng Robyn hym to,
   And no man do hym dere.

mot I the] I thrive.   after] behind on.   dere] injury.

LX

John toke his leve at oure Kyng,
  The sothe as I yow say;
The next way to Notyngham
  To take, he yede the way.

LXI

Whan John came to Notyngham
  The yatis were sparred ychon;
John callid up the porter,
  He answerid sone anon.

LXII

'What is the cause,' seid Litull John,
  'Thou sparris the yates so fast?'—
'Because of Robyn Hode,' seid the porter,
  'In depe prison is cast.

LXIII

'John and Moch and Wyll Scathlok,
  Ffor sothe as I yow say,
Thei slew oure men upon our wallis,
  And sawten us every day.'

LXIV

Litull John spyrred after the Schereff,
  And sone he hym fonde;
He oppyned the Kyngus prive seell,
  And gaf hym in his honde.

LXV

Whan the Scheref saw the Kyngus seell,
  He did of his hode anon:
'Wher is the munke that bare the letturs?'
  He seid to Litull John.

next] nighest.   yede] went.   ychon] each one.   sawten]
assault.   did of his hode] took off his hat.

LXVI

'He is so fayn of hym,' seid Litull John,
  'Fforsothe as I yow say,
He has made hym abot of Westmynster,
  A lorde of that abbay.'

LXVII

The Scheref made John godè chere,
  And gaf hym wyne of the best;
At nyght thei went to her beddè,
  And every man to his rest.

LXVIII

When the Scheref was on slepe,
  Dronken of wyne and ale,
Litull John and Moch forsothe
  Toke the way unto the jale.

LXIX

Litull John callid up the jayler,
  And bade hym rise anon;
He seyd Robyn Hode had brokyn prison,
  And out of hit was gon.

LXX

The porter rose anon sertan,
  As sone as he herd John calle;
Litull John was redy with a swerd,
  And bare hym to the walle.

LXXI

'Now wil I be porter,' seid Litull John,
  'And take the keyes in honde:'
He toke the way to Robyn Hode,
  And sone he hym unbonde.
        her] their.

LXXII

He gaf hym a gode swerd in his hond,
    His hed therwith for to kepe,
And ther as the walle was lowyst
    Anon down can thei lepe.

LXXIII

Be that the cok began to crow,
    The day began to spryng,
The Scheref fond the jaylier ded ;
    The comyn bell made he ryng.

LXXIV

He made a crye thoroout al the town,
    Wheder he be yoman or knave,
That cowthè bryng hym Robyn Hode,
    His warison he shuld have.

LXXV

' Ffor I dar never,' said the Scheref,
    ' Cum before oure Kyng ;
Ffor if I do, I wot serten
    Ffor sothe he wil me heng.'

LXXVI

The Scheref made to seke Notyngham,
    Bothe be strete and stye,
And Robyn was in mery Scherwode,
    As light as lef on lynde.

LXXVII

Then bespake gode Litull John,
    To Robyn Hode can he say,
' I have done the a gode turne for an evyll,
    Quyte the whan thou may.

comyn bell] town bell.   warison] reward.   stye] path, alley.

LXXVIII

'I have done the a gode turne,' seid Litull John,
  ' Fforsothe as I yow say ;
I have brought the under grene-wode lyne ;
  Ffare wel, and have gode day.'

LXXIX

' Nay, be my trouth,' seid Robyn Hode,
  ' So shall hit never be ;
I make the maister,' seid Robyn Hode,
  ' Off alle my men and me.'

LXXX

'Nay, be my trouth,' seid Litull John,
  ' So shalle hit never be ;
But lat me be a felow,' seid Litull John,
  ' No noder kepe I be.'

LXXXI

Thus John gate Robyn Hode out of prison,
  Sertan withoutyn layn ;
Whan his men saw hym hol and sounde,
  Fforsothe they were full fayne.

LXXXII

They fillèd in wyne, and made hem glad,
  Under the levys smale,
And yete pastès of venyson,
  That godè was with ale.

LXXXIII

Than wordè came to oure Kyng
  How Robyn Hode was gon,
And how the Scheref of Notyngham
  Durst never loke hym upon.

    kepe I be] care I to be.   yete] ate.

598

LXXXIV

Then bespake oure cumly Kyng,
    In an angur hye:
'Litull John hase begyled the Schereff,
    In faith so hase he me.

LXXXV

'Litull John has begyled us bothe
    And that full wel I se;
Or ellis the Schereff of Notyngham
    Hye hongut shulde he be.

LXXXVI

' I made hem yemen of the crowne,
    And gaf hem fee with my hond;
I gaf hem grith,' seid oure Kyng,
    ' Thorowout all mery Inglond.

LXXXVII

' I gaf theym grith,' then seid oure Kyng;
    ' I say, so mot I the,
Fforsothe soch a yeman as he is on
    In all Inglond ar not thre.

LXXXVIII

' He is trew to his maister,' seid our Kyng;
    ' I sey, be swete Seynt John,
He lovys better Robyn Hode
    Then he dose us ychon.

LXXXIX

' Robyn Hode is ever bond to hym,
    Bothe in strete and stalle;
Speke no more of this mater,' seid oure Kyng,
    ' But John has begyled us alle.'

grith] charter of peace.

XC

Thus endys the talkyng of the munke
And Robyn Hode i-wysse ;
God, that is ever a crowned kyng,
Bryng us all to his blisse !

118. *Robin Hood and the Curtal Friar*

But how many months be in the year ?
There are thirteen, I say ;
The midsummer moon is the merryest of all
Next to the merry month of May.

I

IN summer time, when leaves grow green,
And flowers are fresh and gay,
Robin Hood and his merry men
Were [all] disposed to play.

II

Then some would leap, and some would run,
And some use artillery :
' Which of you can a good bow draw,
A good archer to be ?

III

' Which of you can kill a buck ?
Or who can kill a doe ?
Or who can kill a hart of grease,
Five hundred foot him fro ? '

IV

Will Scadlock he kill'd a buck,
And Midge he kill'd a doe,
And Little John kill'd a hart of grease,
Five hundred foot him fro.

V

' God's blessing on thy heart,' said Robin Hood,
  ' That hath [shot] such a shot for me ;
I would ride my horse an hundred miles,
  To finde one could match with thee.'

VI

That caus'd Will Scadlock to laugh,
  He laugh'd full heartily :
' There lives a curtal friar in Fountains Abbey
  Will beat both him and thee.

VII

' That curtal friar in Fountains Abbey
  Well can a strong bow draw ;
He will beat you and your yeomen,
  Set them all on a row.'

VIII

Robin Hood took a solemn oath,
  It was by Mary free,
That he would neither eat nor drink
  Till the friar he did see.

IX

Robin Hood put on his harness good,
  And on his head a cap of steel,
Broad sword and buckler by his side,
  And they became him weel.

X

He took his bow into his hand,
  It was made of a trusty tree,
With a sheaf of arrows at his belt,
  To the Fountains Dale went he.

XI

And coming unto Fountain[s] Dale,
 No further would he ride ;
There was he aware of a curtal friar,
 Walking by the water-side.

XII

The friar had on a harness good,
 And on his head a cap of steel,
Broad sword and buckler by his side,
 And they became him weel.

XIII

Robin Hood lighted off his horse,
 And tied him to a thorn :
' Carry me over the water, thou curtal friar,
 Or else thy life 's forlorn.'

XIV

The friar took Robin Hood on his back,
 Deep water he did bestride,
And spake neither good word nor bad,
 Till he came at the other side.

XV

Lightly leapt Robin Hood off the friar's back ;
 The friar said to him again,
' Carry me over this water, fine fellow,
 Or it shall breed thy pain.'

XVI

Robin Hood took the friar on 's back,
 Deep water he did bestride,
And spake neither good word nor bad,
 Till he came at the other side.

XVII

Lightly leapt the friar off Robin Hood's back;
  Robin Hood said to him again,
'Carry me over this water, thou curtal friar,
  Or it shall breed thy pain.'

XVIII

The friar took Robin Hood on's back again,
  And stept up to the knee;
Till he came at the middle stream,
  Neither good nor bad spake he.

XIX

And coming to the middle stream,
  There he threw Robin in:
'And chuse thee, chuse thee, fine fellow,
  Whether thou wilt sink or swim!'

XX

Robin Hood swam to a bush of broom,
  The friar to a wicker wand;
Bold Robin Hood is gone to shore,
  And took his bow in hand.

XXI

One of his best arrows under his belt
  To the friar he let flye;
The curtal friar, with his steel buckler,
  He put that arrow by.

XXII

'Shoot on, shoot on, thou fine fellòw,
  Shoot on as thou hast begun;
If thou shoot here a summer's day,
  Thy mark I will not shun.'

XXIII

Robin Hood shot passing well,
　　Till his arrows all were gone;
They took their swords and steel bucklers,
　　And fought with might and maine;

XXIV

From ten o' th' clock that day,
　　Till four i' th' afternoon;
Then Robin Hood came to his knees,
　　Of the friar to beg a boon.

XXV

'A boon, a boon, thou curtal friar!
　　I beg it on my knee;
Give me leave to set my horn to my mouth,
　　And to blow blasts three.'

XXVI

' That will I do,' said the curtal friar!
　　' Of thy blasts I have no doubt;
I hope thou 'lt blow so passing well
　　Till both thy eyes fall out.'

XXVII

Robin Hood set his horn to his mouth
　　He blew but blasts three;
Half a hundred yeomen, with bows bent,
　　Came raking over the lee.

XXVIII

' Whose men are these,' said the friar,
　　' That come so hastily?'
' These men are mine,' said Robin Hood
　　' Friar, what is that to thee?'

raking] advancing.

XXIX

'A boon, a boon,' said the curtal friar,
  'The like I gave to thee!
Give me leave to set my fist to my mouth,
  And to whute whutès three.'

XXX

'That will I do,' said Robin Hood,
  'Or else I were to blame;
Three whutès in a friar's fist
  Would make me glad and fain.'

XXXI

The friar he set his fist to his mouth,
  And whuted whutès three;
Half a hundred good ban-dogs
  Came running the friar unto.

XXXII

'Here's for every man of thine a dog,
  And I my self for thee!'—
'Nay, by my faith,' quoth Robin Hood,
  'Friar, that may not be.'

XXXIII

Two dogs at once to Robin Hood did go,
  T' one behind, the other before;
Robin Hood's mantle of Lincoln green
  Off from his back they tore.

XXXIV

And whether his men shot east or west,
  Or they shot north or south,
The curtal dogs, so taught they were,
  They kept their arrows in their mouth.

whute] whistle.

XXXV

' Take up thy dogs,' said Little John,
  ' Friar, at my bidding be.'—
' Whose man art thou,' said the curtal friar,
  ' Comes here to prate with me ? '—

XXXVI

' I am Little John, Robin Hood's man,
  Friar, I will not lie ;
If thou take not up thy dogs soon,
  I'le take up them and thee.'

XXXVII

Little John had a bow in his hand,
  He shot with might and main ;
Soon half a score of the friar's dogs
  Lay dead upon the plain.

XXXVIII

'Hold thy hand, good fellow,' said the curtal friar,
  ' Thy master and I will agree ;
And we will have new orders taken,
  With all the haste that may be.'

XXXIX

' If thou wilt forsake fair Fountains Dale,
  And Fountains Abbey free,
Every Sunday throughout the year,
  A noble shall be thy fee.

XL

' And every holy day throughout the year,
  Changed shall thy garment be,
If thou wilt go to fair Nottingham,
  And there remain with me.'

XLI

This curtal friar had kept Fountains Dale
  Seven long years or more ;
There was neither knight, lord, nor earl
  Could make him yield before.

119. *Robin Hood and the Butcher*

I

COME, all you brave gallants, and listen a while,
  That are in the bowers within ;
For of Robin Hood, that archer good,
  A song I intend for to sing.

II

Upon a time it chancèd so
  Bold Robin in forrest did spy
A jolly butchèr, with a bonny fine mare,
  With his flesh to the market did hye.

III

'Good morrow, good fellow !' said jolly Robìn,
  'What food hast ? tell unto me ;
And thy trade to me tell, and where thou dost dwell,
  For I like well thy company.'

IV

The butcher he answered jolly Robin :
  'No matter where I dwell ;
For a butcher I am, and to Notingham
  I am going, my flesh to sell.'

V

'What price thy flesh?' said jolly Robin,
  'Come, tell it soon unto me;
And the price of thy mare, be she never so dear,
  For a butcher fain would I be.'

VI

'The price of my flesh,' the butcher repli'd,
  'I soon will tell unto thee;
With my bonny mare, and they are not dear,
  Four mark thou must give unto me.'

VII

'Four mark I will give thee,' saith jolly Robin,
  'Four mark it shall be thy fee;
Thy mony come count, and let me mount,
  For a butcher I fain would be.'

VIII

Now Robin he is to Notingham gone,
  His butcher's trade for to begin;
With good intent, to the Sheriff he went,
  And there he took up his inn.

IX

When other butchers they opened their meat,
  Bold Robin he then begun;
But how for to sell he knew not well,
  For a butcher he was but young.

X

When other butchers no meat could sell,
  Robin got both gold and fee;
For he sold more meat for one peny
  Than others could do for three.

608

XI

But when he sold his meat so fast,
  No butcher by him could thrive ;
For he sold more meat for one peny
  Than others could do for five.

XII

Which made the butchers of Notingham
  To study as they did stand,
Saying, surely he was some prodigal,
  That had sold his father's land.

XIII

The butchers they stepped to jolly Robin,
  Acquainted with him for to be ;
'Come, brother,' one said, ' we be all of one trade,
  Come, will you go dine with me ? '

XIV

' Accurst of his heart,' said jolly Robìn,
  ' That a butcher doth deny !
I will go with you, my brethren true,
  And as fast as I can hie.'

XV

But when to the Sheriff's house they came,
  To dinner they hied apace,
And Robin Hood he the man must be
  Before them all to say grace.

XVI

' Pray God bless us all,' said jolly Robìn,
  ' And our meat within this place ;
A cup of sack good, to nourish our blood,
  And so I do end my grace.

1225   X

XVII

' Come fill us more wine,' said jolly Robìn,
  ' Let us merry be while we do stay ;
For wine and good cheer, be it never so dear,
  I vow I the reck'ning will pay.

XVIII

' Come, brothers, be merry,' said jolly Robìn,
  ' Let us drink, and never give o'er ;
For the shot I will pay, ere I go my way,
  If it cost me five pounds and more.'

XIX

' This is a mad blade,' the butchers then said ;
  Says the Sheriff, ' He 's some prodigal,
That his land has sold, for silver and gold,
  And meaneth to spend it all.'

XX

' Hast thou any horn-beasts,' the Sheriff inquired,
  ' Good fellow, to sell unto me ? '—
' Yea, a plenty I have, good Master Sheriff,
  I have hundreds two or three.

XXI

' And a hundred acre of good free land,
  An it please you go for to see ;
And I'le make you as good assurance of it
  As ever my father made me.'

XXII

The Sheriff he saddled a good palfrèy,
  With three hundred pound in gold,
And away he went with bold Robin Hood,
  His hornèd beasts to behold.

XXIII

Away then the Sheriff and Robin did ride,
    To the forest of merry Sherwood;
Then the Sheriff did say, 'God bless us this day
    From a man they call Robin Hood!'

XXIV

But when that a little further they came,
    Bold Robin he chancèd to spy
A hundred head of the good red deer,
    Come tripping the Sheriff full nigh.

XXV

'How like you my horn'd beasts, Master Sheriff?
    They be fat and fair for to see;'
'I tell thee, good fellow, I would I were gone,
    For I like not thy company.'

XXVI

Then Robin he set his horn to his mouth,
    And blew but blastès three;
Then quickly anon there came Little John,
    And all his company.

XXVII

'What is your will?' then said Little John,
    'Good master come tell it to me;'
'I have brought hither the Sheriff of Notingham,
    This day to dine with thee.'

XXVIII

'He is welcome to me,' then said Little John,
    'I hope he will honestly pay;
I know he has gold, if it be but well told,
    Will serve us to drink a whole day.'

XXIX

Robin Hood took his mantle from his back,
    And laid it upon the ground,
And out of the Sheriff's portmantle
    He told three hundred pound.

XXX

Then Robin he brought him thorow the wood,
    Set him on his dapple gray :
' O have me commended, good sir, to your wife ! '—
    So Robin went laughing away.

120. *Robin Hood and the Bishop of Hereford*

I

COME, gentlemen all, and listen a while ;
    A story I'll to you unfold—
How Robin Hood servèd the Bishop,
    When he robb'd him of his gold.

II

As it befel in merry Barnsdale,
    And under the green-wood tree,
The Bishop of Hereford was to come by,
    With all his companye.

III

' Come, kill a ven'son,' said bold Robin Hood,
    ' Come, kill me a good fat deer ;
The Bishop 's to dine with me to day,
    And he shall pay well for his cheer.

612

IV

'We'll kill a fat ven'son,' said bold Robin Hood,
  'And dress't by the highway-side,
And narrowly watch for the Bishop,
  Lest some other way he should ride.'

V

He dress'd himself up in shepherd's attire,
  With six of his men also;
And the Bishop of Hereford came thereby,
  As about the fire they did go.

VI

'What matter is this?' said the Bishop;
  'Or for whom do you make this a-do?
Or why do you kill the King's ven'son,
  When your company is so few?'

VII

'We are shepherds,' said bold Robin Hood,
  'And we keep sheep all the year;
And we are disposed to be merry this day,
  And to kill of the King's fat deer.'

VIII

'You are brave fellowes,' said the Bishop,
  'And the King of your doings shall know;
Therefore make haste, come along with me,
  For before the King you shall go.'

IX

'O pardon, O pardon,' says bold Robin Hood,
  'O pardon, I thee pray!
For it never becomes your lordship's coat
  To take so many lives away.'

613

X

' No pardon, no pardon ! ' the Bishop says ;
  ' No pardon I thee owe ;
Therefore make haste, come along with me,
  For before the King you shall go.'

XI

Robin set his back against a tree,
  And his foot against a thorn,
And from underneath his shepherd's coat
  He pull'd out a bugle horn.

XII

He put the little end to his mouth,
  And a loud blast did he blow,
Till threescore and ten of bold Robin's men
  Came running all on a row ;

XIII

All making obeisance to bold Robin Hood ;
  —'Twas a comely sight for to see :
' What matter, my master,' said Little John,
  ' That you blow so hastilye ? '—

XIV

' O here is the Bishop of Hereford,
  And no pardon we shall have.'—
' Cut off his head, master,' said Little John,
  ' And throw him into his grave.'—

XV

' O pardon, O pardon,' said the Bishop,
  ' O pardon, I thee pray !
For if I had known it had been you,
  I'd have gone some other way.'—
614

XVI

' No pardon, no pardon ! ' said Robin Hood ;
    ' No pardon I thee owe ;
Therefore make haste, come along with me,
    For to merry Barnsdale you shall go.'

XVII

Then Robin has taken the Bishop's hand
    And led him to merry Barnsdale ;
He made him to stay and sup with him that night,
    And to drink wine, beer and ale.

XVIII

' Call in the reckoning,' said the Bishòp,
    ' For methinks it grows wondrous high.'—
' Lend me your purse, Bishop,' said Little John,
    ' And I'll tell you by-and-by.'

XIX

Then Little John took the Bishop's cloak,
    And spread it upon the ground,
And out of the Bishop's portmantua
    He told three hundred pound.

XX

' So now let him go,' said Robin Hood ;
    Said Little John, ' That may not be ;
For I vow and protest he shall sing us a mass
    Before that he go from me.'

XXI

Robin Hood took the Bishop by the hand,
    And bound him fast to a tree,
And made him to sing a mass, God wot,
    To him and his yeomandrye.

XXII

Then Robin Hood brought him through the wood
    And causèd the music to play,
And he made the Bishop to dance in his boots,
    And they set him on 's dapple-grey,
And they gave the tail within his hand—
    And glad he could so get away!

121.   *Robin Hood and Alan a Dale*

I

COME listen to me, you gallants so free,
    All you that love mirth for to hear,
And I will you tell of a bold outlàw,
    That lived in Nottinghamshire.

II

As Robin Hood in the forest stood,
    All under the green-wood tree,
There was he ware of a brave young man,
    As fine as fine might be.

III

The youngster was clothed in scarlet red,
    In scarlet fine and gay,
And he did frisk it over the plain,
    And chanted a roundelay.

IV

As Robin Hood next morning stood,
    Amongst the leaves so gay,
There did he espy the same young man
    Come drooping along the way.

616

V

The scarlet he wore the day before,
    It was clean cast away;
And every step he fetcht a sigh,
    ' Alack and a well a day!'

VI

Then steppèd forth brave Little John,
    And Much the miller's son,
Which made the young man bend his bow,
    When as he saw them come.

VII

' Stand off, stand off!' the young man said,
    ' What is your will with me?'—
' You must come before our master straight,
    Under yon green-wood tree.'

VIII

And when he came bold Robin before,
    Robin askt him courteously,
' O hast thou any money to spare,
    For my merry men and me?'

IX

' I have no money,' the young man said,
    ' But five shillings and a ring;
And that I have kept this seven long years,
    To have it at my wedding.

X

' Yesterday I should have married a maid,
    But she is now from me tane,
And chosen to be an old knight's delight,
    Whereby my poor heart is slain.'

XI

'What is thy name?' then said Robin Hood,
  'Come tell me, without any fail.'—
'By the faith of my body,' then said the young man,
  'My name it is Alan a Dale.'

XII

'What wilt thou give me,' said Robin Hood,
  'In ready gold or fee,
To help thee to thy true-love again,
  And deliver her unto thee?'

XIII

'I have no money,' then quoth the young man,
  'No ready gold nor fee,
But I will swear upon a book
  Thy true servant for to be.'—

XIV

'But how many miles to thy true-love?
  Come tell me without any guile.'—
'By the faith of my body,' then said the young man,
  'It is but five little mile.'

XV

Then Robin he hasted over the plain,
  He did neither stint nor lin,
Until he came unto the church
  Where Alan should keep his wedding.

XVI

'What dost thou do here?' the Bishop he said,
  'I prithee now tell to me:'
'I am a bold harper,' quoth Robin Hood,
  'And the best in the north countrey.'

lin] stop.

618

XVII

' O welcome, O welcome ! ' the Bishop he said,
  ' That musick best pleaseth me.'—
' You shall have no musick,' quoth Robin Hood,
  ' Till the bride and the bridegroom I see.'

XVIII

With that came in a wealthy knight,
  Which was both grave and old,
And after him a finikin lass,
  Did shine like glistering gold.

XIX

' This is no fit match,' quoth bold Robin Hood,
  ' That you do seem to make here ;
For since we are come unto the church,
  The bride she shall chuse her own dear.'

XX

Then Robin Hood put his horn to his mouth,
  And blew blasts two or three ;
When four and twenty bowmen bold
  Come leaping over the lee.

XXI

And when they came into the churchyard,
  Marching all on a row,
The first man was Alan a Dale,
  To give bold Robin his bow.

XXII

' This is thy true-love,' Robin he said,
  ' Young Alan, as I hear say ;
And you shall be married at this same time,
  Before we depart away.'

ROBIN HOOD AND ALAN A DALE

XXIII

'That shall not be,' the Bishop he said,
'For thy word it shall not stand;
They shall be three times askt in the church,
As the law is of our land.'

XXIV

Robin Hood pull'd off the Bishop's coat,
And put it upon Little John;
'By the faith of my body,' then Robin said,
'This cloath doth make thee a man.'

XXV

When Little John went into the quire,
The people began for to laugh;
He askt them seven times in the church,
Least three should not be enough.

XXVI

'Who gives me this maid?' then said Little John;
Quoth Robin, 'That do I!
And he that doth take her from Alan a Dale
Full dearly he shall her buy.'

XXVII

And thus having ended this merry wedding,
The bride lookt as fresh as a queen,
And so they return'd to the merry green-wood,
Amongst the leaves so green.

122. *Robin Hood and the Widow's Three Sons*

I

THERE are twelve months in all the year,
  As I hear many men say,
But the merriest month in all the year
  Is the merry month of May.

II

Now Robin Hood is to Nottingham gone,
  With a link a down and a day,
And there he met a silly old woman,
  Was weeping on the way.

III

'What news? what news, thou silly old woman?
  What news hast thou for me?'
Said she, 'There's three squires in Nottingham town
  To-day is condemn'd to die.'

IV

'O have they parishes burnt?' he said,
  'Or have they ministers slain?
Or have they robb'd any virgin,
  Or other men's wives have ta'en?'—

V

'They have no parishes burnt, good sir,
  Nor yet have ministers slain,
Nor have they robbed any virgin,
  Nor other men's wives have ta'en.'

VI

'O what have they done?' said bold Robin Hood,
　'I pray thee tell to me.'—
'It's for slaying of the King's fallow deer,
　Bearing their long bows with thee.'—

VII

'Dost thou not mind, old woman,' he said,
　'Since thou made me sup and dine?
By the truth of my body,' quoth bold Robin Hood,
　'You could tell it in no better time.'

VIII

Now Robin Hood is to Nottingham gone,
　With a link a down and a day,
And there he met with a silly old palmer,
　Was walking along the highway.

IX

'What news? what news, thou silly old man?
　What news, I do thee pray?'—
Said he, 'Three squires in Nottingham town
　Are condemned to die this day.'—

X

'Come change thy apparel with me, old man,
　Come change thy apparel for mine;
Here is forty shillings in good silver,
　Go drink it in beer or wine.'—

XI

'O thine apparel is good,' he said,
　'And mine is ragged and torn;
Wherever you go, wherever you ride,
　Laugh ne'er an old man to scorn.'—

622

ROBIN HOOD AND WIDOW'S THREE SONS

XII

'Come change thy apparel with me, old churl,
   Come change thy apparel with mine;
Here are twenty pieces of good broad gold,
   Go feast thy brethren with wine.'

XIII

Then he put on the old man's hat,
   It stood full high on the crown:
'The first bold bargain that I come at,
   It shall make thee come down.'

XIV

Then he put on the old man's cloak,
   Was patch'd black, blue, and red;
He thought no shame, all the day long,
   To wear the bags of bread.

XV

Then he put on the old man's breeks,
   Was patch'd from ballup to side;
'By the truth of my body,' bold Robin can say,
   'This man lov'd little pride!'

XVI

Then he put on the old man's hose,
   Were patch'd from knee to wrist;
'By the truth of my body,' said bold Robin Hood,
   'I'd laugh if I had any list.'

XVII

Then he put on the old man's shoes,
   Were patch'd both beneath and aboon;
Then Robin Hood swore a solemn oath,
   'It's good habit that makes a man!'

ballup] front, or flap.   list] inclination, desire for it.

XVIII

Now Robin Hood is to Nottingham gone,
    With a link a down and a down,
And there he met with the proud Sheriff,
    Was walking along the town.

XIX

' O save, O save, O Sheriff,' he said,
    ' O save, and you may see !
And what will you give to a silly old man
    To-day will your hangman be ? '

XX

' Some suits, some suits,' the Sheriff he said,
    ' Some suits I'll give to thee ;
Some suits, some suits, and pence thirteen
    To-day 's a hangman's fee.'

XXI

Then Robin he turns him round about,
    And jumps from stock to stone ;
' By the truth of my body,' the Sheriff he said,
    ' That 's well jumpt, thou nimble old man.'—

XXII

' I was ne'er a hangman in all my life,
    Nor yet intends to trade ;
But curst be he,' said bold Robin,
    ' That first a hangman was made !

XXIII

' I've a bag for meal, and a bag for malt,
    And a bag for barley and corn ;
A bag for bread, and a bag for beef,
    And a bag for my little small horn.

XXIV

' I have a horn in my pockèt,
  I got it from Robin Hood,
And still when I set it to my mouth,
  For thee it blows little good.'—

XXV

' O wind thy horn, thou proud fellòw,
  Of thee I have no doubt ;
I wish that thou give such a blast
  Till both thy eyes fall out.'

XXVI

The first loud blast that he did blow,
  He blew both loud and shrill ;
A hundred and fifty of Robin Hood's men
  Came riding over the hill.

XXVII

The next loud blast that he did give,
  He blew both loud and amain ;
And quickly sixty of Robin Hood's men
  Came shining over the plain.

XXVIII

' O who are yon,' the Sheriff he said,
  ' Come tripping over the lee ? '
' They're my attendants,' brave Robin did say,
  ' They'll pay a visit to thee.'

XXIX

They took the gallows from the slack,
  They set it in the glen,
They hang'd the proud Sheriff on that,
  And releas'd their own three men.

slack] hollow, dell.

I

I HAVE heard talk of bold Robin Hood,
  And of brave Little John,
Of Friar Tuck, and Will Scarlet,
  Locksley, and Maid Marion.

II

But such a tale as this before
  I think there was never none ;
For Robin Hood disguised himself,
  And to the wood is gone.

III

Like to a friar bold Robin Hood
  Was accouter'd in his array ;
With hood, gown, beads and crucifix,
  He pass'd upon the way.

IV

He had not gone miles two or three,
  But it was his chance to spy
Two lusty priests, clad all in black,
  Come riding gallantly.

V

' Benedicite,' then said Robin Hood,
  ' Some pity on me take ;
Cross you my hand with a silver groat,
  For Our dear Ladye's sake !

VI

' For I have been wand'ring all this day,
  And nothing could I get ;
Not so much as one poor cup or drink,
  Nor bit of bread to eat.'

VII

' By my holydame,' the priests repli'd,
  ' We never a penny have ;
For we this morning have been robb'd,
  And could no money save.'

VIII

' I am much afraid,' said bold Robin Hood,
  ' That you both do tell a lye ;
And now before that you go hence,
  I am resolv'd to try.'

IX

When as the priests heard him say so,
  They rode away amain ;
But Robin betook him to his heels,
  And soon overtook them again.

X

Then Robin Hood laid hold of them both,
  And pull'd them down from their horse :
' O spare us, friar ! ' the priests cry'd out,
  ' On us have some remorse ! '

XI

' You said you had no money,' quoth he ;
  ' Wherefore without delay
We three will fall down on our knees,
  And for money we will pray.'

XII

The priests they could not him gainsay,
  But down they kneel'd with speed ;
' Send us, O send us,' then quoth they,
  ' Some money to serve our need ! '

627

XIII

The priests did pray with mournful chear,
  Sometimes their hands did wring,
Sometimes they wept and cried aloud,
  Whilst Robin did merrily sing.

XIV

When they had pray'd an hour's space,
  The priests did still lament ;
Then quoth bold Robin, ' Now let 's see
  What money heaven hath us sent.

XV

' We will be sharers all alike
  Of the money that we have ;
And there is never a one of us
  That his fellows shall deceive.'

XVI

The priests their hands in their pockets put,
  But money would find none :
' We'll search ourselves,' said Robin Hood,
  ' Each other, one by one.'

XVII

Then Robin took pains to search them both,
  And he found good store of gold ;
Five hundred pieces presently
  Upon the grass was told.

XVIII

' Here 's a brave show,' said Robin Hood,
  ' Such store of gold to see !
And you shall each one have a part,
  'Cause you pray'd so heartily.'

XIX

He gave them fifty pound a-piece,
   And the rest for himself did keep ;
The priests they durst not speak one word,
   But they sighèd wondrous deep.

XX

With that the priests rose up from their knees,
   And thought to have parted so ;
' Nay, stay,' said Robin Hood, ' one thing more
   I have to say ere you go.

XXI

' You shall be sworn,' said Robin Hood,
   ' Upon this holy grass,
That you will never tell lies again,
   Which way soever you pass.

XXII

' The second oath that you here must take,
   All the days of your lives
You never shall tempt maids to sin,
   Nor covet other men's wives.

XXIII

' The last oath you shall take, it is this,
   Be charitable to the poor ;
Say you have met with a holy friar,
   And I desire no more.'

XXIV

He set them upon their horses again,
   And away then they did ride ;
And he return'd to the merry green-wood,
   With great joy, mirth and pride.

The Noble Fisherman

or Robin Hood's Preferment

I

IN summer time, when leaves grow green,
   When they doe grow both green and long,
Of a bold outlaw call'd Robin Hood
   It is of him I sing this song.

II

When the lilly leafe and the elephant
   Doth bud and spring with a merry good cheere,
This outlaw was weary of the wood-side,
   And chasing of the fallow deere.

III

' The fisherman brave more mony have
   Then any merchant, two or three ;
Therefore I will to Scarboro' goe,
   That I a fisherman brave may be.'

IV

This outlaw call'd his merry men all,
   As they sate under the green-wood tree :
' If any of you have gold to spend,
   I pray you heartily spend it with me.

V

' Now,' quoth Robin, ' I'le to Scarboro' goe,
   It seemes to be a very faire day '—
He tooke up his inne at a widdow-woman's house,
   Hard by upon the water gray :

elephant] a weed of the scabious order.

THE NOBLE FISHERMAN

VI

Who asked of him, ' Where wert thou born ?
  Or tell to me, where dost thou fare ? '—
' I am a poore fisherman,' saith he then,
  ' This day intrappèd all in care.'

VII

' What is thy name, thou fine fellòw ?
  I pray thee heartily tell to me ' ;
' In mine own country where I was born,
  Men called me Simon over the Lee.'

VIII

' Simon, Simon,' said the good wife,
  ' I wish thou maist well brook thy name ' ;
The outlaw was ware of her courtesie,
  And rejoyc'd he had got such a dame.

IX

' Simon, wilt thou be my man ?
  And good round wages I'le give thee ;
I have as good a ship of mine owne
  As any sayle upon the sea.

X

' Anchors and planks thou shalt want none,
  Masts and ropes that are so long '—
' And if that you thus furnish me,'
  Said Simon, ' nothing shall goe wrong.'

XI

They pluckt up anchor, and away did sayle,
  More of a day then two or three ;
When others cast in their baited hooks,
  The bare lines into the sea cast he.

brook] enjoy, or earn the name of Simon, as a fisherman.

XII

' It will be long,' said the master then,
  ' Ere this great lubber do thrive on the sea ;
I'le assure you he shall have no part of our fish,
  For in truth he is of no part worthy.'

XIII

' O woe is me,' said Simon then,
  ' This day that ever I came here !
I wish I were in Plomton Parke,
  In chasing of the fallow deere.

XIV

' For every clowne laughs me to scorne,
  And they by me set nought at all ;
If I had them in Plomton Park,
  I would set as little by them all.'

XV

They pluckt up anchor, and away did sayle,
  More of a day then two or three ;
But Simon spied a ship of warre,
  That sayld towards them most valourouslie.

XVI

' O woe is me,' said the master then,
  ' This day that ever I was borne !
For all our fish we have got to-day
  Is every bit lost and forlorne.

XVII

' For your French robbers on the sea,
  They will not spare of us one man,
But carry us to the coast of France,
  And ligge us in the prison strong.'

forlorne] lost

632

XVIII

But Simon said, 'Doe not feare them,
    Neither, master, take you no care;
Give me my bent bow in my hand,
    And never a Frenchman will I spare.'—

XIX

' Hold thy peace, thou long lubber,
    For thou art nought but braggs and boast;
If I should cast thee over-board,
    There were nothing but a lubber lost.'

XX

Simon grew angry at these words,
    And so angry then was he
That he tooke his bent bow in his hand,
    And to the ship-hatch goeth he.

XXI

' Master, tye me to the mast,' saith he,
    ' That at my mark I may stand fair,
And give me my bended bow in my hand,
    And never a Frenchman will I spare.'

XXII

He drew his arrow to the very head,
    And drew it with all might and maine,
And straightway, in the twinkling of an eye,
    To the Frenchman's heart the arrow did gain.

XXIII

The Frenchman fell downe on the ship-hatch,
    And under the hatches down below;
Another Frenchman that him espy'd
    The dead corps into the sea doth throw.

XXIV

'O master, loose me from the mast,
  And for them all take you no care;
And give me my bent bow in my hand,
  And never a Frenchman will I spare!'

XXV

Then straight they did board the Frenchman's ship,
  They lying all dead in their sight;
They found within the ship of warre
  Twelve thousand pound of money bright.

XXVI

'One halfe of the ship,' said Simon then,
  'I'le give to my dame and children small;
The other halfe of the ship I'le bestow
  On you that are my fellowes all.'

XXVII

But now bespake the master then,
  'For so, Simon, it shall not be;
For you have won her with your own hand,
  And the owner of it you shall bee.'—

XXVIII

'It shall be so, as you have said;
  And, with this gold, for the opprest
An habitation I will build,
  Where they shall live in peace and rest.'

125. *The Death of Robin Hood*

I

WHEN Robin Hood and Little John
  Down a-down, a-down, a-down
Went o'er yon bank of broom,
Said Robin Hood bold to Little John,
  'We have shot for many a pound
    Hey, down a-down, a-down!

II

'But I am not able to shoot one shot more,
  My broad arrows will not flee;
But I have a cousin lives down below,
  Please God, she will bleed me.

III

'I will never eat nor drink,' he said,
  'Nor meat will do me good,
Till I have been to merry Kirkleys
  My veins for to let blood.

IV

'The dame prior is my aunt's daughter,
  And nigh unto my kin;
I know she wo'ld me no harm this day,
  For all the world to win.'

V

'That I rede not,' said Little John,
  'Master, by th'assent of me,
Without half a hundred of your best bowmen
  You take to go with yee.'—

rede] advise.

VI

' An thou be afear'd, thou Little John,
    At home I rede thee be.'—
' An you be wroth, my deare mastèr
    You shall never hear more of me.'

VII

Now Robin is gone to merry Kirkleys
    And knockèd upon the pin :
Up then rose Dame Priorèss
    And let good Robin in.

VIII

Then Robin gave to Dame Priorèss
    Twenty pound in gold,
And bade her spend while that did last,
    She sho'ld have more when she wo'ld.

IX

' Will you please to sit down, cousin Robin,
    And drink some beer with me ? '—
' No, I will neither eat nor drink
    Till I am blooded by thee.'

X

Down then came Dame Priorèss
    Down she came in that ilk,
With a pair of blood-irons in her hands,
    Were wrappèd all in silk.

XI

' Set a chafing-dish to the fire,' she said,
    ' And strip thou up thy sleeve.'
—I hold him but an unwise man
    That will no warning 'leeve !

in that ilk] in that same (moment), then and there.   'leeve]
believe.

XII

She laid the blood-irons to Robin's vein,
    Alack, the more pitye !
And pierc'd the vein, and let out the blood
    That full red was to see.

XIII

And first it bled the thick, thick blood,
    And afterwards the thin,
And well then wist good Robin Hood
    Treason there was within.

XIV

And there she blooded bold Robin Hood
    While one drop of blood wou'd run ;
There did he bleed the live-long day,
    Until the next at noon.

XV

He bethought him then of a casement there,
    Being lockèd up in the room ;
But was so weak he could not leap,
    He could not get him down.

XVI

He bethought him then of his bugle-horn,
    That hung low down to his knee ;
He set his horn unto his mouth,
    And blew out weak blasts three.

XVII

Then Little John he heard the horn
    Where he sat under a tree :
' I fear my master is now near dead,
    He blows so wearilye.'

XVIII

Little John is gone to merry Kirkleys,
    As fast as he can dree ;
And when he came to merry Kirkleys,
    He broke locks two or three :

XIX

Until he came bold Robin to see,
    Then he fell on his knee ;
' A boon, a boon ! ' cries Little John,
    ' Master, I beg of thee ! '

XX

' What is that boon,' said Robin Hood,
    ' Little John, thou begs of me ? '—
' It is to burn fair Kirkleys-hall,
    And all their nunnerye.'

XXI

' Now nay, now nay,' quoth Robin Hood,
    ' That boon I'll not grant thee ;
I never hurt woman in all my life,
    Nor men in their company.

XXII

' I never hurt maid in all my time,
    Nor at mine end shall it be ;
But give me my bent bow in my hand,
    And a broad arrow I'll let flee ;
And where this arrow is taken up
    There shall my grave digg'd be.

XXIII

' But lay me a green sod under my head,
   And another at my feet;
And lay my bent bow at my side,
   Which was my music sweet;
And make my grave of gravel and green,
   Which is most right and meet.

XXIV

' Let me have length and breadth enough,
   And under my head a sod;
That they may say when I am dead,
   —Here lies bold Robin Hood! '

BOOK VI

BOOK VI

126. *Durham Field*

I

LORDINGS, listen, and hold you still;
Hearken to me a spell;
I shall you tell of the fairest battell
That ever in England befell.

II

It befell in Edward the Third's dayes,
When in England he ware the crowne,
That all the chief chivalry of England
They buskèd and made them bowne.

III

They have chosen all the best archers
That in England might be found,
And all was to fight with the King of France,
Within a litle stounde

IV

And when our King was over the water,
And on the salt sea gone,
Then tydings into Scotland came
That all England was gone.

V

Bowes and arrowes they all were forth;
At home was not left a man
But shepards and millers both,
And preists with shaven crownes.

buskèd] dressed.   bowne] ready.   stounde] time.

DURHAM FIELD

VI

Then the King of Scotts in a study stood,
  As he was a man of great might;
He sware he would hold his parlament in leeve London,
  If he cold ryde there right.

VII

Then bespake a Squire, of Scottland borne,
  And sayd, ' My leege, ha' peace,
Before you come to leeve London,
  Full sore you'le rue that race.

VIII

'Ther beene bold yeomen in merry England,
  Husbandmen stiffe and strong;
Sharpè swords they done weare,
  Bearen bowes and arrowes longe.'

IX

The King was angrye at that word;
  A long sword out he drew,
And there before his royall companye
  His ownè Squire hee slew.

X

Hard hansell had the Scottes that day,
  That wrought them woe enoughe,
For a Scott then durst not speake a word
  Ffor hanging att a boughe.

XI

' The Earle of Anguish, where art thou ?
  In my coate-armour thou shalt bee,
And thou shalt lead the forward
  Thorow the English countrye.

leeve] dear, pleasant.   hansell] foretaste.   Anguish] Angus.
        1225   Y   641

XII

'Take thee Yorke,' then sayd the King,
   'In stead wheras it doth stand;
I'le make thy eldest sonne after thee
   Heyre of all Northumberland.

XIII

'The Earle of Buchan, where be yee?
   In my coate-armour thou shalt bee;
The high Peak and all Darbyshire
   I give it thee to thy fee.'

XIV

The famous Douglas then came in,
   Saies, 'What shall my meede bee?
And I will lead the vanward, lord,
   Thorow the English countrye.'

XV

'Take thee Worster,' sayd the King,
   'Tuxburye, Killingworth, Burton on Trent;
Doe thou not say another day
   But I gave thee lands and rent.

XVI

'Sir Richard of Edenborrow, where are yee?
   A wise man in this warr!
I'le give thee Bristow and the shire
   The time that wee come there.

XVII

'Thou, my lord Nevill, where art thou?
   Thou must in this warres bee;
I'le give thee Shrewsburye,' saies the King,
   'And Coventrye faire and free.

642

XVIII

' My lord of Hambleton, where art thou?
   Thou art of my kin full nye;
I'le give thee Lincolne and Lincolneshire,
   And that's enoughe for thee.'

XIX

By then came in William Douglas,
   As breeme as any bore;
He kneelèd him downe upon his knees,
   In his heart he sighèd sore.

XX

' I have servèd you, my lovelye liege,
   This thirty winters and four,
And in the Scottish Marches
   Have beene wounded and beaten sore.

XXI

' For all the good service that I have done,
   What now shall my meed bee?
And I will lead the vanward
   Thorow the English countrye.'

XXII

' Now aske on, Douglas,' said the King,
   ' And granted it shall bee.'—
' Why then, I aske litle London,' saies Douglas,
   ' Gotten gif that it bee.'

XXIII

The King was wroth, and rose away,
   Saies, ' Nay, that cannot bee !
For that I will keepe for my cheefe chamber,
   Gotten gif that it bee.

Hambleton] Hamilton.   breeme] fierce.

XXIV

' But take thee North Wales and Weschester,
    The countrye all round about,
And rewarded thou shalt bee,
    Of that take thou noe doubt.'

XXV

Five score knights he made on a day,
    And dubb'd them with his hands ;
Rewarded them right worthilye
    With the townes in merry England.

XXVI

And when the fresh knights they were made,
    To battell they buske them bowne ;
Jamès Douglas he went before,
    And he thought to have wonnen him shoone.

XXVII

But they were mett in a morning of May
    With the comminaltye of litle England ;
But there scapèd never a man away,
    Through the might of Christès hand.

XXVIII

But all onely Jamès Douglas ;
    In Durham in the ffeild
An arrow stroke him in the thye ;
    Fast flinges he towards the King.

XXIX

The King looked toward litle Durham,
    Saies, ' All things is not weel !
For James Douglas beares an arrow in his thye,
    The head of it is of steele.

      buske] addressed.   bowne] ready.

XXX

How now, James ? ' then said the King,
   ' How now, how may this bee ?
And where beene all thy merrymen
   That thou tooke hence with thee ? '

XXXI

' But cease, my King,' saies James Douglas,
   ' Alive is not left a man ! '
' Now by my faith,' saies the King of Scotts,
   ' That gate was evil gone.

XXXII

' But I'le revenge thy quarrell well,
   And of that thou may be fain ;
For one Scott will beate five Englishmen,
   If they meeten them on the plaine.'

XXXIII

' Now hold your tongue,' saies James Douglas,
   ' For in faith that is not soe ;
For one English man is worth five Scotts,
   When they meeten together thoe.

XXXIV

' For they are as eager men to fight
   As a faulcon upon a prey ;
Alas ! if ever they winne the vanward,
   There scapes noe man away.'

XXXV

' O peace thy talking,' said the King,
   ' They bee but English knaves,
But shepards and millers both,
   And priestès with their staves.'

thoe] those.

645

XXXVI

The King sent forth one of his heralds of armes
  To vew the Englishmen :
' Be of good cheere,' the herald said,
  ' For against one we be ten.'

XXXVII

' Who leads those lads ? ' said the King of Scotts,
  ' Thou herald, tell thou mee : '
The herald said, ' The Bishop of Durham
  Is captaine of that companye.

XXXVIII

' For the Bishop hath spred the King's banner,
  And to battell he buskes him bowne ' ;
' I sweare by St Andrewes bones,' saies the King,
  ' I'le rapp that priest on the crowne ! '

XXXIX

The King look'd towards litle Durham,
  And that hee well beheld,
That the Earle Percy was well arm'd,
  With his battell-axe entred the feild.

XL

The King look'd again towards litle Durham,
  Four ancyents there saw he ;
There were two standards, six in a valley,
  He cold not see them with his eye.

XLI

My Lord of Yorke was one of them,
  My Lord of Carlile was the other,
And my Lord Fitzwilliams,
  The Bishop came with the other.

ancyents] ensigns.

646

DURHAM FIELD

XLII

The Bishop of Durham commanded his men,
  And shortlye he them bade,
That never a man shold goe to fight
  Till he had served his God.

XLIII

Five hundred priests said mass that day
  In Durham in the field,
And afterwards, as I hard say,
  They bare both spear and shield.

XLIV

The Bishop orders himselfe to fight,
  With his battell-axe in his hand ;
He said, 'This day now I will fight
  As long as I can stand ! '

XLV

' And soe will I,' sayd my Lord of Carlile,
  ' In this faire morning gay ' ;
' And soe will I,' said my Lord Fitzwilliams,
  ' For Mary, that mild may.'

XLVI

Our English archers bent their bowes
  Shortly and anon ;
They shot over the Scottish oast
  And scantly toucht a man.

XLVII

' Hold downe your hands,' sayd the Bishop of Durham,
  ' My archers good and true ' !
The second shootè that they shott,
  Full sore the Scots it rue.

may] maiden.

647

DURHAM FIELD

XLVIII

The Bishop of Durham spoke on hie,
 That both partyes might heare:
'Be of good cheere, my merrymen all,
 They flyen and changen their cheere!'

XLIX

But as they saidden, see they didden,
 They fell on heapès hie;
Our Englishmen laid on with their bowes,
 As fast as they might drie.

L

The King of Scotts in a study stood
 Amongst his companye;
An arrow stoke him thoro' the nose,
 And thoro' his armorye.

LI

The King went to a marsh-side
 And light beside his steede;
He leanèd him downe on his swordhilts,
 To let his nosè bleede.

LII

There follow'd him a yeaman of merry England,
 His name was John of Coplande:
'Yeeld thee, traytor!' saies Coplande then,
 'Thy life lies in my hand.'

LIII

'How shold I yeeld me,' sayes the King,
 'And thou art noe gentleman?'—
'Noe, by my troth,' sayes Copland there,
 'I am but a poore yeaman.

648

LIV

'What art thou better then I, Sir King?
  Tell me if that thou can!
What art thou better then I, Sir King,
  Now we be but man to man?'

LV

The King smote angerly at Copland,
  Angerly in that stonde;
Then Copland was a bold yeaman,
  And bore the King to the ground.

LVI

He sett the King on a palfrey,
  Himselfe upon a steede;
He tooke him by the bridle-rayne,
  Towards London he can him lead.

LVII

And when to London that he came,
  The King from Ffrance was come home,
And there unto the King of Scotts
  He sayd these words anon.—

LVIII

'How like you my shepards and my millers?
  My priests with shaven crownes?'—
'By my fayth, they are the sorest fighters
  That ever I mett on the ground.

LIX

'There was never a yeaman in merry England
  But was worth a Scottish knight.'—
'Ay, by my troth,' said King Edward, and laughe,
  'For you fought all against the right.'

Y 3   649

LX

But now the prince of merry England,
    Worthilye under his sheelde,
Hath taken captive the King of France,
    At Poytiers in the field.

LXI

The prince did present his father
    With the lovely King of France,
And forward of his journey he is gone :
    God send us all good chance !

LXII

Sayd the King of Scots to the King of France,
    ' Well met, brother, too soone !
Christ leeve that I had taken my way
    Unto the court of Roome ! '

LXIII

' And soe wold I,' said the King of France,
    ' When I came over the streame,
That I had taken my journey
    Unto Jerusalem ! '

LXIV

Thus ends the battell of fair Durham.
    In one morning of May ;
The battells of Cressey and of Poytiers,
    All within one monthes day.

LXV

Then was wealthe and welfare in merry England,
    Solaces, game, and glee,
And every man loved other well,
    And the King loved good yeomanrye.

LXVI

But God that made the grasse to growe,
    And leaves on greenwoode tree,
Now save and keepe our noble King,
    And maintaine good yeomanrye!

127. *The Battle of Otterburn*

I

IT fell about the Lammas tide
    When husbands win their hay,
The doughty Douglas bound him to ride
    In England to take a prey.

II

He has chosen the Graemes, and the Lindsays light,
    And the gallant Gordons gay;
And the Earl of Fyfe withouten strife,
    He's bound him over Solwày.

III

They come in over Ottercap Hill,
    So down by Rodeley Cragge;
Upon Green Leyton they lighted down
    Styrande many a stagge.

IV

And they have brent the dales of Tyne,
    And harryed Bamborowe shire,
And the Otter Dale they have brent it hale
    And left it a' on fire.

husbands] husbandmen.   Styrande] stirring, rousing.
brent] burned.   hale] whole.

THE BATTLE OF OTTERBURN

V

Then spake a berne upon the bent,
  Of comfort that was not cold,
And said, 'We have brent Northumberland,
  We have all wealth in hold.

VI

'Now we have harryed all Bamborowe shire,
  All the wealth in the world have we :
I rede we ryde to Newcastell
  So still and stalworthlye.'

VII

Upon the morrow, when it was day,
  The standards shone full bright ;
To Newcastell they took the way,
  And thither they came full right.

VIII

To Newcastell when that they came,
  The Douglas cry'd on hyght :
'Harry Percy, an thou bidest within,
  Come to the field, and fight !—

IX

'For we have brent Northumberland,
  Thy herytage good and right ;
And syne my lodging I have ta'en,
  With my brand dubb'd many a knight.'

X

Sir Harry Percy came to the walls
  The Scottish host for to see,
Sayd, 'An thou hast brent Northumberland,
  Full sore it rueth me.

berne] fighting-man.   bent] coarse grass.   rede] counsel.

XI

If thou hast haryed all Bamborowe shire,
   Thou hast done me great envye ;
For this trespasse thou hast me done
   The tone of us shall die.'

XII

' Where shall I bide thee ? ' sayd the Douglas,
   ' Or where wilt thou come to me ? '—
' But gae ye up to Otterbourne,
   And wait there dayès three.

XIII

' The roe full rekeles there she rins,
   To make the game and glee ;
The falcon and the phesant both,
   To fend thy men and thee.

XIV

' There may'st thou have thy wealth at will,
   Well lodg'd thou there may'st be :
It shall not be long ere I come thee till,'
   Sayd Sir Harry Percy.

XV

' There shall I bide thee,' sayd the Douglas,
   ' By the faith of my bodye.'—
' There shall I come,' said Sir Harry Percy,
   ' My troth I plight to thee.'

XVI

A pipe of wine over the wall,
   He gave them [to their pay],
There he made the Douglas drinke,
   And all his host that day.

tone] one of two.   rekeles] reckless, wild.   fend] provide for.
till] to.   pay] satisfaction.

XVII

The Douglas turn'd him homeward again,
  [And rode withouten stay];
He pyght his standard at Otterbourne
  Upon a Wedensday.

XVIII

And syne he warned his men to go
  To choose their geldings grass;
[And he that had no man to send]
  His own servant he was.

XIX

A Scottish knight hoved on the bent
  At watch, I dare well say,
So was he ware of the noble Percy
  In the dawning of the day.

XX

He pryck'd to his pavilion door
  As fast as he might run :
' Awaken, Douglas ! ' cried the knight,
  ' For his sake that sits in throne !

XXI

' Awaken, Douglas ! ' cried the knight,
  ' For thou mayst wake with wynne !
Yonder have I spied the proud Percy,
  And seven standards with him.'

XXII

' Now by my troth,' the Douglas sayd,
  ' It is but a faynèd tale !
He durst not look on my broad banner
  [Were all England in] hail !

pyght] pitched.   hoved] abode.   bent] grass.   pavilion]
tent.   wynne] joy.   faynèd] feigned.

THE BATTLE OF OTTERBURN

XXIII

'Was I not yesterday at Newcastell
    That stands so fair on Tyne?
For all the men the Percy had
    He could not gar me to dine.'

XXIV

He stepp'd out at his pavilion-door
    To look an it were lease:
'Array you, lordings, one and all!
    For here begins no peace.

XXV

'The Earl of Menteith, thou art my eme,
    The vaward I give to thee:
The Earl of Huntley, cante and keen,
    Take him to go with thee.

XXVI

'The Lord of Buchan, in armure bright,
    On the other side he shall be;
Lord Johnstone and Lord Maxwell
    They two shall go with me.

XXVII

'Swynton, fair fall upon your pride!
    To battle make you bowne.—
Sir Davy Scott, Sir Walter Steward,
    Sir John of Agerstone!'

XXVIII

The Percy came before his host,
    He was ever a gentil knight:
Upon the Douglas loud can he cry
    'I will hold that I have hyght.'

gar me to dine] give me my fill, entertain me (at fighting).
lease] leasing, falsehood.   eme] uncle.   vaward] vanguard.
cante] spirited.   bowne] ready.   that I have hyght] what
I have promised.

XXIX

'For thou hast brent Northumberland,
  And done me great envye,
For this trespasse thou hast me done
  The tone of us shall die.'

XXX

The Douglas answer'd him again
  With great words upon hie,
And sayd, ' I have twenty against thy one :
  Behold, and thou mayst see ! '

XXXI

With that the Percy was grievèd sore,
  Forsooth as I you say :
He lighted down upon his foot
  And schoote his horse away.

XXXII

Every man saw that he did so,
  That ryal was ever in rowghte :
Every man schoote his horse him fro
  And lighted him round about.

XXXIII

Sir Harry Percy took the field
  Even thus, as I you say ;
Jesus Christe in hevyn on height
  Did help him well that day.

XXXIV

But nine thousand, there was no more—
  The chronicle will not layne—
Forty thousand of Scots and four
  That day fought them again.

schoote] thrust, sent quickly.   ryal in rowghte] royal in rout,
a king amongst men.   layne] conceal.   them again] against
them.

XXXV

But when the battel began to join,
  In haste there came a knight ;
And letters fair forth hath he ta'en,
  And thus he sayd full right :

XXXVI

' My lord your father greets you well,
  With many a noble knight ;
He doth desire you now to bide,
  That he may see this fight.

XXXVII

' The Baron of Graystoke is out of the west
  With a noble companye :
All they lodge at your father's this night,
  And the battel fayn would they see.'

XXXVIII

' For Jesus' love,' sayd Sir Harry Percy,
  ' That died for you and me,
Wend to my lord my father agayn,
  Say thou saw me not with thee.

XXXIX

' My troth is plight to yon Scottish knight,
  —It nede's me not to layne—
That I should bide him upon this bent,
  And I have his troth agayn.

XL

' And if that I wend off this growende,
  Forsooth, unfoughten away,
He would call me but a coward knight
  In his land another day.

growende] ground.

XLI

'Yet had I liefer be rynde and rent,
—By Mary, that mickle may!—
Than ever my manhood be reproved
With a Scot another day.

XLII

'Wherefore shoot, archers, for my sake!
And let sharp arrows flee.
Minstrels, play up for your waryson!
And well quit it shall be.

XLIII

'Every man thynke on his true-love,
And mark him to the Trinitye:
For unto God I make mine avowe
This day will I not flee.'

XLIV

The blodye herte in the Douglas arms
His standard stood on hie,
That every man might full wel knowe;
Bysyde stood starrès three.

XLV

The white lyon on the English part,
Forsooth as I you sayn,
The lucettes and the cressants both
The Scot fought them again.

XLVI

Upon Seynt Andrewe loud can they crye,
And thrice they showt on hyght,
Syne mark'd them on our English men,
As I have told you right.

rynde] riven, or flayed.   mickle may] mighty maid.
waryson] reward.   lucettes] luces, pikes (heraldic).
658

THE BATTLE OF OTTERBURN

XLVII

Seynt George the bryght, Our Ladye's knyght,
   To name they were full fayne;
Our English men they cry'd on hyght,
   And thrice they shot agayne.

XLVIII

With that sharp arrows began to flee,
   I tell you in certayne:
Men of arms began to joyne,
   Many a doughty man was slayne.

XLIX

The Percy and the Douglas met
   That either of other was fayne;
They swapp'd together while they swet
   With swords of fyne Collayne:

L

Until the blood from their bassonets ran
   As the roke doth in the rayne;
' Yield thou to me,' sayd the Douglas,
   ' Or elles thou shalt be slayne.

LI

' For I see by thy bryght bassonet
   Thou art some man of myght:
And so I do by thy burnysh'd brand,
   Thou'rt an earl or elles a knyght.'

LII

' By my good faith,' said the noble Percye,
   ' Now hast thou rede full ryght;
Yet will I never yield me to thee,
   While I may stand and fyght.'

swapp'd] smote.   swet] sweated.   Collayne]
Cologne steel.   bassonets] steel skull-caps.   roke] reek,
mist.

LIII

They swapp'd together, while that they swet,
  With swordès sharp and long;
Each on other so fast they bette,
  Their helms came in pieces down.

LIV

The Percy was a man of strength,
  I tell you in this stounde :
He smote the Douglas at the sword's length
  That he fell to the grounde.

LV

The Douglas call'd to his little foot-page,
  And sayd, ' Run speedilye,
And fetch my ain dear sister's son,
  Sir Hugh Montgomery.

LVI

' My nephew good,' the Douglas sayd,
  ' What recks the death of ane ?
' Last night I dream'd a dreary dream,
  And I ken the day's thy ain.

LVII

'My wound is deep : I am fayn to sleep,
  Take thou the vaward of me,
And hide me by the bracken bush
  Grows on yon lilye-lee.'

LVIII

He has lifted up that noble lord
  With the saut tears in his e'e ;
He has hidden him in the bracken bush
  That his merry men might not see.

bette] beat.   stounde] time.

LIX

The standards stood still on eke side ;
  With many a grievous groan
They fought that day, and all the night ;
  Many a doughtye man was slone.

LX

The morn was clear, the day drew nie,
  —Yet stiffly in stowre they stood ;
Echone hewing another while they might drie,
  Till aye ran down the blood.

LXI

The Percy and Montgomery met
  That either of other was fayn :
They swappèd swords, and they two met
  Till the blood ran down between.

LXII

' Now yield thee, yield thee, Percy,' he said,
  ' Or I vow I'le lay thee low ! '
' To whom shall I yield ? ' said Earl Percy,
  ' Now I see it maun be so.'—

LXIII

' Thou shalt not yield to lord nor loun,
  Nor yet shalt thou to me ;
But yield thee to the bracken bush
  Grows on yon lilye-lee.'—

LXIV

' I winna yield to a bracken bush,
  Nor yet I will to a brere ;
But I would yield to Earl Douglas,
  Or Montgomery if he was here.'

stowre] press of battle.   brere] briar.

LXV

As soon as he knew Montgomery,
  He stuck his sword's point in ground ;
The Montgomery was a courteous knight,
  And quickly took him by the hand.

LXVI

There was slayne upon the Scottès' side,
  For sooth and certaynlye,
Sir James a Douglas there was slayne,
  That day that he cou'd dye.

LXVII

The Earl of Menteith he was slayne,
  And gryselye groan'd on the groun' ;
Sir Davy Scott, Sir Walter Steward,
  Sir John of Agerstone.

LXVIII

Sir Charlès Murray in that place
  That never a foot would flee ;
Sir Hew Maxwell, a lord he was,
  With the Douglas did he dee.

LXIX

There was slayne upon the Scottès' side
  For sooth as I you say,
Of four and fifty thousand Scottes
  Went but eighteen away.

LXX

There was slayne upon the English side
  For sooth and certaynlye,
A gentle Knight, Sir John Fitzhughe,
  It was the more pitye.

  gryselye] in a grisly manner, terribly.

LXXI

Sir James Hardbotell there was slayne,
   For him their heartes were sore ;
The gentle Lovell there was slayne,
   That the Percy's standard bore.

LXXII

There was slayne upon the English part
   For sooth as I you say,
Of ninè thousand English men
   Five hundred came away.

LXXIII

The others slayne were in the field ;
   Christ keep their souls from woe !
Seeing there was so fewè friends
   Against so many a foe.

LXXIV

Then on the morn they made them bieres
   Of birch and hazell gray :
Many a widow with weeping teares
   Their makes they fette away.

LXXV

This fray was fought at Otterbourne,
   Between the night and the day ;
Earl Douglas was buried at the bracken bush,
   And the Percy led captive away.

LXXVI

Now let us all for the Percy pray
   To Jesu most of might,
To bring his soul to the bliss of heaven,
   For he was a gentle knight.

makes] mates.   fette] fetched.

Fytte I

I

THE Percy out of Northumberland,
    An avow to God made he
That he would hunt in the mountains
    Of Cheviot within days three,
In the maugre of doughty Douglas,
    And all that e'er with him be.

II

The fattest harts in all Cheviot
    He would kill and carry away.—
' By my faith,' said the doughty Douglas again,
    ' I will let that hunting if I may ! '

III

Then the Percy out of Banborowe came,
    With him a mighty meinye,
With fifteen hundred archers bold
    Chosen out of shirès three.

IV

This began on a Monday at morn,
    In Cheviot the hills so hye ;
The child may rue that is unborn,
    It was the more pitye.

V

The drivers through the woodès went
    [All] for to raise the deer,
Bowmen bicker'd upon the bent
    With their broad arrows clear.

---

maugre] despite.   let] hinder.   meinye] company.
bicker'd] attacked, skirmished.   bent] rough grass.

CHEVY CHASE

VI

Then the wild thoro' the woodès went
    On every sidè shear;
Grayhounds thoro' the grevès glent
    For to kill their deer.

VII

This began on Cheviot the hills abune
    Early on a Monenday;
By that it drew to the hour of noon
    A hundred fat harts dead there lay.

VIII

They blew a mort upon the bent,
    They 'sembled on sidès shear;
To the quarry then the Percy went
    To the brittling of the deer.

IX

He said, ' It was the Douglas' promise
    This day to meet me here;
But I wist he would fail, verament!'
    —A great oath the Percy sware.

X

At the last a squire of Northumberland
    Lookèd at his hand full nigh;
He was ware o' the doughty Douglas coming,
    With him a great meinye.

XI

Both with speär, bill and brand,—
    'Twas a mighty sight to see;
Hardier men both of heart nor hand
    Were not in Christiantè.

---

wild] game, deer.   shear] several   grevès] groves.
glent] glanced, darted.   mort] death of the deer.   quarry]
dead game.   brittling] cutting up.

XII

They were twenty hundred spearmen good,
  Withouten any fail :
They were born along by the water o' Tweed
  I' the boun's o' Teviotdale.

XIII

' Leave off the brittling of deer,' he said ;
  ' To your bows look ye take good heed,
For sith ye were on your mothers born
  Had ye never so mickle need.'

XIV

The doughty Douglas on a steed
  Rode all his men beforn ;
His armour glitter'd as did a gleed,
  Bolder bairn was never born.

XV

' Tell me whose men ye are,' he says,
  ' Or whose men that ye be ;
Who gave you leave in this Cheviot chase
  In the spite of mine and of me ? '

XVI

The first man that him answer made
  It was the good Lord Percye :
' We will not tell thee whose men we are,
  Nor whose men that we be ;
But we will hunt here in this chase
  In the spite of thine and of thee.

XVII

' The fattest harts in all Cheviot
  We have kill'd, to carry away.'—
' By my troth,' said the doughty Douglas again,
  ' The one of us dies this day.

boun's] boundaries.   gleed] live coal.   bairn] fighting man.
666

XVIII

'[Yet] to kill allè these guiltless men
    Alas, it were great pitye !
But, Percy, thou art a lord of land,
    I an earl in my countrye—
Let all our men on a party stand,
    And do battle of thee and me ! '

XIX

' Christ's curse on his crown,' said the lord Percye,
    ' Whosoever thereto says nay !
By my troth, thou doughty Douglas,' he says,
    ' Thou shalt never see that day—

XX

—' Neither in England, Scotland nor France,
    Nor for no man of woman born,
But, that (and fortune be my chance)
    I dare meet him, one man for one.'

XXI

Then bespake a squire of Northumberland,
    Richard Witherington was his name ;
' It shall never be told in South England
    To King Harry the Fourth for shame.

XXII

' I wot you bin great lordès two,
    I am a poor squire of land ;
[Yet] I'll ne'er see my captain fight on a field
    And stand myself and look on.
But while that I may my weapon wield
    I'll not fail, both heart and hand.'

on a party] apart.

XXIII

That day, that day, that dreadful day !—
  The first fytte here I find :
An you'll hear any more o' the hunting of Cheviot,
  Yet there is more behind.

Fytte II

XXIV

The Englishmen had their bows y-bent,
  Their hearts were good enow ;
The first of arrows that they shot off
  Seven score spearmen they slew.

XXV

Yet bides the Earl Douglas upon the bent,
  A captain good enoghe ;
And that was seenè verament,
  For he wrought them both woe and wouche.

XXVI

The Douglas parted his host in three,
  Like a chief chieftain of pride ;
With surè spears of mighty tree
  They came in on every side ;

XXVII

—Throughè our English archery
  Gave many a woond full wide ;
Many a doughty they gar'd to dye,
  Which gainèd them no pride.

XXVIII

The Englishmen let their bowès be,
  And pull'd out brands that were bright ;
It was a heavy sight to see
  Bright swords on basnets light.

fytte] division of a ballad.   wouche] evil.   tree]
timber.   doughty] doughty man.   basnets] steel caps.

CHEVY CHASE

XXIX

Thoro' rich mail and manoplie
    Many stern they struck down straight ;
Many a freyke that was full free
    There under foot did light.

XXX

At last the Douglas and the Percy met,
    Like to captains of might and of main ;
They swapt together till they both swat
    With swordès of fine Milan.

XXXI

These worthy freykès for to fight
    Thereto they were full fain,
Till the blood out of their basnets sprent
    As ever did hail or rain.

XXXII

' Yield thee, Percy,' said the Douglas,
    ' And i' faith I shall thee bring
Where thou shalt have an Earl's wages
    Of Jamie our Scottish king.

XXXIII

' Thou shaltè have thy ransom free,
    —I hight thee here this thing ;
For the manfullest man thou art that e'er
    I conquer'd in field fighting.'

XXXIV

But ' Nay ', then said the lord Percye,
    ' I told it thee beforn
That I would never yielded be
    To man of a woman born.'

  manoplie] long gauntlet.   stern] stern men, warriors.
freyke] bold fellow.   swapt] smote.   swat] sweated.
sprent] spurted.   hight] promise.

XXXV

With that an arrow came hastily
  Forth of a mighty wane ;
And it hath stricken the Earl Douglas
  In at the breastè-bane.

XXXVI

Thoro' liver and lungès both
  The sharp arròw is gone,
That never after in his life-days
  He spake mo words but one :
'Twas, ' Fight ye, my merry men, whiles ye may,
  For my life-days bin gone ! '

XXXVII

The Percy leanèd on his brand
  And saw the Douglas dee ;
He took the dead man by the hand,
  And said, ' Woe is me for thee !

XXXVIII

' To have sav'd thy life I'd have parted with
  My lands for yearès three,
For a better man of heart nor of hand
  Was not in the north countrye.'

XXXIX

[All this there saw] a Scottish knight,
  Sir Hugh the Montgomerye :
When he saw Douglas to the death was dight,
  Through a hundred archerye
He never stint nor he never blint
  Till he came to the lord Percye.

wane] host, multitude.   dight] done, doomed.   stint]
stayed.   blint] stopped.

XL

He set upon the lord Percỳ
  A dint that was full sore ;
With a surè spear of a mighty tree
  Thro' the body him he bore,
O' the t'other side that a man might see
  A large cloth-yard and more.

XLI

An archer of Northumberland
  Saw slain was the lord Percye :
He bare a bent bow in his hand,
  Was made of a trusty tree.

XLII

An arrow that was a cloth-yard long
  To the hard steel halèd he,
A dint that was both sad and sair
  He set on Montgomerye.

XLIII

The dint it was both sad and sair
  That he on Montgomerye set ;
The swan-feathers that his arrow bare
  With his heart-blood they were wet.

XLIV

There was never a freykè one foot would flee,
  But still in stoure did stand ;
Hewing on each other, while they might dree,
  With many a baleful brand.

XLV

This battle began in Cheviot
  An hour before the noon,
And when the even-song bell was rung
  The battle was not half done.

dint] stroke, lunge.   halèd] pulled.   stoure] press of
battle.   dree] endure.

CHEVY CHASE

XLVI

They took [their stand] on either hand
  By the [lee] light of the moon ;
Many had no strength for to stand
  In Cheviot the hills abune.

XLVII

Of fifteen hundred archers of England
  Went away but seventy-and-three ;
Of twenty hundred spearmen of Scotland
  But even five-and-fifty.

XLVIII

There was slain with the bold Percye
  Sir John of Agerstoune,
Sir Roger, the hendè Hartley,
  Sir William, the bold Herone.

XLIX

Sir George, the worthy Loumlye,
  A knight of great renown,
Sir Ralph, the richè Rabye,
  With dints were beaten down.

L

For Witherington my heart was woe
  That ever he slain should be :
For when both his legs were hewn in two
  Yet he kneel'd and fought on his knee.

LI

There was slayn with the doughty Douglas
  Sir Hugh the Montgomerye,
Sir Davy Lambwell, that worthy was,
  His sister's son was he.

lee] fair, bright.   hendè] courteous, gentle.

CHEVY CHASE

LII

Sir Charles a Murray in that place,
 That never a foot would flee :
Sir Hew Maxwell, a lord he was,
 With the Douglas did he dee.

LIII

So on the morrow they made them biers
 Of birch and hazel so gray ;
Many widows with weeping tears
 Came to fetch their makes away.

LIV

Teviotdale may carp of care,
 Northumberland may make moan,
For two such captains as slain were there
 On the March-parts shall never be none.

LV

Word is come to Edinboro',
 To Jamie the Scottish King,
Earl Douglas, lieutenant of the Marches,
 Lay slain Cheviot within.

LVI

His hands the King did weal and wring,
 Said, 'Alas ! and woe is me !
Such another captain Scotland within
 I' faith shall never be ! '

LVII

Word is come to lovely London
 To the fourth Harry, our King,
Lord Percy, lieutenant of the Marches,
 Lay slain Cheviot within.

makes] mates. carp] talk. weal] clench.

CHEVY CHASE

LVIII

' God have mercy on his soul,' said King Harry,
   ' Good Lord, if thy will it be !
I've a hundred captains in England,' he said,
   ' As good as ever was he :
But Percy, an I brook my life,
   Thy death well quit shall be.'

LIX

And as our King made his avow
   Like a noble prince of renown,
For Percy he did it well perform
   After, on Homble-down ;

LX

Where six-and-thirty Scottish knights
   On a day were beaten down ;
Glendale glitter'd on their armour bright
   Over castle, tower and town.

LXI

This was the Hunting of the Cheviot ;
   That e'er began this spurn !
Old men, that knowen the ground well,
   Call it of Otterburn.

LXII

There was never a time on the Marche-partès
   Since the Douglas and Percy met,
But 'tis marvel an the red blood run not
   As the reane does in the street.

brook] retain.   Glendale] one of the six ' wards ' of
Northumberland. Homildon was here.   spurn] fray (?).
reane] gutter.

LXIII

Jesu Christ ! our balès bete,
  And to the bliss us bring !
This was the Hunting of the Cheviot :
  God send us all good endìng !

129. *Northumberland Betrayed by Douglas*

I

NOW list and lithe, you gentlemen,
  And I'st tell you the veretye,
How they have dealt with a banish'd man,
  Driven out of his owne countrye.

II

When as he came on Scottish ground,
  As woe and wonder be them amonge !
Full much was there traitorye
  They wrought the Erle of Northumberland.

III

When they were at the supper set,
  Before many goodly gentlemen,
They fell a flouting and mocking both,
  And said to the Erle of Northumberland :

IV

'What makes you be soe sad, my lord,
  And in your mind soe sorrowfullye ?
In the north to-morrow there is a shooting,
  And thither thou'st goe, my Lord Percye.

balès] woes.   bete] better, relieve.

675

V

'The buttes are sett, and the shooting is made,
   And there is like to be great royaltye,
And I am sworne into my bill
   Thither to bring my Lord Percye.'

VI

'I'le give thee my hand, Douglas,' he says,
   'And by the faith in my bodye,
If that thou wilt ryde to the worldis end,
   Then I'le ryde in thy companye.'

VII

And then bespake the good ladye,
   Mary a Douglas was her name:
'You shall byde here, good English lord;
   My brother is a traitorous man.

VIII

'He is a traitor stout and stronge,
   As I'st tell you the veretye;
For he hath ta'en 'liverance of the Erle,
   And into England he will 'liver thee.'—·

IX

'Now hold thy tongue, thou goodly ladye,
   Now all this talking let a-bee;
For all the gold that's in Lough Leven,
   William wo'ld not 'liver mee.

X

'It wo'ld breake truce betweene England and Scottland,
   And freinds againe they wo'ld never bee,
If he sho'ld 'liver a banisht erle,
   Was driven out of his owne countrye.'—

into my bill] on paper, in writing.

676

XI

'Hold your tounge, my lord,' she sayes,
  'There is much falsehood them amonge;
Soone they will part them freinds againe,
  When you are dead, then they are done.

XII

'If you will give me any trust, my lord,
  I'le tell you how you best may bee;
You'st let my brother ryde his wayes,
  And tell those English lords, trulye,

XIII

'How that you cannot with them ryde,
  Because you are in an isle of the sea;
Then, ere my brother come againe,
  To Edenborrow castle I'le carry thee.

XIV

'I'le 'liver you unto the Lord Hume,
  And you know a trew Scothe lord is hee,
For he hath lost both land and goods
  In ayding of your good bodye.'—

XV

'Marry, I am woe, woman,' he sayes,
  'That any freind fares worse for me;
For where one saith it is a true tale,
  Then two will say it is a lee.

XVI

'When that I was at home in my realme,
  Amonge my tennants all trulye,
In my time of losse, wherin my need stoode,
  They came to ayd me honestlye.

XVII

'Therefore I left a many a child fatherlese,
　And many a widdow to looke wanne;
Therefore do thou blame nothing, ladye,
　But the woeffull warres which I began.'—

XVIII

'If you will give me noe trust, my lord,
　Nor noe credence you will give mee,
An you'le come hither to my right hand,
　Indeed, my lord, I'le let you see.'—

XIX

Says, 'I never loved noe witchcraft,
　Nor never dealt with treacherye,
But evermore held the hye way;
　Alas, that may be seene by mee!'—

XX

'If you will not come your selfe, my lord,
　You'le lett your chamberlaine goe with me,
Three words that I may to him speake,
　And soone he shall come againe to thee.'

XXI

When James Swynard came that lady before,
　She let him see thro' the weme of her ring
How many there was of English lords
　To wayte there for his master and him.

XXII

'But who beene yonder, my good ladye,
　That walkes soe royallye on yond greene?'—
'Yond is Lord Hunsden, Jamye,' she sayd,
　'Alas, he'le doe you both tree and teene!'—

weme] inward.　　wayte] wait in ambush.　　tree and teene]
injury and grief.
678

XXIII

'And who beene yonder, thou gay ladye,
  That walkes soe royallye him beside?'—
'Yond's Sir William Drurye, Jamye,' she sayd,
  'And a keene captain he is, and tryde.'—

XXIV

'How many miles is't, thou good ladye,
  Betwixt yond English lord and mee?'—
'Marry, thrice fifty mile, Jamye,' she sayd,
  'And even to sayle and by the sea.

XXV

'I never was on English ground,
  Nor never see it with mine eye,
But as my wit and wisedome serves,
  And as the booke it telleth mee.

XXVI

'My mother, she was a witch woman,
  And part of it she learnèd mee;
She wo'ld let me see out of Lough Leven
  What they dyd in London citye.'—

XXVII

'But who is yond, thou good ladye,
  Comes yonder with an osterne face?'
'Yond's Sir John Forster, Jamye,' she sayd;
  Alas! he'll do ye sore disgrace.'

XXVIII

He pulled his hat downe over his eyes,
  And, Lord, he wept soe tenderlye!
He is gone unto his master againe,
  And even to tell him the veretye.

osterne] austere.

XXIX

'Now hast thou beene with Mary,' he sayd,
    'Even as thy tounge will tell to mee;
But if thou trust any woman's words,
    Thou must refraine good companye.'

XXX

'It is noe words, my lord,' he sayes;
    'Yonder the men she lets me see,
How many English lords there is
    Is wayting there for you and mee.

XXXI

'Yonder I see the Lord Hunsden,
    And he and you is of third degree;
A greater enemye, indeed, my Lord,
    In England never a one have yee.'—

XXXII

'And I have beene in Lough Leven
    The most part of these yeerès three:
Yet had I never noe out-rake,
    Nor good gamès that I co'ld see.

XXXIII

'And I am thus bidden to yonder shooting
    By William Douglas all trulye;
Therfore speake never a word of thy mouth
    That thou thinkès will hinder me.'

XXXIV

Then he writhe the gold ring of his fingar
    And gave it to that gay ladye;
Sayes, 'That was a legacye left unto mee
    In Harley woods where I co'ld bee.'—

of third degree] third cousins.   out-rake] holiday.
680

XXXV

'Then ffarewell hart, and farewell hand,
 And ffarwell all good companye !
That woman shall never beare a sonne
 Shall know soe much of your privitye.'—

XXXVI

'Now hold thy tongue, ladye,' he sayde,
 'And make not all this dole for me,
For I may well drinke, but I'st never eate,
 Till ance againe in Lough Leven I bee.'

XXXVII

He tooke his boate at the Lough Leven,
 For to sayle now over the sea,
And he hath cast up a silver wand,
 Says, 'Fare thou well, my good ladye ! '
The ladye looked owre her left sholder ;
 In a dead swoone there down fell she.

XXXVIII

'Goe backe againe, Douglas ! ' he sayd,
 'And I will goe in thy companye ;
For sudden sicknesse yonder lady has tane,
 And ever, alas, she will but dye !

XXXIX

'If ought come to yonder ladye but good,
 Then blamèd sore that I shall bee,
Because a banish'd man I am,
 And driven out of my owne countrye.'—

XL

'Come on, come on, my lord,' he sayes,
 'And all such talking let a-bee ;
There 's ladyes enow left in Lough Leven
 For to cheere yonder gay ladye.'

XLI

' An you will not goe your selfe, my lord,
  You will lett my chamberlaine go with mee ;
We shall now take our boate againe,
  And soone wee shall overtake thee.'—

XLII

' Come on, come on, my lord,' he sayes,
  ' And all this talking now let a-bee ;
For my sister is craftye enoughe
  For to beguile thousands such as you and mee.'

XLIII

When they had saylèd fifty myle,
  Now fifty myle upon the sea,
Hee asked, ' How ffarr is it to that shooting
  That William Douglas promised me ? '—

XLIV

'Now faire words makès foolès faine,
  And that may be seene by thy master and thee ;
For happen you'll think it soone enoughe
  Whenever you that shooting see.'

XLV

Jamye pulled his hat now over his browe,
  I wot the teares fell in his e'e ;
And he is to his master againe,
  And for to tell him the veretye.

XLVI

' He says fayre words makes foolès faine,
  And that may be seene by you and mee,
For happen we'll thinke it soone enoughe
  Whenever we that shooting see.'

XLVII

' Hold upp thy head, Jamye,' the Erle sayd,
   ' And never let thy hart fayle thee ;
He did it but to prove thee with,
   And see how thow wo'ld take with death trulye.'

XLVIII

When they had sayl'd other fifty mile,
   Other fifty mile upon the sea,
Lord Percye called to him, himselfe,
   Sayd, ' Douglas, what wilt thou doe with mee ? '

XLIX

' Looke that your brydle be wight, my lord,
   That you may goe as a shipp at sea ;
Looke that your spurres be bright and sharpe,
   That you may pricke her while she'le awaye.'

L

' What needeth this, Douglas,' he sayth,
   ' That thou needest to ffloutè mee ?
For I was counted a horsseman good
   Before that ever I met with thee.

LI

' A ffalsè Hector hath my horsse,
   And ever an evill death may hee dye !
And Willye Armestronge hath my spurres
   And all the geere belongs to mee.'

LII

When they had sayled other fifty mile,
   Other fifty mile upon the sea,
They landed low by Berwicke-side ;
   [Soe Douglas betray'd the] Lord Percye.

      wight] strong.

I

A S it befel in midsummer-time,
  When birds singe sweetlye on every tree,
Our noble king, King Henry the Eighth,
  Over the river of Thames pass'd he.

II

He was no sooner over the river,
  Downe in a forrest to take the ayre,
But eighty merchants of London citye
  Came kneeling before King Henry there.

III

'O ye are welcome, rich merchànts,
  Good saylers, welcome unto me!'
They swore by the rood they were saylers good,
  But rich merchànts they co'ld not be.

IV

'To France nor Flanders dare we not passe,
  Nor Bourdeaux voyage we dare not fare,
All for a false robber that lyes on the seas,
  And robbs us of our merchants-ware.'

V

King Henry was stout, and he turned him about,
  And swore by the Lord that was mickle of might,
'I thought he'd not been in the world throughout
  That durst have wrought England such unright.'

VI

But ever they sighèd, and said, alas!
  Unto King Harry this answer againe:
'He is a proud Scott that will robb us all
  Were we twenty shipps and he but one.'

684

VII

The King looket over his left shouldèr,
  Amongst his lords and barrons so free :
' Have I never a lord in all my realme
  Will fetch yond traitor unto me ? '

VIII

' Yes, that dare I ! ' says my lord Charles Howard,
  Neere to the King wheras he did stand ;
' If that Your Grace will give me leave,
  My self will perform what you command.'

IX

' Thou shalt have six hundred men,' saith our King,
  ' And chuse them out of my realme so free ;
[Moreover] mariners and ship boyes,
  To guide the great ship on the sea.'

X

' I'le goe speake with Sir Andrew,' says my Lord Howard ;
  ' Upon the sea, if he be there ;
I will bring him and his ship to shore,
  Or before my prince I will ne'er come neere.'

XI

The first of all my Lord did call,
  A noble gunner he was one ;
This man was three score yeares and ten,
  And Peter Simon was his name.

XII

' Peter,' says he, ' I must sayle to the sea,
  To seek out an enemy ; God be my speed !
Before all others I have chosen thee ;
  Of a hundred gunners thou'st be my head.'

XIII

'My lord,' says he, 'if you've chosen me
　Of a hundred gunners to be the head,
You may hang me at your maine-mast tree
　If I miss my mark past three pence bread.'

XIV

The next of all my lord he did call,
　A noble bowman he was one;
In Yorkshire was this gentleman borne,
　And William Horsley was his name.

XV

'Horsley,' says he, 'I must sayle to the sea,
　To seek out an enemy; God be my speede!
Before all others I have chosen thee;
　Of a hundred bowemen thou'st be my head.'

XVI

'My lord,' says he, 'if you've chosen me
　Of a hundred bowemen to be the head,
Hang me at your main-mast tree
　If I miss my mark past twelve pence bread.'

XVII

With pikes, and gunnes, and bowmen bold,
　This noble Howard is gone to the sea
On the day before Midsummer-even,
　And out at Thames' mouth saylèd they.

XVIII

They had not saylèd dayès three
　Upon their journey they took in hand,
But there they met with a noble ship,
　And stoutely made it both stay and stand.

three pence bread] the breadth of a threepenny piece.
686

XIX

'Thou must tell me thy name,' says Charles my lord
      Howard,
  'Or who thou art, or from whence thou came,
Yea, and where thy dwelling is,
    To whom and where thy ship does belong.'

XX

'My name,' says he, 'is Henery Hunt,
    With a pure hart and a penitent mind ;
I and my ship they doe belong
    Unto the New-castle that stands upon Tyne.'—

XXI

'Now thou must tell me, Henery Hunt,
    As thou hast saylèd by day and by night
Hast thou not heard of a stout robbèr ?
    Men calls him Sir Andrew Barton, Knight.'

XXII

But ever he sighèd, and said, 'Alas !
    Full well, my lord, I know that wight ;
He has robb'd me of my merchants-ware,
    And I was his pris'ner but yesternight.

XXIII

'As I was sayling upon the sea,
    And a Bourdeaux voyage as I did fare,
He claspèd me to his archèborde,
    And robb'd me of all my merchants-ware.

XXIV

'And I am a man both poor and bare,
    Every man will have his own of me ;
And I am bound towards London to fare,
    To complain unto my prince Henrye.

archèborde] hatch-board.

687

SIR ANDREW BARTON

XXV

'That shall not need,' says my Lord Howard;
  'If thou canst let me this robber see,
For every penny he hath taken thee fro'
  Thou shalt be rewarded a shilling,' quoth he.

XXVI

'Now God forfend,' says Henery Hunt,
  'My lord, you sho'ld work so far amisse!
God keep you out of that traitor's hands!
  For you wot full little what man he is.

XXVII

'He is brasse within, and steele without,
  And beams he bears in his topcastle stronge;
His ship hath ordinance clean round about;
  Besides, my lord, he is very well mann'd.

XXVIII

'He hath a pinnace is dearlye dight,
  Saint Andrew's cross, that is his guide;
His pinnace bears nine-score men and more,
  With fifteen cannons on every side.

XXIX

'Were you twenty ships, and he but one,
  Either in archbord or in hall,
He wo'ld overcome you everye one,
  An if his beams they doe down fall.'

XXX

'This is cold comfort,' says my Lord Howard,
  'To welcome a stranger thus to the sea;
I'le bring him and his ship to shore,
  Or else into Scotland he shall carry me.'

dearlye dight] expensively fitted, or ornamented.   guide]
guidon, signal flag.   hall] hull.

688

XXXI

' Then, my lord, you must get a noble gunner ;
  One that can set well with his e'e,
And sink his pinnace into the sea,
  And soon then overcome will he be.

XXXII

' And when that you have done all this,
  If you chance Sir Andrew for to board,
Let no man to his topcastle go ;
  And I will give you a glass, my lord,

XXXIII

' And then you need to fear no Scot,
  Whether you sayle by day or by night ;
And to-morrow, by seven of the clocke,
  You shall meete with Sir Andrew Barton, Knight.'

XXXIV

The merchant set Lord Howard a glass
  So well apparent in his sight
That on the morrow by seven of the clock
  He spy'd Sir Andrew Barton, Knight.

XXXV

Lord Howard he swore a mighty oath
  When he saw his hache-bords dearly dight ;
' Now by my faith and by my troth,
  Yonder proud Scott is a worthy wight.

XXXVI

' Take in your ancients and your standards,
  Yea, that no man shall them see,
And put me forth a white willow wand,
  As merchants use to sayle the sea.'

glass] a lantern to guide the man-of-war's course by the mer-
chantman's.   ancients] ensigns.

XXXVII

But they stirr'd neither top nor mast,
    But Sir Andrew they passèd by.—
'What English are yonder,' said Sir Andrew,
    'That can so little curtesye?

XXXVIII

'I have been admiral over the sea
    [Methinketh] more then these yeeres three;
There is never an English nor Portingall dog,
    Can pass this way without leave of me.

XXXIX

'But now yonder pedlars, they are pass'd,
    Which is no little grief to me:
Fetch them backe,' sayes Sir Andrew Barton,
    'They shall all hang at my maine-mast tree.'

XL

With that the pinnace it shot off,
    That my Lord Howard might it well ken;
It strokè down my lord's fore-màst,
    And kill'd fourteen of my lord his men.

XLI

'Come hither, Simon!' says my Lord Howard,
    'Look that thy words be true thou said;
I'le hang thee at my maine-mast tree
    If thou miss thy mark past three pence bread.'

XLII

Simon was old, but his hart it was bold;
    He tooke downe a piece, and laid it full low;
Chaine yeards nine he put therein,
    Besides other great shot less and moe.

stirr'd] moved, lowered.   can] ken, know.

SIR ANDREW BARTON

XLIII

With that he let his gun-shot go;
  So well he settled it with his e'e,
The first sight that Sir Andrew saw,
  He saw his pinnace sunk in the sea.

XLIV

When Sir Andrew saw his pinnace sunk,
  Lord! in his heart he was not well!
'Cut my ropes! it is time to be gone!
  I'le goe fetch yond pedlars back mysell!'

XLV

When my Lord Howard saw Sir Andrew loose,
  Lord! in his heart that he was faine!
'Strike on your drums! spread out your ancients!
  Sound out your trumpets! sound out amain!'

XLVI

'Fight on, my men!' says Sir Andrew Barton;
  'Weate, howsoever this geare will sway,
It is my Lord Admiral of England
  Is come to seek me on the sea.'

XLVII

Simon had a sone; with shot of a gun—
  Well Sir Andrew might it ken—
He shot it in at the middle deck,
  And killed sixty more of Sir Andrew's men.

XLVIII

[Bold] Hunt came in at the other side,
  And at Sir Andrew he shot then;
He drove down his fore-mast tree,
  And kill'd eighty more of Sir Andrew's men.

Weate] wit ye, know.   geare] business, fighting.   sway]
go, turn out.

SIR ANDREW BARTON

XLIX

'I have done a good turne,' sayes Henery Hunt;
　'Sir Andrew is not our King's friend;
He hoped t' have undone me yesternight,
　But I hope I have quit him well in the end.'

L

'Ever alas!' sayd Sir Andrew Barton,
　'What sho'ld a man either thinke or say?
Yonder false thief is my strongest enemy,
　Who was my prisoner but yesterday.

LI

'Come hither to me, thou Gourden good,
　And be thou ready at my call,
And I will give thee three hundred pound
　If thou wilt let my beames downe fall.'

LII

With that hee swarm'd the main-mast tree,
　Soe did he it with might and maine;
But Horsley, with a bearing arrow,
　Stroke the Gourden through the braine.

LIII

And he fell into the hatches againe,
　And sore of his wound that he did bleed;
Then word went through Sir Andrew's men,
　How that the Gourden he was dead.

LIV

'Come hither to me, James Hamilton,
　Thou'rt my sister's son, I have no more;
I will give thee six hundred pound
　If thou wilt let my beames downe fall.'

　　swarm'd] climbed.　　bearing arrow] a long arrow for distant
shooting.
　　692

LV

With that he swarm'd the main-mast tree,
    Soe did he it with might and main:
Horsley, with another broad arrow,
    Strake the yeaman thoro' the brain.

LVI

That he fell downe to the hatches againe;
    Sore of his wound that hee did bleed;
Covetousness gets no gaine,
    It is very true, as the Welshman said.

LVII

But when he saw his nephew slaine,
    Lord! in his heart he was not well!
'Go fetch me downe my armour of proof,
    For I will to the topcastle mysell.

LVIII

'Go fetch me downe my armour of proof,
    For it is gilded with gold so cleere;
God be with my brother, John of Barton!
    Amongst the Portingalls he did it weare.'

LIX

But when he had his armour of proof,
    And on his body he had it on,
Every man that lookèd at him
    Said, Gun nor arrow he need fear none.

LX

'Come hither, Horsley!' says my Lord Howard,
    'And look your shaft that it goe right;
Shoot a good shoote in the time of need,
    And for thy shooting thou'st be made knight.'

SIR ANDREW BARTON

LXI

'I'le do my best,' sayes Horsley then,
  'Your Honour shall see before I goe ;
If I sho'ld be hang'd at your maine-mast tree,
  I have in my ship but arrows two.'

LXII

But at Sir Andrew he shot then ;
  He made so sure to hit his mark ;
Under the spole of his right arme
  He smote Sir Andrew quite thro' the heart.

LXIII

Yet from the tree he wo'ld not start,
  But he cling'd to it with might and main ;
Under the collar then of his jacke,
  He stroke Sir Andrew thoro' the brain.

LXIV

'Fight on, my men !' says Sir Andrew Barton,
  'I am hurt, but I am not slain ;
I'le lay me downe and bleed a-while,
  And then I'le rise and fight again.

LXV

'Fight on, my men !' says Sir Andrew Barton,
  'These English dogs they bite so lowe ;
Fight on for Scotland and Saint Andrew
  While that you hear my whistle blowe !'

LXVI

But when they co'ld not hear his whistle,
  Says Henery Hunt, 'I'le lay my head
You may board yonder noble ship, my lord,
  For I know Sir Andrew he is dead.'

spole] shoulder, *épaule*. jacke] jacket, short coat of mail.

694

LXVII

With that they boarded this noble ship,
  So did they it with might and main ;
They found eighteen score Scots alive,
  Besides the rest were maim'd and slaine.

LXVIII

Lord Howard took a sword in his hand,
  And so smote off Sir Andrew's head ;
The Scots stood by did weepe and mourne,
  But never a word they spoke or sayd.

LXIX

He caused his body to be taken downe,
  And over the hatch-bord cast into the sea,
And about his middle three hundred crownes :
  ' Wheresoever thou lands, it will bury thee ! '

LXX

With his head they sayl'd into England againe,
  With right good will and force and main,
And on the day before New-Year's Even
  Into Thames' mouth they came againe.

LXXI

Lord Howard wrote to King Henry's grace,
  With all the newes hee co'ld him bring :
' Such a New Year's gift I have brought to your Grace
  As never did subject to any King.

LXXII

' For merchandise, yea and manhood,
  The like is nowhere to be found ;
The sight of these wo'ld do you good,
  For you have not the like in your English ground.'

695

LXXIII

When the King heard tell that they were come,
　Full royally he welcomed them home;
Sir Andrew's ship was his New-Year's gift;
　A braver ship you never saw none.

LXXIV

Now hath our King Sir Andrew's ship,
　Beset with pearles and precyous stones;
And now hath England two ships of war,
　Two ships of war, before but one.

LXXV

'Who holpe to this?' says King Henrye,
　'That I may reward him for his paine.'—
'Henery Hunt, and Peter Simon,
　William Horsley, and I the same.'—

LXXVI

' Harry Hunt shall have his whistle and chaine,
　And all his jewels whatsoe'er they be,
And other rich gifts that I will not name,
　For his good service he hath done me.

LXXVII

·Horsley, right thou'st be a knight,
　Lands and livings thou shalt have store;
Howard shall be Earl of Nottingham,
　And so was never Howard before.

LXXVIII

' Now, Peter Simon, thou art old;
　I will maintaine thee and thy son;
Thou shalt have five hundred pound all in gold
　For the good service that thou hast done.'

696

LXXIX

With that King Henrye shifted his room;
  In came the Queene and ladyes bright;
Other arrands they had none
  But to see Sir Andrew Barton, Knight.

LXXX

But when they saw his deadly face,
  His eyes were hollow in his head;
' I wo'ld give a hundred pound,' says his Grace,
  ' The man were alive as he is dead!

LXXXI

' Yet for the manful part he hath play'd,
  Both here at home and beyond the sea,
His men shall have half-a-crowne a day
  Till they come to my brother, King Jamie.'

131.   *The ' George-Aloe '*

I

THE *George-Aloe*, and the *Sweepstake*, too,
  With hey, with hoe, for and a nony no,
O, there were two Merchant-men, a sailing for Safee
  And alongst the Coast of Barbarye.

II

The *George-Aloe* came to anchor in the bay,
  With hey, &c.
But the jolly *Sweepstake* kept on her way,
  And alongst, &c.

III

They had not sayl'd but leagues two or three,
  With hey, &c.
But they met with a French Man-of-War upon the Sea,
  And alongst, &c.

shifted his room] made place.

THE 'GEORGE-ALOE'

IV

' All haile, all haile, you lusty Gallants all !
    With hey, &c.
Of whence is your fair Ship, and whither do ye call ? '
    And alongst, &c.

V

' We are Englishmen, and bound for Safee,'—
    With hey, &c.
' Ay, and we are Frenchmen, and war upon the sea,
    And alongst, &c.

VI

' Amaine, Amaine, you English dogs, hail ! '—
    With hey, &c.
' Come aboard you French swads, and strike down your
    sayle,'
    And alongst, &c.

VII

They laid us aboard on the Starboard side,
    With hey, &c.
And they threw us into the Sea so wide,
    And alongst, &c.

VIII

When tidings to the *George-Aloe* came,
    With hey, &c.
That the jolly *Sweepstake* by a Frenchman was ta'en,
    And alongst, &c.

IX

' To top, to top, thou little Cabin-boy,
    With hey, &c.
And see if this French Man-of-War thou canst descry,'—
    And alongst, &c.

swads] peascods, a cant term for soldiers.

THE 'GEORGE-ALOE'

X

'A Sayle, a Sayle, under our lee!
    With hey, &c.
Yea, and another that is under her obey!'
    And alongst, &c.

XI

'Weigh anchor, weigh anchor, O jolly Boat-swain!
    With hey, &c.
We will take this Frenchman, if we can,'
    And alongst, &c.

XII

We had not sayl'd leagues two or three,
    With hey, &c.
But we met the French Man-of-War upon the Sea,
    And alongst, &c.

XIII

'All haile, All haile, you lusty Gallants hail!
    With hey, &c.
Of whence is your faire Ship, and whither do ye sayl?'
    And alongst, &c.

XIV

'O, we are Merchant-men and bound for Safee,'—
    With hey, &c.
'Ay, and we are Frenchmen, and war upon the sea,
    And alongst, &c.

XV

'Amaine, Amaine, you English Dogges, hail!'—
    With hey, &c.
'Come aboard, you French rogues, and strike down your
    sayl!'
    And alongst, &c.

XVI

The first good shot that the *George-Aloe* shot,
    With hey, &c.
He made the Frenchman's heart sore afraid,
    And alongst, &c.

XVII

The second shot the *George-Aloe* did afford,
    With hey, &c.
He struck their main-mast over the board,
    And alongst, &c.

XVIII

' Have mercy, have mercy, you brave English Men ! '—
    With hey, &c.
' O, what have you done with our merry Brethren ? '—
    As they sayl'd in Barbarye ?

XIX

' We laid them aboard the starboard side,
    With hey, &c.
And we threw them into the Sea so wide,'—
    And alongst, &c.

XX

'Such mercy as you have shewed unto them,
    With hey, &c.
Then the like mercy shall you have again,'—
    And alongst, &c.

XXI

We laid them aboard the larboard side,
    With hey, &c.
And we threw them into the Sea so wide,
    And alongst, &c.

700

THE 'GEORGE-ALOE'

XXII

Lord, how it grieved our hearts full Sore,
  With hey, &c.
To see the drowned Frenchmen to swim along the shore!
  And alongst, &c.

XXIII

Now gallant Seamen I bid you all adieu,
  With hey, &c.
This is the last Newes I can write to you,
  To England's Coast from Barbarye.

132.   *The 'Golden Vanity'*

I

A SHIP I have got in the North Country
 And she goes by the name of the *Golden Vanity*,
O I fear she'll be taken by a Spanish Ga-la-lee,
  As she sails by the Low-lands low.

II

To the Captain then upspake the little Cabin-boy,
He said, 'What is my fee, if the galley I destroy?
The Spanish Ga-la-lee, if no more it shall anoy,
  As you sail by the Low-lands low.'

III

'Of silver and of gold I will give to you a store;
And my pretty little daughter that dwelleth on the shore,
Of treasure and of fee as well, I'll give to thee galore,
  As we sail by the Low-lands low.'

701

IV

Then they row'd him up tight in a black bull's skin,
And he held all in his hand an augur sharp and thin,
And he swam until he came to the Spanish Gal-a-lin,
    As she lay by the Low-lands low.

V

He bored with his augur, he bored once and twice,
And some were playing cards, and some were playing dice,
When the water flowèd in it dazzled their eyes,
    And she sank by the Low-lands low.

VI

So the Cabin-boy did swim all to the larboard side,
Saying 'Captain! take me in, I am drifting with the tide!'
'I will shoot you! I will kill you!' the cruel Captain cried,
    'You may sink by the Low-lands low.'

VII

Then the Cabin-boy did swim all to the starboard side,
Saying, 'Messmates, take me in, I am drifting with the tide!'
Then they laid him on the deck, and he closed his eyes
        and died,
    As they sailed by the Low-lands low.

VIII

They sew'd his body tight in an old cow's hide,
And they cast the gallant cabin-boy out over the ship side,
And left him without more ado to drift with the tide,
    And to sink by the Low-lands low.

I

AS it fell on a holy-day,
   And upon a holy-tide-a,
John Dory bought him an ambling nag,
   To Paris for to ride-a.

II

And when John Dory to Paris was come,
   A little before the gate-a,
John Dory was fitted, the porter was witted
   To let him in thereat-a.

III

The first man that John Dory did meet
   Was good King John of France-a;
John Dory could well of his courtesie,
   But fell downe in a trance-a.

IV

'A pardon, a pardon, my liege and my king,
   For my merry men and for me-a,
And all the churls in merry England,
   I'le bring them all bound to thee-a.'

V

And Nichol was then a Cornish man,
   A little beside Bohyde-a,
He mann'd him forth a good black barke,
   With fifty good oars of a side-a.

VI

'Run up, my boy, unto the maine top,
   And look what thou canst spy-a:'
'Who ho! who ho! a good ship I do see,
   I trow it be John Dory-a.'

703

VII

They hoist their sailes, both top and top,
　　The mizzen and all was tride-a,
And every man stood to his lot,
　　Whatever should betide-a.

VIII

The roring cannons then were plied,
　　And dub-a-dub went the drum-a ;
The braying trumpets loud they cried
　　To courage both all and some-a.

IX

The grappling-hooks were brought at length,
　　The brown bill and the sword-a,
John Dory at length, for all his strength,
　　Was clapt fast under board-a.

134.　　*Willie Macintosh*

I

'TURN, Willie Macintosh,
　　Turn, I bid you ;
Gin ye burn Auchindown,
　　Huntly wili head you.'—

II

' Head me or hang me,
　　That canna fley me ;
I'll burn Auchindown
　　Ere the life lea' me.'

III

Coming down Deeside,
　　In a clear morning,
Auchindown was in flame,
　　Ere the cock-crawing.

IV

But coming o'er Cairn Croom,
  And looking down, man,
I saw Willie Macintosh
  Burn Auchindown, man.

V

' Bonnie Willie Macintosh,
  Whare left ye your men ? '—
' I left them in the Stapler,
  But they'll never come hame.'

VI

' Bonny Willie Macintosh,
  Whare now is your men ? '—
' I left them in the Stapler,
  Sleeping in their sheen.'

135. The Bonnie House o' Airlie

I

IT fell on a day, and a bonnie simmer day,
  When green grew aits and barley,
That there fell out a great dispute
  Between Argyll and Airlie.

II

Argyll has raised an hunder men,
  An hunder harness'd rarely,
And he 's awa' by the back of Dunkell,
  To plunder the castle of Airlie.

III

Lady Ogilvie looks o'er her bower-window,
  And O but she looks warely !
And there she spied the great Argyll,
  Come to plunder the bonnie house of Airlie.

sheen] shoes.   aits] oats.

IV

'Come down, come down, my Lady Ogilvie,
  Come down and kiss me fairly.'—
'O I winna kiss the fause Argyll,
  If he shouldna leave a standing stane in Airlie.'

V

He hath taken her by the left shoulder,
  Says, 'Dame, where lies thy dowry?'—
'O it's east and west yon wan water side,
  And it's down by the banks of the Airlie.'

VI

They hae sought it up, they hae sought it down,
  They hae sought it maist severely,
Till they fand it in the fair plum-tree
  That shines on the bowling-green of Airlie.

VII

He hath taken her by the middle sae small,
  And O but she grat sairly!
And laid her down by the bonnie burn-side,
  Till they plunder'd the castle of Airlie.

VIII

'Gif my gude lord war here this night,
  As he is with King Charlie,
Neither you, nor ony ither Scottish lord,
  Durst avow to the plundering of Airlie.

IX

'Gif my gude lord war now at hame,
  And he is with his king,
There durst nae a Campbell in a' Argyll
  Set fit on Airlie green.

grat] cried.   fit] foot.

706

X

'Ten bonnie sons I have borne unto him,
    The eleventh ne'er saw his daddy;
But though I had an hunder mair,
    I'd gie them a' to King Charlie!'

136.   *Johnnie of Cockerslee*

I

JOHNNIE rose up in a May morning,
    Call'd for water to wash his hands;
'Gar loose to me the gude gray dogs,
    That are bound wi' iron bands.'

II

When Johnnie's mother gat word o' that,
    Her hands for dule she wrang;
'O Johnnie, for my benison,
    To the greenwood dinna gang!

III

'Eneugh ye hae o' gude wheat bread,
    And eneugh o' the blude-red wine;
And therefore for nae venison, Johnnie,
    I pray ye, stir frae hame.

IV

'There are Seven For'sters at Hislinton side,
    At Hislinton where they dwell,
And for ae drap o' thy heart's blude
    They wad ride the fords o' hell.'

V

But Johnnie has buskit his gude bend-bow,
    His arrows, ane by ane,
And he has gane to Durrisdeer
    To ding the dun deer down.

707

VI

He 's lookit east, and he 's lookit west,
    And a little below the sun;
And there he spied the dun deer lying
    Aneath **a** buss o' broom.

VII

Johnnie he shot and the dun deer lap,
    And he wounded her on the side;
But atween the wood and the wan water
    His hounds they laid her pride.

VIII

And Johnnie has brittled the deer sae well,
    Had out her liver and lungs;
And wi' these he has feasted his bluidy hounds
    As if they had been Earl's sons.

IX

They ate sae much o' the venison,
    And drank sae much o' the blude,
That Johnnie and his gude gray hounds
    Fell asleep by yonder wood.

X

By there came a silly auld carle,
    An ill death mote he die!
And he 's awa' to Hislinton,
    Where the Seven Foresters did lie.

XI

'What news, what news, ye gray-headed carle?
    What news? come tell to me.'—
'I bring nae news,' said the gray-headed carle,
    'But what these eyes did see.

buss] bush, clump.   lap] leapt.   brittled] 'broken', cut up venison.

XII

'High up in Braidislee, low down in Braidislee,
    And under a buss o' scroggs,
The bonniest childe that ever I saw
    Lay sleeping atween his dogs.

XIII

'The sark he had upon his back
    It was o' the holland fine,
The doublet he had over that
    It was o' the Lincoln twine.

XIV

'The buttons that were on his sleeve
    Were o' the gowd sae gude;
The twa gray dogs he lay atween,
    Their mouths were dyed wi' blude.'

XV

Then out and spak' the First Forester,
    The head man owre them a';
'If this be Johnnie o' Cockerslee
    Nae nearer will we draw.'

XVI

But up and spak' the Sixth Forester,
    (His sister's son was he,)
'If this be Johnnie o' Cockerslee,
    We soon shall gar him dee!'

XVII

The first flight of arrows the Foresters shot,
    They wounded him on the knee;
And out and spak' the Seventh Forester,
    'The next will gar him dee.'

scroggs] stunted, or scraggy, trees.   twine] thread, texture.

XVIII

'O some they count ye well-wight men,
    But I do count ye nane;
For you might well ha' waken'd me,
    And ask'd gin I wad be ta'en.

XIX

'The wildest wolf in a' this wood
    Wad no ha' done sae by me;
She ha' wet her foot i' the wan water,
    And sprinkled it owre my bree,
And if that wad not ha' waken'd me,
    Wad ha' gone an' let me be.

XX

'O bows of yew, if ye be true,
    In London where ye were bought;
And, silver strings, value me sma' things
    Till I get this vengeance wrought!
And, fingers five, get up belive:
    And Manhood fail me nought!

XXI

'Stand stout, stand stout, my noble dogs,
    Stand stout and dinna flee!
Stand fast, stand fast, my good gray hounds,
    And we will gar them dee!'

XXII

Johnnie has set his back to an aik,
    His foot against a stane,
And he has slain the Seven Foresters,
    He has slain them a' but ane.

---

well-wight] sturdy, here brave.   bree] brow.   belive]
nimbly, at once.

JOHNNIE OF COCKERSLEE

XXIII

He has broke three ribs in that ane's side,
    But and his collar bane ;
He 's flung him twa-fald owre his steed,
    Bade him carry the tidings hame . . .

XXIV

' Is there no a bird in a' this forest
    Will do as mickle for me
As dip its wing in the wan water
    And straik it on my e'e-bree ?

XXV

' Is there no a bird in a' this forest
    Can sing as I can say,—
Can flee away to my mother's bower
    And tell to fetch Johnnie away ? '

XXVI

The starling flew to her window-stane,
    It whistled and it sang ;
And aye the owre-word o' the tune
    Was, *Johnnie tarries lang !*

XXVII

They made a rod o' the hazel-bush,
    Another o' the slae-thorn tree,
And mony, mony were the men
    At the fetching our Johnnie.

XXVIII

Then out and spak' his auld mother,
    And fast her tears did fa' :
' Ye wadna be warn'd, my son Johnnie,
    Frae the hunting to bide awa' ! '

XXIX

Now Johnnie's gude bend-bow is broke,
  And his gude gray dogs are slain;
And his body lies dead in Durrisdeer,
  And his hunting it is done.

137.   *Kinmont Willie*

I

O HAVE ye na heard o' the fause Sakelde?
  O have ye na heard o' the keen Lord Scroope?
How they hae ta'en bauld Kinmont Willie,
  On Haribee to hang him up?

II

Had Willie had but twenty men,
  But twenty men as stout as he,
Fause Sakelde had never the Kinmont ta'en,
  Wi' eight score in his companie.

III

They band his legs beneath the steed,
  They tied his hands behind his back;
They guarded him, fivesome on each side,
  And they brought him ower the Liddel-rack.

IV

They led him thro' the Liddel-rack,
  And also thro' the Carlisle sands;
They brought him in to Carlisle castell,
  To be at my Lord Scroope's commands.

V

'My hands are tied, but my tongue is free,
  And whae will dare this deed avow?
Or answer by the Border law?
  Or answer to the bauld Buccleuch?'—

        Liddel-rack] a ford on the Liddel.

KINMONT WILLIE

VI

'Now haud thy tongue, thou rank reiver!
   There's never a Scot shall set thee free:
Before ye cross my castle yate,
   I trow ye shall take farewell o' me.'

VII

'Fear na ye that, my lord,' quo' Willie:
   'By the faith o' my body, Lord Scroope,' he said,
'I never yet lodged in a hostelrie
   But I paid my lawing before I gaed.'

VIII

Now word is gane to the bauld Keeper,
   In Branksome Ha', where that he lay,
That Lord Scroope has ta'en the Kinmont Willie,
   Between the hours of night and day.

IX

He has ta'en the table wi' his hand,
   He garr'd the red wine spring on hie—
'Now Christ's curse on my head,' he said,
   'But avengèd of Lord Scroope I'll be!

X

'O is my basnet a widow's curch?
   Or my lance a wand of the willow-tree?
Or my arm a ladye's lilye hand,
   That an English lord should lightly me!

XI

'And have they ta'en him, Kinmont Willie,
   Against the truce of Border tide?
And forgotten that the bauld Buccleuch
   Is Keeper here on the Scottish side?

lawing] reckoning.   curch] kerchief, coif.   lightly]
treat disrespectfully.

XII

' And have they e'en ta'en him, Kinmont Willie,
    Withouten either dread or fear ?
And forgotten that the bauld Buccleuch
    Can back a steed, or shake a spear ?

XIII

' O were there war between the lands,
    As well I wot that there is nane,
I would slight Carlisle castell high,
    Though it were builded of marble stane.

XIV

' I would set that castell in a low,
    And sloken it with English blood !
There 's never a man in Cumberland
    Should ken where Carlisle castell stood.

XV

' But since nae war 's between the lands,
    And there is peace, and peace should be ;
I'll neither harm English lad or lass,
    And yet the Kinmont freed shall be ! '

XVI

He has call'd him forty Marchmen bauld,
    I trow they were of his ain name,
Except Sir Gilbert Elliot, call'd
    The Laird of Stobs, I mean the same.

XVII

He has call'd him forty Marchmen bauld,
    Were kinsmen to the bauld Buccleuch ;
With spur on heel, and splent on spauld,
    And gleuves of green, and feathers blue.

low] flame.   splent] split, or overlapping armour.   spauld]
shoulder, épaule.

XVIII

There were five and five before them a',
   Wi' hunting-horns and bugles bright :
And five and five came wi' Buccleuch,
   Like Warden's men, array'd for fight.

XIX

And five and five, like a mason-gang,
   That carried the ladders lang and hie ;
And five and five, like broken men ;
   And so they reach'd the Woodhouselee.

XX

And as we cross'd the Bateable Land,
   When to the English side we held,
The first o' men that we met wi',
   Whae sould it be but fause Sakelde ?

XXI

' Where be ye gaun, ye hunters keen ? '
   Quo' fause Sakelde ; ' come tell to me ! '—
' We go to hunt an English stag,
   Has trespass'd on the Scots countrie.'

XXII

' Where be ye gaun, ye marshal men ? '
   Quo' fause Sakelde ; ' come tell me true ! '—
' We go to catch a rank reiver,
   Has broken faith wi' the bauld Buccleuch.'

XXIII

' Where be ye gaun, ye mason lads,
   Wi' a' your ladders, lang and hie ? '—
' We gang to herry a corbie's nest,
   That wons not far frae Woodhouselee.'—

Bateable Land] debateable land; a stretch of frontier between
the Solway Frith and Scots Dyke, claimed by both nations.

XXIV

'Where be ye gaun, ye broken men?'
  Quo' fause Sakelde; 'come tell to me!'—
Now Dickie of Dryhope led that band,
    And the never a word of lear had he.

XXV

'Why trespass ye on the English side?
  Row-footed outlaws, stand!' quo' he;
The never a word had Dickie to say,
    Sae he thrust the lance through his fause bodie.

XXVI

Then on we held for Carlisle toun,
  And at Staneshaw-bank the Eden we cross'd;
The water was great and meikle of spate,
    But the never a horse nor man we lost.

XXVII

And when we reach'd the Staneshaw-bank,
  The wind was rising loud and hie;
And there the Laird gar'd leave our steeds,
    For fear that they should stamp and neigh.

XXVIII

And when we left the Staneshaw-bank,
  The wind began fu' loud to blaw;
But 'twas wind and weet, and fire and sleet,
    When we came beneath the castle wa'.

XXIX

We crept on knees, and held our breath,
  Till we placed the ladders against the wa';
And sae ready was Buccleuch himsell
    To mount the first before us a'.

lear] lore.   row-footed] rough-footed.

XXX

He has ta'en the watchman by the throat,
  He flung him down upon the lead—
' Had there not been peace between our lands,
  Upon the other side thou hadst gaed!—

XXXI

' Now sound out, trumpets!' quo' Buccleuch;
  'Let's waken Lord Scroope right merrilie!'
Then loud the Warden's trumpet blew—
  O wha dare meddle wi' me?

XXXII

Then speedilie to wark we gaed,
  And raised the slogan ane and a',
And cut a hole through a sheet of lead,
  And so we wan to the castle ha'.

XXXIII

They thought King James and a' his men
  Had won the house wi' bow and spear;
It was but twenty Scots and ten,
  That put a thousand in sic a stear!

XXXIV

Wi' coulters, and wi' forehammers,
  We gar'd the bars bang merrilie,
Until we came to the inner prison,
  Where Willie o' Kinmont he did lie.

XXXV

And when we cam to the lower prison,
  Where Willie o' Kinmont he did lie—
' O sleep ye, wake ye, Kinmont Willie,
  Upon the morn that thou's to die?'—

stear] stir, commotion.   forehammers] sledge-hammers.

XXXVI

' O I sleep saft, and I wake aft ;
  It 's lang since sleeping was fley'd frae me !
Gie my service back to my wife and bairns,
  And a' gude fellows that spier for me.'

XXXVII

The Red Rowan has hente him up,
  The starkest man in Teviotdale—
' Abide, abide now, Red Rowan,
  Till of my Lord Scroope I take farewell.

XXXVIII

' Farewell, farewell, my gude Lord Scroope !
  My gude Lord Scroope, farewell ! ' he cried ;
' I'll pay you for my lodging mail,
  When first we meet on the Border side.'—

XXXIX

Then shoulder high, with shout and cry,
  We bore him down the ladder lang ;
At every stride Red Rowan made,
  I wot the Kinmont's airns play'd clang !

XL

' O mony a time,' quo' Kinmont Willie,
  ' I have ridden horse baith wild and wood ;
But a rougher beast than Red Rowan
  I ween my legs have ne'er bestrode.

XLI

' And mony a time,' quo' Kinmont Willie,
  ' I've prick'd a horse out oure the furs ;
But since the day I back'd a steed,
  I never wore sic cumbrous spurs !'

fley'd] scared.   spier] inquire.   mail] rent.   wood]
mad.   furs] furrows.

KINMONT WILLIE

We scarce had won the Staneshaw-bank
  When a' the Carlisle bells were rung,
And a thousand men on horse and foot
  Cam wi' the keen Lord Scroope along.

Buccleuch has turn'd to Eden Water,
  Even where it flow'd frae bank to brim,
And he has plunged in wi' a' his band,
  And safely swam them through the stream.

He turn'd him on the other side,
  And at Lord Scroope his glove flung he ;
' If ye like na my visit in merry England,
  In fair Scotland come visit me ! '

All sore astonish'd stood Lord Scroope,
  He stood as still as rock of stane ;
He scarcely dared to trew his eyes,
  When through the water they had gane.

' He is either himsell a devil frae hell,
  Or else his mother a witch maun be ;
I wadna have ridden that wan water
  For a' the gowd in Christentie.'

trew] trust.

I

NOW Liddesdale has ridden a raid,
     But I wat they had better hae staid at hame ;
For Michael o' Winfield he is dead,
     And Jock o' the Side is prisoner ta'en.

II

To Sybill o' the Side the tidings came ;
     By the waterside there as she ran
She took her kirtle by the hem
     And fast to Mangerton she 's gane.

III

Then up and spoke her Lord Mangerton—
     ' What news, what news, my sister to me ? '—
' Bad news, bad news ! My Michael is slain ;
     And they ha'e taken my son Johnie.'

IV

The lords they wrang their fingers white,
     Ladyes did pull themsells by the hair,
Crying ' Alas and well-a-day !
     For Jock o' the Side we'll never see mair ! '

V

—' Ne'er fear, sister Sybill,' quo' Mangerton ;
     ' I have yokes of ousen, eighty and three ;
My barns, my byres, and my faulds, a' weil fill'd,
     I'll part wi' them a' ere Johnie shall dee.

VI

' Three men I'll send to set him free,
     Well harness'd a' wi' the best o' steel ;
The English louns may hear, and drie
     The weight o' their braid-swords to feel.

720

JOCK O' THE SIDE

VII

'The Laird's Jock ane, the Laird's Wat twa,
  O Hobbie Noble, thou ane maun be!
Thy coat is blue, thou hast been true,
  Since England banish'd thee, to me.'

VIII

Now Hobbie was an English man,
  In Bewcastle dale was bred and born;
But his misdeeds they were sae great,
  They banish'd him ne'er to return.

IX

Lord Mangerton them orders gave,
  'Your horses the wrang way maun be shod,
Like gentlemen ye mauna seem,
  But look like corn-caugers ga'en the road.

X

'Your armour gude ye mauna shaw,
  Nor yet appear like men o' war;
As country lads be a' array'd,
  Wi' branks and brecham on each mare.'

XI

Their horses are the wrang way shod,
  And Hobbie has mounted his grey sae fine;
Wat on his auld horse, Jock on his bey,
  And on they rode for the water of Tyne.

XII

But when they came to Cholerton ford
  They lighted down by the light o' the moon,
And a tree they cut, wi' nogs on each side,
  To climb up the wa' of Newcastle toun.

corn-caugers] corn hucksters.   branks] wooden halter.
brecham] straw collar.

JOCK O' THE SIDE

XIII

But when they cam to Newcastle toun,
  And down were alighted at the wa',
They fand thair tree three ells ower laigh,
  They fand their stick baith short and sma'.

XIV

Then up spake the Laird's ain Jock:
  'There's naething for't; the gates we maun force.'—
But when they cam the gate until,
  The porter withstood baith men and horse.

XV

His neck in twa the Armstrangs wrang;
  Wi' fute or hand he ne'er play'd pa!
His life and his keys at anes they hae ta'en,
  And cast the body ahint the wa'.

XVI

Now sune they reach Newcastle jail,
  And to the prisoner thus they call:
'Sleeps thou, wakes thou, Jock o' the Side,
  Or art thou weary of thy thrall?'

XVII

Jock answers thus, wi' dolefu' tone:
  'Aft, aft I wake—I seldom sleep:
But whae's this kens my name sae weel,
  And thus to mese my waes does seek?'—

XVIII

Then out and spak the gude Laird's Jock,
  'Now fear ye na, my billie,' quo' he;
'For here are the Laird's Jock, the Laird's Wat,
  And Hobbie Noble to set thee free.'—

laigh] low.   pa] paw.   mese] soothe.   billie] comrade.

722

XIX

'Now haud thy tongue, my gude Laird's Jock,
    For ever, alas! this canna be;
For if a' Liddesdale were here the night,
    The morn's the day that I maun dee.

XX

'Full fifteen stane o' Spanish iron,
    They hae laid a' right sair on me;
Wi' locks and keys I am fast bound
    In this dungeon dark and dreirie.'

XXI

'Fear ye na that,' quo' the Laird's Jock;
    'A faint heart ne'er wan a fair ladie;
Work thou within, we'll work without,
    And I'll be sworn we'll set thee free.'

XXII

The first strong door that they cam at,
    They loosèd it without a key;
The next chain'd door that they cam at,
    They garr'd it a' to flinders flee.

XXIII

The prisoner now upon his back
    The Laird's Jock has gotten up fu' hie;
And, airns and a', down the tolbooth stair,
    Wi' nae sma' speed and joy brings he.

XXIV

'Now, Jock, my man,' quo' Hobbie Noble,
    'Some o' his weight ye may lay on me.'—
'I wat weel no!' quo' the Laird's ain Jock,
    'I count him lighter than a flee.'

tolbooth] gaol.

723

XXV

Sae out at the gates they a' are gane,
    The prisoner 's set on horseback hie ;
And now wi' speed they've ta'en the gate,
    While ilk ane jokes fu' wantonlie :

XXVI

' O Jock ! sae winsomely ye sit,
    Wi' baith your feet upon ae side ;
Sae weel ye're harneist, and sae trig,
    In troth ye sit like ony bride !'

XXVII

The night, tho' wat, they did na mind,
    But hied them on fu' merrilie,
Until they cam to Cholerton brae,
    Where the water ran like mountains hie.

XXVIII

But when they cam to Cholerton ford,
    There they met with an auld man ;
Says—' Honest man, will the water ride ?
    Tell us in haste, if that ye can.'—

XXIX

' I wat weel no,' quo' the gude auld man ;
    ' I hae lived here thretty years and three ;
Nor man nor horse can go ower Tyne,
    Except it were a horse of tree.'—

XXX

Then out and spoke the Laird's saft Wat,
    The greatest coward in the companie :
' Now halt, now halt ! we need na try't ;
    The day is come we a' maun die !'—

JOCK O' THE SIDE

XXXI

' Puir faint-hearted thief!' cried the Laird's ain Jock,
  ' There'll nae man die but him that 's fie ;
I'll guide ye a' right safely thro' ;
  Lift ye the pris'ner on ahint me.'

XXXII

Wi' that the water they hae ta'en,
  By ane's and twa's they a' swam thro' ;
' Here are we a' safe,' quo' the Laird's Jock,
  ' And, puir faint Wat, what think ye now?'

XXXIII

They scarce the other brae had won,
  When twenty men they saw pursue ;
Frae Newcastle toun they had been sent,
  A' English lads baith stout and true.

XXXIV

But when the Land-sergeant the water saw,
  ' It winna ride, my lads,' says he ;
Then cried aloud—' The prisoner take,
  But leave the fetters, I pray, to me !'

XXXV

' I wat weel no,' quo' the Laird's ain Jock,
  ' I'll keep them, shoon to my mare to be :
My gude bay mare—for I am sure,
  She has bought them a' right dear frae thee.'—

XXXVI

Sae now they are on to Liddesdale,
  E'en as fast as they could them hie ;
The prisoner is brought to his ain fireside,
  And there o' his airns they mak him free.

fie] fey, doomed.

XXXVII

'Now, Jock, my billie,' quo' a' the three,
  'The day is comed thou was to die;
But thou's as weel at thy ain ingle-side,
  Now sitting, I think, 'twixt thee and me.'

139.   *Hobbie Noble*

I

FOUL fa' the breast first treason bred in!
  That Liddesdale may safely say,
For in it there was baith meat and drink,
  And corn unto our geldings gay.

II

We were stout-hearted men and true,
  As England it did often say;
But now we may turn our backs and fly,
  Since brave Noble is seld away.

III

Now Hobbie he was an English man,
  And born into Bewcastle dale,
But his misdeeds they were sae great,
  They banish'd him to Liddesdale.

IV

At Kershope-foot the tryst was set,
  Kershope of the lily lee;
And there was traitour Sim o' the Mains,
  With him a private companie.

V

Then Hobbie has graith'd his body weel,
  I wat wi' baith good iron and steel;
And he has pull'd out his fringed grey,
  And there, brave Hobbie, he rade him weel.

seld] sold.   graith'd] clad in **armour.**   fringed] long-
haired at fetlocks.
726

VI

Then Hobbie is down the water gane,
    Even as fast as he may drie ;
Tho' they shou'd a' brusten and broken their hearts,
    Frae that riding-tryst he would not be.

VII

' Weel may ye be, my feiries five !
    And aye, what is your wills wi' me ? '
Then they cryd a' wi' ae consent :
    ' Thou'rt welcome here, brave Noble, to me.

VIII

' Wilt thou with us into England ride ?
    And thy safe-warrand we will be,
If we get a horse worth a hundred punds,
    Upon his back that thou shalt be.'—

IX

' I dare not with you into England ride,
    The Land-sergeant has me at feid ;
I know not what evil may betide
    For Peter of Whitfield his brother is dead.

X

' And Antony Shiel he loves not me,
    For I gat twa drifts of his sheep ;
The great Earl of Whitfield loves me not,
    For nae gear frae me he e'er could keep.

XI

' But will ye stay till the day gae down,
    Until the night come owre the grund,
And I'll be a guide worth ony twa
    That may in Liddesdale be found.

       feiries] feres, comrades.   feid] feud.

XII

'Tho' dark the night as pick and tar,
  I'll guide ye owre yon hills sae hie,
And bring ye a' in safety back,
  If you will be true and follow me.'

XIII

He has guided them owre moss and muir,
  O'er hill and houp, and mony a down,
Til they came to the Foulbogshiel,
  And there brave Noble he lighted down.

XIV

Then word is gane to the Land-sergeant,
  In Askerton where that he lay:
'The deer that ye hae hunted sae lang
  Is seen into the Waste this day.'—

XV

'Then Hobbie Noble is that deer;
  I wat he carries the style fu' hie!
Aft has he beat your slough-hounds back,
  And set yourselves at little eie.

XVI

'Gar warn the bows of Hartlie-burn,
  See they sharp their arrows on the wa!
Warn Willeva and Spear Edom,
  And see the morn they meet me a'.

XVII

'Gar meet me on the Rodric-haugh,
  And see it be by break o' day;
And we will on to Conscouthart Green,
  For there, I think, we'll get our prey.'

pick] pitch.   houp] 'hope,' a hollow between two hills.
slough-hounds] sleuth-hounds.   eie] awe.

HOBBIE NOBLE

XVIII

Then Hobbie Noble has dreamit a dream,
  In the Foulbogshiel where that he lay;
He thought his horse was aneath him shot,
  And he himself got hard away.

XIX

The cocks could craw, and the day could daw',
  And I wat sae even down fell the rain;
Had Hobbie na waken'd at that time,
  In the Foulbogshiel he'd been ta'en or slain.

XX

' Get up, get up, my feiries five,
  For I wat here makes a fu' ill day;
And the warst clock of this companie
  I hope shall cross the Waste this day.

XXI

Now Hobbie thought the gates were clear,
  But, ever alas! it was not sae;
They were beset wi' cruel men and keen,
  That away brave Noble could not gae.

XXII

' Yet follow me, my feiries five,
  And see of me ye keep good array;
And the worst clock of this companie
  I hope shall cross the Waste this day.'

XXIII

There was heaps of men now Hobbie before,
  And other heaps was him behin',
That had he been wight as Wallace was
  Away brave Noble he could not win.

clock] lame one, hobbler.

XXIV

Then Hobbie he had but a laddie's sword,
But he did more than a laddie's deed;
Till in the midst of Conscouthart Green,
He brake it o'er Jers-a-Wigham's head.

XXV

Now they have ta'en brave Hobbie Noble,
Wi' his ain bowstring they band him sae;
And I wat his heart was neer sae sair
As when his ain five band him on the brae.

XXVI

They have ta'en him on for West Carlisle;
They ask'd him if he kenn'd the way;
Whate'er he thought, yet little he said;
He knew that gate as well as they.

XXVII

They hae ta'en him up the Ricker-gate;
The wives they cast their windows wide,
And ilka wife to anither can say,
'That's the man loos'd Jock o' the Side!'—

XXVIII

'Fy on ye, women! why ca' ye me man?
For it's nae man that I'm used like;
I'm but like a forfoughen hound,
Has been fighting in a dirty syke.'

XXIX

Then they hae ta'en him up thro' Carlisle town,
And set him by the chimney-fire;
They gave brave Noble a wheat loaf to eat,
And that was little his desire.

forfoughen] out-wearied.   syke] ditch.

HOBBIE NOBLE

XXX

They gave him a wheaten loaf to eat
  And after that a can of beer ;
Then they cried a', wi' ae consent,
    ' Eat, brave Noble, and make good cheer !

XXXI

' Confess my lord's horse, Hobbie,' they say,
  ' And the morn in Carlisle thou'se no dee.'—
' How shall I confess them ? ' Hobbie says,
    ' For I never saw them with mine e'e.'

XXXII

Then Hobbie has sworn a fu' great aith,
  By the day that he was gotten or born,
He never had onything o' my lord's
    That either ate him grass or corn.

XXXIII

' Now fare thee weel, sweet Mangerton !
  For I think again I'll ne'er thee see ;
I wad betray nae lad alive,
    For a' the gowd in Christentie.

XXXIV

' And fare thee well now, Liddesdale,
  Baith the hie land and the law !
Keep ye weel frae traitor Mains !
    For gowd and gear he'll sell ye a'.

XXXV

' I'd rather be ca'd Hobbie Noble,
  In Carlisle, where he suffers for his faut,
Before I were ca'd the traitor Mains,
    That eats and drinks o' the meal and maut.'

Archie of Cawfield

I

AS I was a-walking mine alane,
  It was by the dawning of the day,
I heard twa brithers make their mane,
  And I listen'd weel what they did say.

II

The youngest to the eldest said :
  'Blythe and merrie how can we be?
There were three brithren of us born,
  And ane of us is condemn'd to die.'—

III

'An ye wad be merrie, an ye wad be sad,
  What the better wad billy Archie be?
Unless I had thirty men to mysell,
  And a' to ride in my companie.

IV

'Ten to hald the horses' heads,
  And other ten the watch to be,
And ten to break up the strong prison
  Where billy Archie he does lie.

V

'Had I but thirty well-wight men,
  Thirty o' the best in Christiantie,
I wad go on to fair Dumfries,
  I wad loose my brother and set him free.'

VI

Then up and spak him mettled John Ha'
  (For leugh o' Liddesdale crackit he) :
'An I had eleven men to mysell,
  It 's aye the twalt man I wad be.'—

billy] brother, comrade.   well-wight] stout, sturdy.   For
leugh, etc.] He boasted to be of lower Liddesdale. εὔχετο εἶναι.
732

VII

Then up bespak him coarse Ca'field,
  (I wot and little gude worth was he):
'Thirty men is few anew,
  And a' to ride in our companie.'

VIII

There was horsing, horsing in haste,
  And cracking of whips out owre the lee;
Until they cam to the Murraywhat,
  And they lighted there right speedilie.

IX

'A smith! a smith!' Dickie he cries,
  'A smith, a smith, right speedilie,
To turn back the caukers of our horses' shoon!
  For it 's unkensome we wad be.

X

'There lives a smith on the water-side,
  Will shoe my little black mare for me;
And I've a crown in my pockét,
  And every groat of it I wad gie.'—

XI

'The night is mirk, and it 's very mirk,
  And by candle-light I canna weel see;
The night is mirk, and it 's very pit mirk,
  And there will never a nail ca' right for me.'—

XII

'Shame fa' you and your trade baith,
  Canna beet a good fellow by your mystery;
But leeze me on thee, my little black mare,
  Thou 's worth thy weight in gold to me.'

caukers] calkins.   unkensome] unknown.   beet] abet, aid.
mystery] craft.   leeze me on] commend me to.

XIII

There was horsing, horsing in haste,
   And cracking of whips out owre the lee,
Until they came to the Bonshaw wood,
   Where they held their council privately.

XIV

Some says, 'We'll gang the Annan road;
   It is the better road,' said they;
But up bespake then Dicky Ha',
   The wisest of that company:

XV·

Says, 'Annan road's a public road,
   It's no the road that makes for me;
But we will through at the Hoddam ford,
   It is the better road,' quo' he.

XVI

There was horsing, horsing in haste,
   And crackin' of whips out owre the lee;
Until they cam to Dumfries port,
   And they lighted there right speedilie.

XVII

'There's five of us will hold the horse,
   And other five will watchmen be:
But wha's the man among ye a',
   Will gae to the tolbooth door wi' me?'—

XVIII

O up then spak him mettled John Ha',
   (For leugh o' Liddesdale crackit he):
'If it should cost my life this very night,
   I'll gae to the tolbooth door wi' thee.'—

port] gate.   tolbooth] gaol.

ARCHIE OF CAWFIELD

XIX

'Be of gude cheir, now, Archie, lad !
  Be of gude cheir, now, dear billie !
Work thou within, and we without,
  And the morn thou'se dine at Ca'field wi' me !'

XX

O Jockie Ha' stepp'd to the door,
  And he bended low back on his knee,
And he made the bolts that the door hang on,
  Loup frae the wa' right wantonlie.

XXI

He took the prisoner on his back,
  And down the tolbooth stair cam he ;
The black mare stood ready at the door,
  I wot a foot ne'er stirrèd she.

XXII

They laid the links out owre her neck,
  And that was her gold twist to be ;
And they cam doun thro' Dumfries toun,
  And wow but they cam speedilie.

XXIII

The live-lang night these twelve men rade,
  And aye till they were right wearie,
Until they cam to the Murraywhat,
  And they lighted there right speedilie.

XXIV

' A smith ! a smith ! ' then Dickie he cries,
  ' A smith, a smith, right speedilie,
To file the irons frae my dear brither !
  For forward, forward we wad be.'—

735

XXV

They hadna filed a shackle of iron,
    A shackle of iron but barely three,
When out and spak young Simon brave :
    ' O dinna you see what I do see ?

XXVI

' Lo ! yonder comes Lieutenant Gordon,
    Wi' a hundred men in his companie ;
This night will be our lyke-wake night,
    The morn the day we a' maun die.'—

XXVII

O there was mounting, mounting in haste,
    And cracking of whips out owre the lee ;
Until they cam to Annan water,
    And it was flowing like the sea.

XXVIII

' My mare is young and very skeigh,
    And in o' the weil she will drown me ! '—
' But ye'll take mine, and I'll take thine,
    And sune through the water we sall be.'

XXIX

Then up and spak him coarse Ca'field
    (I wot and little gude worth was he),
' We had better lose ane than lose a' the lave ;
    We'll lose the prisoner, we'll gae free.'—

XXX

' Shame fa' you and your lands baith !
    Wad ye e'en your lands to your born billy ?
But hey ! bear up, my bonnie black mare,
    And yet thro' the water we sall be.'—

skeigh] shy.   weil] eddy.   lave] rest.   e'en] even, count as equal.

XXXI

Now they did swim that wan water,
    And wow but they swam bonnilie !
Until they cam to the other side,
    And they wrang their cloathes right drunkily.

XXXII

'Come thro', come thro', Lieutenant Gordon !
    Come thro' and drink some wine wi' me !
For there is an ale-house here hard by,
    And it shall not cost thee ae penny.'—

XXXIII

'Throw me my irons,' quo' Lieutenant Gordon ;
    'I wot they cost me dear eneugh.'—
'The shame a ma,' quo' mettled John Ha',
    'They'll be gude shackles to my pleugh.'—

XXXIV

'Come thro', come thro', Lieutenant Gordon !
    Come thro' and drink some wine wi' me !
Yestreen I was your prisoner,
    But now this morning am I free.'

shame a ma] devil a bit.

I

IT fell about the Martinmas tyde,
   When our Border steeds get corn and hay,
The Captain of Bewcastle bound him to ryde,
   And he's ower to Tividale to drive a prey.

II

The first ae guide that they met wi',
   It was high up in Hardhaughswire;
The second guide that they met wi',
   It was laigh down in Borthwick water.

III

'What tidings, what tidings, my trusty guide?'—
   'Nae tidings, nae tidings, I hae to thee;
But gin ye'll gae to the fair Dodhead,
   Mony a cow's cauf I'll let thee see.'

IV

And when they cam to the fair Dodhead,
   Right hastily they clam the peel;
They loosed the kye out, ane and a',
   And ranshackled the house right weel.

V

Now Jamie Telfer's heart was sair,
   The tear aye rowing in his ee;
He pled wi' the Captain to hae his gear,
   Or else revengèd he wad be.

VI

The Captain turned him round and leugh;
   Said—'Man, there's naething in thy house,
But ae auld sword without a sheath,
   That hardly now would fell a mouse.'

laigh] low.   peel] stronghold, keep.   rowing] rolling.

VII

The sun wasna up, but the moon was down,
    It was the gryming of a new-fa'n snaw,
Jamie Telfer has run ten myles a-foot,
    Between the Dodhead and the Stobs's Ha'.

VIII

And when he cam to the fair tower-yate,
    He shouted loud, and cried weel hie,
Till out bespak auld Gibby Elliot—
    'Whae's this that brings the fraye to me?'—

IX

' It's I, Jamie Telfer in the fair Dodhead,
    And a harried man I think I be!
There's naething left at the fair Dodhead,
    But a waefu' wife and bairnies three.'

X

' Gae seek your succour at Branksome Ha',
    For succour ye'se get nane frae me!
Gae seek your succour where ye paid black-mail,
    For, man, ye ne'er paid money to me.'—

XI

Jamie has turned him round about,
    I wat the tear blinded his ee—
' I'll ne'er pay mail to Elliot again,
    And the fair Dodhead I'll never see.

XII

' My hounds may a' rin masterless,
    My hawks may fly frae tree to tree,
My lord may grip my vassal lands,
    For there again maun I never be!'—

gryming] sprinkling.   fraye] fright, alarm.

XIII

He has turn'd him to the Tiviot-side,
 E'en as fast as he could drie,
Till he cam to the Coultart Cleugh,
 And there he shouted baith loud and hie.

XIV

Then up bespak him auld Jock Grieve,
 ' Whae 's this that brings the fraye to me ? '—
' It 's I, Jamie Telfer in the fair Dodhead,
 A harried man I trow I be.

XV

' There 's naething left in the fair Dodhead,
 But a greeting wife and bairnies three,
And sax poor ca's stand in the sta',
 A' routing loud for their minnie.'—

XVI

' Alack a wae ! ' quo' auld Jock Grieve,
 ' Alack ! my heart is sair for thee !
For I was married on the elder sister,
 And you on the youngest of a' the three.'

XVII

Then he has ta'en out a bonny black,
 Was right weel fed with corn and hay,
And he 's set Jamie Telfer on his back,
 To the Catslockhill to tak the fraye.

XVIII

And whan he cam to the Catslockhill,
 He shouted loud, and cried weel hie,
Till out and spak him William's Wat,
 ' O whae 's this brings the fraye to me ? '—

ca's] calves.   minnie] mother.

740

JAMIE TELFER IN THE FAIR DODHEAD

XIX

' It 's I, Jamie Telfer in the fair Dodhead,
    A harried man I think I be !
The Captain of Bewcastle has driven my gear ;
    For God's sake rise, and succour me ! '—

XX

' Alas for wae ! ' quoth William's Wat,
    ' Alack, for thee my heart is sair !
I never cam by the fair Dodhead,
    That ever I fand thy basket bare.'

XXI

He 's set his twa sons on coal-black steeds,
    Himsell upon a freckled gray,
And they are on wi' Jamie Telfer,
    To Branksome Ha' to tak the fraye.

XXII

And when they cam to Branksome Ha',
    They shouted a' baith loud and hie,
Till up and spak him auld Buccleuch,
    Said, ' Whae 's this brings the fraye to me ?'—

XXIII

' It 's I, Jamie Telfer in the fair Dodhead,
    And a harried man I think I be !
There 's nought left in the fair Dodhead,
    But a greeting wife and bairnies three.'—

XXIV

' Alack for wae ! ' quoth the gude auld lord,
    ' And ever my heart is wae for thee !
But fye gar cry on Willie, my son,
    And see that he come to me speedilie !

XXV

' Gar warn the water, braid and wide,
    Gar warn it sune and hastilie !
They that winna ride for Telfer's kye,
    Let them never look in the face o' me !

XXVI

' Warn Wat o' Harden, and his sons,
    Wi' them will Borthwick Water ride ;
Warn Gaudilands, and Allanhaugh,
    And Gilmanscleugh, and Commonside.

XXVII

' Ride by the gate at Priesthaughswire,
    And warn the Currors o' the Lee ;
As ye cum down the Hermitage Slack,
    Warn doughty Willie o' Gorrinberry.'

XXVIII

The Scotts they rade, the Scotts they ran,
    Sae starkly and sae steadilie !
And aye the ower-word o' the thrang
    Was—' Rise for Branksome readilie ! '

XXIX

The gear was driven the Frostylee up,
    Frae the Frostylee unto the plain,
Whan Willie has look'd his men before,
    And saw the kye right fast drivand.

XXX

' Whae drives thir kye ? ' ' 'gan Willie say,
    ' To make an outspeckle o' me ? '—
' It 's I, the Captain o' Bewcastle, Willie;
    I winna layne my name for thee.'—

warn the water] raise the cry along the waterside.   outspeckle]
laughing-stock.   layne] lie, falsen.

XXXI

' O will ye let Telfer's kye gae back ?
Or will ye do aught for regard o' me ?
Or, by the faith of my body,' quo' Willie Scott,
' I'se ware my dame's cauf skin on thee ! '—

XXXII

' I winna let the kye gae back,
Neither for thy love, nor yet thy fear ;
But I will drive Jamie Telfer's kye,
In spite of every Scott that's here.'—

XXXIII

' Set on them, lads ! ' quo' Willie than ;
' Fye, lads, set on them cruellie !
For ere they win to the Ritterford,
Mony a toom saddle there sall be ! '

XXXIV

Then till 't they gaed wi' heart and hand,
The blows fell thick as bickering hail ;
And mony a horse ran masterless,
And mony a comely cheek was pale.

XXXV

But Willie was stricken ower the head,
And thro' the knapscap the sword has gane ;
And Harden grat for very rage,
Whan Willie on the grund lay slane.

XXXVI

But he 's ta'en aff his gude steel cap,
And thrice he 's waved it in the air—
The Dinlay snaw was ne'er mair white
Nor the lyart locks of Harden's hair.

ware, &c.] spend, use my mother's calf-skin whip.　　toom]
empty.　　till 't] to it.　　knapscap] headpiece.　　grat] wept.
lyart] grizzled.

XXXVII

'Revenge! revenge!' auld Wat 'gan cry;
    'Fye, lads, lay on them cruellie!
We'll ne'er see Tiviot-side again,
    Or Willie's death revenged sall be.'

XXXVIII

O mony a horse ran masterless,
    The splinter'd lances flew on hie;
But or they wan to the Kershope ford,
    The Scotts had gotten the victory.

XXXIX

John o' Brigham there was slane,
    And John o' Barlow, as I heard say;
And thirty mae o' the Captain's men
    Lay bleeding on the grund that day.

XL

The Captain was run through the thick of the thigh,
    And broken was his right leg-bane;
If he had lived this hundred years,
    He had never been loved by woman again.

XLI

'Hae back the kye!' the Captain said;
    'Dear kye, I trow, to some they be!
For gin I suld live a hundred years,
    There will ne'er fair lady smile on me.'

XLII

Then word is gane to the Captain's bride,
    Even in the bower where that she lay,
That her lord was prisoner in enemy's land,
    Since into Tividale he had led the way.

744

XLIII

' I wad lourd have had a winding-sheet,
    And helped to put it ower his head,
Ere he had been disgraced by the Border Scot,
    Whan he ower Liddel his men did lead ! '

XLIV

There was a wild gallant amang us a',
    His name was Watty wi' the Wudspurs,
Cried—' On for his house in Stanegirthside,
    If ony man will ride with us ! '

XLV

When they cam to the Stanegirthside,
    They dang wi' trees, and burst the door ;
They loosed out a' the Captain's kye,
    And set them forth our lads before.

XLVI

There was an auld wyfe ayont the fire,
    A wee bit o' the Captain's kin—
' Whae dar loose out the Captain's kye
    Or answer to him and his men ? '—

XLVII

' It 's I, Watty Wudspurs, loose the kye,
    I winna layne my name frae thee !
And I will loose out the Captain's kye,
    In scorn of a' his men and he.'

XLVIII

Whan they cam to the fair Dodhead,
    They were a wellcum sight to see !
For instead of his ain ten milk kye,
    Jamie Telfer has gotten thirty and three.

lourd] liefer, rather.   wudspurs] hotspur, or madspur.

XLIX

And he has paid the rescue shot,
    Baith wi' gowd and white monie ;
And at the burial o' Willie Scott,
    I wat was mony a weeping e'e.

142.   *Dick o' the Cow*

I

NOW Liddesdale has lain lang in,
    There is na ryding there at a' ;
The horses are a' grown sae lither fat,
    They downa stir out o' the sta'.

II

Fair Johnie Armstrong to Willie did say—
    ' Billie, a-ryding then will we ;
England and us have been lang at feid ;
    Aiblins we'll light on some bootie.'—

III

Then they're come on to Hutton Ha' ;
    They rade that proper place about.
But the laird he was the wiser man,
    For he had left nae gear without :

IV

For he had left nae gear to steal,
    Except sax sheep upon a lea :
Quo' Johnie—' I'd rather in England die,
    Ere thir sax sheep gae to Liddesdale wi' me.

ryding] raiding.   lither] *here an adverb,* vilely.   aiblins]
perchance.

DICK O' THE COW

V

' But how ca' they the man we last met,
    Billie, as we cam owre the know ? '—
' That same he is an innocent fule,
    And men they call him Dick o' the Cow.'

VI

' That fule has three as good kye o' his ain,
    As there are in a' Cumberland, billie,' quo' he.
' Betide me life, betide me death,
    These kye shall go to Liddesdale wi' me.'

VII

Then they're come on to the pure fule's house,
    And they hae broken his wa's sae wide;
They have loosed out Dick o' the Cow 's three kye,
    And ta'en three co'erlets off his wife's bed.

VIII

Then on the morn when the day grew light,
    The shouts and cries raise loud and hie :
' O haud thy tongue, my wife,' he says,
    ' And o' thy crying let me be !

IX

' O haud thy tongue, my wife,' he says,
    ' And o' thy crying let me be ;
And aye where thou hast lost ae cow,
    In gude sooth I shall bring thee three.'

X

Now Dickie 's gane to the gude Lord Scroope,
    And I wat a dreirie fule was he ;
' Now haud thy tongue, my fule,' he says,
    ' For I may not stand to jest wi' thee.'

know] knop of the hill.

DICK O' THE COW

XI

' Shame fa' your jesting, my lord ! ' quo' Dickie,
  ' For nae sic jesting grees wi' me ;
Liddesdale 's been in my house last night,
  And they hae awa' my three kye frae me.

XII

' But I may nae langer in Cumberland dwell,
  To be your puir fule and your leal,
Unless you gie me leave, my lord,
  To gae to Liddesdale and steal.'—

XIII

' I gie thee leave, my fule ! ' he says ;
  ' Thou speakest against my honour and me,
Unless thou gie me thy troth and thy hand,
  Thou'lt steal frae nane but wha sta' frae thee.'—

XIV

' There is my troth, and my right hand !
  My head shall hang on Hairibee ;
I'll never cross Carlisle sands again,
  If I steal frae a man but wha sta' frae me.'

XV

Dickie 's ta'en leave o' lord and master ;
  I wat a merry fule was he !
He 's bought a bridle and a pair o' new spurs,
  And packed them up in his breek thie.

XVI

Then Dickie 's come on to Puddingburn house,
  Even as fast as he might dree :
Then Dickie 's come on to Puddingburn,
  Where there were thirty Armstrangs and three.

Hairibee] the place of execution at Carlisle.   breek thie]
thigh-pocket of his breeches.   dree] last, endure.

748

DICK O' THE COW

XVII

' O what's this come o' me now?' quo' Dickie;
  'What mickle wae is this?' quo' he;
' For here is but ae innocent fule,
  And there are thirty Armstrangs and three!'

XVIII

Yet he has come up to the fair ha' board,
  Sae well he became his courtesie!
' Well may ye be, my gude Laird's Jock!
  But the dèil bless a' your companie.

XIX

' I'm come to plain o' your man, Johnie Armstrang,
  And syne o' his billie Willie,' quo' he;
' How they hae been in my house last night,
  And they hae ta'en my three kye frae me.'—

XX

' Ha!' quo' Johnie Armstrang, ' we will him hang.'
  —' Na,' quo' Willie, ' we'll him slae.'—
Then up and spak another young Armstrang,
  ' We'll gie him his batts, and let him gae.'

XXI

But up and spak the gude Laird's Jock,
  The best in a' the companie,
' Sit down thy ways a little while, Dickie,
  And a piece o' thy ain cow's hough I'll gie ye.'

XXII

But Dickie's heart it grew sae grit,
  That the ne'er a bit o't he dought to eat—
Then he was aware of an auld peat-house,
  Where a' the night he thought for to sleep.

plain] complain.   batts] beating.   grit] great, i.e.
his heart swelled so.   dought to] could.

XXIII

Then Dickie was ware of an auld peat-house,
 Where a' the night he thought for to lye—
And a' the prayers the puir fule pray'd,
 Were, 'I wish I had mends for my gude three kye!'

XXIV

It was then the use of Puddingburn house,
 And the house of Mangerton, all hail,
Them that cam na at the first ca',
 Gat nae mair meat till the neist meal.

XXV

The lads, that hungry and weary were,
 Abune the door-head they threw the key;
Dickie he took gude notice o' that,
 Says—'There will be a bootie for me.'

XXVI

Then Dickie has into the stable gane,
 Where there stood thirty horses and three;
He has tied them a' wi' St. Mary's knot,
 A' these horses but barely three.

XXVII

He has tied them a' wi' St. Mary's knot,
 A' these horses but barely three;
He 's loupen on ane, ta'en another in hand,
 And out at the door is gane Dickie.

XXVIII

But on the morn, when the day grew light,
 The shouts and cries raise loud and hie.
'Ah! wha has done this?' quo' the gude Laird's Jock,
 'Tell me the truth and the verity!

mends] amends.   tied wi' St. Mary's knot] hamstrung.

DICK O' THE COW

XXIX

'Wha has done this deed?' quo' the gude Laird's Jock;
  'See that to me ye dinna lee!'—
'Dickie has been in the stable last night,
  And my brother's horse and mine's frae me.'—

XXX

'Ye wad ne'er be tauld,' quo' the gude Laird's Jock;
  'Have ye not found my tales fu' leil?
Ye never wad out o' England bide,
  Till crooked and blind and a' would steal.'—

XXXI

'But lend me thy bay,' fair Johnie can say;
  'There's nae horse loose in the stable save he;
And I'll either fetch Dick o' the Cow again,
  Or the day is come that he shall dee.'—

XXXII

'To lend thee my bay!' the Laird's Jock 'gan say;
  'He's baith worth gowd and gude monie:
Dick o' the Cow has awa' twa horse:
  I wish na thou may make him three.'

XXXIII

He has ta'en the laird's jack on his back,
  A twa-handed sword to hang by his thie;
He has ta'en a steel cap on his head,
  And on he is to follow Dickie.

XXXIV

Dickie was na a mile aff the town,
  I wat a mile but barely three,
When he was o'erta'en by Johnie Armstrong,
  Hand for hand, on Cannobie lee.

jack] short coat-of-mail.

XXXV

' Abide, abide, thou traitour thiefe !
  The day is come that thou maun dee ! '
Then Dickie look't ower his left shoulder,
  —' Johnie, hast thou nae mae in thy companie ?

XXXVI

' There is a preacher in our chapell,
  And a' the lee-lang day teaches he :
When day is gane and night is come,
  There 's ne'er a word I mark but three.

XXXVII

' The first and second is—*Faith* and *Conscience ;*
  The third—*Johnie, take heed o' thee !*
But, Johnie, what faith and conscience was thine,
  When thou took awa' my three kye frae me ?

XXXVIII

' And when thou had ta'en awa' my three kye,
  Thou thought in thy heart thou wast no well sped,
Till thou sent thy billie owre the know,
  To tak three co'erlets off my wife's bed ! '—

XXXIX

Then Johnie let a spear fa' laigh by his thie,
  Thought weel to hae run the innocent through,
But the powers above were mair than he,
  For he ran but the pure fule's jerkin through.

XL

Together they ran, or ever they blan ;
  This was Dickie the fule and he !
Dickie couldna win at him wi' the blade o' the sword,
  But fell'd him wi' the plummet under the ee.

laigh] low.   blan] checked, stopped.   plummet]
pommel.

752

XLI

Thus Dickie has fell'd fair Johnie Armstrong,
  The prettiest man in the south country :
' Gramercy ! ' then 'gan Dickie say,
  ' I had but twa horse, thou hast made me three ! '

XLII

He 's ta'en the laird's jack aff Johnie's back,
  The twa-handed sword that hung low by his thie ;
He 's ta'en the steel cap aff his head—
  ' Johnie, I'll tell that I met wi' thee.'

XLIII

When Johnie waken'd out o' his dream,
  I wat a dreirie man was he :
' And is thou gane ? Now, Dickie, than
  The shame and dule is left wi' me.

XLIV

' And is thou gane ? Now, Dickie, than
  The deil gae in thy companie !
For if I should live these hundred years,
  I ne'er shall fight wi' a fule after thee.'

XLV

Then Dickie 's come hame to the gude Lord Scroope,
  E'en as fast as he might hie ;
' Now, Dickie, I'll neither eat nor drink,
  Till hie hangèd that thou shalt be.'—

XLVI

' The shame speed the liars, my lord ! ' quo' Dickie ;
  ' This was na the promise ye made to me !
For I'd ne'er gang to Liddesdale to steal,
  Had I not got my leave frae thee.'—

753

DICK O' THE COW

XLVII

'But what gar'd thee steal the Laird's Jock's horse?
    And, limmer, what gar'd ye steal him?' quo' he;
'For lang thou mightst in Cumberland dwelt
    Or the Laird's Jock had stown aught frae thee.'—

XLVIII

'Indeed I wat ye lied, my lord!
    And e'en sae loud as I hear ye lie!
I wan the horse frae fair Johnie Armstrang,
    Hand to hand, on Cannobie lee.

XLIX

'There is the jack was on his back;
    This twa-handed sword hung laigh by his thie;
And there's the steel cap was on his head;
    I brought a' these tokens to let thee see.'—

L

'If that be true thou to me tells
    (And I think thou dares na tell me a lee),
I'll gie thee fifteen punds for the horse,
    Well tauld on thy cloak lap they shall be.

LI

'I'll gie thee ane o' my best milk kye,
    To maintain thy wife and children three;
And that may be as gude, I think,
    As ony twa o' thine wad be.'—

LII

'The shame speed the liars, my lord!' quo' Dickie;
    'Trow ye aye to make a fule o' me?
I'll either hae twenty punds for the gude horse,
    Or he's gae to Mortan Fair wi' me.'

LIII

He 's gi'en him twenty punds for the gude horse,
    A' in the goud and gude monie ;
He 's gi'en him ane o' his best milk kye,
    To maintain his wife and children three.

LIV

Then Dickie 's come down thro' Carlisle toun,
    E'en as fast as he could drie :
The first o' men that he met wi'
    Was my Lord's brother, Bailiff Glozenburrie.

LV

' Weil be ye met, my gude Ralph Scroope ! '—
    ' Welcome, my brother's fule ! ' quo' he ;
' Where didst thou get Johnie Armstrang's horse ? '—
    ' Where did I get him, but steal him,' quo' he.

LVI

' But wilt thou sell me the bonny horse ?
    And, billie, wilt thou sell him to me ? ' quo' he.—
' Ay ; if thou'lt tell me the monie on my cloak lap :
    For there 's never ae penny I'll trust thee.'—

LVII

' I'll gie thee ten punds for the gude horse,
    Weil tauld on thy cloak lap they shall be ;
And I'll gie thee ane o' the best milk kye,
    To maintain thy wife and children three.'—

LVIII

' The shame speed the liars, my lord ! ' quo' Dickie ;
    ' Trow ye aye to make a fule o' me !
I'll either hae twenty punds for the gude horse,
    Or he 's gae to Mortan Fair wi' me.'—

755

DICK O' THE COW

LIX

He 's gi'en him twenty punds for the gude horse,
    Baith in goud and gude monie;
He 's gi'en him ane o' his milk kye,
    To maintain his wife and children three.

LX

Then Dickie lap a loup fu' hie,
    And I wat a loud laugh laughèd he:
'I wish the neck o' the third horse was broken,
    If ony of the twa were better than he!'

LXI

Then Dickie 's come hame to his wife again;
    Judge ye how the puir fule had sped!
He has gi'en her twa score English punds,
    For the three auld co'erlets ta'en aff her bed.

LXII

' And tak thee these twa as gude kye,
    I trow, as a' thy three might be;
And yet here is a white-footed nag,
    I trow he'll carry baith thee and me.

LXIII

' But I may nae langer in Cumberland bide;
    The Armstrangs they would hang me hie.'—
So Dickie 's ta'en leave at lord and master,
    And at Burgh under Stanmuir dwells Dickie.

lap a loup] leapt a leap.

Hughie the Graeme

I

GUDE Lord Scroope's to the hunting gane,
He has ridden o'er moss and muir;
And he has grippit Hughie the Graeme,
   For stealing o' the Bishop's mare.

II

'Now, good Lord Scroope, this may not be!
   Here hangs a broadsword by my side;
And if that thou canst conquer me,
   The matter it may soon be tryed.'—

III

'I ne'er was afraid of a traitor thief;
   Although thy name be Hughie the Graeme,
I'll make thee repent thee of thy deeds,
   If God but grant me life and time.'—

IV

'Then do your worst now, good Lord Scroope,
   And deal your blows as hard as you can!
It shall be tried within an hour,
   Which of us two is the better man.'—

V

But as they were dealing their blows so free,
   And both so bloody at the time,
Over the moss came ten yeomen so tall,
   All for to take brave Hughie the Graeme.

VI

Then they hae grippit Hughie the Graeme,
   And brought him up through Carlisle town:
The lasses and lads stood on the walls,
   Crying, 'Hughie the Graeme, thou'se ne'er gae down!'

VII

Then they hae chosen a jury of men,
    The best that were in Carlisle town ;
And twelve of them cried out at once,
    ' Hughie the Graeme, thou must gae down ! '

VIII

Then up bespak him gude Lord Hume,
    As he sat by the judge's knee ;
' Twenty white owsen, my gude lord,
    If you'll grant Hughie the Graeme to me.'—

IX

' O no, O no, my gude Lord Hume !
    For sooth and sae it mauna be ;
For, were there but three Graemes of the name,
    They suld be hangèd a' for me.'—

X

'Twas up and spake the gude Lady Hume,
    As she sat by the judge's knee ;
' A peck of white pennies, my gude lord judge,
    If you'll grant Hughie the Graeme to me !'—

XI

' O no, O no, my gude Lady Hume,
    Forsooth and so it must na be ;
Were he but the one Graeme of the name,
    He suld be hangèd high for me.'—

XII

' If I be guilty,' said Hughie the Graeme,
    ' Of me my friends shall have small talk ' ;
And he 's loupèd fifteen feet and three,
    Though his hands they were tied behind his back.

758

XIII

He lookèd over his left shoulder,
  And for to see what he might see ;
There was he aware of his auld father,
  Came tearing his hair most piteouslie.

XIV

' O hald your tongue, my father,' he says,
  ' And see that ye dinna weep for me !
For they may ravish me o' my life,
  But they canna banish me fro' Heaven hie.

XV

' Here, Johnie Armstrang, take thou my sword,
  That is made o' the metal sae fine ;
And when thou comest to the English side,
  Remember the death of Hughie the Graeme.'

144. *The Lochmaben Harper*

I

O HEARD ye na o' the silly blind Harper,
  How long he lived in Lochmaben town ?
And how he wad gang to fair England,
  To steal King Henry's Wanton Brown ?

II

But first he gaed to his gude wyfe,
  Wi' a' the haste that he could thole—
' This wark,' quo' he, ' will ne'er gae weel,
  Without a mare that has a foal.'—

thole] suffer, be capable of.

III

Quo' she, ' Thou hast a gude gray mare,
    That'll rin o'er hills baith laigh and hie ;
Sae set thee on the gray mare's back,
    And leave the foal at hame wi' me.'

IV

So he is up to England gane,
    And even as fast as he can hie ;
And when he cam to Carlisle gate,
    O whae was there but the King Henrye ?

V

' Come into my hall, thou silly blind Harper,
    And of thy harping let me hear ! '—
' O, by my sooth,' quo' the silly blind Harper,
    ' I'd rather hae stabling for my mare.'

VI

The King look'd ower his left shoulder,
    And said unto his stable groom ;
' Gae take the silly blind Harper's mare,
    And tie her beside my Wanton Brown.'

VII

Then aye he harpit, and aye he carpit,
    Till a' the lordlings footed the floor ;
They thought the music was sae sweet,
    They had nae mind o' the stable door.

VIII

And aye he harpit, and aye he carpit,
    Till a' the nobles were fast asleep ;
Then quietly he took aff his shoon,
    And saftly down the stair did creep.

laigh] low.   carpit] sang, recited.

THE LOCHMABEN HARPER

IX

Syne to the stable door he hied,
    Wi' tread as light as light could be;
And when he open'd and gaed in,
    There he fand thirty steeds and three.

X

He took a colt halter frae his hose,
    And o' his purpose he didna fail;
He slipt it owre the Wanton's nose,
    And tied it to his gray mare's tail.

XI

He turn'd them loose at the castle gate,
    Owre muir and moss and ilka dale;
And she ne'er let the Wanton bait,
    But kept him still gaun to her tail.

XII

The mare she was right swift o' foot,
    She didna fail to find the way;
For she was at Lochmaben gate
    Fu' lang three hours before the day.

XIII

When she came to the Harper's door,
    There she gave mony a nicker and sneer—
'Rise up,' quo' the wife, 'thou lazy lass;
    Let in thy master and his mare!'

XIV

Then up she rose, put on her clothes,
    And keekit out through the lock-hole—
'O! by my sooth,' then cried the lass,
    'Our mare has gotten a braw brown foal!'—

nicker and sneer] whinny and snort.

XV

'Come haud thy tongue, thou foolish lass !
    The moon 's but glancing in your ee.
I'll wad my hail fee against a groat,
    He 's bigger than e'er our foal will be.'

XVI

Now all this while in merry Carlisle
    The Harper harpit to hie and law ;
And the fiend dought they do but listen him to,
    Until that the day began to daw.

XVII

But on the morn at fair daylight,
    When they had ended a' their cheer,
Behold the Wanton Brown was gane,
    And eke the poor blind Harper's mare !

XVIII

'Allace ! allace ! ' quo' the silly blind Harper,
    ' And ever allace that I cam here !
In Scotland I've tint a braw colt-foal,
    In England they've stown my gude gray mare ! '—

XIX

'Come ! cease thy allacing, thou silly blind Harper,
    And again of thy harping let us hear ;
And weel paid sall thy colt-foal be,
    And thou sall have a far better mare.'

XX

Then aye he harpit, and aye he carpit ;
    Sae sweet were the harpings he let them hear !
He was paid for the foal he had never lost,
    And three times ower for the gude gray mare.

wad my hail fee] bet my whole wages.   fiend dought they do]
the deuce could they do.

I

THE eighteenth of October,
　A dismal tale to hear
How good Lord John and Rothiemay
　Was both burnt in the fire.

II

When steeds was saddled and well bridled,
　And ready for to ride,
Then out it came her false Frendraught,
　Inviting them to bide.

III

Said, ' Stay this night untill we sup,
　The morn untill we dine ;
'Twill be a token of good greement
　'Twixt your good lord and mine.'

IV

' We'll turn again,' said good Lord John ;
　' But no,' said Rothiemay,
' My steed 's trapan'd, my bridle 's broken,
　I fear the day I'm fey.'

V

When mass was sung, and bells was rung,
　And all men bound for bed,
Then good Lord John and Rothiemay
　In one chamber was laid.

VI

They had not long cast off their cloaths,
　And were but now asleep,
When the weary smoke began to rise,
　Likewise the scorching heat.

trapan'd] tampered with.　　　fey] doomed, having my fate
on me.

VII

'O waken, waken, Rothiemay!
  O waken, brother dear!
And turn you to our Saviour;
  There is strong treason here.'

VIII

When they were dressèd in their cloaths,
  And ready for to boun,
The doors and windows was all secur'd,
  The roof-tree burning down.

IX

He did him to the wire-window,
  As fast as he could gang;
Says, Wae to the hands put in the stancheons!
  For out we'll never win.

X

When he stood at the wire-window,
  Most doleful to be seen,
He did espy her Lady Frendraught,
  Who stood upon the green.

XI

Cried, 'Mercy, mercy, Lady Frendraught!
  Will ye not sink with sin?
For first your husband killed my father,
  And now you burn his son.'

XII

O then out spoke her Lady Frendraught,
  And loudly did she cry;
'It were great pity for good Lord John,
  But none for Rothiemay;
But the keys are casten in the deep draw-well,
  Ye cannot get away.'

wire-window] grated window.

764

THE FIRE OF FRENDRAUGHT

XIII

While he stood in this dreadful plight,
    Most piteous to be seen,
There callèd out his servant Gordon,
    As he had frantic been :

XIV

' O loup, O loup, my dear master !
    O loup and come to me !
I'll catch you in my arms twa,
    One foot I will not flee.

XV

' O loup, O loup, my dear master !
    O loup and come away !
I'll catch you in my arms twa,
    But Rothiemay may lie.'—

XVI

' The fish shall never swim in the flood,
    Nor corn grow through the clay,
Nor the fiercest fire that ever was kindled
    Twin me and Rothiemay.

XVII

' But I cannot loup, I cannot come,
    I cannot win to thee ;
My head 's fast in the wire-window,
    My feet burning from me.

XVIII

' My eyes are seething in my head,
    My flesh roasting also,
My bowels are boiling with my blood ;
    Is not that a woeful woe ?

twin] part.

XIX

' Take here the rings from my white fingers,
    That are so long and small,
And give them to my lady fair,
    Where she sits in her hall.

XX

' So I cannot loup, I cannot come,
    I cannot loup to thee ;
My earthly part is all consumed,
    My spirit but speaks to thee.'

XXI

Wringing her hands, tearing her hair,
    His lady she was seen,
And thus address'd his servant Gordon,
    Where he stood on the green.

XXII

' O wae be to you, George Gordon !
    An ill death may you die !
So safe and sound as you stand there,
    And my lord bereaved for me ! '—

XXIII

' I bad him loup, I bad him come,
    I bad him loup to me ;
I'd catch him in my arms twa,
    A foot I should not flee.

XXIV

' He threw me the rings from his white fingers,
    Which were so long and small,
To give to you, his lady fair,
    Where you sat in your hall.'

XXV

Sophia Hay, Sophia Hay,
  O bonny Sophia was her name,
Her waiting maid put on her cloaths,
  But I wot she tore them off again!

XXVI

And aft she cried, ' Ohon! alas!
  A sair heart's ill to win;
I wan a sair heart when I married him,
  And to-day it's return'd again.'

146. *The Death of Parcy Reed*

I

GOD send the land deliverance
  Frae every reaving, riding Scot;
We'll sune hae neither cow nor ewe,
  We'll sune hae neither staig nor stot.

II

The outlaws come frae Liddesdale,
  They herry Redesdale far and near;
The rich man's gelding it maun gang,
  They canna pass the puir man's mare.

III

Sure it were weel, had ilka thief
  Around his neck a halter strang;
And curses heavy may they light
  On traitors vile oursels amang!

Sophia Hay] wife of Lord John [Gordon], burned in this fire.
She had jilted the young lord of Tolquhon to marry him, which
explains the allusion in the last stanza.   stot] steer.

IV

Now Parcy Reed has Crosier taen,
  He has delivered him to the law ;
But Crosier says he'll do waur than that,
  He'll make the tower o' Troughend fa'.

V

And Crosier says he will do waur,
  He will do waur if waur can be ;
He'll make the bairns a' fatherless,
  And then, the land it may lie lee.

VI

'To the hunting, ho !' cried Parcy Reed,
  'The morning sun is on the dew ;
The cauler breeze frae off the fells
  Will lead the dogs to the quarry true.

VII

'To the hunting, ho !' cried Parcy Reed,
  And to the hunting he has gane ;
And the three fause Ha's o' Girsonsfield
  Alang wi' him he has them taen.

VIII

They hunted high, they hunted low,
  By heathery hill and birken shaw ;
They raised a buck on Rooken Edge,
  And blew the mort at fair Ealylawe.

IX

They hunted high, they hunted low,
  They made the echoes ring amain ;
With music sweet o' horn and hound,
  They merry made fair Redesdale glen.

mort] death of the deer.

THE DEATH OF PARCY REED

X

They hunted high, they hunted low,
 They hunted up, they hunted down,
Until the day was past the prime,
 And it grew late in the afternoon.

XI

They hunted high in Batinghope,
 When as the sun was sinking low ;
Says Parcy then, 'Ca' off the dogs,
 We'll bait our steeds and homeward go.'

XII

They lighted high in Batinghope,
 Atween the brown and benty ground ;
They had but rested a little while
 Till Parcy Reed was sleeping sound.

XIII

There 's nane may lean on a rotten staff,
 But him that risks to get a fa' ;
There 's nane may in a traitor trust,
 And traitors black were every Ha'.

XIV

They've stown the bridle off his steed,
 And they've put water in his lang gun ;
They've fixed his sword within the sheath
 That out again it winna come.

XV

'Awaken ye, waken ye, Parcy Reed,
 Or by your enemies be ta'en !
For yonder are the five Crosiers
 A-coming owre the Hingin-stane ! '—

XVI

'If they be five, and we be four,
    Sae that ye stand alang wi' me,
Then every man ye will take one,
    And only leave but two to me :
We will them meet as brave men ought,
    And make them either fight or flee.'—

XVII

'We mayna stand, we canna stand,
    We daurna stand alang wi' thee ;
The Crosiers haud thee at a feud,
    And they wad kill baith thee and we.'—

XVIII

'O turn thee, turn thee, Johnie Ha',
    O turn thee, man, and fight wi' me ;
When ye come to Troughend again,
    My gude black naig I will gie thee ;
He cost full twenty pound o' gowd,
    Atween my brother John and me.'—

XIX

'I mayna turn, I canna turn,
    I daurna turn and fight wi' thee ;
The Crosiers haud thee at a feud,
    And they wad kill baith thee and me.'—

XX

'O turn thee, turn thee, Willie Ha',
    O turn thee, man, and fight wi' me ;
When ye come to Troughend again,
    A yoke o' owsen I'll gie thee.'—

XXI

'I mayna turn, I canna turn,
  I daurna turn and fight wi' thee ;
The Crosiers haud thee at a feud,
  And they wad kill baith thee and me.'—

XXII

'O turn thee, turn thee, Tommy Ha',
  O turn now, man, and fight wi' me ;
If ever we come to Troughend again,
  My daughter Jean I'll gie to thee.'—

XXIII

'I mayna turn, I canna turn,
  I daurna turn and fight wi' thee ;
The Crosiers haud thee at a feud,
  And they wad kill baith thee and me.'—

XXIV

'O shame upon ye, traitors a'!
  I wish your hames ye may never see ;
Ye've stown the bridle off my naig,
  And I can neither fight nor flee.

XXV

'Ye've stown the bridle off my naig,
  And ye've put water i' my lang gun ;
Ye've fixed my sword within the sheath
  That out again it winna come.'

XXVI

He had but time to cross himsel',
  A prayer he hadna time to say,
Till round him came the Crosiers keen,
  All riding graith'd and in array.

graith'd] harnessed, in armour.

THE DEATH OF PARCY REED

' Weel met, weel met, now, Parcy Reed,
    Thou art the very man we sought ;
Owre lang hae we been in your debt,
    Now will we pay you as we ought.

' We'll pay thee at the nearest tree,
    Where we shall hang thee like a hound.'—
Brave Parcy rais'd his fankit sword,
    And fell'd the foremost to the ground.

Alake, and wae for Parcy Reed !
    Alake, he was an unarmed man !
Four weapons pierced him all at once,
    As they assail'd him there and than.

They fell upon him all at once,
    They mangled him most cruellie ;
The slightest wound might caused his deid,
    And they hae gi'en him thirty-three ;
They hackit off his hands and feet,
    And left him lying on the lee.

' Now, Parcy Reed, we've paid our debt,
    Ye canna weel dispute the tale,'
The Crosiers said, and off they rade ;
    They rade the airt o' Liddesdale.

It was the hour o' gloaming gray,
    When herds come in frae fauld and pen ;
A herd he saw a huntsman lie,
    Says he, ' Can this be Laird Troughen' ? '—

fankit] entangled.   airt] direction.

THE DEATH OF PARCY REED

'There's some will ca' me Parcy Reed,
  And some will ca' me Laird Troughen';
It's little matter what they ca' me,
  My faes hae made me ill to ken.

'There's some will ca' me Parcy Reed,
  And speak my praise in tower and town;
It's little matter what they do now,
  My life-blood rudds the heather brown.

'There's some will ca' me Parcy Reed,
  And a' my virtues say and sing;
I would much rather have just now
  A draught o' water frae the spring.'

The herd flung aff his clouted shoon
  And to the nearest fountain ran;
He made his bonnet serve a cup,
  And wan the blessing o' the dying man.

'Now, honest herd, ye maun do mair,
  Ye maun do mair, as I you tell;
Ye maun bear tidings to Troughend,
  And bear likewise my last farewell.

' A farewell to my wedded wife,
  A·farewell to my brother John,
Wha sits into the Troughend tower
  Wi' heart as black as any stone.

773

XXXIX

'A farewell to my daughter Jean,
    A farewell to my young sons five;
Had they been at their father's hand,
    I had this night been man alive.

XL

'A farewell to my followers a',
    And a' my neighbours gude at need;
Bid them think how the treacherous Ha's
    Betrayed the life o' Parcy Reed.

XLI

'The laird o' Clennel bears my bow,
    The laird o' Brandon bears my brand;
Whene'er they ride i' the Border-side,
    They'll mind the fate o' the laird Troughend.'

147.   *Baby Livingston*

I

O BONNY Baby Livingston
    Went forth to view the hay,
And by it came him Glenlyon,
    Sta' bonny Baby away.

II

O first he's ta'en her silken coat,
    And neist her satten gown,
Syne row'd her in a tartan plaid,
    And hap'd her roun' and roun'.

III

He has set her upon his steed
    And roundly rode away,
And ne'er loot her look back again
    The live-long summer's day.

row'd] wrapped.

774

IV

He 's carried her o'er hills and muirs
   Till they came to a Highland glen,
And there he 's met his brother John,
   With twenty armèd men.

V

O there were cows, and there were ewes,
   And lasses milking there !
But Baby ne'er ance look'd about,
   Her heart was fill'd wi' care.

VI

Glenlyon took her in his arms,
   And kiss'd her, cheek and chin ;
Says, ' I'd gie a' these cows and ewes
   But ae kind look to win.'—

VII

' O ae kind look ye ne'er shall get,
   Nor win a smile frae me,
Unless to me you'll favour shew,
   And take me to Dundee.'—

VIII

' Dundee, Baby ?   Dundee, Baby ?
   Dundee you ne'er shall see
Till I've carried you to Glenlyon
   And have my bride made thee.

IX

' We'll stay a while at Auchingour,
   And get sweet milk and cheese,
And syne we'll gang to Glenlyon,
   And there live at our ease.'—

775

X

'I winna stay at Auchingour,
  Nor eat sweet milk and cheese,
Nor go with thee to Glenlyon,
  For there I'll ne'er find ease.'

XI

Then out it spake his brother John,
  'O were I in your place,
I'd take that lady hame again,
  For a' her bonny face.

XII

'Commend me to the lass that's kind,
  Tho' na so gently born;
And, gin her heart I coudna gain,
  To take her hand I'd scorn.'—

XIII

'O haud your tongue now, John,' he says,
  'You wis na what you say;
For I have lo'ed that bonny face
  This twelve month and a day.

XIV

'And tho' I've lo'ed her lang and sair,
  A smile I ne'er cou'd win;
Yet what I've got ance in my power
  To keep I think nae sin.'

XV

When they came to Glenlyon Castle,
  They lighted at the yate,
And out it came his sisters three,
  Wha did them kindly greet.

XVI

O they've ta'en Baby by the hands
 And led her o'er the green,
And ilka lady spake a word,
 But bonny Baby spake nane.

XVII

Then out it spake her bonny Jean,
 The youngest o' the three;
'O lady, dinna look sae sad,
 But tell your grief to me.'—

XVIII

'O wherefore should I tell my grief,
 Since lax I canna find?
I'm stown frae a' my kin and friends,
 And my love I left behind.

XIX

'But had I paper, pen, and ink,
 Before that it were day,
I yet might get a letter sent
 In time to Johny Hay.'

XX

O she's got paper, pen, and ink,
 And candle that she might see,
And she has written a broad letter
 To Johny at Dundee.

XXI

And she has gotten a bonny boy,
 That was baith swift and strang,
Wi' philabeg and bonnet blue,
 Her errand for to gang.

lax] relief.

XXII

' O boy, gin ye'd my blessing win
　　And help me in my need,
Run wi' this letter to my love,
　　And bid him come wi' speed.

XXIII

' And here 's a chain of good red gowd,
　　And gowden guineas three,
And when you've well your errand done,
　　You'll get them for your fee.'

XXIV

The boy he ran o'er hill and dale,
　　Fast as a bird cou'd flee,
And ere the sun was twa hours height
　　The boy was at Dundee.

XXV

And when he came to Johny's door
　　He knockèd loud and sair ;
Then Johny to the window came,
　　And loudly cry'd, ' Wha 's there ? '—

XXVI

' O here 's a letter I have brought,
　　Which ye maun quickly read,
And, gin ye wou'd your lady save,
　　Gang back wi' me wi' speed.'

XXVII

O when he had the letter read,
　　An angry man was he ;
He says, ' Glenlyon, thou shalt rue
　　This deed of villany !

778

BABY LIVINGSTON

XXVIII

'Woe be to thee, Glenlyon!' he says,
  'An ill death may thou dee!
Thou micht hae ta'en anither woman,
  And let my lady be.

XXIX

'O saddle to me the black, the black,
  O saddle to me the brown,
O saddle to me the swiftest steed
  That e'er rade frae the town.

XXX

'And arm ye well, my merry men a',
  And follow me to the glen,
For I vow I'll neither eat nor sleep
  Till I get my love again.'

XXXI

He's mounted on a milk-white steed,
  The boy upon a gray,
And they got to Glenlyon's castle
  About the close of day.

XXXII

As Baby at her window stood,
  The west wind saft did bla';
She heard her Johny's well-kent voice
  Beneath the castle wa'.

XXXIII

'O Baby, haste, the window jump!
  I'll kep you in my arm;
My merry men a' are at the yate,
  To rescue you frae harm.'

XXXIV

She 's to the window fixt her sheets
  And slippèd safely down,
And Johny catch'd her in his arms,
  Ne'er loot her touch the ground.

XXXV

She 's mounted on her Johny's horse,
  Fu' blithely can she say,—
' Glenlyon, you hae lost your bride!
  She 's aff wi' Johny Hay!'

XXXVI

Glenlyon and his brother John
  Were birling in the ha',
When they heard Johny's bridle ring,
  As fast he rade awa'.

XXXVII

' Rise, Jock! gang out and meet the priest,
  I hear his bridle ring!
My Baby now shall be my wife
  Before the laverocks sing.'—

XXXVIII

' O brother, this is not the priest;
  I fear he'll come owre late;
For armèd men with shining brands
  Stand at the castle-yate.'—

XXXIX

' Haste Donald, Duncan, Dugald, Hugh!
  Haste, take your sword and spier!
We'll gar these traytors rue the hour
  That e'er they ventured here.'

XL

The Highland men drew their claymores,
    And gae a warlike shout,
But Johny's merry men kept the yate,
    Nae ane durst venture out.

XLI

The lovers rade the live-lang night,
    And safe gat on their way,
And bonny Baby Livingston
    Has gotten Johny Hay.

XLII

' Awa', Glenlyon ! fy for shame !
    Gae hide ye in some den !
You've latten your bride be stown frae you,
    For a' your armed men.'

148. *The Gypsy Countess*

I

THERE cam' seven Egyptians on a day,
    And wow, but they sang bonny !
And they sang sae sweet, and sae very complete,
    Down cam' Earl Cassilis' lady.

II

She cam' tripping down the stair,
    And a' her maids before her ;
As soon as they saw her weel-faur'd face
    They cast the glamourie owre her.

III

They gave to her the nutmeg,
    And they gave to her the ginger ;
But she gave to them a far better thing,
    The seven gold rings off her fingers.

THE GYPSY COUNTESS

IV

And when the Earl he did come home,
    Enquiring for his ladie,
One of the servants made this reply,
    'She 's awa' with the gypsie laddie.'

V

'Come saddle for me the brown,' he said,
    'For the black was ne'er so speedy,
And I will travel night and day
    Till I find out my wanton ladie.'

VI

'Will you come home, my dear ?' he said,
    'Oh will you come home, my honey ?
And by the point of my broad sword,
    A hand I'll ne'er lay on you.'. . .

VII

'Yestreen I rade this water deep,
    And my own gude lord beside me ;
But this night I maun wet my little pretty feet
    With a wheen blackguards to wade me.

VIII

'Yestreen I lay on a good feather-bed,
    And my own wedded lord beyond me,
And to-night I'll lie in the ash-corner,
    With the gypsies all around me.

IX

'They took off my high-heeled shoes,
    That were made of Spanish leather,
And I have put on coarse Lowland brogues,
    To trip it o'er the heather.

782

X

'The Earl of Cassilis is lying sick;
  Not one hair I'm sorry;
I'd rather have a kiss from Johnny Faa's lips
  Than all his gold and his money.'

149.   *The Baron of Brackley*

I

INVEREY cam' doun Deeside, whistlin' and playin';
He was at brave Brackley's yates ere it was dawin'.

II

Says, 'Baron of Brackley, are ye within?
There's sharp swords at your yate will gar your blood spin.

III

'Open the yate, Brackley, let us within,
Till on the green turf we gar your blood spin.'

IV

The lady rase up, to the window she went;
She heard the kye lowin' o'er hill and o'er bent.

V

'O rise up, John,' she says, 'turn back your kye;
They're o'er the hills rinnin', they're skippin awye!'—

VI

'Come to bed, Peggie, and let the kye rin:
For were I to gang out, I'd never get in.

VII

'For there is na gentlemen, nor yet pretty lads,
But a curn o' hired widdifu's, wears belted plaids.'

dawin'] dawn.   curn] pack.   widdifu's] gallows-birds,
fit to fill a 'widdie' or halter.

THE BARON OF BRACKLEY

Then she cry'd on her women, they quickly came ben:
'Tak' up your rocks, lasses, and fight a' like men!

IX

'Tho' I'm but a woman, to head you I'll try,
Nor let these vile Hielandmen steal a' our kye.'

X

Then up gat the Baron and cry'd for his graith;
Says, 'Lady, I'll gang, tho' to leave you I'm laith.

XI

'Come kiss me, my Peggie, and get me my gun;
For I well may gang out, but I'll never win in.'

XII

When the Baron of Brackley he rade thro' the close,
A gallanter gentleman ne'er mounted horse.

XIII

Tho' there cam' in with Inverey thirty and three,
There was nane wi' bold Brackley but his brither and he.

XIV

Twa gallanter Gordons did never sword draw:
But against four and thirty, wae's me, what was twa?

XV

Wi' swords and wi' daggers they did him surround,
And they've pierced the bold Brackley wi' mony a wound.

XVI

Frae the head o' the Dee to the banks o' the Spey
The Gordons may mourn him and ban Inverey.

graith] harness, arms.

THE BARON OF BRACKLEY

XVII

' O cam' ye in by Brackley, and was ye in there ?
Or saw ye his Peggy dear riving her hair ? '—

XVIII

' O I cam' by Brackley, and I was in there,
But I saw-na his Peggy dear riving her hair.'—

XIX

' O fye on ye, ladye ! how could ye do sae ?
You open'd your yate to the fause Inverey.'

XX

She ate wi' him, drank wi' him, welcomed him in ;
She 's welcomed the villain that slew her Baròn.

XXI

She kept him till morning, syne bade him be gane,
And show'd him the road that he wouldna be ta'en.

XXII

' Thro' Bires and Aboyne,' she says, ' lyin' in a tour
O'er the hills o' Glentanor ye'll skip in an hour.'

XXIII

There is dule in the kitchen, and mirth in the ha',
For the Baron of Brackley is dead and awa'.

XXIV

But and up spak' the babe on his nourice's knee—
' Gin I live to be man, it 's revenged I will be.'

riving] tearing.   yate] gate.

The Dowie Houms of Yarrow

I

LATE at een, drinkin' the wine,
And ere they paid the lawin',
They set a combat them between,
   To fight it in the dawin'.

II

'O stay at hame, my noble lord !
   O stay at hame, my marrow !
My cruel brother will you betray,
   On the dowie houms o' Yarrow.'—

III

'O fare ye weel, my lady gay !
   O fare ye weel, my Sarah !
For I maun gae, tho' I ne'er return
   Frae the dowie banks o' Yarrow.'

IV

She kiss'd his cheek, she kamed his hair,
   As she had done before, O ;
She belted on his noble brand,
   An' he 's awa to Yarrow.

V

O he 's gane up yon high, high hill—
   I wat he gaed wi' sorrow—
An' in a den spied nine arm'd men,
   I' the dowie houms o' Yarrow.

lawin'] reckoning.   marrow] married mate.   dowie]
doleful.   houms] water-meads.

786

THE DOWIE HOUMS OF YARROW

VI

'O are ye come to drink the wine,
  As ye hae doon before, O ?
Or are ye come to wield the brand,
  On the dowie houms o' Yarrow ?'—

VII

'I am no come to drink the wine,
  As I hae done before, O,
But I am come to wield the brand,
  On the dowie houms o' Yarrow.'

VIII

Four he hurt an' five he slew,
  On the dowie houms o' Yarrow,
Till that stubborn knight came him behind,
  An' ran his body thorrow.

IX

'Gae hame, gae hame, good brother John,
  An' tell your sister Sarah
To come an' lift her noble lord,
  Who's sleepin' sound on Yarrow.'

X

'Yestreen I dream'd a dolefu' dream ;
  I ken'd there wad be sorrow ;
I dream'd I pu'd the heather green,
  On the dowie banks o' Yarrow.'

XI

She gaed up yon high, high hill—
  I wat she gaed wi' sorrow—
An' in a den spied nine dead men,
  On the dowie houms o' Yarrow.

XII

She kiss'd his cheek, she kamed his hair,
    As oft she did before, O ;
She drank the red blood frae him ran,
    On the dowie houms o' Yarrow.

XIII

' O haud your tongue, my douchter dear,
    For what needs a' this sorrow ?
I'll wed you on a better lord
    Than him you lost on Yarrow.'—

XIV

' O haud your tongue, my father dear,
    An' dinna grieve your Sarah ;
A better lord was never born
    Than him I lost on Yarrow.

XV

' Tak hame your ousen, tak hame your kye,
    For they hae bred our sorrow ;
I wiss that they had a' gane mad
    Whan they cam' first to Yarrow.'

ousen] oxen.

151. *Lord Maxwell's Last Goodnight*

I

' ADIEU, madame, my mother dear,
But and my sisters three !
Adieu, fair Robert of Orchardstane !
My heart is wae for thee.

II

' Adieu, the lily and the rose,
The primrose fair to see ;
Adieu, my ladye, and only joy !
For I may not stay with thee.

III

' Though I hae slain the Lord Johnstone,
What care I for their feid ?
My noble mind does still incline—
He was my father's deid.

IV

' Both night and day I labour'd oft
Of him avenged to be ;
But now I've got what lang I sought
And I may not stay with thee.

V

' Adieu ! Drumlanrig, false wert aye,
And Closeburn in a band !
The Laird of Lag, frae my father that fled,
When the Johnstone struck aff his hand.

my father's deid] the death of my father.

VI

'They were three brethren in a band—
  Joy may they never see!
Their treacherous art, and cowardly heart,
  Has twined my love and me.

VII

'Adieu! Dumfries, my proper place,
  But and Carlaverock fair!
Adieu! my castle of the Thrieve,
  Wi' a' my buildings there!

VIII

'Adieu! Lochmaben's gate sae fair,
  And Langholm, where birks there be;
Adieu! my ladye, and only joy,
  For I may not stay wi' thee.

IX

'Adieu! Fair Eskdale up and down,
  Where my puir friends do dwell;
The bangisters will ding them down,
  And will them sair compell.

X

'But I'll avenge their feid mysell,
  When I come o'er the sea;
Adieu! my ladye, and only joy,
  For I may not stay wi' thee.'—

XI

'Lord of the land, will you go then
  Unto my father's place,
And walk into their gardens green,
  And I will you embrace.

twined] parted.   bangisters] lawless folk.

XII

'There Hamiltons, and Douglas baith,
    Shall rise to succour thee.'—
'Thanks for thy kindness, fair my dame,
    But I may not stay wi' thee.'—

XIII

Then he tuik aff a gay gold ring,
    Thereat hang signets three;
'Hae, tak thee that, mine ain kind thing,
    And still hae mind o' me!

XIV

'But if thou take another lord,
    Ere I come ower the sea,
His life is but a three days' lease,
    Though I may not stay wi' thee.'

XV

The wind was fair, the ship was clear,
    That good lord went away;
And most part of his friends were there,
    To give him a fair convey.

XVI

They drank the wine, they didna spare
    Even in that gude lord's sight—
Sae now he's o'er the floods sae gray,
    And Lord Maxwell has ta'en his Goodnight.

Helen of Kirkconnell

I

I WISH I were where Helen lies,
Night and day on me she cries;
O that I were where Helen lies,
On fair Kirkconnell lea!

II

Curst be the heart that thought the thought,
And curst the hand that fired the shot,
When in my arms burd Helen dropt,
And died to succour me!

III

O think na ye my heart was sair,
When my Love dropp'd and spak nae mair!
There did she swoon wi' meikle care,
On fair Kirkconnell lea.

IV

As I went down the water side,
None but my foe to be my guide,
None but my foe to be my guide,
On fair Kirkconnell lea;

V

I lighted down my sword to draw,
I hackèd him in pieces sma',
I hackèd him in pieces sma',
For her sake that died for me.

VI

O Helen fair, beyond compare!
I'll mak a garland o' thy hair,
Shall bind my heart for evermair,
Until the day I dee!

VII

O that I were where Helen lies!
Night and day on me she cries;
Out of my bed she bids me rise,
    Says, ' Haste, and come to me!'

VIII

O Helen fair!   O Helen chaste!
If I were with thee, I'd be blest,
Where thou lies low and taks thy rest,
    On fair Kirkconnell lea.

IX

I wish my grave were growing green,
A winding-sheet drawn owre my een,
And I in Helen's arms lying,
    On fair Kirkconnell lea.

X

I wish I were where Helen lies!
Night and day on me she cries;
And I am weary of the skies,
    For her sake that died for me

153. *The Lament of the Border Widow*

I

MY love he built me a bonny bower,
    And clad it a' wi' lilye flour;
A brawer bower ye ne'er did see,
Than my true love he built for me.

II

There came a man, by middle day,
He spied his sport, and went away;
And brought the King that very night,
Who brake my bower, and slew my knight.

THE LAMENT OF THE BORDER WIDOW

III

He slew my knight, to me sae dear ;
He slew my knight, and poin'd his gear ;
My servants all for life did flee,
And left me in extremitie.

IV

I sew'd his sheet, making my mane ;
I watch'd the corpse, myself alane ;
I watch'd his body, night and day ;
No living creature came that way.

V

I took his body on my back,
And whiles I gaed, and whiles I sat ;
I digg'd a grave, and laid him in,
And happ'd him with the sod sae green.

VI

But think na ye my heart was sair,
When I laid the moul' on his yellow hair ;
O think na ye my heart was wae,
When I turn'd about, away to gae ?

VII

Nae living man I'll love again,
Since that my lovely knight is slain ;
Wi' ae lock of his yellow hair
I'll chain my heart for evermair.

poin'd] made forfeit.

BOOK VII

Lady Alice

I

LADY ALICE was sitting in her bower-window,
  Mending her midnight quoif,
And there she saw as fine a corpse
  As ever she saw in her life.

II

' What bear ye, what bear ye, ye six men tall?
  What bear ye on your shouldèrs?'—
' We bear the corpse of Giles Collins,
  An old and true lover of yours.'—

III

' O lay him down gently, ye six men tall,
  All on the grass so green,
And to-morrow, when the sun goes down,
  Lady Alice a corpse shall be seen.

IV

' And bury me in Saint Mary's church,
  All for my love so true,
And make me a garland of marjoram,
  And of lemon-thyme, and rue.'

V

Giles Collins was buried all in the east,
  Lady Alice all in the west,
And the roses that grew on Giles Collins's grave,
  They reached Lady Alice's breast.

LADY ALICE

VI

The priest of the parish he chanced to pass,
  And he sever'd those roses in twain;
Sure never were seen such true lovers before,
  Nor e'er will there be again.

155.   *Lord Lovel*

I

LORD LOVEL he stood at his castle-gate,
  Combing his milk-white steed,
When up came Lady Nancy Belle,
  To wish her lover good speed.

II

'Where are you going, Lord Lovel?' she said,
  'Oh where are you going?' said she.
'I'm going, my Lady Nancy Belle,
  Strange countries for to see.'

III

'When will you be back, Lord Lovel?' she said,
  'Oh when will you come back?' said she.
'In a year, or two, or three at the most,
  I'll return to my fair Nancy.'

IV

But he had not been gone a year and a day,
  Strange countries for to see,
When languishing thoughts came into his head,
  Lady Nancy Belle he would go see.

796

LORD LOVEL

V

So he rode, and he rode, on his milk-white steed,
    Till he came to London town,
And there he heard St. Pancras' bells,
    And the people all mourning round.

VI

'Oh what is the matter?' Lord Lovel he said,
    'Oh what is the matter?' said he;
'A lord's lady is dead,' a woman replied,
    'And some call her Lady Nancy.'

VII

So he order'd the grave to be open'd wide,
    And the shroud he turnèd down,
And there he kiss'd her clay-cold lips,
    Till the tears came trickling down.

VIII

Lady Nancy she died, as it might be, today,
    Lord Lovel he died as tomorrow;
Lady Nancy she died out of pure, pure grief,
    Lord Lovel he died out of sorrow.

IX

Lady Nancy was laid in St. Pancras' Church,
    Lord Lovel was laid in the choir;
And out of her bosom there grew a red rose,
    And out of her lover's a briar.

X

They grew, and they grew, to the church-steeple top,
    And then they could grow no higher;
So there they entwined in a true-lovers' knot,
    For all lovers true to admire.

I

ALL the trees they are so high,
  The leaves they are so green,
The day is past and gone, sweet-heart,
   That you and I have seen.
     It is cold winter's night,
     You and I must bide alone :
       Whilst my pretty lad is young
         And is growing.

II

In a garden as I walked,
  I heard them laugh and call ;
There were four and twenty playing there,
  They played with bat and ball.
     O the rain on the roof,
     Here and I must make my moan :
       Whilst my pretty lad is young
         And is growing.

III

I listen'd in the garden,
  I lookèd o'er the wall ;
'Midst five and twenty gallants there
  My love exceeded all.
     O the wind on the thatch,
     Here and I alone must weep :
       Whilst my pretty lad is young
         And is growing.

IV

O father, father dear,
  Great wrong to me is done,
That I should married be this day,
  Before the set of sun.

THE TREES SO HIGH

At the huffle of the gale,
 Here I toss and cannot sleep :
  Whilst my pretty lad is young
   And is growing.

v

My daughter, daughter dear,
 If better be, more fit,
I'll send him to the court awhile,
 To point his pretty wit.
  But the snow, snowflakes fall,
   O and I am chill as dead :
    Whilst my pretty lad is young
     And is growing.

vi

To let the lovely ladies know
 They may not touch and taste,
I'll bind a bunch of ribbons red
 About his little waist.
  But the raven hoarsely croaks,
   And I shiver in my bed ;
    Whilst my pretty lad is young
     And is growing.

vii

I married was, alas,
 A lady high to be,
In court and stall and stately hall,
 And bower of tapestry.
  But the bell did only knell,
   And I shuddered as one cold :
    When I wed the pretty lad
     Not done growing.

VIII

At fourteen he wedded was,
  A father at fifteen,
At sixteen 's face was white as milk,
  And then his grave was green;
      And the daisies were outspread,
      And buttercups of gold,
          O'er my pretty lad so young
              Now ceased growing.

157.   *The Brown Girl*

I

'I AM as brown as brown can be,
  My eyes as black as a sloe;
I am as brisk as a nightingale,
  And as wild as any doe.

II

'My love has sent me a love-letter,
  Not far from yonder town,
That he could not fancy me,
  Because I was so brown.

III

'I sent him his letter back again,
  For his love I valu'd not,
Whether that he could fancy me
  Or whether he could not.

IV

'He sent me his letter back again,
  That he lay sick to death,
That I might then go speedily
  To give him up his faith.'

800

THE BROWN GIRL

V

Now you shall hear what love she had
   Then for this love-sick man;
She was a whole long summer's day
   In a mile a going on.

VI

When she came to her love's bed-side,
   Where he lay dangerous sick,
She could not for laughing stand
   Upright upon her feet.

VII

She had a white wand all in her hand,
   And smooth'd it all on his breast;
'In faith and troth come pardon me,
   I hope your soul 's at rest.'—

VIII

'Prithee,' said he, 'forget, forget,
   Prithee forget, forgive;
O grant me yet a little space,
   That I may be well and live.'—

IX

'O never will I forget, forgive,
   So long as I have breath;
I'll dance above your green, green grave
   Where you do lie beneath.

X

'I'll do as much for my true-love
   As other maidens may;
I'll dance and sing on my love's grave
   A whole twelvemonth and a day.'

158. *Barbara Allen's Cruelty*

I

IN Scarlet town, where I was born,
  There was a fair maid dwellin',
Made every youth cry *Well-a-way!*
  Her name was Barbara Allen.

II

All in the merry month of May,
  When green buds they were swellin',
Young Jemmy Grove on his death-bed lay,
  For love of Barbara Allen.

III

He sent his man in to her then,
  To the town where she was dwellin';
'O haste and come to my master dear,
  If your name be Barbara Allen.'

IV

So slowly, slowly rase she up,
  And slowly she came nigh him,
And when she drew the curtain by—
  'Young man, I think you're dyin'.'

V

'O it's I am sick and very very sick,
  And it's all for Barbara Allen.'—
'O the better for me ye'se never be,
  Tho' your heart's blood were a-spillin'!

VI

'O dinna ye mind, young man,' says she,
    'When the red wine ye were fillin',
That ye made the healths go round and round,
    And slighted Barbara Allen?'

VII

He turn'd his face unto the wall,
    And death was with him dealin':
'Adieu, adieu, my dear friends all,
    And be kind to Barbara Allen!'

VIII

As she was walking o'er the fields,
    She heard the dead-bell knellin';
And every jow the dead-bell gave
    Cried 'Woe to Barbara Allen.'

IX

'O mother, mother, make my bed,
    O make it saft and narrow:
My love has died for me to-day,
    I'll die for him to-morrow.

X

'Farewell,' she said, 'ye virgins all,
    And shun the fault I fell in:
Henceforth take warning by the fall
    Of cruel Barbara Allen.'

jow] beat, toll.

The Gardener

I

THE gardener stands in his bower-door,
   With a primrose in his hand,
And by there came a leal maiden
   As jimp as a willow wand.

II

' O lady, can you fancy me,
   For to be my bride?
Ye'se get a' the flowers in my garden
   To be to you a weed.

III

' The lily white sall be your smock
   Becomes your body best ;
Your head sall be busk'd wi' gillyflower
   And the primrose in your breast.

IV

' Your gown sall be the sweet-william,
   Your coat the camovine,
Your apron a' the salluds neat
   That taste baith sweet and fine.

V

' Your stockings sall be o' the braid kail-blade,
   That is baith braid and lang ;
And narrow, narrow at the cute,
   And braid, braid at the brawn.

leal] true.   jimp] slender.   weed] clothing.
camovine] camomile.   cute] ankle.   brawn] calf.

THE GARDENER

VI

' Your gloves sall be the marigold,
    All glittering to your hand,
Well spread o'er wi' the blue blaewort
    That grows amang corn-land.' —

VII

' O fare ye well, young man,' she says,
    ' Farewell, and I bid adieu ;
If you can fancy me,' she says,
    ' O I cannot fancy you.

VIII

' Sin ye've provided a weed for me
    Amang the summer flowers,
Then I'se provide anither for you
    Amang the winter showers. —

IX

' The new-fa'n snaw to be your smock
    Becomes your body best ;
An' your head sall be wound wi' the eastern wind,
    An' the cauld rain on your breast.'

blaewort] corn bluebottle.

160. *The Lowlands o' Holland*

I

' MY love has built a bonny ship, and set her on the sea,
    With seven score good mariners to bear her company;
There's three score is sunk, and three score dead at sea,
And the Lowlands o' Holland has twin'd my love and me.

II

' My love he built another ship, and set her on the main,
And nane but twenty mariners for to bring her hame;
But the weary wind began to rise, and the sea began to rout,
My love then and his bonny ship turn'd withershins about.

III

' Then shall neither coif come on my head nor comb come
    in my hair;
Then shall neither coal nor candle-light shine in my bower
    mair;
Nor will I love another one until the day I die,
Sin' the Lowlands o' Holland has twin'd my love and me.'—

IV

'O haud your tongue, my daughter dear, be still and be
    content;
There are mair lads in Galloway, ye neen nae sair lament.'—
' O there is none in Gallow, there 's none at a' for me,
For I never loved a love but one, and he 's drown'd in the
    sea.'

twin'd] parted.   withershins] around against the sun.

161. The Spanish Lady's Love

I

WILL you hear a Spanish lady
    How she woo'd an English man?
Garments gay and rich as may be,
    Decked with jewels, she had on;
Of a comely countenance and grace was she,
And by birth and parentage of high degree.

II

As his prisoner there he kept her,
    In his hands her life did lie;
Cupid's bands did tie her faster,
    By the liking of an eye;
In his courteous company was all her joy,
To favour him in any thing she was not coy.

III

At the last there came commandment
    For to set the ladies free,
With their jewels still adornèd,
    None to do them injury:
'Alas!' then said this lady gay, 'full woe is me;
O let me still sustain this kind captivity!

IV

'Gallant captain, show some pity
    To a lady in distress;
Leave me not within this city,
    For to die in heaviness;
Thou hast set this present day my body free,
But my heart in prison strong remains with thee.'—

807

THE SPANISH LADY'S LOVE

V

'How should'st thou, fair lady, love me,
    Whom thou know'st thy country's foe?
Thy fair words make me suspect thee;
    Serpents lie where flowers grow.'—
'All the harm I think to thee, most gracious knight,
God grant unto myself the same may fully light:

VI

'Blessèd be the time and season
    That you came on Spanish ground;
If our foes you may be termèd,
    Gentle foes we have you found.
With our city you have won our hearts each one;
Then to your country bear away that is your own.'—

VII

'Rest you still, most gallant lady,
    Rest you still, and weep no more;
Of fair lovers there are plenty;
    Spain doth yield a wondrous store.'—
'Spaniards fraught with jealousy we often find,
But Englishmen through all the world are counted kind.

VIII

'Leave me not unto a Spaniard;
    You alone enjoy my heart;
I am lovely, young, and tender,
    And so love is my desart.
Still to serve thee day and night my mind is press'd;
The wife of every Englishman is counted blest.'—

808

THE SPANISH LADY'S LOVE

IX

'It would be a shame, fair lady,
  For to bear a woman hence ;
English soldiers never carry
  Any such without offence.'—
'I will quickly change myself if it be so,
And like a page I'll follow thee where'er thou go.'—

X

'I have neither gold nor silver
  To maintain thee in this case,
And to travel, 'tis great charges,
  As you know, in every place.'—
'My chains and jewels every one shall be thine own,
And eke five hundred pounds in gold that lies unknown.'—

XI

'On the seas are many dangers ;
  Many storms do there arise,
Which will be to ladies dreadful,
  And force tears from watery eyes.'—
'Well in truth I shall endure extremity,
For I could find in heart to lose my life for thee.'—

XII

'Courteous lady, leave this fancy ;
  Here comes all that breeds the strife ;
I in England have already
  A sweet woman to my wife :
I will not falsify my vow for gold or gain,
Nor yet for all the fairest dames that live in Spain.'—

THE SPANISH LADY'S LOVE

XIII

'Oh how happy is that woman,
    That enjoys so true a friend!
Many happy days God send you!
    Of my suit I'll make an end:
On my knees I pardon crave for this offence,
Which did from love and true affection first commence.

XIV

'Commend me to thy loving lady:
    Bear to her this chain of gold,
And these bracelets for a token;
    Grieving that I was so bold.
All my jewels in like sort bear thou with thee,
For they are fitting for thy wife, but not for me.

XV

'I will spend my days in prayer,
    Love and all his laws defy,
In a nunnery will I shroud me,
    Far from any company:
But ere my prayers have end, be sure of this,
To pray for thee and for thy love I will not miss.

XVI

'Thus farewell, most gentle captain,
    Farewell too my heart's content!
Count not Spanish ladies wayward,
    Though to thee my love was bent:
Joy and true prosperity go still with thee!'—
'The like fall ever to thy share, most fair lady!'

162. *The Bailiff's Daughter of Islington*

I

THERE was a youth, and a well-belovèd youth,
    And he was an esquire's son,
He loved the bailiff's daughter dear,
    That lived in Islington.'

II

But she was coy, and she would not believe
    That he did love her so,
No, nor at any time she would
    Any countenance to him show.

III

But when his friends did understand
    His fond and foolish mind,
They sent him up to fair London,
    An apprentice for to bind.

IV

And when he had been seven long years,
    And his love he had not seen ;
'Many a tear have I shed for her sake
    When she little thought of me.'

V

All the maids of Islington
    Went forth to sport and play ;
All but the bailiff's daughter dear ;
    She secretly stole away.

VI

She put off her gown of gray,
    And put on her puggish attire ;
She 's up to fair London gone,
    Her true-love to require.

puggish] tramp's.

VII

As she went along the road,
    The weather being hot and dry,
There was she aware of her true-love,
    At length came riding by.

VIII

She stept to him, as red as any rose,
    And took him by the bridle-ring:
'I pray you, kind sir, give me one penny,
    To ease my weary limb.'—

IX

'I prithee, sweetheart, canst thou tell me
    Where that thou wast born?'—
'At Islington, kind sir,' said she,
    'Where I have had many a scorn.'—

X

'I prithee, sweetheart, canst thou tell me
    Whether thou dost know
The bailiff's daughter of Islington?'—
    'She's dead, sir, long ago.'—

XI

'Then will I sell my goodly steed,
    My saddle and my bow;
I will into some far countrey,
    Where no man doth me know.'—

XII

'Oh stay, O stay, thou goodly youth!
    She's alive, she is not dead;
Here she standeth by thy side,
    And is ready to be thy bride.'—

XIII

'O farewell grief, and welcome joy,
   Ten thousand times and o'er!
For now I have seen my own true-love,
   That I thought I should have seen no more.'

163. *The Blind Beggar's Daughter of Bednall-Green*

I

IT was a blind beggar, had long lost his sight,
He had a fair daughter of beauty most bright;
And many a gallant brave suitor had she,
For none was so comely as pretty Bessee.

II

And though she was of favour most faire,
Yet seeing she was but a poor beggar's heyre,
Of ancyent housekeepers despisèd was she,
Whose sons came as suitors to pretty Bessee.

III

Wherefore in great sorrow fair Bessy did say,
'Good father, and mother, let me go away
To seek out my fortune, whatever it be.'
This suit then they granted to pretty Bessee.

IV

Then Bessy, that was of beauty so bright,
All clad in grey russet, and late in the night,
From father and mother alone parted she;
Who sighèd and sobbèd for pretty Bessee.

813

V

She went till she came to Stratford-le-Bow;
Then knew she not whither, nor which way to go:
With tears she lamented her hard destinìe,
So sad and so heavy was pretty Bessee.

VI

She kept on her journey until it was day,
She went unto Rumford along the high way;
Where at the Queen's Arms entertainèd was she:
So fair and well favoured was pretty Bessee.

VII

She had not been there a month to an end,
But master and mistress and all was her friend:
And every brave gallant, that once did her see,
Was straightway enamour'd of pretty Bessee.

VIII

Great gifts they did send her of silver and gold,
And in their songs daily her love was extoll'd;
Her beauty was blazèd in every degree;
So fair and so comely was pretty Bessee.

IX

The young men of Rumford in her had their joy;
She showed herself courteous, and modestly coy;
And at her commandèment still would they be;
So fair and so comely was pretty Bessee.

X

Four suitors at once unto her did go;
They cravèd her favour, but still she said 'no;
I would not wish gentles to marry with me.'—
Yet ever they honoured pretty Bessee.

XI

The first of them was a gallant young knight,
And he came unto her disguised in the night :
The second a gentleman of good degree,
Who wooèd and suèd for pretty Bessee.

XII

A merchant of London, whose wealth was not small,
He was the third suitor, and proper withal :
Her master's own son the fourth man must be,
Who swore he would die for pretty Bessee.

XIII

'And, if thou wilt marry with me,' quoth the knight,
'I'll make thee a lady with joy and delight ;
My heart so enthrallèd is by thy beautìe,
That soon I shall die for pretty Bessee.'

XIV

The gentleman said, 'Come, marry with me,
As fine as a lady my Bessy shall be :
My life is distressèd : O hear me,' quoth he ;
'And grant me thy love, my pretty Bessee.'—

XV

'Let me be thy husband,' the merchant did say,
'Thou shalt live in London both gallant and gay ;
My ships shall bring home rich jewels for thee,
And I will for ever love pretty Bessee.'

XVI

Then Bessy she sighed, and thus she did say,
'My father and mother I mean to obey ;
First get their good will, and be faithful to me,
And then you shall marry your pretty Bessee.'

XVII

To every one this answer she made,
Wherefore unto her they joyfully said,
'This thing to fulfil we all do agree ;
But where dwells thy father, my pretty Bessee ? '

XVIII

'My father,' she said, 'is soon to be seen :
The silly blind beggar of Bednall-green,
That daily sits begging for charitìe,
He is the good father of pretty Bessee.

XIX

' His marks and his tokens are known very well ;
He always is led with a dog and a bell :
A silly old man, God knoweth, is he,
Yet he is the father of pretty Bessee.'

XX

'Nay then,' quoth the merchant, 'thou art not for me ! '
'Nor,' quoth the innholder, 'my wife thou shalt be.'
'I lothe,' said the gentle, 'a beggar's degree,
And therefore adieu, my pretty Bessee ! '

XXI

'Why then,' quoth the knight, ' hap better or worse,
I weigh not true love by the weight of the purse,
And beauty is beauty in every degree ;
Then welcome unto me, my pretty Bessee.

XXII

'With thee to thy father forthwith I will go.'—
'Nay soft,' quoth his kinsmen, 'it must not be so ;
A poor beggar's daughter no lady shall be,
Then take thy adieu of pretty Bessee.'

XXIII

But soon after this, by break of the day
The Knight had from Rumford stole Bessy away.
The young men of Rumford, as thick as might be,
Rode after to fetch again pretty Bessee.

XXIV

As swift as the wind to ryde they were seen,
Until they came near unto Bednall-green ;
And as the Knight lighted most courteouslie,
They all fought against him for pretty Bessee.

XXV

But rescue came speedily over the plain,
Or else the young Knight for his love had been slain.
This fray being ended, then straightway he see
His kinsmen come railing at pretty Bessee.

XXVI

Then spake the blind beggar, 'Although I be poor,
Yet rail not against my child at my own door :
Though she be not deckèd in velvet and pearl,
Yet will I drop angels with you for my girl.

XXVII

' And then, if my gold may better her birth,
And equal the gold that you lay on the earth,
Then neither rail nor grudge you to see
The blind beggar's daughter a lady to be.

XXVIII

' But first you shall promise, and have it well known,
The gold that you dropt shall all be your own.'
With that they replied, ' Contented be we.'
' Then here's,' quoth the beggar, ' for pretty Bessee ! '

THE BLIND BEGGAR'S DAUGHTER

XXIX

With that an angel he cast on the ground,
And dropped in angels full three thousand pound ;
And oftentimes it was provèd most plain,
For the gentlemen's one the beggar dropt twain :

XXX

So that the place, wherein they did sit,
With gold it was coverèd every whit.
The gentlemen then, having dropt all their store,
Said, 'Now, beggar, hold, for we have no more,

XXXI

'Thou hast fulfilled thy promise aright.'—
'Then marry,' quoth he, 'my girl to this Knight;
And here,' added he, 'I will now throw you down
A hundred pounds more to buy her a gown.'

XXXII

The gentlemen all, that this treasure had seen,
Admirèd the beggar of Bednall-green :
And all those, that were her suitors before,
Their flesh for very anger they tore.

XXXIII

Thus was fair Bessy match'd to the Knight,
And then made a lady in others' despite :
A fairer lady there never was seen
Than the blind beggar's daughter of Bednall-green.

XXXIV

But of their sumptuous marriage and feast,
What brave lords and knights thither were prest,
The second fitt shall set forth to your sight
With marvellous pleasure and wished delight.

818

Part II

XXXV

Of a blind beggar's daughter most bright,
That late was betrothed unto a young Knight;
All the discourse thereof you did see:
But now comes the wedding of pretty Bessee.

XXXVI

Within a gorgeous palace most brave,
Adornèd with all the cost they could have,
This wedding was kept most sumptuouslìe,
And all for the credit of pretty Bessee.

XXXVII

All kind of dainties and delicates sweet
Were bought for the banquet, as it was most meet;
Partridge, and plover, and venison most free,
Against the brave wedding of pretty Bessee.

XXXVIII

This marriage through England was spread by report,
So that a great number thereto did resort
Of nobles and gentles in every degree;
And all for the fame of pretty Bessee.

XXXIX

To church then went this gallant young Knight;
His bride followed after, an angel most bright,
With troops of ladies—the like ne'er was seen
As went with sweet Bessy of Bednall-green.

THE BLIND BEGGAR'S DAUGHTER

XL

This marriage being solemnized then,
With musick performed by the skilfullest men,
The nobles and gentles sat down at that tide,
Each one admiring the beautiful bride.

XLI

Now, after the sumptuous dinner was done,
To talk and to reason a number begun :
They talk'd of the blind beggar's daughter most bright,
And what with his daughter he gave to the Knight.

XLII

Then spake the nobles, 'Much marvel have we,
This jolly blind beggar we cannot here see.'
'My lords,' quoth the bride, 'my father's so base,
He is loth with his presence these states to disgrace.'—

XLIII

'The praise of a woman in question to bring,
Before her own face, were a flattering thing,
But we think thy father's baseness,' quoth they,
'Might by thy beauty be clean put away.'

XLIV

They had no sooner these pleasant words spoke,
But in comes the beggar clad in a silk cloak ;
A fair velvet cap, and a feather had he,
And now a musician forsooth he would be.

XLV

He had a dainty lute under his arm,
He touchèd the strings, which made such a charm,
Says, 'Please you to hear any musick of me,
I'll sing you a song of pretty Bessee.'

820

XLVI

With that his lute he twangèd straightway,
And thereon began most sweetly to play;
And after that lessons were played two or three,
He strain'd out this song most delicatelìe.

XLVII

' A poor beggar's daughter did dwell on a green,
Who for her fairness might well be a queen:
A blithe bonny lass, and a dainty was she,
And many one callèd her pretty Bessee.

XLVIII

' Her father he had no goods, nor no land,
But begg'd for a penny all day with his hand;
And yet to her marriage he gave thousands three,
And still he hath somewhat for pretty Bessee.

XLIX

' And if any one here her birth do disdain,
Her father is ready, with might and with main,
To prove she is come of noble degree:
Therefore never flout at pretty Bessee.'

L

With that the lords and the company round
With hearty laughter were ready to swound;
At last said the lords, ' Full well we may see,
The bride and the beggar's beholden to thee.'

LI

On this the bride all blushing did rise,
The pearly drops standing within her fair eyes,
' O pardon my father, grave nobles,' quoth she,
' That through blind affection thus doteth on me.'

THE BLIND BEGGAR'S DAUGHTER

LII

'If this be thy father,' the nobles did say,
'Well may he be proud of this happy day;
Yet by his countenance well may we see,
His birth and his fortune did never agree:

LIII

And therefore, blind man, we pray thee bewray
(And look that the truth thou to us do say)
Thy birth and thy parentage, what it may be;
For the love that thou bearest to pretty Bessee.'—

LIV

.'Then give me leave, nobles and gentles, each one,
One song more to sing, and then I have done;
And if that it may not win good report,
Then do not give me a groat for my sport.

LV

'Sir Simon de Montfort my subject shall be;
Once chief of all the great barons was he,
Yet fortune so cruel this lord did abase,
Now lost and forgotten are he and his race.

LVI

'When the barons in arms did King Henry oppose,
Sir Simon de Montfort their leader they chose;
A leader of courage undaunted was he,
And ofttimes he made their enemies flee.

LVII

'At length in the battle on Evesham plain,
The barons were routed, and Montfort was slain;
Most fatal that battle did prove unto thee,
Though thou wast not born then, my pretty Bessee!

822

LVIII

' Along with the nobles, that fell at that tide,
His eldest son Henry, who fought by his side,
Was fell'd by a blow he received in the fight ;
A blow that deprived him for ever of sight.

LIX

' Among the dead bodies all lifeless he lay,
Till evening drew on of the following day ;
When by a young lady discovered was he ;
And this was thy mother, my pretty Bessee !

LX

' A baron's fair daughter stept forth in the night
To search for her father, who fell in the fight,
And seeing young Montfort, where gasping he lay,
Was movèd with pity, and brought him away.

LXI

' In secret she nurst him, and swagèd his pain,
While he through the realm was believed to be slain :
At length his fair bride she consented to be,
And made him glad father of pretty Bessee.

LXII

' And now, lest our foes our lives should betray,
We clothèd ourselves in beggars' array ;
Her jewels she sold, and hither came we :
All our comfort and care was our pretty Bessee.

LXIII

' And here have we livèd in fortune's despite,
Though poor, yet contented with humble delight :
Full forty winters thus have I been
A silly blind beggar of Bednall-green.

THE BLIND BEGGAR'S DAUGHTER

LXIV

' And here, noble lords, is ended the song
Of one that once to your own rank did belong :
And thus have you learnèd a secret from me,
That ne'er had been known, but for pretty Bessee.'

LXV

Now when the fair company every one,
Had heard the strange tale in the song he had shown,
They all were amazèd, as well they might be,
Both at the blind beggar, and pretty Bessee.

LXVI

With that the fair bride they all did embrace,
Saying, ' Sure thou art come of an hon'rable race ;
Thy father likewise is of noble degree,
And thou art well worthy a lady to be.'

LXVII

Thus was the feast ended with joy and delight,
A bridegroom most happy then was the young Knight,
In joy and felicitie long livèd he,
All with his fair lady, the pretty Bessee.

164. *The Loving Ballad of Lord Bateman*

A Broadside Version of 'Young Beichan'

I

LORD BATEMAN was a noble lord,
  A noble lord of high degree;
He shipp'd himself all aboard of a ship,
  Some foreign country for to see.

II

He sailèd east, he sailèd west,
  Until he came to famed Turkey,
Where he was taken and put to prison,
  Until his life was quite weary.

III

All in this prison there grew a tree,
  O there it grew so stout and strong!
Where he was chain'd all by the middle,
  Until his life was almost gone.

IV

This Turk he had one only daughter,
  The fairest my two eyes e'er see;
She stole the keys of her father's prison,
  And swore Lord Bateman she would let go free.

V

O she took him to her father's cellar,
  And gave to him the best of wine;
And every health she drank unto him
  Was, 'I wish, Lord Bateman, as you was mine.'

VI

'O have you got houses, have you got land,
 And does Northumberland belong to thee?
And what would you give to the fair young lady
 As out of prison would let you go free?'—

VII

'O I've got houses and I've got land,
 And half Northumberland belongs to me;
And I will give it all to the fair young lady
 As out of prison would let me go free.'—

VIII

'O in seven long years, I'll make a vow
 For seven long years, and keep it strong,
That if you'll wed no other woman,
 O I will wed no other man.'

IX

O she took him to her father's harbour,
 And gave to him a ship of fame,
Saying, 'Farewell, farewell to you, Lord Bateman,
 I fear I never shall see you again!'

X

Now seven long years is gone and past,
 And fourteen days, well known to me;
She packèd up all her gay clothing,
 And swore Lord Bateman she would go see.

XI

O when she arrived at Lord Bateman's castle,
 How boldly then she rang the bell!
'Who's there? who's there?' cries the proud young porter,
 'O come unto me pray quickly tell.'—

826

XII

'O is this here Lord Bateman's castle,
   And is his lordship here within ?—
'O yes, O yes,' cries the proud young porter
   'He 's just now taking his young bride in.'—

XIII

'O bid him to send me a slice of bread,
   And a bottle of the very best wine,
And not forgetting the fair young lady
   As did release him when close confine.'

XIV

O away and away went this proud young porter,
   O away and away and away went he,
Until he come to Lord Bateman's chamber,
   When he went down on his bended knee.

XV

'What news, what news, my proud young porter ?
   What news, what news ?   Come tell to me.'—
'O there is the fairest young lady
   As ever my two eyes did see.

XVI

'She has got rings on every finger,
   And on one finger she has got three ;
With as much gay gold about her middle
   As would buy half Northumberlee.

XVII

'O she bids you to send her a slice of bread,
   And a bottle of the very best wine,
And not forgetting the fair young lady
   As did release you when close confine.'

XVIII

Lord Bateman then in passion flew,
  And broke his sword in splinters three,
Saying, ' I will give half of my father's land,
  If so be as Sophia has crossed the sea.'

XIX

Then up and spoke this young bride's mother,
  Who never was heard to speak so free ;
Saying, ' You'll not forget my only daughter,
  If so be as Sophia has crossed the sea.'—

XX

' O it's true I made a bride of your daughter,
  But she's neither the better nor the worse for me ;
She came to me with a horse and saddle,
  But she may go home in a coach and three.'

XXI

Lord Bateman then prepared another marriage,
  With both their hearts so full of glee,
Saying, ' I'll roam no more to foreign countries,
  Now that Sophia has crossed the sea.'

Mary Ambree

I

WHEN captains couragious, whom death could not
    daunte,
Did march to the siege of the citty of Gaunt,
They muster'd their souldiers by two and by three,
And the foremost in battle was Mary Ambree.

II

When brave Sir John Major was slaine in her sight,
Who was her true lover, her joy, and delight,
Because he was slaine most treacherouslie,
She vow'd to revenge him, did Mary Ambree.

III

She clothèd herselfe from the top to the toe
In buffe of the bravest, most seemelye to showe ;
A faire shirt of mail then slippèd on she ;
Was not this a brave bonny lass, Mary Ambree ?

IV

A helmet of proofe she strait did provide,
A strong arminge sword she girt by her side,
And on each hand a goodly faire gauntlett put shee ;
Was not this a brave bonny lass, Mary Ambree ?

V

Then tooke she her sworde and her target in hand,
Bidding all such as wo'ld to be sworn of her band ;
To wayte on her person came thousand and three :
Was not this a brave bonny lass, Mary Ambree ?

      Gaunt] Ghent.

MARY AMBREE

VI

' My soldiers,' she saith, ' soe valiant and bold,
Nowe follow your captaine, whom you doe beholde ;
Still foremost in battel myself will I be ' :
Was not this a brave bonny lass, Mary Ambree ?

VII

Then cry'd out her souldiers, and loude they did say,
' Soe well thou becomest this gallant array,
Thy harte and thy weapons soe well do agree,
There was none that was ever like Mary Ambree.'

VIII

She chearèd her souldiers, that foughten for life,
With ancyent and standard, with drum and with fyfe,
With brave clanging trumpetts, that sounded so free ;
Was not this a brave bonny lass, Marv Ambree ?

IX

' Before I will see the worst of you all
To come into danger of death or of thrall,
This hand and this life I will venture so free ' :
Was not this a brave bonny lass, Mary Ambree ?

X

She led up her souldiers in battaile array
Gainst three times theyr number by break of the daye ;
Seven howers in skirmish continuèd shee :
Was not this a brave bonny lass, Mary Ambree ?

XI

She fillèd the skyes with the smoke of her shott,
And her enemyes bodyes with bullets soe hott ;
For one of her owne men a score killèd shee :
Was not this a brave bonny lass, Mary Ambree ?

ancyent] ensign.

XII

And when her false gunner, to spoyle her intent,
Away all her pellets and powder had sent,
Straight with her keen weapon she slasht him in three:
Was not this a brave bonny lass, Mary Ambree!

XIII

Being falselye betrayèd for lucre of hyre,
At length she was forcèd to make a retyre;
Then her souldiers into a strong castle drew she:
Was not this a brave bonny lass, Mary Ambree?

XIV

Her foes they beset her on everye side,
As thinking close siege shee co'ld never abide;
To beate down the wallès they all did decree:
But stoutlye defyed them brave Mary Ambree.

XV

Then tooke she her sword and her target in hand,
And mounting the walls all undaunted did stand,
There daring their captaines to match any three:
O what a brave captaine was Mary Ambree!

XVI

'Now saye, English captaine, what woldest thou give
To ransome thy selfe, which else must not live?
Come yield thy selfe quicklye, or slaine thou must bee.'—
O then smilèd sweetlye brave Mary Ambree.

XVII

'Ye captaines couragious, of valour so bold,
Whom thinke you before you now you doe behold?'—
'A knight, sir, of England, and captaine soe free,
Who shortèlye with us a pris'ner must bee.'—

831

XVIII

'No captaine of England; behold in your sight
Two brests in my bosome, and therfore no knight:
Noe knight, sirs, of England, nor captaine you see,
But a poor simple lass, callèd Mary Ambree.'—

XIX

'But art thou a woman, as thou dost declare,
Whose valor hath prov'd so undaunted in warre?
If England doth yield such brave lasses as thee,
Full well may they conquer, faire Mary Ambree!'

XX

Then to her owne country shee backe did returne,
Still holding the foes of faire England in scorne:
Therfore, English captaines of every degree,
Sing forth the brave valours of Mary Ambree!

166. *The Lady turned Serving-Man*

I

YOU beauteous ladies great and small,
I write unto you, one and all,
Whereby that you may understand
What I have suffer'd in this land.

II

I was by birth a lady fair,
My father's chief and only heir;
But when my good old father died,
Then I was made a young knight's bride.

III

And then my love built me a bower,
Bedeck'd with many a fragrant flower;
A braver bower you ne'er did see
Than my true love did build for me.

832

IV

But there came thieves late in the night,
They robb'd my bower, and slew my knight,
And after that my knight was slain
I could no longer there remain.

V

My servants all from me did fly
In the midst of my extremity,
And left me by myself alone
With a heart more cold than any stone.

VI

Yet, though my heart was full of care,
Heaven would not suffer me to despair;
Wherefore in haste I changed my name
From fair Elise to Sweet William.

VII

And therewithal I cut my hair,
And dress'd myself in man's attire;
And in my beaver, hose, and band,
I travell'd far through many a land.

VIII

With a silver rapier by my side,
So like a gallant I did ride;
The thing that I delighted on,
It was to be a serving-man.

IX

Thus in my sumptuous man's array
I bravely rode along the way;
And at the last it chancèd so
That I to the King's court did go.

X

Then to the King I bow'd full low,
My love and duty for to show;
And so much favour I did crave,
That I a serving-man's place might have.

XI

'Stand up, brave youth,' the King replied,
'Thy service shall not be denied;
But tell me first what thou canst do;
Thou shalt be fitted thereunto.

XII

'Wilt thou be usher of my hall,
To wait upon my nobles all?
Or wilt thou be taster of my wine,
To wait on me when I do dine?

XIII

'Or wilt thou be my chamberlain,
To make my bed both soft and fine?
Or wilt thou be one of my guard?
And I will give thee thy reward.'

XIV

Sweet William, with a smiling face,
Said to the King, 'If 't please your Grace
To show such favour unto me,
Your chamberlain I fain would be.'

XV

The King then did the nobles call,
To ask the counsel of them all;
Who gave consent Sweet William he
The King's own chamberlain should be.

THE LADY TURNED SERVING-MAN

XVI

Now mark what strange thing came to pass:
As the King one day a-hunting was,
With all his lords and noble train,
Sweet William did at home remain.

XVII

Sweet William had no company then
With him at home, but an old man:
And when he saw the house was clear,
He took a lute which he had there:

XVIII

Upon the lute Sweet William play'd,
And to the same he sang and said,
With a sweet and noble voice
Which made the old man to rejoice:

XIX

' My father was as brave a lord
As ever Europe did afford,
My mother was a lady bright,
My husband was a valiant knight:

XX

' And I myself a lady gay,
Bedeck'd with gorgeous rich array;
The bravest lady in the land
Had not more pleasure at command.

XXI

' I had my music every day,
Harmonious lessons for to play;
I had my virgins fair and free
Continually to wait on me.

XXII

' But now, alas ! my husband's dead,
And all my friends are from me fled ;
My former joys are pass'd and gone,
For I am now a serving-man.'

XXIII

At last the King from hunting came,
And presently, upon the same,
He callèd for this good old man,
And thus to speak the King began :

XXIV

' What news, what news, old man ? ' quoth he ;
' What news hast thou to tell to me ? '—
' Brave news,' the old man he did say,
' Sweet William is a lady gay.'—

XXV

' If this be true thou tell'st to me,
I'll make thee lord of high degree ;
But if thy words do prove a lie,
Thou shalt be hang'd up presently.'

XXVI

But when the King the truth had found,
His joys did more and more abound :
According as the old man did say,
Sweet William was a lady gay.

XXVII

Therefore the King without delay
Put on her glorious rich array,
And upon her head a crown of gold
Which was most famous to behold.

XXVIII

And then, for fear of further strife,
He took Sweet William for his wife:
The like before was never seen,
A serving-man to be a queen.

167.   *The Simple Ploughboy*

I

O THE Ploughboy was a-ploughing
With his horses on the plain,
   And was singing of a song as on went he:
'Since that I have fall'n in love,
If the parents disapprove,
   'Tis the first thing that will send me to the sea.'

II

When the parents came to know
That their daughter loved him so,
   Then they sent a gang, and press'd him for the sea.
And they made of him a tar,
To be slain in cruel war;
   Of the simple Ploughboy singing on the lea.

III

The maiden sore did grieve,
And without a word of leave,
   From her father's house she fled secretlie,
In male attire dress'd,
With a star upon her breast,
   All to seek her simple Ploughboy on the sea.

837

THE SIMPLE PLOUGHBOY

IV

Then she went o'er hill and plain,
And she walked in wind and rain,
   Till she came to the brink of the blue sea,
Saying, ' I am forced to rove,
For the loss of my true love,
   Who is but a simple Ploughboy from the lea.'

V

Now the first she did behold,
O it was a sailor bold,
   ' Have you seen my simple Ploughboy ? ' then said she.
' They have press'd him to the fleet,
Sent him tossing on the deep,
   Who is but a simple Ploughboy from the lea.'

VI

Then she went to the Captain,
And to him she made complain,
   ' O a silly Ploughboy's run away from me ! '
Then the Captain smiled and said,
' Why Sir ! surely you're a maid !
   So the Ploughboy I will render up to thee.'

VII

Then she pullèd out a store,
Of five hundred crowns and more,
   And she strew'd them on the deck, did she.
Then she took him by the hand,
And she row'd him to the land,
   Where she wed the simple Ploughboy back from sea.

I

IN Cawsand Bay lying, with the Blue Peter flying,
  And all hands on deck for the anchor to weigh,
When off came a lady, as fresh as a daisy,
  And modestly hailing, the damsel did say :

II

' Ship ahoy ! bear a hand there ! I wants a young man there,
  So heave us a man-rope, or send him to me ;
His name 's Henry Grady, and I am a lady,
  Arrived to prevent him from going to sea.'

III

Now the captain, his honour, when he looked upon her,
  He ran down the side for to hand her on board.
Cried he, with emotion, ' What son of the ocean
  Can thus be looked after by Helena Ford ? '

IV

Then the lady made answer, ' That there is a man, sir,
  I'll make him as free as a Duke or a Lord.'—
' Oh no ! ' says the capp'en, ' That can't very well happen,
  I've got sailing orders—you, sir, stop on board.'

V

But up spoke the lady, ' Don't you mind him, Hal Grady,
  He once was your capp'en, but now you're at large.
You shan't stop on board her, for all that chap's order ! '
  Then out of her bosom she drew his discharge.

CAWSAND BAY

VI

Said the captain, 'I'm hang'd now, you're cool, and I'm
    bang'd now!'
  Said Hal, 'Here, old Weatherface, take all my clothes.'
And ashore then he steer'd her; the lads they all cheer'd
    her;
  But the captain was jealous, and looked down his nose.

VII

Then she got a shore tailor to rig up her sailor
  In white nankeen trowsers and long blue-tail'd coat;
And he looked like a squire, for all to admire,
  With a dimity handkercher tied round his throat.

VIII

They'd a house that was greater than any first-rater,
  With footmen in livery handing the drink,
And a garden to go in, where flowers were blowing,
  The buttercup, daisy, the lily, the pink.

IX

And he got edication befitting his station
  (For we all of us know we're not too old to larn);
And his messmates they found him, his little ones round
    him,
  All chips of the old block from the stem to the starn.

I

IN seventeen hundred and ninety-four,
On March the twentieth day ;
We hoist our colours to the mast,
   And for Greenland bore away, brave boys !
   And for Greenland bore away.

II

We were twelve gallant men aboard,
   And to the North did steer :
Old England left we in our wake—
   We sailors knew no fear, brave boys !
   We sailors knew no fear.

III

Our boatswain to the mast-head went,
   Wi' a spy glass in his hand ;
He cries, ' A whale ! a whale doth blow,
   She blows at every span, brave boys !
   She blows at every span.'

IV

Our Captain on the master deck
   (A very good man was he),
' Overhaul ! overhaul ! let the boat tackle fall,
   And launch your boat to sea, brave boys !
   And launch your boat to sea.'

V

Our boat being launch'd, and all hands in,
   The whale was full in view ;
Resolved was then each seaman bold
   To steer where the whale-fish blew, brave boys !
   To steer where the whale-fish blew.

THE GREENLAND FISHERY

VI

The whale was struck, and the line paid out,
  She gave a flash with her tail;
The boat capsized, and we lost four men,
  And we never caught that whale, brave boys!
  And we never caught that whale.

VII

Bad news we to the Captain brought,
  The loss of four men true.
A sorrowful man was our Captain then,
  And the colours down he drew, brave boys!
  And the colours down he drew.

VIII

'The losing of this whale,' said he,
  'Doth grieve my heart full sore;
But the losing of four gallant men
  Doth hurt me ten times more, brave boys!
  Doth hurt me ten times more.

IX

'The winter star doth now appear,
  So, boys, the anchor weigh;
'Tis time to leave this cold country,
  And for England bear away, brave boys!
  And for England bear away.

X

'For Greenland is a barren place,
  A land where grows no green,
But ice and snow, and the whale-fish blow,
  And the daylight's seldom seen, brave boys!
  And the daylight's seldom seen!'

The Old Cloak

I

THIS winter's weather it waxeth cold,
    And frost it freezeth on every hill,
And Boreas blows his blast so bold
    That all our cattle are like to spill.
Bell, my wife, she loves no strife;
    She said unto me quietlye,
'Rise up, and save cow Crumbock's life!
    Man, put thine old cloak about thee!'

II

He. O Bell my wife, why dost thou flyte?
    Thou kens my cloak is very thin:
It is so bare and over worn,
    A crickè thereon cannot renn.
Then I'll no longer borrow nor lend;
    For once I'll new apparell'd be;
To-morrow I'll to town and spend;
    For I'll have a new cloak about me.

III

She. Cow Crumbock is a very good cow:
    She has been always true to the pail;
She has help'd us to butter and cheese, I trow,
    And other things she will not fail.
I would be loth to see her pine.
    Good husband, counsel take of me:
It is not for us to go so fine—
    Man, take thine old cloak about thee!

flyte] scold.

THE OLD CLOAK

He. My cloak it was a very good cloak,
　　It hath been always true to the wear ;
　But now it is not worth a groat :
　　I have had it four and forty year'.
　Sometime it was of cloth in grain :
　　'Tis now but a sigh clout, as you may see :
　It will neither hold out wind nor rain ;
　　And I'll have a new cloak about me.

V

She. It is four and forty years ago
　　Sine the one of us the other did ken ;
　And we have had, betwixt us two,
　　Of children either nine or ten :
　We have brought them up to women and men :
　　In the fear of God I trow they be :
　And why wilt thou thyself misken ?
　　Man, take thine old cloak about thee !

VI

He. O Bell my wife, why dost thou flyte ?
　　Now is now, and then was then :
　Seek now all the world throughout,
　　Thou kens not clowns from gentlemen :
　They are clad in black, green, yellow and blue,
　　So far above their own degree.
　Once in my life I'll take a view ;
　　For I'll have a new cloak about me.

VII

She. King Stephen was a worthy peer ;
　　His breeches cost him but a crown ;
　He held them sixpence all too dear,
　　Therefore he called the tailor ' lown.'

cloth in grain] scarlet cloth.　　　sigh clout] a rag for straining.
844

He was a king and wore the crown,
    And thou'se but of a low degree :
It's pride that puts this country down :
    Man, take thy old cloak about thee !

VIII

He.   Bell my wife, she loves not strife,
    Yet she will lead me, if she can :
And to maintain an easy life
    I oft must yield, though I'm good-man.
It's not for a man with a woman to threap,
    Unless he first give o'er the plea :
As we began, so will we keep,
    And I'll take my old cloak about me.

171.   *Widdicombe Fair*

I

'TOM PEARSE, Tom Pearse, lend me your grey mare,
    All along, down along, out along, lee.
For I want for to go to Widdicombe Fair,
    Wi' Bill Brewer, Jan Stewer, Peter Gurney, Peter Davy,
      Dan'l Whiddon, Harry Hawk,
    Old Uncle Tom Cobbleigh and all.'
          Chorus. Old Uncle Tom Cobbleigh and all.

II

' And when shall I see again my grey mare ? '—
    All along, down along, out along, lee.
' By Friday soon, or Saturday noon,
    Wi' Bill Brewer, Jan Stewer,' &c.
          threap] argue.

845

WIDDICOMBE FAIR

III

Then Friday came, and Saturday noon,
    All along, down along, out along, lee.
But Tom Pearse's old mare hath not trotted home,
    Wi' Bill Brewer, &c.

IV

So Tom Pearse he got up to the top o' the hill,
    All along, down along, out along, lee.
And he seed his old mare down a-making her will
    Wi' Bill Brewer, &c.

V

So Tom Pearse's old mare, her took sick and her died.
    All along, down along, out along, lee.
And Tom he sat down on a stone, and he cried
    Wi' Bill Brewer, &c.

VI

But this isn't the end o' this shocking affair,
    All along, down along, out along, lee.
Nor, though they be dead, of the horrid career
    Of Bill Brewer, &c.

VII

When the wind whistles cold on the moor of a night,
    All along, down along, out along, lee.
Tom Pearse's old mare doth appear, gashly white,
    Wi' Bill Brewer, &c.

VIII

And all the long night be heard skirling and groans,
    All along, down along, out along, lee.
From Tom Pearse's old mare in her rattling bones,
      And from Bill Brewer, Jan Stewer, Peter Gurney,
        Peter Davy, Dan'l Whiddon, Harry Hawk,
    Old Uncle Tom Cobbleigh and all.
            Chorus. Old Uncle Tom Cobbleigh and all.

172. *Get up and Bar the Door*

I

IT fell about the Martinmas time,
    And a gay time it was then,
When our goodwife got puddings to make,
    And she's boil'd them in the pan.

II

The wind sae cauld blew south and north,
    And blew into the floor ;
Quoth our goodman to our goodwife,
    'Gae out and bar the door.'—

III

'My hand is in my hussyfskap,
    Goodman, as ye may see ;
An' it shou'dna be barr'd this hundred year,
    It's no be barr'd for me.'

IV

They made a paction 'tween them twa,
    They made it firm and sure,
That the first word whae'er shou'd speak,
    Shou'd rise and bar the door.

V

Then by there came two gentlemen,
    At twelve o' clock at night,
And they could neither see house nor hall,
    Nor coal nor candle-light.

GET UP AND BAR THE DOOR

'Now whether is this a rich man's house,
    Or whether is it a poor?'
But ne'er a word wad ane o' them speak,
    For barring of the door.

VII

And first they ate the white puddings,
    And then they ate the black.
Tho' muckle thought the goodwife to hersel'
    Yet ne'er a word she spake.

VIII

Then said the one unto the other,
    'Here, man, tak ye my knife;
Do ye tak aff the auld man's beard,
    And I'll kiss the goodwife.'—

IX

'But there's nae water in the house,
    And what shall we do than?'—
'What ails ye at the pudding-broo,
    That boils into the pan?'

X

O up then started our goodman,
    An angry man was he:
'Will ye kiss my wife before my een,
    And sca'd me wi' pudding-bree?'

XI

Then up and started our goodwife,
    Gied three skips on the floor:
'Goodman, you've spoken the foremost word!
    Get up and bar the door.'

848

172. *King John and the Abbot of Canterbury*

I

AN ancient story I'll tell you anon
Of a notable prince, that was callèd King John;
And he rulèd England with maine and with might,
For he did great wrong, and maintein'd little right.

II

And I'll tell you a story, a story so merrye,
Concerning the Abbot of Canterbùrye;
How, for his house-keeping and high renowne,
They rode poste for him to fair London towne.

III

An hundred men, the King did heare say,
The Abbot kept in his house every day;
And fifty golde chaynes, without any doubt,
In velvet coates waited the Abbot about.

IV

'How now, Father Abbot, I heare it of thee
Thou keepest a farre better house than mee,
And for thy house-keeping and high renowne,
I feare thou work'st treason against my crown.'—

V

'My liege,' quo' the Abbot, 'I would it were knowne,
I never spend nothing, but what is my owne;
And I trust your Grace will doe me no deere
For spending of my owne true-gotten geere.'

VI

' Yes, yes, Father Abbot, thy fault it is highe,
And now for the same thou needest must dye;
For except thou canst answer me questions three,
Thy head shall be smitten from thy bodìe.

VII

'And first,' quo' the King, ' when I'm in this stead,
With my crowne of golde so faire on my head,
Among all my liege-men so noble of birthe,
Thou must tell me to one penny what I am worthe.

VIII

' Secondlye, tell me, without any doubt,
How soone I may ride the whole worlde about.
And at the third question thou must not shrinke,
But tell me here truly what I do thinke.'—

IX

' O, these are hard questions for my shallow witt,
Nor I cannot answer your Grace as yet:
But if you will give me but three weekes space,
I'll do my endeavour to answer your Grace.

X

' Now three weekes space to thee will I give,
And that is the longest time thou hast to live;
For if thou dost not answer my questions three,
Thy lands and thy livings are forfeit to mee.'

XI

Away rode the Abbot all sad at that word,
And he rode to Cambridge, and Oxenford;
But never a doctor there was so wise,
That could with his learning an answer devise.

850

ABBOT OF CANTERBURY

XII

Then home rode the Abbot of comfort so cold,
And he mett with his shepheard a-going to fold:
'How now, my lord Abbot, you are welcome home;
What newes do you bring us from good King John?'—

XIII

'Sad newes, sad newes, shepheard, I must give;
That I have but three days more to live:
For if I do not answer him questions three,
My head will be smitten from my bodìe.

XIV

'The first is to tell him there in that stead,
With his crowne of golde so fair on his head,
Among all his liege-men so noble of birthe,
To within one penny of what he is worthe.

XV

'The seconde, to tell him, without any doubt,
How soone he may ride this whole worlde about:
And at the third question I must not shrinke,
But tell him there truly what he does thinke.'—

XVI

'Now cheare up, sire Abbot, did you never hear yet,
That a fool he may learn a wise man witt?
Lend me horse, and serving-men, and your apparel,
And I'll ride to London to answere your quarrel.

XVII

'Nay frowne not, if it hath bin told unto mee,
I am like your lordship, as ever may bee:
And if you will but lend me your gowne,
There is none shall knowe us at fair London towne.'—

851

XVIII

' Now horses and serving-men thou shalt have,
With sumptuous array most gallant and brave ;
With crozier, and miter, and rochet, and cope,
Fit to appeare 'fore our Father the Pope.' —

XIX

' Now welcome, sire Abbot,' the King he did say,
' 'Tis well thou'rt come back to keepe thy day ;
For and if thou canst answer my questions three,
Thy life and thy living both savèd shall bee.

XX

' And first, when thou seest me here in this stead,
With my crown of golde so fair on my head,
Among all my liege-men so noble of birthe,
Tell me to one penny what I am worthe.' —

XXI

' For thirty pence our Saviour was sold
Amonge the false Jewes, as I have bin told ;
And twenty-nine is the worthe of thee,
For I thinke thou art one penny worser than hee.'

XXII

The King he laughed, and swore by St. Bittel,
' I did not thinke I had been worthe so littel !
— Now secondly tell me, without any doubt,
How soone I may ride this whole world about.' —

ABBOT OF CANTERBURY

XXIII

'You must rise with the sun, and ride with the same,
Until the next morning he riseth againe;
And then your Grace need not make any doubt,
But in twenty-four hours you'll ride it about.'

XXIV

The King he laughed, and swore by St. Jone,
'I did not think it could be gone so soone!
—Now from the third question thou must not shrinke,
But tell me here truly what I do thinke.'—

XXV

'Yea, that shall I do, and make your Grace merry:
You thinke I'm the Abbot of Canterbùrye;
But I'm his poor shepheard, as plain you may see,
That am come to beg pardon for him and for mee.'

XXVI

The King he laughed, and swore by the Masse,
'I'll make thee Lord Abbot this day in his place!'—
'Now naye, my liege, be not in such speede,
For alacke I can neither write, ne reade.'—

XXVII

'Four nobles a weeke, then, I will give thee
For this merry jest thou hast showne unto mee;
And tell the old Abbot when thou comest home,
Thou hast brought him a pardon from good King John.

I

NOW ponder well, you parents dear,
  These words which I shall write;
A doleful story you shall hear,
  In time brought forth to light.
A gentleman of good account
  In Norfolk dwelt of late,
Who did in honour far surmount
  Most men of his estate.

II

Sore sick he was and like to die,
  No help his life could save;
His wife by him as sick did lie,
  And both possest one grave.
No love between these two was lost,
  Each was to other kind;
In love they lived, in love they died,
  And left two babes behind:

III

The one a fine and pretty boy
  Not passing three years old,
The other a girl more young than he,
  And framed in beauty's mould.
The father left his little son,
  As plainly did appear,
When he to perfect age should come,
  Three hundred pounds a year;

THE CHILDREN IN THE WOOD

IV

And to his little daughter Jane
   Five hundred pounds in gold,
To be paid down on marriage-day,
   Which might not be controll'd.
But if the children chanced to die
   Ere they to age should come,
Their uncle should possess their wealth;
   For so the will did run.

V

'Now, brother,' said the dying man,
   'Look to my children dear;
Be good unto my boy and girl,
   No friends else have they here:
To God and you I recommend
   My children dear this day;
But little while be sure we have
   Within this world to stay.

VI

'You must be father and mother both,
   And uncle, all in one;
God knows what will become of them
   When I am dead and gone.'
With that bespake their mother dear:
   'O brother kind,' quoth she,
'You are the man must bring our babes
   To wealth or misery!

VII

'And if you keep them carefully,
   Then God will you reward;
But if you otherwise should deal,
   God will your deeds regard.'

With lips as cold as any stone,
    They kiss'd their children small:
' God bless you both, my children dear ! '
    With that the tears did fall.

VIII

These speeches then their brother spake
    To this sick couple there :
' The keeping of your little ones,
    Sweet sister, do not fear ;
God never prosper me nor mine,
    Nor aught else that I have,
If I do wrong your children dear
    When you are laid in grave ! '

IX

The parents being dead and gone,
    The children home he takes,
And brings them straight unto his house,
    Where much of them he makes.
He had not kept these pretty babes
    A twelvemonth and a day,
But, for their wealth, he did devise
    To make them both away.

X

He bargain'd with two ruffians strong,
    Which were of furious mood,
That they should take these children young,
    And slay them in a wood.
He told his wife an artful tale :
    He would the children send
To be brought up in London town
    With one that was his friend.

THE CHILDREN IN THE WOOD

XI

Away then went those pretty babes,
    Rejoicing at that tide,
Rejoicing with a merry mind
    They should on cock-horse ride.
They prate and prattle pleasantly,
    As they ride on the way,
To those that should their butchers be
    And work their lives' decay:

XII

So that the pretty speech they had
    Made Murder's heart relent;
And they that undertook the deed
    Full sore did now repent.
Yet one of them, more hard of heart,
    Did vow to do his charge,
Because the wretch that hirèd him
    Had paid him very large.

XIII

The other won't agree thereto,
    So here they fall to strife;
With one another they did fight
    About the children's life:
And he that was of mildest mood
    Did slay the other there,
Within an unfrequented wood.—
    The babes did quake for fear!

XIV

He took the children by the hand,
    Tears standing in their eye,
And bade them straightway follow him,
    And look they did not cry;

And two long miles he led them on,
　　While they for food complain:
'Stay here,' quoth he ; 'I'll bring you bread
　　When I come back again.'

XV

These pretty babes, with hand in hand,
　　Went wandering up and down ;
But never more could see the man
　　Approaching from the town.
Their pretty lips with blackberries
　　Were all besmear'd and dyed ;
And when they saw the darksome night,
　　They sat them down and cried.

XVI

Thus wander'd these poor innocents,
　　Till death did end their grief ;
In one another's arms they died,
　　As wanting due relief :
No burial this pretty pair
　　From any man receives,
Till Robin Redbreast piously
　　Did cover them with leaves.

XVII

And now the heavy wrath of God
　　Upon their uncle fell ;
Yea, fearful fiends did haunt his house,
　　His conscience felt an hell :
His barns were fired, his goods consumed,
　　His lands were barren made,
His cattle died within the field,
　　And nothing with him stay'd.

XVIII

And in a voyage to Portugal
  Two of his sons did die;
And, to conclude, himself was brought
  To want and misery:
He pawn'd and mortgaged all his land
  Ere seven years came about.
And now at last his wicked act
  Did by this means come out.

XIX

The fellow that did take in hand
  These children for to kill,
Was for a robbery judged to die,
  Such was God's blessed will:
Who did confess the very truth,
  As here hath been display'd:
The uncle having died in jail,
  Where he for debt was laid.

XX

You that executors be made,
  And overseërs eke,
Of children that be fatherless,
  And infants mild and meek,
Take you example by this thing,
  And yield to each his right,
Lest God with suchlike misery
  Your wicked minds requite.

The Suffolk Miracle

I

A WONDER stranger ne'er was known
Than what I now shall treat upon.
In Suffolk there did lately dwell
A farmer rich and known full well.

II

He had a daughter fair and bright,
On whom he placed his chief delight;
Her beauty was beyond compare,
She was both virtuous and fair.

III

A young man there was living by,
Who was so charmèd with her eye,
That he could never be at rest;
He was by love so much possest.

IV

He made address to her, and she
Did grant him love immediately;
But when her father came to hear,
He parted her and her poor dear.

V

Forty miles distant was she sent,
Unto his brother's, with intent
That she should there so long remain,
Till she had changed her mind again.

THE SUFFOLK MIRACLE

VI

Hereat this young man sadly grieved,
But knew not how to be relieved ;
He sigh'd and sobb'd continually
That his true love he could not see.

VII

She by no means could to him send,
Who was her heart's espousèd friend ;
He sigh'd, he grieved, but all in vain,
For she confined must still remain.

VIII

He mourn'd so much that doctor's art
Could give no ease unto his heart,
Who was so strangely terrified
That in short time for love he died.

IX

She that from him was sent away
Knew nothing of his dying day ;
But constant still she did remain,
And loved the dead, although in vain.

X

After he had in grave been laid
A month or more, unto this maid
He comes in middle of the night,
Who joy'd to see her heart's delight.

XI

Her father's horse which well she knew,
Her mother's hood and safeguard too,
He brought with him to testify
Her parents' order he came by.

safeguard] riding-skirt.

XII

Which when her uncle understood,
He hoped it would be for her good,
And gave consent to her straightway
That with him she should come away.

XIII

When she was got her love behind,
They pass'd as swift as any wind,
That in two hours, or little more,
He brought her to her father's door.

XIV

But as they did this great haste make,
He did complain his head did ache ;
Her handkerchief she then took out,
And tied the same his head about.

XV

And unto him she thus did say :
' Thou art as cold as any clay,
When we come home a fire we'll have ' ;
But little dream'd he went to grave.

XVI

Soon were they at her father's door,
And after she ne'er saw him more ;
' I'll set the horse up,' then he said,
And there he left this harmless maid.

XVII

She knock'd, and straight a man he cried,
' Who's there ? ' ' 'Tis I,' she then replied ;
Who wonder'd much her voice to hear,
And was possest with dread and fear.

THE SUFFOLK MIRACLE

XVIII

Her father he did tell, and then
He stared like an affrighted man:
Down stairs he ran, and when he see her,
Cried out, 'My child, how cam'st thou here?'

XIX

'Pray, sir, did you not send for me
By such a messenger?' said she:
Which made his hair stand on his head,
As knowing well that he was dead.

XX

'Where is he?' then to her he said.—
'He's in the stable,' quoth the maid.—
'Go in,' said he, 'and go to bed;
I'll see the horse well litterèd.'

XXI

He stared about, and there could he
No shape of any mankind see,
But found his horse all on a sweat;
Which made him in a deadly fret.

XXII

His daughter he said nothing to,
Nor no-one else (though well they knew
That he was dead a month before),
For fear of grieving her full sore.

XXIII

Her father to his father went
Who was deceased, with full intent
To tell him what his daughter said;
So both came back unto this maid.

THE SUFFOLK MIRACLE

XXIV

They ask'd her, and she still did say
'Twas he that then brought her away;
Which when they heard, they were amazed,
And on each other strangely gazed.

XXV

A handkerchief she said she tied
About his head, and that they tried;
The sexton they did speak unto
That he the grave would then undo.

XXVI

Affrighted then they did behold
His body turning into mould,
And though he had a month been dead
This kerchief was about his head.

XXVII

This thing unto her then they told,
And the whole truth they did unfold.
She was thereat so terrified
And grieved, she quickly after died.

176. Bessie Bell and Mary Gray

I

O BESSIE BELL and Mary Gray,
    They war twa bonnie lasses ;
They biggit a bower on yon burn-brae,
    And theekit it o'er wi' rashes.

II

They theekit it o'er wi' rashes green,
    They theekit it o'er wi' heather ;
But the pest cam frae the burrows-town,
    And slew them baith thegither.

III

They thought to lye in Methven kirkyard,
    Amang their noble kin ;
But they maun lye in Stronach haugh,
    To biek forenent the sin.

IV

And Bessie Bell and Mary Gray,
    They war twa bonnie lasses ;
They biggit a bower on yon burn-brae,
    And theekit it o'er wi' rashes.

biggit] built.   theekit] thatched.   haugh] water-mead.
biek] bask.   sin] sun.

INDEX OF FIRST LINES

INDEX OF FIRST LINES

868

INDEX OF FIRST LINES

INDEX OF FIRST LINES

870

INDEX OF FIRST LINES

PRINTED IN GREAT BRITAIN AT THE UNIVERSITY PRESS, OXFORD
BY JOHN JOHNSON, PRINTER TO THE UNIVERSITY

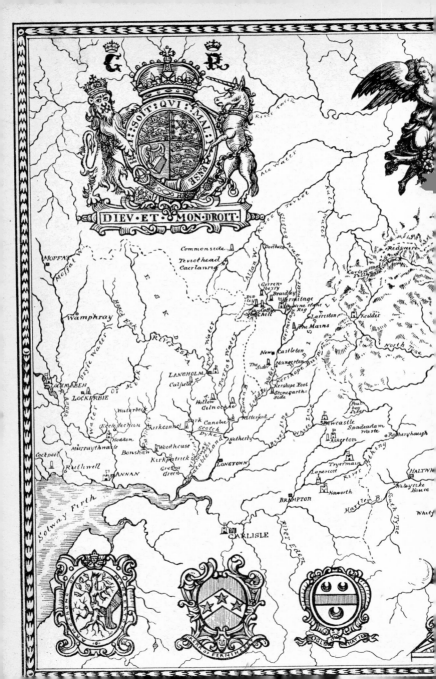